MW01060427

SAGE was founded in 1965 by Sara Miller McCune to support the dissemination of usable knowledge by publishing innovative and high-quality research and teaching content. Today, we publish over 900 journals, including those of more than 400 learned societies, more than 800 new books per year, and a growing range of library products including archives, data, case studies, reports, and video. SAGE remains majority-owned by our founder, and after Sara's lifetime will become owned by a charitable trust that secures our continued independence.

Los Angeles | London | New Delhi | Singapore | Washington DC | Melbourne

Advance Praise

A nation is as strong as its higher educational and research institutions. Professor Jalote has created one such institution and nurtured it carefully for over a decade to make it a widely respected research institution in the world. This book is a winning recipe for how to create a globally respected research institution in any country. A must-read for everyone interested in higher education and research.

N. R. Narayana Murthy,
Founder, Infosys

This book describes in depth the fundamental issues in Indian universities and the need to improve the research ecosystem to enable the potential of faculty and students to be fully realized. This insightful and well-written volume will benefit all those involved with the governance of higher education, especially the administrators and policymakers.

Professor Sudhir Sopory,
Former VC, JNU

Higher education in India has grown tremendously. However, much remains to be done on the quality of research and its application for practical problems. The author has gone into the fact sheet and challenges that lie ahead for building world-class research universities. This book comes at an appropriate time when the new National Education Policy is on the anvil, and will open new vistas for policymakers, educationists, administrators and students of higher education.

Professor Anil Sahasrabudhe,
Chairman, AICTE

The book presents a very comprehensive view of the current standing of research ambience in the university system in India, and the way forward to building world-class universities through a conscious promotion of the research culture in universities. This is a must-read for all academics and leaders of higher education who are seriously interested in promoting high-end academic research in universities, especially in India.

Professor Surendra Prasad,
Former Director, IIT Delhi

India urgently needs world-class research universities. This book by Pankaj Jalote, who is one of a rare breed of 'Thinker Doers' in our country, shares the roadmap for building strong research universities in India. Anyone involved in higher education can benefit from this book!

Nandan Nilekani,
Chairman, Infosys

This book, based on the insights from Pankaj Jalote's success in developing an India-based research university in IIIT-Delhi, offers many lessons for building a research-based HE system, which is innovative and cutting-edge as new India grows into a knowledge-based economy.

T. V. Mohandas Pai,
Chairman, Manipal Global Education Services

Knowledge without action is meaningless. Pankaj embodies this value principle at its best. He built a first-rate institution and has now put down his insights into a book through a larger perspective. This is a much-needed book that should be mandatory reading for educators, policymakers and anyone interested in learning about the right way to take higher education forward across the globe.

Professor Dinesh Singh,
Former VC, Delhi University

Higher education in India is huge and complex. Professor Jalote, an educator, researcher and an institution-builder who is admired for the way he brought up IIIT-Delhi, makes an effort to unravel it and presents a vision for building future universities and how our institutions can stay relevant.

Professor V. Ramgopal Rao,
Director, IIT Delhi

IIIT-Delhi has become a world-class institution in a short time due to the vision, passion and commitment of Pankaj Jalote. *Building Research Universities in India* will help readers learn what it takes to build an institution while remaining focused on the vision and borrowing best practices globally.

Professor Bijendra Jain,
Former Vice Chancellor, BITS Pilani,
and Deputy Director, IIT Delhi

The analysis presented in this book thoughtfully reveals the origins, forms and effects of the underperformance of Indian higher education system, together with many signposts for turning things around.

Professor Fazal Rizvi,
The University of Melbourne, Australia

This is a comprehensive book that provides a foundation for understanding research universities and suggests ways to make them internationally competitive. A must-read for everyone interested in Indian research universities and their future.

Professor Satish K. Tripathi,
President, State University of New York at Buffalo

Jalote's argument for improving the research culture and ethics in Indian institutions is compelling. He makes a strong case for encouraging them to become research universities through scale, funding, by both government and industry, and impact. He calls for a higher expectation from and deeper support of universities. Listen to him.

Professor Pankaj Chandra,
Vice Chancellor, Ahmedabad University,
Former Director, IIM Bangalore

For thriving in the knowledge-based global economy, India needs to enhance its quality, relevance and diversity of research. This book, written by someone who has built a fine research university himself, can help all the stakeholders of our HE system in understanding and implementing the structures and processes required to develop world-class universities.

Professor Ashutosh Sharma,
Secretary, DST

In this powerfully argued book, Pankaj Jalote provides a primer for policymakers, university leaders and their governing bodies on fostering a high-quality research culture—a necessary prerequisite for Indian universities to take their place among their global peers. Essential reading from someone who has spent the past decade successfully building a research-intensive institution from scratch.

Arun Sharma, AM,
Distinguished Professor Emeritus and
Former Deputy Vice Chancellor and Vice-President, QUT

India needs many more research universities which can reach the global standard of excellence in innovation, invention and academic research. Pankaj Jalote's new book offers comprehensive guidance to build successful research institutions. This is a welcome book on an important topic which will be useful for all universities and thinkers.

Prof. K. Vijay Raghavan,
Principal Scientific Adviser to the Government of India

Jayant V. Narlikar once stated, 'Just as a teacher who does not add to his knowledge through research becomes stale, so can a researcher devoid of teaching experience become sterile.' A potent system of higher education must, therefore, lay equal emphasis on teaching and research. Pankaj Jalote's book serves as a practical guide and roadmap for translating this idea into action.

Furqan Qamar,
Professor of Management, Jamia Millia Islamia

BUILDING
RESEARCH
UNIVERSITIES
IN INDIA

SAGE Studies in Higher Education

Higher Education has become an important player in the global economy and has a dynamic and growing role in every society. Massification, differentiation, human resource development, knowledge development and transfer, internationalization and privatization are key characteristics of the global higher education landscape, although they manifest themselves in different ways depending on the type of institution, country and/or region of the world. Traditional divisions—such as those between North and South, high-income and lower-middle income economies, universities and vocational schools, and so on—are no longer adequate to describe the dynamic and complex patterns of postsecondary education worldwide. *SAGE Studies in Higher Education* provides cogent discussion, analysis and debate of key themes in global higher education.

Series Editors

Philip G. Altbach
Research Professor and
Founding Director
Center for International
Higher Education
Boston College, USA

Hans de Wit
Director
Center for International
Higher Education
Boston College, USA

Laura Rumbley
Associate Director
Center for International
Higher Education
Boston College, USA

Simon Marginson
Professor of International
Higher Education
UCL Institute of Education
University College London, UK

Claire Callender
Professor of Higher Education
Studies
UCL Institute of Education and
Birkbeck University of London,
UK

SAGE Studies in Higher Education

BUILDING RESEARCH UNIVERSITIES IN INDIA

Pankaj Jalote

Los Angeles | London | New Delhi
Singapore | Washington DC | Melbourne

First published in 2021 by

SAGE Publications India Pvt Ltd
B1/I-1 Mohan Cooperative Industrial Area
Mathura Road, New Delhi 110 044, India
www.sagepub.in

SAGE Publications Inc
2455 Teller Road
Thousand Oaks, California 91320, USA

SAGE Publications Ltd
1 Oliver's Yard, 55 City Road
London EC1Y 1SP, United Kingdom

SAGE Publications Asia-Pacific Pte Ltd
18 Cross Street #10-10/11/12
China Square Central
Singapore 048423

Published by Vivek Mehra for SAGE Publications India Pvt Ltd. Typeset in 10.5/13 pt Sabon by Zaza Eunice, Hosur, Tamil Nadu, India.

Library of Congress Control Number: 2020946913

ISBN: 978-93-5388-502-1 (HB)

SAGE Team: Rajesh Dey, Ankit Verma and Rajinder Kaur

*Dedicated to the board, faculty,
staff and students of IIIT Delhi who made
it possible to build a strong research university.*

Contents

Preface

In July 2008, I was informed that I had been selected as the Founding Director of Indraprastha Institute of Information Technology, Delhi (IIIT Delhi), an institute for which the state of Delhi had passed a legislative act but which did not exist as yet. As I thought about the possibilities, it soon became clear that despite many challenges, this was a unique opportunity to develop a fine institution from scratch—an opportunity that very few get. So, I took it up with enthusiasm.

Very early on, we established that the institute would focus strongly on research, besides fulfilling its role in education, that is, it would be what we call a research university in this book. We convinced the government and other stakeholders that the need of the time in the country was to establish a university that could conduct research at an international level while providing education of the highest quality. We set the vision of the institute as follows: be a world-class research and development (R&D)–led institute that is globally respected for research and education, has thriving undergraduate and postgraduate programmes, and is socially relevant, industry facing and globally connected.

We were also clear that the institute would not be a replica of any existing institute and would innovate and emerge as a model system. Many innovative policies and systems were put in place in the first few years for achieving the vision. As a result, within a decade, the institute was ranked in the BRICS top 200 universities by QS (out of the 9,000+ they assessed) and is widely respected in academic circles in India for the standards it has set in research, education and governance. (Recently it was also ranked in World University Rankings of THE.)

Given that I was the first and only employee in the beginning and there was no other senior faculty for many years, I gained hands-on experience in all aspects of a research university—education and curriculum design, research management, PhD programme, faculty recruitment and management, finance, governance and administration, and so on. When my term as Founding Director ended after I had served for a decade, I decided to use this unique experience of successfully building a research university from scratch to write a book on research universities in India. I felt that covering all the major aspects in one book and providing an overall view of a research university would be very useful to administrators, academics, policymakers, and so on, who are involved in higher education but often are not scholars of higher education and would like to get a view of the different aspects in one volume.

The aim of this book is to provide an overall view of a research university, with different chapters covering key aspects of a research university. The rationale of the topics covered in different chapters in the book emerges naturally from the aim of the book. The first two chapters set the context: Chapter 1 discusses the Indian higher education system briefly, with special emphasis on research universities. Chapter 2 discusses research, research universities and their relevance and importance. Chapters 3–5 discuss the three missions of a research university: education, research and contribution to society. A strong PhD programme distinguishes research universities from others, and faculty is at the heart of a research university—Chapters 6 and 7 discuss these aspects. A research university needs strong governance that understands the needs of such a university and good finances—Chapters 8 and 9 discuss these topics. Finally, Chapter 10 discusses the road ahead from an Indian perspective—what research universities may do and what is needed in the higher education ecosystem to support these universities.

To provide a broad perspective covering the major aspects of a research university in one book, I have discussed each aspect briefly, covering only the key issues involved. Where appropriate, the relationship with the recommendations of the new National Education Policy of India (2019) is also mentioned. The discussions are based largely on my experience and understanding but also contain ideas and concepts from the rich literature that exists. It is not the aim of the book to provide an in-depth study of any of the topics—indeed, it cannot be done, as each topic is in itself complex and comes with considerable literature. It is hoped that this approach will provide a decent understanding of the different aspects of a research university, and a reader can delve into the rich literature available for any topic for a deeper understanding.

No book is currently available on Indian higher education that discusses research universities—an area of growing interest in India. This book fills this gap in the higher education literature on India. I believe the book also contributes to the global higher education literature by providing an overall view of a research university, with a chapter on the key aspects—most existing books tend to focus on some specific aspects.

The book should be of value to all those interested in higher education in India, as all aspects of a research university are also present in any higher education institution with perhaps a different emphasis. The book should be of interest to academicians in India, academic leaders, policymakers and education thinkers, and those who are involved in developing a university.

Many other developing countries have evolving higher education systems; these countries aspire to strengthen or build research universities. The book should also be of interest to academicians and policymakers in such countries. Globally, the book can be useful to those interested in the Indian higher education system, and to any academician or thinker who might not be a scholar of higher education but is interested in getting an overall understanding of research universities.

In some ways, for me, the book is like taking a path taken earlier—a sense of *déjà vu*. In 1996, I went on a 2-year sabbatical to Infosys as Vice President of Quality, during which I successfully led the transition of the quality system to high levels of maturity of the Capability Maturity Model framework. On returning back to academics, I wrote two books to share the experience: *CMM in Practice* and *Project Management in Practice* (both published by Addison Wesley). These books had a substantial influence on the software industry across the world and were translated in many languages such as Chinese, Japanese, French and so on. This journey followed the same paradigm—do first and then write about it. The only difference was that for this book, the doing was a 10-year journey and just laid the foundations from an institutional perspective. I hope that, like my previous endeavour, this sharing of my experience and understanding will be useful to others who might be interested in either creating or nurturing universities.

I would like to thank a number of people who provided invaluable help during this project. During the course of this work, I visited some universities and higher education research centres—in particular Queensland University of Technology (QUT) in Brisbane, Centre for the Study of Higher Education (CSHE) in University of Melbourne and the Department of Education Leadership in University at Buffalo. My heartful thanks to my hosts in these universities—Professors Arun Sharma at QUT, Fazal Rizvi at Melbourne and Satish Tripathi at Buffalo—and the various administrators and scholars who took time out to meet with me and give their inputs.

I would like to thank Professor Philip G. Altbach, one of the most respected researchers in the field of higher education and research universities and an author of many books, who not only consistently encouraged me for this project but also kindly agreed to write the introduction for the book. A special thanks to Mr Kiran Karnik, who kindly agreed to write the foreword of the book. Mr Karnik is a well-known intellectual in India and was the Chairman, Board of Governors of IIIT Delhi—his support and guidance greatly helped in conceptualizing and implementing various initiatives.

I would also like to thank IIIT Delhi for the experience it provided me, which formed the basis of this book, and also for granting me the sabbatical for writing. I would like to thank all my faculty and staff colleagues, who helped create a world-class institution in a short time under rather challenging circumstances. (As a token of my appreciation, the royalties from the book will be donated to IIIT Delhi.) Finally, I would like to thank my wife, Shikha, for supporting me in the years while I was the Director, despite the cost it incurred on family time, and my daughters Sumedha and Sunanda for their understanding and support.

Foreword

India's higher education has long been schizophrenic—some fine institutions, and almost all the others of a rather poor quality. On the one hand, the older Indian Institutes of Management (IIMs), the Indian Institute of Science, some of the Indian Institutes of Technology (IITs), and possibly four or five others, are among the few—the very few—that have won global recognition and peer respect. On the other hand, there are thousands of universities that churn out a few million badly educated, unemployable graduates each year, and next to nothing by way of quality research. Even in the best institutions, the amount and quality of research is hardly comparable with that in leading global universities. If they have made a name for themselves, it is more through the quality and achievements of their graduates, rather than through their research output. The ambition of having many Indian universities in the top 500 global ones, and at least a few in the top 100, has remained a dream.

Apart from government committees, a few scholars have looked in detail at the state of university-level education in India. However, such studies have rarely focused specifically on research in these institutions and how it can be nurtured. In many countries, the importance of research has been recognized through the creation of 'research universities'—institutions that generally have a strong education programme but where the primary focus is research. In the best of these places, the two are linked, and a synergistic relationship develops as an upward spiral. Such research universities were set up in Europe and USA over a century ago. Over the last two decades or so, a few other countries (notably China) have tried to emulate them.

India has been a slow (or even non-) starter and has less than 10 universities ranked in the top 500 of the Times Higher Education (THE) ranking. Global rankings have some drawbacks and flaws but are undoubtedly reflective of the overall standing of a university. The poor rankings of Indian universities are, therefore, worth taking note of, even though they reflect many external constraints, including those relating to foreign faculty and international students. Fortunately, there is growing awareness in India about the need to generally upgrade the quality of higher education and the importance of research—not only for its own sake but also as a vital input for the economic growth and development of the country. India can reap the true benefit of its demographic dividend only if the vast number of people entering the workforce (around 9 million each year) are well-educated.

For a country of India's size and ambition with regard to its global role, research universities that can generate human resources and IPRs (Intellectual Property Rights) at scale (and high quality) are a necessity. While many aspects may be unique to India, there is much that India can emulate—and even more that it can learn—from the experience of others.

An important issue for research in universities relates to research projects and funding. In most countries, much of the research funding goes to universities. A substantial part of the R&D spending by the government—including that related to defence and strategic sectors—as also by private industry, goes to universities as projects and grants. This has encouraged research and ensured funding support, leading to the growth of research universities. It has promoted cutting-edge work in universities and built strong industry–academia connections.

In India, on the other hand, a very large proportion of R&D funds goes to dedicated research laboratories/organizations within the government, and only small amounts find their way to universities. These not only absorb large funds but also researchers, making it difficult for universities to attract funds or people. This is changing, but only slowly. Meanwhile, industry–academia connections are yet weak and not conducive to industry-relevant research.

These factors have greatly inhibited the development of research universities, as also of a research culture in other universities. The recent thrust towards greater research in universities has focused attention on factors that would help to create the right institutional setting for this. Many of the obstacles have been long-recognized and inhibit not only research but also the overall quality of universities. The first of these is at the overall level: over-centralization and over-regulation. In a country as diverse as India, it is obvious that a central diktat, a one-size-fits-all model, will not work effectively. Yet, this is the long-prevalent approach. Not only do central regulators like the University Grants Commission (UGC) and All India Council for Technical Education (AICTE) issue detailed instructions, but the Ministry of Human Resources Development (HRD) also often issues even more specific 'orders'. This completely erodes the autonomy of universities, and—as always—standardization means lowering all to the least common denominator. Excellence, the hallmark of research, is the obvious casualty.

Financial autonomy is crucial. In India, practically all central and state universities are dependent on yearly government grants, and their fees are capped and set at levels that make financial independence infeasible. Around the world, there are a number of alternative models, but India has so far stayed with the yearly grant model, rather than moving to a formula-based financial support model. An important part of financial autonomy is with regard to the deployment of funds: can they be used for special research grants to faculty, or to reward the publication of papers, or for professional development (society memberships, conference travel, buying books), or for performance-based incentives?

Centralized and standardized admission tests are another challenge. In many universities abroad, even when such a standard test is used, individual universities add their own supplementary tests to decide on admission. In India, on the other hand, the model is the IIT–Joint Entrance Examination and a single 'merit list', common to all IITs. The IIMs have followed a different model, supplementing the standard Common Admission Test with their own screening and interviews, but there is pressure to regress to the IIT common/single-merit list.

Another factor is the trend of creating single-discipline institutions. While this method has resulted in some high-quality institutes—notably in management, law, design, technology and science—it is not conducive to innovation (which typically happens at the interface of or interaction between two disciplines), nor to the growing cross-disciplinary products (and needs) that are emerging. Most top global research universities are multidisciplinary.

These and other factors severely inhibit innovation and excellence in the Indian higher education system. Amidst this, the IIM Act, passed by the parliament two years ago, came as a breath of fresh air reflecting new thinking in governance and financial autonomy. It is far from ideal, and many of the suggestions made to provide greater autonomy were rejected, but it is certainly a step forward from the existing rules applicable to other institutions.

Fortunately, there are some in the government who recognize the need for drastic systemic reform and see research universities as a means to drive excellence in higher education. There are also many good leaders in various universities who are keen to consider steps to improve the quality of education and research. As they look at how best to do this and consider the various possibilities, a good starting point would be to look at examples and experiences from different countries. Collating and analysing these is, therefore, particularly useful.

It is in this context that this book is of special value. It takes a close look at India's higher education system, and at universities in various other countries, with a focus on research. The author has a deep and long experience of teaching and researching at two of India's top institutions (IIT Kanpur and IIT Delhi), combined with industry experience (in world-renowned Infosys). Following this, he served for a decade as Founder Director of Indraprastha Institute of Information Technology, Delhi (IIIT-D), a unique university set up by the Government of Delhi and conceived as a research-led teaching institution—in many ways, a 'research university'. This path-breaking initiative—setting new benchmarks in governance, academic and financial autonomy—deserves wider dissemination and adoption; a first-hand description is, therefore, of special value.

Professor Jalote's experience enables him to bring an overall perspective based on deep immersion in the higher education system, supplemented by his study of and discussions with key people in foreign universities, and visits to some of these universities. Apart from his own knowledge, he brings a lot of very useful data to the table and analyses it in ways that highlight key variables for success. Based on these, he synthesizes recommendations for what might be done in India. These would be of immense value to policymakers, institution heads and all interested in higher education. I do hope this will stir up debate and dialogue, leading to concrete action by way of systemic changes.

Kiran Karnik
Chairman Board of Governors, IIIT Delhi, and
Former President, NASSCOM, New Delhi, India

Introduction

The truth is that India in 2020 does not now have any world-class research universities. It has several outstanding research institutes in various scientific fields. It also has some world-class technology and management institutions—the Indian Institutes of Technology and the Indian Institutes of Management—a few excellent public institutions, such as the Indian Institute of Science, and some private initiatives such as Manipal, Ashoka and a few others. But none of these are comprehensive research universities that can compare with the best universities globally—or which are recognized by any of the global higher education rankings.

Without question, India needs a small number of top research universities. India has an expanding economy and plays an increasingly important role in global affairs. However, it is not yet a scientific or research power. For India to be fully successful, it needs research universities. This requirement has finally been recognized in several of the impressive initiatives proposed by the Government of India. Such programmes as the Global Initiatives of Academic Networks, the National Institutional Ranking Framework and, especially, the effort to identify and fund top universities, if appropriately funded and implemented, will greatly improve the top of India's higher education system.

Building Research Universities in India provides a useful roadmap for the development of these universities. It identifies the key elements for developing successful research universities. By examining how successful universities in other countries are organized and interpreting these aspects for the Indian reality, the book provides useful lessons.

xxii | Building Research Universities in India

Some have argued that India needs to develop its own university model. While a research university, or any academic institution, needs to take into account national realities, the basic model of the research university, as this book convincingly points out, is well established and necessarily reflects the patterns followed by the best universities globally. China, which has been quite successful in developing a number of successful research universities by, among other things, spending vast sums of money on the effort, talked about 'universities with Chinese characteristic'—but in fact their successful universities follow established, mainly Western, models. Indeed, the main elements that are 'Chinese' are negative—limitations on academic freedom, restrictions on access to some information and too much bureaucracy—and actually slow down progress. Thus, successful Indian research universities will inevitably resemble the best universities worldwide.

India has several important advantages as it emerges as an academic power. The widespread use of English means that India is immediately part of the global scientific communication. India also has a sizeable cadre of accomplished academics and researchers—both within the country and as part of the diaspora. Creating a productive academic environment for the most talented academics requires careful attention, good organization and adequate funding. Involving the diaspora is quite important, as the talent pool is immense—a significant number of Indians currently serve as university presidents and provosts of, for example, American universities and could contribute knowledge about building research universities, even if they do not actually return to India. Similarly, Indian professors in the diaspora can contribute to building research capacity by participating in collaborative research and other initiatives.

As Pankaj Jalote points out, research universities are necessarily a small but central part of a differentiated academic system. India, which now has the second largest student enrolments in the world, has a highly complex but poorly articulated academic system. It is important to recognize the importance of the research universities at the pinnacle of that system, but at the same time also to understand that the number of such institutions is a small part of the total—and that choosing which universities will be research-intensive is quite important.

The 'stars are aligned' for India to play an important part in the global knowledge system and to build world-class research universities. The talent exists, the need is clear, and there are some promising initiatives from the government. *Building Research Universities in India* provides guidelines for successful research universities in the Indian context.

Philip G. Altbach
Research Professor and Founding Director of
the Center for International Higher Education,
Boston College, Chestnut Hill, MA, USA

Chapter 1

Higher Education and Research in India

India has a very large and relatively young higher education (HE) system, which is also expanding rapidly. It has over 900 degree-granting institutions and over 40,000 colleges, with more than two-thirds of the universities and colleges being created in this century. While there are a few higher education institutions (HEIs) that have a global reputation for research, the focus and discourse of the HE system have generally been on education, with research-focused universities not getting due attention. As a consequence, despite having one of the largest HE systems in the world, the presence of Indian universities is minimal in global rankings, which are based largely on the research capability and contributions of universities.

In this chapter, we discuss the scenario of HE in India with a focus on issues more relevant from the research university perspective. For our discussions, we use the general understanding of what a research university is—one that strongly emphasizes its research mission, while continuing to offer high-quality education, and has internal systems and policies to support and promote the research mission.

In this book, we refer to all degree-granting HE institutions as universities—including institutions that may not have 'university' in their name but grant degrees, for example, the Indian Institute of Technology (IIT), Indian Institute of Science (IISc),

Indraprastha Institute of Information Technology, Delhi (IIIT-Delhi), etc. However, a college which is affiliated to a university is not a university. Also, much of the discussion in the book refers to public universities, as most research universities in India currently are public universities.

In this chapter, we have provided a brief discussion on the HE system and its growth and the evolution of research universities. Then, we have discussed some key aspects of the HE system that are crucial to research universities—the PhD programme and research funding. We have also presented an analysis on how the top universities in India compare with the top universities worldwide on a few parameters.

1.1 INDIAN HIGHER EDUCATION SYSTEM

In this section, we briefly look at the evolution of the Indian HE system and the current situation. The Indian HE seems to have evolved uniquely. Most HEIs have focused more on education and less on research. As engagement in research is known to be important for quality of education, as well as the quality of the culture that prevails in a university, most HEIs in India do not offer high-quality education. The quality of education is a pressing need and a demand—an examination of the various deficiencies in the Indian HEIs and the poor quality of education is given in Chandra (2017) and Kapur and Mehta (2017).

However, the importance of research has increased now, resulting in a shift of focus from only education to research and education in many universities. This is not very different from the evolution in most other countries, where universities generally started with a focus on education, and with a lapse of time, some gradually transformed into research universities by emphasizing on research. The key difference is the timing of transition. In most developed countries, this transition took place in the early 20th century, with the World War II giving a further impetus. In India, whose basic literacy rate was less than 20 per cent at the time of independence in 1947, this transformation seems to be happening now.

1.1.1 Structure of Higher Education System

In India, HE is a concurrent subject, which means that both the central and the state governments have jurisdiction over it. Both governments actively participate and have created hundreds of HEIs that they support. Universities in India can also be private. All HEIs are required by law to be not-for-profit.

Generally, universities are created by an Act of a state government or the central government. In addition to the universities that are created by the central or state government through an Act, there are also deemed universities that are given the university status by the University Grants Commission (UGC). However, in the recent past, this mode of establishing universities has not been much in use, and most of the universities have been created through an Act of the state or central government.

Also, unlike in most parts of the world, India has the system of affiliated colleges, which means that there are universities to which hundreds of colleges may be affiliated. Overall, the HE system in India is much more complicated than that in most countries. Universities in India can be categorized in different ways as follows:

- **Deemed or act-created.** There are only two ways to create a university in India—either through an Act of the central or state government or by being granted a deemed university status by the UGC. Many central government institutions have also been declared as institutes of national importance through a central Act. A list of all universities is maintained by the UGC (2018) and is available on its website. A list of HEIs, declared as institutes of national importance, is maintained by the Ministry of Human Resource Development (MHRD; now called Ministry of Education) and is available on its website.

While these institutions are sometimes not listed as universities, as mentioned earlier, we have considered these also as universities in this book because they have degree-granting powers.

- **Central, state or private.** This is about the ownership or who financially supports the university. Central government institutions are funded either by a central government ministry or by a department/agency. Some of these are called central universities (e.g., Delhi University, Banaras Hindu University [BHU]), while others are called institutes of national importance (e.g., IITs, National Institutes of Technology [NITs]). The state government funds state universities. Private universities, though generally created through an Act of a state government, do not get any budgetary support from the centre or a state. It is worth mentioning that as per the current laws, government institutions have to follow the reservation policies for admissions while private universities do not have to follow these. (Reservation is a complicated subject, which is not discussed in this book—it requires that, of the total number of seats for the incoming student cohort, certain fractions have to be reserved for students from some categories. Reservations often also apply to employees.)
- **Affiliating or non-affiliating.** Affiliating universities can affiliate colleges, while non-affiliating universities cannot affiliate any colleges. For example, in Delhi, IP University is an affiliating university, while IIIT-Delhi (Indraprastha Institute of Information Technology Delhi) and IIT Delhi are both non-affiliating universities. In the affiliation model, the education programme design, the course syllabus and so forth are all decided by the affiliating university—the colleges affiliated to the university have to teach these courses as per the prescribed curriculum. The exam assessment is carried out mainly by the university, although some part of the assessment may be given to colleges. Finally, the degree is also granted by the university. The university often has a separate unit that deals with the affairs of its affiliated colleges—setting the syllabus, conducting exams, getting the exam copies graded, giving degrees, interacting with colleges and so forth. Most colleges

have their own faculty, management structure (with representation from the affiliating university) and finances. The affiliating approach is a peculiarity of the Indian HE system, which has been abolished in most parts of the world.

The bulk of undergraduate (UG) education happens in affiliated colleges—India has more than 40,000 colleges, and more than 80 per cent of students get their bachelor's degrees through colleges. Almost no research is expected in colleges. As this book is about research universities, we have focused only on universities and not on colleges. It should be mentioned that India is one of the few countries where this model of affiliated colleges still exists. The recently proposed National Education Policy (NEP) of the Government of India (NEP 2019) recognizes that lack of autonomy for teachers regarding what they teach and how they teach is demotivating and therefore proposes to abolish the affiliation system and convert all affiliated colleges into autonomous colleges with full control over their programmes, courses, syllabus, assessment, etc. It envisages that there will be some amalgamation of colleges leading to about 10,000 to 20,000 such colleges each with an enrolment of 2,000 to 5,000 students.

Let us look at how universities are distributed with respect to the aforementioned parameters. The distribution of universities is shown in Table 1.1 (AISHE 2018, 31).

Of these universities, about 280 universities are affiliating, that is, they have colleges affiliated to them where much of the UG teaching is carried out based on the syllabus developed by the affiliating university. On an average, an affiliating university has more than 125 colleges affiliated to it, and according to some reports, a few of these universities have more than 500 colleges affiliated to them, the largest having almost 1,000 colleges.

An affiliating university often has regular programmes at the master's and PhD levels, which are taught and managed within the university and not in colleges (although some colleges may be allowed to have master's programmes). Hence, an affiliating

Table 1.1 *Distribution of Universities*

S. No.	Type of University	2013–2014	2014–2015	2015–2016	2016–2017	2017–2018
1	Central university	42	43	43	44	45
2	Institute of national importance	68	75	75	100	101
3	State public university	309	316	329	345	351
6	State private university	153	181	197	233	262
4	Deemed university—government	36	32	32	33	33
5	Deemed university—private	80	79	79	79	80

Source: AISHE (2018, 31).

university may also be a respected research university—for example, Delhi University—which has many affiliated colleges but is also considered a good research university. For discussion on research universities, universities without their affiliated colleges can be treated as regular universities.

For the base funding for public universities (i.e., the yearly grant for running the institution), there are three main sources. The first is the Central Government Ministry dealing with education, namely MHRD, most central governments created technical institutions such as IITs, NITs, Indian Institutes of Science Engineering and Research (IISERs), central government's IIITs and Indian Institutes of Management who get their base funding through this channel. The second is the UGC, which gets its funds from the MHRD. This channel is used by most central government universities, such as Delhi University, University of Hyderabad, and Jawaharlal Nehru University (JNU). The third is the state governments—most state universities receive funding through this channel, although a few of them may also get some support from the UGC.

However, this is not the complete picture. Some of the specialized institutions, which are universities and grant degrees, are associated with different ministries. For example, for many of the universities focusing on medicine, the funding is provided by the Ministry of Health and Family Welfare. Similarly, the Ministry of Law and Justice provides funds to some of the law universities and the Ministry of Agriculture & Farmer Welfare supports some of the agricultural universities.

Public universities get their annual grant mainly to cover their establishment and running expenses. The level of annual grant is typically decided based on the last year's grant with a suitable increase to cover for inflation. Funds may also be provided for any special needs the university may have in the current year. A university submits the request for funds with details about the level of funds needed for different expenditure heads, and the funds are granted to the university for expenses such as salary, pension and maintenance. Any fund that is not used in the current year has to be returned to the government (or accommodated in the budget for the following year).

We have just given a short overview of the structure of the HE system. A detailed discussion on the various aspects of the Indian HE system including the structure and growth, access and equity, role of private sector, regulatory framework, financing, etc. is given in Agarwal (2009).

1.1.2 Growth of Higher Education

Much has been written about the HE set-up in India and its growth, and an annual report also comes out giving the figures and discussing different aspects (AISHE 2018; Varghese et al. India Higher Education Report). The intent of this book is not to discuss the growth of HE in general; rather, it focuses on research universities and their education system. However, to provide the context, let us briefly look at the growth of universities, colleges and student enrolment in India. The growth of degree-granting institutions, which comprise all universities, including the ones

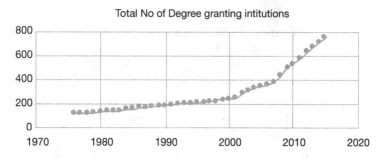

Figure 1.1 *Growth of Universities and Institutes in India*
Source: DST (2017, Table 8).

created by the central or state government, deemed universities and institutes of national importance created by the government of India, is shown in Figure 1.1 (data from DST [2017, Table 8]).

As shown in Figure 1.1, the rate of growth has increased significantly in this century. As a result, the number of universities increased from 240 in 2000 to more than 750 in 2015.

As mentioned earlier, a vast majority of UG education takes place in affiliated colleges. Hence, colleges are high in number. The total number of colleges and their growth, as well as the enrolment of students in HE and their growth, is shown in Figure 1.2—the y-axis on left represents the number of colleges (data from DST [2017, Table 8]).

The model of affiliated colleges permitted the private sector players to become active participants in HE. Private universities were still uncommon, and establishing one was difficult. The requirements for establishing colleges were generally modest in terms of capital, labs, land and so forth, allowing more private players to establish them. With the robust control being exercised by the affiliating university, not only in curriculum and programmes but also in tuition fees, it was probably felt that a broader private participation helped satisfy the demand for HE without the adverse potential side effects of profiteering. This

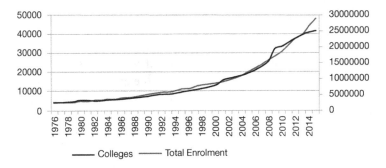

Figure 1.2 *Growth of Colleges and the Total Enrolment*
Source: DST (2017, Table 8).

allowed rapid expansion of HE with lesser investment by the governments. Most affiliating universities kept control on the fees. Although the cost of education was ensured to be modest, the quality of faculty was a challenge, as their compensation had to be correspondingly adjusted. Consequently, the quality of education suffered in many of these colleges.

It should also be mentioned that the gross enrolment ratio (GER)—which captures the percentage of students eligible for HE who actually get enrolled—is currently around 25 per cent in India and is expected to reach 30 per cent in the next few years. In many developed countries, such as the USA, Australia and European countries, the GER is generally more than 80 per cent. In China, it is about 40 per cent.

It is a stated goal of the Indian government to further increase the GER. It is also known that the demographics in India is biased towards the youth, for example, more than 20 per cent of the population is between the ages of 0 and 10 years and another 20 per cent is between the ages of 10 and 20 years. This means that the HE system needs to grow just to accommodate the larger number of young people graduating from schools to maintain the existing GER. And to increase GER, the HE system will have to continue to grow at a fast pace for the next couple of decades.

1.1.3 Evolution of Research Universities

We have discussed earlier the overall HE system in India and the growth of education. As the focus of the book is on research universities, in this section, we look at the evolution of research universities in India. We continue our discussion using the general understanding that a research university is one that focuses strongly on research (in addition to ensuring high-quality education), which gets reflected in a high-quality and extensive PhD programme and research output in terms of research papers. It should be mentioned that this narrative of evolution is broad and loose, as no extensive research has been performed to study the evolution of research universities in India.

1.1.3.1 Early Universities: Before Independence

The modern university system in India was started with the establishment of university of Calcutta by the British. This was followed by universities of Bombay and Madras. These universities were set up with a clear purpose of developing educated human resources for the British administrative machinery in India. (This is one of the main reasons why, after some debate, English was chosen as the medium of instruction in these universities.)

Although these universities were created mainly with the purpose of education, they did have research programmes. Given that they had some outstanding faculty and were perhaps the only places with PhD programmes, they emerged as centres for research. In that sense, these were the first research universities in India. Based on the data on the production of PhDs, as discussed later in the chapter, some of the top research universities around the time of independence were the University of Calcutta, the University of Madras, the University of Bombay, Lucknow University, Allahabad University, BHU), Agra University, Punjab University, Aligarh Muslim University (AMU) and so forth.

However, the focus of these institutions remained on education, which was indeed an important need of the country at the time. The data show that the total number of PhDs produced till the 1920s was less than one per year, and it was just about three per year in the entire country even in the 1930s (the decade before independence). A very senior academician in a prominent university at the time of independence informally mentioned that, as faculty, they were expected to only teach. Some of the talented faculty were involved in research not because they were expected to but because they wanted to, and thankfully, the university had leadership that allowed research to be pursued.

1.1.3.2 Establishment of Universities with Research as a Mission, Such As IITs, IISc and JNU

Between 1950 and 1975, about 100 universities were established in India, many of which had research as a mission. These included the original five IITs, All India Institute of Medical Sciences (AIIMS), IISc, Tata Institute of Fundamental Research (TIFR), Tata Institute of Social Sciences, Birla Institute of Technology & Science (a private university), University of Hyderabad, Jadavpur University, Indian Agricultural Research Institute, JNU, Indian Statistical Institute (ISI) and so forth. Seven of the top 10 engineering institutions as per the National Institutional Ranking Framework, 2018 (NIRF 2018), and about 8 of the top 10 universities (as per the rankings) were created during this period or earlier. Hence, we can say that these are the initial set of research universities established in India.

This period also saw the establishment of national research lab systems such as Indian Space Research Organization (ISRO), Defence Research and Development Organization (DRDO), Department of Atomic Energy (DAE) and Council of Scientific and Industrial Research (CSIR) (some of them were actually established earlier but got support for growth in this period). This dual system with research labs expected to do mission-oriented research and universities mainly for education and academic research diluted the research agenda for universities. Universities were largely perceived as having the mission of improving HE in the country—establishing new models of education, new programmes, admission approaches and so forth—besides training the next generation of researchers through their PhD programmes. The support for research provided to them was also modest. As a result, many universities focused more on teaching. Following the Soviet model of having research for national needs in research labs has had some gains, but those have not been sufficient and much more could have been done in terms of research output as well as the quality of research, if such labs were established in partnership with universities, as is the case in countries like Germany and USA. (Chandra 2017, Chapter 6). Overall, this division hurt the evolution of universities as important and high-quality research centres (Hatakenaka 2017). Universities, however, tend to attract talent from everywhere in the world— given the academic freedom and education programmes to train the next generation of researchers and other professionals. As a result, many of these institutions evolved as research institutions with some fine researchers.

Some of the institutions, particularly the IITs, were set up with strong collaboration and support from different developed countries. For example, IIT Bombay was established with the help from Russia, IIT Delhi with the help from the UK, IIT Madras with the collaboration of Germany and IIT Kanpur with the collaboration of the USA and a Kanpur Indo-American Program in which some of the top universities such as Caltech, Carnegie Mellon University, Massachusetts Institute of Technology, Purdue, Princeton, Ohio State and so forth participated actively. Collaboration with such research universities also helped research take roots in such institutions in India.

1.1.3.3 Growth of Research-Oriented Universities in this Century

After the establishment of the leading research institutions, the next few decades in HE focused more on increasing educational opportunities for the youth. This period saw a tremendous rise in demand for HE, and getting into premier institutions became harder and harder. This increased demand was met mostly by starting new colleges and teaching-focused universities.

This century has seen a significant expansion of universities with research as a key mission. As these universities are young, many may not have yet evolved into full research universities by a quantitative definition (e.g., the number of PhDs graduated or the number of full-time PhD scholars), but they have research as a key mission and recruit faculty suitably. Some facts about the growth of universities in India in this century are as follows:

- The number of IITs expanded from 6 to 23. IIT, as a system, aims to have research as an integral part of the mission.
- Seven IISERs were established—somewhat along the lines of the successful IISc.
- Some of the well-recognized research-focused IIITs were established, including Gwalior, Jabalpur, Allahabad, Bangalore, Hyderabad and Delhi (some were established a few years before 2000).
- Eleven new AIIMS have been established, taking their number to 12—earlier there was only 1 in Delhi.

Thus, in the last two decades, there has been a rapid expansion of universities with research as a focus, many of which can evolve into mature research universities.

This century also saw the rise of global rankings of universities. As these rankings are based mainly on research performance, the focus of existing elite institutions on research has also increased. As an example, data for an IIT indicated about 400 publications per year during 1985–2000. However, the yearly publications jumped to more than 900 by 2005, increased to more than 1,400 per year in the subsequent 5 years and again increased to more than 1,800 per year in another 5 years. The trend in many of the other leading research institutions is likely to be similar, suggesting that these research universities have increased their emphasis on research in this century.

The data from Web of Science for 5-year windows also show that for the top 25 institutions, the average growth of publications from 1991–1995 to 1996–2000 was about 20 per cent. For the same institutions, the average growth from the last decade of the previous century to the first decade of this century was 100 per cent. Similarly, data for the top 20 institutions from Scopus suggest that the average ratio of the number of publications in two consecutive 5-year periods in the previous century (1985–1989/1990–1994) was 1.29, but the ratio for two 5-year periods in this century (2006–2009/2000–2004) was 1.88. These indicate that the rate of increase in publications increased substantially in this century.

Overall, we can say that this century has witnessed the expansion of research universities in India, the impact of which will be felt in the coming decades. The current scenario of research universities in India can be summarized as follows:

- A couple of them were established before independence.
- Most were established in the first few decades after independence, many of which have global rankings and aspire to improve their global standing.
- Many young research universities (less than two decades old) exist, which aspire to be globally respected universities. How they would perform in the research mission is to be seen—the coming decade will probably show more evident trends.

It should be added that a few universities have come up or are coming up in the private sector with a stated desire to be globally respected research universities. Also, significant funds are being deployed as philanthropic contributions for establishing and running these universities. While it is early days, some of these can evolve into private research universities in the coming decades, as has happened in the USA.

1.2 PRODUCTION OF PHDS

The concept of PhD degree originated in Europe, where the early PhDs were granted in the 12th century. However, the PhD in its modern form, that is, with a research thesis, took firm roots in Europe in the 1800s—mainly with the establishment of the Humbolt's Model in Germany, which then spread. With changes, it was taken up and expanded in the USA which, by the mid-1900s, became a major producer of PhDs in the world.

An extensive and respected PhD programme is the hallmark of a research university—the size and quality of the PhD programme indirectly indicate the size and quality of the level of research activity, and hence is perhaps the most important feature that distinguishes a research university from others. Some classification frameworks of universities define research universities in terms of the size of the PhD programme—the oldest and most well-known Carnegie Classification of Universities in the USA classifies a university as a research university based only on the size of its PhD programme. (More about classification frameworks for research universities are discussed in Chapter 2.) Given the importance of the PhD programme for research universities, this section briefly discusses the evolution and current status of the PhD programme in India. A more detailed discussion on the PhD programme in India can be found in Jayaram (2008).

1.2.1 Early Stages of the PhD Programme

In India, the PhD programme started towards the end of the 19th century—Calcutta University in 1877 granted the first PhD. The Universities of Calcutta, Madras and Bombay gave the early PhDs—these are the earliest universities in the modern format and were established in 1857 by the British. A few other universities were established in the 19th century, for example, Lucknow University, Allahabad University and Roorkee University. Until the mid-1900s, very few universities granted PhDs, and the production of PhDs was modest. The number of PhDs produced in the early years, in accordance with the reports of Association of Indian Universities (AIU 1975a, 1975b, 1975c, 1975d), is shown in Table 1.2.

As we can see, the production of PhDs in India was quite low until before independence (in 1947). This was because the

Table 1.2 *Total Number of PhDs Graduated in India in the Early Years*

	Up to 1920	1921–1930	1931–1940	1941–1950	1951–1960	1961–1970
Social science	10	12	33	163	687	1,909
Biological science	2	6	51	155	785	3,196
Humanities	15	29	86	308	1,092	3,880
Engineering and technology	0	2	3	30	146	580
Other physical sciences	12	50	152	383	1,533	5,171
Total PhDs	39	99	325	1,039	4,243	14,736

Source: AIU (1975a, 1975b, 1975c, 1975d).

universities set up by the British were intended to develop human resources to support the administration—research was not a goal, although the PhD degree provision was there. We can see that the production of PhDs rose rapidly in the two decades after India's independence. The PhD output in India was a little more than 1 per cent of the output in the USA in the 1930s, which climbed to about 5 per cent in the 1950s—the decade after India's independence. (Data on PhD production in USA are from Chiswick [2010].)

In the early 1900s, PhDs were mostly being granted by the oldest three universities. Others started granting PhDs later, but a few universities dominated the PhD output. These included, besides the oldest three, universities in Lucknow, Allahabad, Banaras and Agra (AIU 1975a, 1975b, 1975c, 1975d).

The first two decades after independence also witnessed the establishment of some of the major research universities, including the original five IITs and the IISc. Many of these focused on engineering and sciences, and within two decades of independence, PhDs were being granted in engineering also in reasonable numbers. Before independence, hardly a few PhDs graduated in engineering. In the decade after independence, the number of PhDs in engineering grew to about 150 (from 30 in the 1940s) and then to 580 in the following decade. The engineering institutions granting most PhDs included the IITs, University of Roorkee, BHU and Jadavpur. Most of these institutions remain as the leading research institutions in engineering and related areas till today. By 1960s, they were graduating almost half of all PhDs in engineering—a clear sign of research in engineering shifting to the engineering institutions.

1.2.2 Recent Trends in the Production of PhDs

In India, about 900 universities have degree-granting powers. Most of them have doctoral programmes. The structure of the modern doctoral programme is what prevails in many countries—the doctoral thesis that reports some original research by the candidate is the main component—one that distinguishes it from most other programmes. Besides the thesis, most universities have a course requirement depending on the degree the candidate has at the time of joining the PhD programme—thus, for example, candidates with a master's degree will have to do fewer courses compared with candidates with bachelor's. Some universities may have publication requirements for submitting a thesis. The approach for thesis examination varies but generally involves some external experts and a thesis defence.

The PhD programme in India is largely research-based. Professional doctorate programmes that exist in many countries (e.g., the UK) are very few—Pharm D (Doctorate in Pharmacy) is one such programme which was started in 2008. The PhD degree may sometimes have a different name, for example, some of the management institutions call it Fellow Program in Management.

The production of PhDs in India has continued to grow in almost all fields of study. Organisation for Economic Co-operation and Development (OECD) has data on the pro-duction of PhDs in many countries on its website. The data show that, in terms of the total number of PhDs produced, India stands fifth. It is worth noting that, although the number of

PhDs produced in India was tiny compared with the USA around independence (around 5%), the situation is quite different at present—India graduates about one-third the number of PhDs graduated by the USA.

The total production of PhDs in recent years has continued to rise (despite a dip in 1 year). The overall production of PhDs in India and the total number of PhDs in different fields of study are shown in Table 1.3 (data obtained from All India Survey of Higher Education annual reports for different years, e.g., AISHE (2018)—they are available online).

With the emergence of IITs and other research-focused HEIs after independence, the production of PhDs shifted more to these institutions towards the end of the previous century, as discussed earlier. For the recent few years, which are more indicative of the existing situation, data from the NIRF are an excellent source. The NIRF, in its 2018 edition (NIRF 2018), has compiled and published data of the top 100 universities and the top 100 engineering institutions—the two largest groups—as well as the top few institutions in different specializations such as management, law and medicine. The data suggest that the top 10 institutions, in terms of number of PhDs produced, on an average produced about 160 PhDs per year for engineering institutions and about 400 per year for universities during 2014–2017.

In any large HE system, it is expected that only top universities will be research-focused, with the rest focusing on education. It is clearly desirable that these top research universities grant most of the PhDs. The PhD production data in the USA indicates that the top 50 universities, out of a about 400 PhD-granting institutions, graduate about half of the total PhDs (Nerad 2008). This is a sign of a healthy HE system—the top universities are almost always research-focused and are most likely to have the best and most rigorous PhD programmes, leading to high-quality PhD graduates.

For a similar analysis, we have considered the top 25 universities and the top 25 engineering institutions (as per the NIRF ranking; referred to as 25 + 25) and their PhD graduation data

Table 1.3 *Production of PhDs in India in Different Fields in Recent Years*

	2011–2012	2012–2013	2013–2014	2014–2015	2015–2016	2016–2017	2017–2018
Humanities	2,994	3,463	3,570	2,759	3,191	3,015	3,727
Social sciences	4,271	4,770	5,403	4,785	4,950	6,462	6,700
Biological sciences	5,659	6,406	5,063	4,253	5,063	5,542	8,212
Engineering and technology	2,081	2,186	2,583	2,597	2,785	3,366	4,907
Other physical sciences	2,678	2,571	2,551	2,533	2,923	3,495	3,924
Others	3,874	4,257	4,695	4,914	5,263	6,921	6,938
Total	21,557	23,653	23,865	21,841	24,175	28,801	34,408

Source: AISHE (2018).

Table 1.4 *PhDs Produced by Top 25 + 25 Institutions*

	2015	2016	2017
PhDs from top 25 engineering institutes	2,437 (11.16%)	2,633 (10.89%)	2,903 (10.08%)
PhDs from top 25 universities	6,536 (29.94%)	6,438 (26.63%)	6,331 (21.99%)
Percentage of total PhDs from these top 25 + 25 institutions	41.1%	37.52%	32.79%

Source: NEP (2019).

and compared them with the overall production of PhDs. The total number of PhDs graduated from these institutions and their contribution to the total number of PhDs in the country are shown in Table 1.4. The trend seems to indicate that the PhD production in universities beyond these 25 + 25 is growing faster than in these universities. The new National Education Policy (NEP) of India (NEP 2019) envisages that the PhD programme in the research universities will be expanded considerably and will produce most of the PhDs in the country.

The fraction of full-time PhDs in top institutions compared with the rest is worth noting. The data indicate that PhD students in the top 25 institutions are mostly full time—about 85 per cent in both engineering institutions and universities. This is expected because top research universities rely on dedicated full-time PhD students (and dedicated postdocs in some advanced countries). This percentage drops significantly in the rest of top 100 institutions (about 45% and 68% in engineering institutions and universities, respectively).

There is a possible explanation for this large number of part-time PhDs. It is quite likely that most of these part-time PhD candidates are working as faculty in some university or college. According to the HE regulators, PhD is essential for high-level positions (e.g., full-time professor) or promotion. Hence, the demand for pursuing a PhD increased because many universities and affiliated colleges had a large number of faculty who did not have PhDs. As these candidates in teaching-focused institutions are working full time as faculty and often have considerable teaching load, they have little motivation for doing research. Such candidates often end up enrolling for PhD in a local university, or in the affiliating university.

In India, the tradition of industry researchers doing part-time PhD is not quite prevalent, and generally, only a small number of such PhD scholars are present. It should be pointed out that only companies having a reasonable internal R&D programme and some part of their business benefiting from research will permit some of their employees to do part-time PhD. Other corporations have no incentive to send their employees for PhD. In most situations, companies and candidates prefer doing PhD in a top research university to get the maximum benefit. Top institutions, particularly in engineering, also encourage such candidates because they bring in a good industry perspective and possible linkages. A decent proportion of part-time PhD candidates in a top research university may be such candidates.

1.3 RESEARCH FUNDING FOR UNIVERSITIES IN INDIA

Let us now discuss the other crucial aspect of a research university—research funding. Research is expensive and research universities need funding to support their research. Without adequate support, research universities cannot thrive. In India, as in most countries, research funding is provided through a few research-sponsoring bodies. The basic budgetary support for a university is mostly for the educational mission, though it may also include support for PhD students.

Research funding to universities is dependent on the overall research expenditure in a country. Therefore, we first consider the overall pattern of research funding in various countries and compare it with India's expenditure. Then, we consider the funds available to universities for research—a context more important when discussing research universities.

1.3.1 R&D Expenditure

Traditionally, research is carried out in a few types of organizations. These can be categorized as follows:

- Universities
- Government R&D (in labs, agencies, etc.)
- Business sector
- Others (nonprofits, focused groups, etc.)

The first three are the major players in research in most countries. The total R&D funding and the main sources for the USA, the UK, and Australia are shown in Table 1.5 (Willetts 2018, 111, ABS Website).

The business sector is the largest investor in R&D in these developed countries, which have a highly respected and globalized HE system besides a strong economy. In developed economies, many businesses thrive and expand on innovation and new developments, for which R&D is essential. Therefore, businesses in developed countries invest heavily in R&D. The business sector accounts for more than half the total R&D expenditure; in the USA, it is 70 per cent.

Another point to note is the ratio of expenditure for R&D in universities compared with government R&D. Much of the

Table 1.5 *R&D Expenditure in Some Developed Countries (in US$ billion)*

Country	Total	Univer-sities	Govt. R&D	Business Sector	Others	Academia/ Govt. R&D
UK (2014)	44	11	3	28	2	3.7
US (2013)	457	65	48	322	22	1.4
Australia (2013)	33	10	4	19	1	2.5

Source: Willetts (2018, 111, ABS Website).

R&D funding in universities comes from government sources. Although companies also fund research in universities, funding by corporations is generally a tiny fraction of the total. The bulk of the research funding for universities comes from sponsored research projects granted by sponsoring agencies, which are themselves sponsored by the government. In other words, the overall government funding mostly goes to two sectors: government R&D labs and centres and universities. Thus, the ratio of expenditure on universities and government R&D set-up indicates how the government research budget is spent. In the developed countries, the R&D expenditure in universities is more than that in the government R&D set-up, often many times more, as shown in Table 1.5. These countries have taken an approach that the government R&D budget is best spent by sponsoring research in universities while keeping sensitive and mission-critical research with the government.

In India, traditionally, the business sector (i.e., called the private sector in India) has not invested significantly in research. This is probably because, earlier, much of the economy was rather low-tech, and the focus was on producing goods using existing technologies and know-how. Consequently, the investment in R&D was felt as not necessary. Also, the size of the economy, as well as the size of corporations, was rather small, leaving little room for research investment. Few data are available on the research investment in the private sector in the decades after independence. However, in the 1970s–1980s, the private sector R&D investment was generally around 10 per cent of the overall R&D expenditure. This increased to 20 per cent by the end of the previous century. It may be noted that the liberalization and opening up of the Indian economy happened in 1991—perhaps this increase was a reflection of the new economy that was more globalized and market-oriented. The R&D expenditure in recent years is given in Table 1.6 (DST 2017, Table 1).

It is worth noting that the private sector expenditure in R&D has continued to increase and has now reached 40 per cent of the total. This is perhaps an indicator of the changing nature

Table 1.6 *R&D Expenditure in ₹100 Crore (i.e., ₹1 billion)*

Sector	2005–2006	2007–2008	2009–2010	2011–2012	2013–2014	2015–2016
Central sector	178	218	316	340	388	460
State sector	23	29	38	51	59	69
Private sector	84	129	153	232	305	378
Higher education	12	16	21	35	40	36

Source: DST (2017).

of the economy, which is now far more globalized, with many global corporations having R&D centres and operations in India. Moreover, many Indian companies have become global corporations, and overall, the economy is far more innovation- and technology-dependent, like the rest of the world.

However, the total R&D expenditure in India is much lesser than in most developed countries—India spends only about 0.7 per cent of the GDP on research, whereas in most developed countries, investments in research and innovation are often more than 2 per cent of GDP (NEP 2019). It is known that return on investment for research is often substantial—much of the growth in most developed countries in the previous decades can be attributed to their investments in research and innovation.

It is also interesting to note that the total expenditure for research in universities in India is less than 10 per cent of the expenditure in the government (central and state) sector. In other words, the R&D budget of the government is largely being spent on government labs and initiatives, and very little of it goes to universities. That is, the government research funding in India is highly in favour of government labs, with universities getting a small fraction of research funding. This is contrary to what happens in some of the developed countries with a vibrant HE system—the R&D expenditure is much more in research universities than the expenditure in government R&D labs. These countries have realized that research is most efficiently done in universities, which also have an extremely valuable by-product in the form of PhDs, who form the research workforce and faculty for the next generation. This funding pattern for research has a significant impact on the nature and volume of research in universities.

Much of the government expenditure on research in India is done through a set of agencies. These agencies spend their funds mainly for three purposes: running the organization; internal R&D, which is used for supporting the research labs they run; and extramural project funding, which is used to sponsor project-based research grants to academic institutions as well as research labs. We have considered the first two together as internal R&D expenditure to study the support available to universities for research. To give an idea of the R&D expenditure of various agencies and the extramural funding available, the R&D expenditures of the top few agencies for the year 2014–2015 are given in Table 1.7 (DST 2015). The table also presents the percentage of total extramural funding given by the agency.

In mission-oriented research organizations (e.g., DRDO DAE, and CSIR), which have labs and research infrastructure of their own, most of the R&D expenditure goes for their own research; only a small portion is spent for extramural funding. In agencies which are primarily into funding research, though they also support some labs (such as DBT and Department of Science and Technology [DST]), a higher portion of the total budget is allocated to extramural funding.

The total extramural funding by all agencies in 2014–2015 (DST 2015) was about ₹2,000 crore. As seen earlier, the total R&D expenditure by the central sector was ₹43,094 crore. In other words, only 5 per cent of the total R&D expenditure by the central sector is extramural, that is, funding that is given for research projects based on their proposals and which universities can apply for.

Table 1.7 *Total and Extramural R&D Spending for a Few Agencies in 2014–2015 (₹ crores; 1 crore = 10 million)*

Agency	Total R&D Expenditure	Extramural Funding (% of total)	% of total Extramural funding
Defence R&D Organization (DRDO)	13,256	77 (0.6)	4
Department of Science and Technology (DST)	2,700	760 (28)	38
Department of Biotechnology (DBT)	1,020	570 (56)	28
Indian Council of Medical Research (ICMR)	843	90 (11)	5
Council of Scientific and Industrial Research (CSIR)	3,335	39 (1)	2
Department of Atomic Energy (DAE)	4,075	101 (3)	5
Ministry of Communication and Information Tech (MoCIT)	-	231	12

Source: DST (2015).

1.3.2 Research Funding to Universities

The primary funding for research in a university comes through sponsored research projects, that is, from research projects funded by various research agencies in the country. It should, however, be mentioned that public universities, in India and elsewhere, also get base funding from their ministry/government for running the institute. We have assumed that much of this base funding is for paying salaries and covering standard expenditure and can be treated as the support for the teaching mission of these HEIs—which is perhaps the most important mission for HEIs in the country and the main reason for government support. However, some part of this support has dual purpose and supports research

Table 1.8 *Extramural Funding Per Year (avg) (in ₹ crore)*

Agency	1990–1995	1995–2000	2000–2005	2005–2010	2010–2015
DRDO	4.09	8.19	19.56	45.06	59.59
DST	30.66	59.68	154.86	516.05	739.35
DBT	26.73	33.61	67.4	255.52	525.74
ICMR	2.61	7.79	29.33	78.61	123.85
CSIR	5.7	12.24	18.66	35.58	60.96
DAE	3.07	8.84	19.28	31.96	68.54
MoCIT			36.43	138.19	262.89
TOTAL (from all agencies)	109.53	268.36	439.56	1266.3	2102.84

Source: DST-Extramural.

also—expenses for library, PhD scholars' stipend and so forth. Also, from time to time, some yearly budget may provide special funding for research to a couple of institutions. We focused only on the sponsored research funding, as that remains as the main source for funding research projects.

In India, universities get sponsored projects from the extramural funding of various agencies. The extramural funding per year, over the years, by the top few agencies, which accounts for more than 90 per cent of the research expenditure, is given in Table 1.8—all values are in crores of rupees (1 crore = 10,000,000; DST-Extramural).

According to a report by DST (DST 2017, Table 4), about 58 per cent of the extramural funding went to HEIs while the rest went to projects from different research labs and other bodies. However, for discussion here, we assume that all the extramural funding is potentially available for universities for research projects. A plot depicting the growth of extramural funding over the years is given in Figure 1.3 (the figures are in ₹ lakhs, 1 lakh = 100,000).

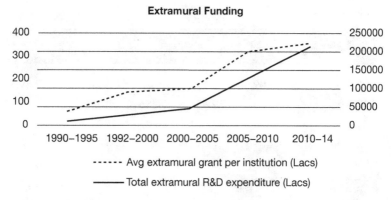

Figure 1.3 *Total and per University Extramural Funding Over the Years (in ₹ lakh)*

Source: Compiled by the author from various sources.

Given the increase in the number of research universities, it is useful to consider the extramural funding available per university. From the data on the number of universities over the years, we determined the average number of universities in the 5-year period. Using this and the data on extramural funding, we can estimate the extramural funding per university over the years. This is also given in Figure 1.3 (the scale on the left *y*-axis represents per university funding).

As we can see, the total extramural funding has continued to increase over the years. However, funding per university seems to have plateaued in the recent past at about ₹350 lakh per year. Even if we assume that 80 per cent of this research funding will go to the top 20 per cent of the universities engaged more actively in research, the average funding per research university will be around ₹1,400 lakh per year (approximately US$2 million.)

We can look at R&D funding available to universities in another way—from their own data—as reported to the NIRF. Using the data from the NIRF for 2018, we have considered the top 100 engineering institutions and the top 100 universities. We determined the average grant per institution for the top 100, as well average for the top 25 universities/engineering institutions.

Table 1.9 *Research Funding in Universities/Institutes (₹ lakh)*

	Average Per University/Institution in 2016–2017	Average Per Faculty in 2016–2017
For top 100 universities	2437.1	4.8
For top 25 universities	5568.3	9.7
For top 100 engineering institutions	1637.6	5.1
For top 25 engineering institutions	5027.9	12.7

Source: NIRF (2018).

These are given in Table 1.9 along with the average grant per faculty.

The average sponsored research funding per institution for the top 100 universities and engineering institutions is about ₹2,000 lakhs (about US$3 million). It is useful to look at per faculty-sponsored research funding in top universities. For computing the average per faculty, we computed the average per faculty of each institution and then took the average of these averages. This is also shown in Table 1.9—the average funding per faculty per year in all institutions and universities is about ₹5 lakh (approximately US$7,000). The average funding per HEI is twice or more in the top 25 institutions as compared with the average in the top 100. This is expected, as sponsored research funding naturally gets concentrated in a few top research institutions in a country. This is also desired, as the places that do the best research get more support. As expected, the average per faculty in the top 25 HEIs is about twice as much as in the top 100.

As we can see, the average research funding even in the top 100 institutions is modest—even for the top 25 HEIs, it is just about US$8 million per institution. (Only four universities and three engineering institutions received grants of more than ₹100 crore, i.e., approximately US$15 million.) Clearly, this level of research funding is insufficient for research universities, which need much more funds to do research at an international quality level. The NEP recognizes that the research funding available to universities is very limited and proposes establishing a National Research Foundation (NRF) to fund research in universities in all the different fields (NEP 2019).

1.4 TOP INDIAN AND GLOBAL UNIVERSITIES

The universities in India have evolved very differently from those in the developed world. Although India has more than 900 universities, very few of them feature in the top 200 in global rankings—none in the Times Higher Education (THE) and Shanghai rankings and some in QS rankings.

Global university rankings depend heavily on the research performance and impact of universities. For example, THE ranking gives 30 per cent weightage to citations and 30 per cent weightage to research, and 8 per cent out of the 30 per cent weightage is given to teaching which is related to the PhD programme. Others consider awards, fellowships, papers in top journals and so forth. As a result, all these top universities are well-known research universities with a strong emphasis on research.

Here we looked at the top 200 universities globally as per the THE ranking and the top HEIs in India as per the NIRF ranking and compare them in terms of a few key features—age, size and funding. For top HEIs in India, we have considered the top 100 in the university and top 100 in the engineering categories according to the NIRF ranking for 2018 (these include IISc, JNU, BHU, Delhi University, Jadavpur, IITs, NITs, IIITs and so forth) but exclude HEIs in the field of medicine, law, pharma, management and so forth. (Much of this analysis and results were reported in Jalote [2019].)

1.4.1 Age

The evolution of research universities took shape as the Humboldt model of HE, which proposed an integration of teaching and research, spread in the 1800s. It started from Germany and was vigorously adopted in the USA after some adaptation. Many new universities were created, which had research as an important goal, and many older universities reoriented themselves to become more research-focused. Many of these universities dominate the world rankings today.

Of the top 200 universities in the THE rankings, more than 65 per cent were created in the 19th century, when the Humboldt model started spreading rapidly. Only 19 per cent were created after 1950, when the current model of research universities with a focus on the PhD programme was firmly established and around the time when India got independence.

Of the top 100 universities and the top 100 engineering institutions in India, the age profile shows that about 60 per cent of them were created after 1975 and only six were created before 1900. The age of the top global institutions and top Indian institutions is shown in Table 1.10.

Late entrants indeed have a significant challenge in reaching the elite club of global top 200. First, establishing a decent research programme takes at least a decade or more, as it may take a few years to start a PhD programme; also, after starting the programme, it takes at least 5 years for the first PhD

Table 1.10 *Year of Establishment of Global Top-Ranked Universities and Top Indian HEIs*

Date of Creation of the University	No. of Global Top 200 Universities	No. of Top 100 Universities in India	No. of Top 100 Engineering Institutes in India
Created before 1900	132	2	4
Between 1900 and 1950	30	10	7
Between 1950 and 1975	23	23	35
After 1975	15	65	54

Source: Jalote (2019).

to graduate. Second, the impact of research is fundamentally time-dependent, and often, it takes decades for the impact to be recognized. Third, the impact the graduates of a university make, through which the perception of the university is strengthened, increases with time. The longer the university has been producing graduates and research, the stronger the impact. Thus, age helps a university in making it to the league of top universities, whereas young institutions face a significant obstacle in making it to this league.

The age distribution of all the HEIs in India is even more skewed towards youth. As of 2019, there were about 900 universities and about 90 HEIs which were listed as institutions of national importance. Of these, only eight HEIs were created before 1900. More than 80 per cent of the current HEIs were created after 1975 and about 70 per cent (670) of the HEIs were created in this century. It is clear that modern India is a late starter in the world of HE (ancient India was a leader with great universities such as Nalanda and Takshashila); much of the expansion in HE, including adding institutions with focus and potential for research, is very recent.

1.4.2 Size and Scope

Another factor that plays a significant role in being a top-class research university is the size of the university. Of the top 200 universities, the size in terms of the number of students is as follows: more than 90 per cent have student strength of more than 10,000 students (more than 60% have actually more than 20,000 students) and just about 2 per cent have a student population of less than 5,000. This distribution is shown in Table 1.11.

In India, in terms of student size, only seven engineering institutions have more than 10,000 students, and only two of them are public institutions. The two engineering institutions with the student population of more than 20,000 are both private universities. (It is important to recognize that in India, most private HEIs, particularly in engineering, are teaching-led and their primary

Table 1.11 *Student Strength in Global Top-Ranked Universities and Top Indian HEIs*

Size in Terms of No. of Students	No. of Global top 200 Universities	No. of Top 100 Universities in India	No. of Top 100 Engineering Institutes in India
Size <5000	5	50	68
Size between 5000 and 10,000	13	27	25
Size >10,000	182	23	7
Size >20,000	125	8	2

Source: Jalote (2019).

aim is to meet the needs of education.) The universities tend to be larger; still half of them have a student strength of less than 5,000, and only two of the eight that have a student strength of more than 20,000 are public universities. The student strength distribution of global top-ranked universities and top Indian HEIs is shown in Table 1.11.

In terms of faculty size, of the global top 200 universities, only 6 per cent have faculty members less than 500 and about 70 per cent have more than 1,000. In India, however, only three HEIs (less than 2%) have more than 1,000 faculty members; the overwhelming majority—more than 80 per cent—of the top-ranked HEIs have less than 500 faculty members. The faculty size distribution of global top-ranked universities and top Indian HEIs is shown in Table 1.12.

In other words, more than 90 per cent in the top 200 universities in the world have a student strength of more than 10,000 as against 15 per cent universities in India. Further, about 70 per cent of the top world universities have a faculty size of more than 1,000 and only 6 per cent have a faculty size of less than 500, as against about 2 per cent with a faculty size of more than 1,000 and about 80 per cent with a faculty size of less than 500 in India.

Table 1.12 *Faculty Size in Global Top-Ranked Universities and Top Indian HEIs*

Size in Terms of No. of Faculty Members	No. of Global top 200 Universities	No. of Top 100 Universities in India	No. of Top 100 Engineering Institutes in India
Size <500	12	79	94
Size between 500 and 1000	49	18	5
Size >1000	139	3	1

Source: Jalote (2019).

A large size will naturally imply that the university has faculty and departments in more disciplines, leading to broader research contribution and scope, as well as interdisciplinary research. A large faculty will also lead to more research, which also increases the chances of high-impact research. Moreover, a larger population of students graduating each year implies their contribution, impact and influence on society are greater. Both of these are important in building the stature and perception of a university.

In India, the approach for HE has been to develop specialized institutions imparting education in a few focused disciplines. Consequently, most universities tend to have a relatively narrow scope. For example, most universities (using the NIRF classification) have UG programmes in social sciences, humanities, natural sciences, arts, commerce and so forth, but do not have UG programmes in engineering. Similarly, most engineering institutions have UG programmes in engineering (e.g., BTech, BE) but generally do not have UG programmes in social sciences, humanities or natural sciences. Most universities or engineering institutions do not have medical schools, most of these being independent universities. A few may have law programmes at the UG level, but these are often offered by specialized law universities.

There is also a regulatory challenge. An engineering degree at the UG level (e.g., BTech, BE and so forth) is stipulated to be of 4-year duration, while the UG degrees in sciences, humanities and commerce (e.g., BA, BSc, BCom and so forth) are stipulated to be of 3-year duration.

Hence, the scope of most universities remains limited. As an example, let us consider a typical IIT—these institutions were created to impart education and conduct research in engineering and technology. A typical IIT has about a dozen or so departments and offers fewer than 10 UG degrees—mostly in engineering disciplines. Let us compare it with the Georgia Institute of Technology in the USA, another technology institution, which started with a single degree in mechanical engineering and then started degree programmes in a few other engineering disciplines such as electrical, civil, textile and chemical. Today, it has 6 colleges with 28 schools, most offering UG programmes. Nanyang Technological University (NTU) is another example, which is currently the second largest university in Singapore with more than 33,000 students and 10,000 faculty. It started in the 1980s with a charter to train engineers and programmes in three engineering disciplines—civil and structural, electrical and electronic and mechanical. It is now a broad-based university with colleges in engineering; business communication and information; education; biological sciences; humanities; social sciences; physical and mathematical sciences; and art, design and media. It offers more than 60 UG programmes in disciplines as diverse as business, art and design, communication, education, engineering, humanities, medicine, natural sciences, social sciences and sport science.

The NEP recognizes that having small and narrowly focused universities is not always conducive to a thriving research environment and proposes to have multidisciplinary research universities of decent size. It envisages that initially about 100 institutions can be converted to multidisciplinary research universities, and over a period of two decades, this number can increase to 150–300, each having 5,000–25,000 or more students (NEP 2019). The importance of multidisciplinary universities is also stressed in (Hatakenaka 2017).

1.4.3 Funding

Research universities are extremely expensive. There are a host of reasons for this (Altbach 2003). The faculty is expensive because these are the best brains who have to be compensated well. This cost is further increased, as such faculty members in these institutions teach fewer courses compared with their counterparts in teaching-focused institutions, thereby requiring more faculty members. These universities have a large doctorate programme, which is highly expensive (as PhD students are mostly paid) and is often missing in teaching-focused institutions. For conducting research, these universities need to have cutting-edge facilities and equipment, suitable library resources and support for travel to attend conferences, meetings etc. for the faculty and PhD students. All these add to substantial costs.

As discussed earlier, regarding R&D funding, the level of research funding available to Indian universities is modest. An analysis of data of the top universities and the engineering institutions (using the 2018 NIRF data) shows that the average research grant per HEI is about ₹24 crore (less than US$4 million) for the top 100 universities and about ₹16 crore for the top 100 engineering institutions. The average per faculty research grant in these HEIs in India is about ₹5 lakh (about US$7,000). While the human resources and some other costs are lower in India, many other costs associated with research such as equipment, international travel and digital library subscriptions, are the same as in other countries. As mentioned earlier, the NEP recognizes that this level of funding is insufficient for research universities to thrive and has proposed to substantially increase research funding for universities by setting up a research foundation.

To put this in a global context, let us look at the data from the Carnegie classification for US universities. For about 330 universities classified as research universities (as per 2015 results and data [Carnegie 2015]), about one-third are in each of the three subcategories—R1, R2 and R3. The average R&D funding per faculty for R1, R2 and R3 is US$300,000, US$150,000 and US$30,000, respectively. Also, research funding in top universities globally is often in hundreds of million USD. We can safely say that R&D expenditure in top universities in India is modest and significantly lower than even the research universities in the R3 subcategory in the USA.

1.5. SUMMARY

The Indian HE system is complex. It has evolved mostly for education, and research has not been given due importance. As a result, research universities of India are mostly quite young, small, often narrow and not adequately funded, compared with their global counterparts.

In this chapter we have briefly looked at the structure and evolution of the Indian HE system and the evolution of research universities in it. It then discussed two important aspects of research universities: PhD production and research funding. To put the Indian research universities in a global perspective, a comparison of the age, size and funding of top Indian universities and the global top universities has been presented.

REFERENCES

Agarwal, Pawan. 2009. *Indian Higher Education—Envisioning the Future*. New Delhi: SAGE Publications.

AISHE. 2018. *All India Survey on Higher Education, 2017–18*. New Delhi: Govt of India, MHRD.

AIU. 1975a. *Humanities: A Bibliography of Doctoral Dissertations Accepted by Indian Universities, 1857–1970*. New Delhi: Inter-University Board of India, Association of Indian Universities.

AIU. 1975b. *Social Sciences: A Bibliography of Doctoral Dissertations Accepted by Indian Universities, 1857–1970*. New Delhi: Inter-University Board of India, Association of Indian Universities.

AIU. 1975c. *Physical Sciences: A Bibliography of Doctoral Dissertations Accepted by Indian Universities, 1857–1970*. New Delhi: Inter-University Board of India, Association of Indian Universities.

AIU. 1975d. *Biological Sciences: A Bibliography of Doctoral Dissertations Accepted by Indian Universities, 1857–1970*. New Delhi: Inter-University Board of India, Association of Indian Universities.

Altbach, Philip G. 2003. *The Costs and Benefits of World-class Universities*. International Higher Education. ejournals.bc.edu.

Australian Bureau of Statistics, 8104.0. 2013–2014. *Research and Experimental Development Businesses*. Australia. https://www.abs.gov.au/AUSSTATS/abs@.nsf/Previousproducts/8104.0Main%20Features42013-14?opendocument&tabname=Summary&prodno=8104.0&issue=2013-14&num=&view=

Carnegie. 2015. carnegieclassifications.iu.edu. Data from the 2015 edition.

Chandra, Pankaj. 2017. *Building Universities that Matter: Where are Indian Institutions Going Wrong?* New Delhi: Orient BlackSwan.

Chiswick, Barry R., Nicholas Larsen, & Paul Pieper. 2010, December. *The Production of PhDs in the United States and Canada* (Discussion Paper No. 5367). Bonn, Germany.

DST. 2015. *Directory of Extramural Research and Development Projects, DST, for year 2014–15*. http://digitalrepository-nstmis-dst.org/files/rnd/yearwise/2014-15/Analysis_2014-15.pdf

DST. 2017, December. *Research and Development Statistics 2017–18*. National Expenditure on Research and Development by Sector. https://dst.gov.in/research-and-development-statistics-2017-18-december-2017.

DST-Extramural. *Analysis of Outcome of Extramural R&D Projects*, NSTMIS Division, Department of Science and Technology, (i) 1995–96 to 1999–2000, Dec 2008. (ii) 2000–01 to 2004–05, March 2013. (iii) 2005–2010, Dec 2016. (iv) Directory of Extramural R&D Projects, 2014–15.

Hatakenaka, Sachi. 2017. 'What is the Point of Multidisciplinary Research Universities in India?' In *Navigating the Labyrinth: Perspectives on India's Higher Education*, edited by Devesh Kapur & Pratap Bhanu Mehta. New Delhi: Orient BlackSwan.

Jalote, Pankaj. 2019, May. 'India's Quest for World-ranked Universities.' *Current Science* 116 (9) (General Article). https://www.currentscience.ac.in/Volumes/116/09/1479.pdf. [A shorter version appeared in International Higher Education as 'India's Research Universities and Global Rankings', No 99, Fall 2019, https://ejournals.bc.edu/index.php/ihe/article/view/11659/9723]

Jayaram, Narayana. 2008. 'Doctoral Education in India.' In *Towards a Global PHD? Forces and Forms in Doctoral Education Worldwide*, edited by M. Nerad & M. Hegellund. Seattle: University of Washington Press. 221–246.

Kapur, Devesh, and Pratap Bhanu Mehta. 2017. 'Introduction.' In *Navigating the Labyrinth—Perspectives on India's Higher Education*. New Delhi: Orient BlackSwan.

MHRD Website. Institutions of National Importance. mhrd.gov.in.

NEP. 2019. *Draft National Education Policy 2019*. Government of India.

Nerad, Maresi. 2008. 'United States of America.' In *Towards a Global PhD? Forces and Forms in Doctoral Education Worldwide*, edited by Maresi Nerad and Mimi Heggelund. Seattle: University of Washington Press.

NIRF. 2018. *Data on the Top 100 Universities and Top 100 Engineering Institutions*. https://www.nirfindia.org/2018/Ranking2018.html.

THE World University Rankings. https://www.timeshighereducation.com/world-university-rankings

Varghese, N. V., et al. *India Higher Education Report 2016, 2017, 2018, 2019*. SAGE Publications.

Willetts, David. 2017. *A University Education*. Oxford: Oxford University Press.

Chapter 2

Research Universities
Characteristics and Classification

Teaching and research have been the two main missions of a university. However, depending on the need and demand, as well as other governing factors, universities may emphasize the two missions differently and be teaching-focused universities, research-focused universities, or balance the two. It is important to recognize that not all universities need to engage with research at the same level as research universities. Indeed, it is desirable to have more universities focusing extensively on education, and only the select few which can cultivate a strong culture and capacity for research proceed along a more research-intensive path.

Most large HE systems naturally evolve as differentiated systems with some universities being research-intensive and others focusing more on teaching; this segregation of emphasis is inherent in their evolution itself. In some cases, as in the California system, HE organization may be designed with some universities specified as research universities, while others focus on teaching. It should be noted that both research-focused and teaching-focused institutions are required for a vibrant HE system.

In this chapter, we will discuss research-focused universities, which we refer to as research universities or research HEIs. We will discuss, among other things, why research universities are important for a country, which characteristics differentiate a research university from the rest, classification of such universities and how such universities can be created. In order to contextualize these issues, it is important to define what we mean by research, and to assess its importance.

2.1 RESEARCH AND RESEARCH UNIVERSITIES

Scientific research has traditionally been an open endeavour, where research findings are published and available to all. Under these circumstances two obvious questions spring up: Should all nations engage in research? Why can't some developing nations simply use the knowledge that is generated by scientists in the developed world for their own purposes? These types of questions are particularly relevant for a country like India, where resources are scarce, and sometimes research is viewed as an unaffordable luxury or an esoteric engagement which may only be supported if funds permit. In this section, we address this question largely in the context of a developing country, though some of these arguments are more general. Before we discuss the need for research and research universities, let us take a look at the nature of research and its relationship with innovation and development.

2.1.1 Research, Innovation and Development

Research is an activity that leads to generation of new knowledge. This new knowledge may help in our understanding of some phenomenon, or may be useful in developing useful products and services for mankind. Generating 'new' knowledge is the main purpose of the research activity and it can only happen if the scientist or researcher (we will refer to someone doing research, as a scientist or a researcher, even if their main job may be of an engineer, student, teacher, etc.) understands the prevailing trail of knowledge that already exists in the subject area.

Let us also understand how new knowledge created by ongoing research is recognized and accepted as knowledge, and how it is shared. A claim for new knowledge is accepted as valid generally only after it has gone through a process of peer review by expert scientists in the field, following which it is published in a suitable journal (or conference proceedings) through which the knowledge is further scrutinized by the global scientific community.

This process has some subtle implications. Not all new knowledge will be accepted by scientists and journals. Only findings that are scientifically relevant or promising are likely to pass through the filter. A scientific contribution is often assessed by its significance and impact. Significance of the work is largely about how useful the research results are to the wider scientific community, to the industry or to society. 'Impact' is how the new knowledge affects or influences the scientific community in particular and the society as a whole. Impact is time-dependent and there are examples of scientific work whose impact was felt decades later. When a new research finding is submitted, it is largely assessed based on the significance of the work, its accuracy and/or reproducibility and potential for impact.

2.1.1.1 Basic and Applied Research

Research is often considered as basic or applied. This categorization was clearly articulated in Bush's seminal work (Bush 1947) which was highly influential, particularly in the USA where it impacted the Science and Technology (S&T) policy. Basic research is largely concerned with generating new knowledge that will help in understanding the laws of nature. The key characteristic is to expand the understanding of the fundamental phenomenon in an area of science. OECD defines it as 'experimental or theoretical work undertaken primarily to acquire new knowledge of the underlying foundation of phenomena and observable facts' (OECD 2015). As understanding is the goal, basic research may be seen as an endeavour that does not set a target of practical usage or application-based use of the knowledge generated.

On the other hand, applied research seeks to create knowledge which can be utilized by society. The knowledge spawned through applied research can help in developing actual uses by reducing the degree of exploration or experimentation needed (Stokes 1997). Development is the activity of applying available knowledge to create new products or solutions for challenges or problems faced by the individual or the society. It should be pointed out that these roles are not limited to each of these categories: it has been found that basic research may also have application-based uses and applied research may also provide understanding of certain phenomena.

One way to view research is as a continuum between applied and basic. Another, perhaps more appropriate view, is to locate 'use' and 'understanding' as two distinct characteristics of research, and any research work may make a contribution to one or both of these. So, using both these dimensions, we can see research as being located in four possible quadrants (Stokes 1997), as shown in Figure 2.1.

In this quadrant model, the nature of research question being asked or the type of problems being worked on decides which quadrant the research will fall in. If deep fundamental questions are being asked without any specific use in mind, the research falls in Bohr's quadrant. If it is driven largely by some applied problem and consideration for use, then it falls in Edison's quadrant. If

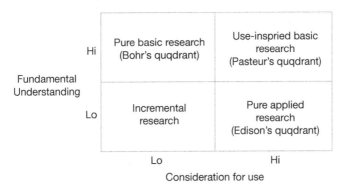

Figure 2.1 *Quadrant Model of Research*
Source: Stokes (1997).

instigated by both, it is in Pasteur's quadrant. It should, however, be added that it is often not possible to foresee the use of some basic knowledge in future—as many examples have shown that their uses may be uncovered decades later.

While it may appear that Pasteur's quadrant is where the best research may fall, as it combines the best of both worlds, this view is too simplistic. There are some fundamental questions about the world and nature to which human curiosity demands answers; these can be given by scientists working in the Bohr's quadrant. Indeed, the work of Bohr and many other top scientists, including Einstein, which has helped humankind better understand the nature of world, falls in this quadrant. And such work is clearly among the best scientific works. Similarly, some of the research that falls in Edison's quadrant may be as impactful as any. We will continue using the terms 'basic' and 'applied' research, while keeping in mind that either type of research may contribute in the other dimension as well.

2.1.1.2 Research and Development

The traditional view of research and its benefits reaching the society is a linear progression of basic research leading to applied research, which in turn leads to development and then to production. This is shown in Figure 2.2 (Stokes 1997). It is implied that basic research generates knowledge, (some of) which is used by applied scientists. The goal of basic research

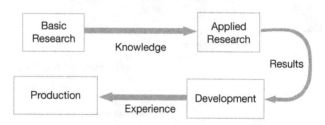

Figure 2.2 *Research, Applied research, Development and Production*
Source: Modified from Stokes (1997).

remains an understanding of some phenomenon, while applied research essentially generates knowledge that is directed towards betterment. Applied research generally aims at evolving new approaches for achieving targeted goals. This applied research may be completely for the benefit of humanity and may provide solutions for problems not articulated so far. Or it may provide new approaches which are better than existing approaches—in terms of cost, duration, feasibility, etc. Much of applied research is about finding better approaches.

Development is the next stage in which the research findings are leveraged to develop useful materials, devices, systems, procedures or other solutions (Stokes 1997). Development also involves limited research, as research rarely provides 'ready-to-use' findings. Adaptation of the research is also often considered part of the research enterprise and that is why the generic phrase 'Research and Development' (R&D) is widely used. This type of development can be considered as an extension of applied research and generates knowledge about how best to use existing information and findings to produce useful products or services. Development leads to production, which is largely a commercial activity carried out by business organizations.

2.1.1.3 Research and Innovation

Currently, innovation is a buzz word across the world. Innovation is concerned with creating value through novel applications of knowledge in practical and feasible ways. So, the goals of the research and innovation endeavours are different—one is about generating knowledge and the other is about generating value. There is, however, a strong synergy between innovation and research, as innovation creates new value, often by using new knowledge in innovative ways to generate value. In other words, research results often provide the basic fodder for innovation.

Innovation often combines results from different disciplines for innovatively addressing some problems in the human domain. Combining knowledge from multiple fields provides a fertile ground for innovation, as often human and societal problems require sound knowledge of various aspects which may come from research in different disciplines. Often gaps emerge in existing knowledge as it may have been created by a researcher who was completely unaware of this potential use. This needs further research. In other words, innovation, while it uses research results, also throws up problems which need further research.

In other words, research is needed to promote innovation—both to generate knowledge to be used for innovation and to address knowledge gaps that come up in the innovation process. One can safely say that without strong research capabilities to rely upon, the scope of innovation will be limited. Research and knowledge creation help in adoption of the innovation, support and expansion of the innovation ecosystem (Hawkins et al. 2006). This is shown in Figure 2.3.

It should, however, be pointed out that not all kinds of innovations require new or latest research results—old and well-established knowledge can also be used for innovation. For example, many e-commerce companies providing new services to specialized groups often use existing knowledge about products and technologies, but innovate in providing better consumer experience or user satisfaction.

2.1.2 Need for Research

The above discussion has shown that research is necessary for development and innovation—both fundamentally rely on

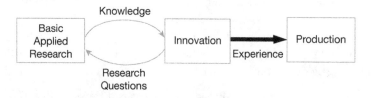

Figure 2.3 *Research and Innovation*
Source: Hawkins et al. (2006).

knowledge created by the research endeavour. It still does not fully address the question why even a developing country like India should engage in research, rather than just relying on the research published in the public domain. Here we briefly discuss some of the other reasons why research is necessary even in a developing country. We do not do any analysis of research in India—for this, we refer the reader to Aggarwal (2018) which discusses various aspects of research in India such as output, impact, comparison with other countries, past, future prospects, research personnel, research productivity, as well as the importance of research for economy and innovation in India.

2.1.2.1 Generation of Knowledge and Membership of the Global S&T Fraternity

Knowledge creation is the fundamental goal of research. Knowledge can also be considered as an intrinsic need of mankind to satisfy its curiosity. There are always some people in a country who are passionate about finding the unknown and contributing to global knowledge and have the capability and drive to do it. Research needs to be supported in a country so that such people can contribute to it and reach the heights they are capable of.

A country cannot be just a consumer of knowledge created elsewhere. It should participate in the global knowledge creation endeavour—at least to the level of its resources and capabilities. Active participating in knowledge creation also provides benefits to the global network of scientists. These networks can be leveraged effectively only if one is a part of that network (Altbach 2009).

Further, given that some of the major research challenges of current times, like pollution or climate change, are inherently global in nature, they require global collaboration to study and address them. This requires an apt system of research in a country which can collaborate with the global network to evolve solutions for such problems.

2.1.2.2 Capacity to Absorb Research

While most research is in the public domain and freely available to anyone, in practice, the knowledge is not really 'off the shelf' for use by all. Many researchers have shown that using knowledge developed elsewhere or externally itself presupposes certain conditions—it requires prior knowledge, an understanding of the field, the ability to qualitatively assess the importance and usefulness of knowledge, etc. Furthermore, there are often details, implicit knowledge and understanding that are missing from the published works, making it hard to use the knowledge if one is not an active researcher in the field. In other words, there is some 'tacit knowledge' which is required to fully leverage the knowledge being shared through research papers, and which active researchers often possess.

Hence, even the effective leveraging of the global research ecosystem producing knowledge requires a strong research ecosystem within the country. Capacity to absorb research therefore requires researchers working on the forefront of knowledge, particularly in areas that may be of importance to a country.

2.1.2.3 Economic Growth

As discussed above, research is intricately tied to development and innovation. As the pace of change of knowledge and technology has increased, and as we move towards a knowledge economy, knowledge becomes an engine of innovation and economic growth. Earlier research results were considered to be a 'resource' for the economy—knowledge produced by research was available as a resource to the industry to help solve its problems. In today's world, innovation is seen as a way to start new companies and create growth, and not just help existing industries in solving their problems. In this model, research plays a much more active role in the economy (Berman 2012). So, earlier where the focus of applied research was to help existing companies, an additional and more compelling dimension has been added—to act as a catalyst for growth of new industries and companies that are based on innovation.

New economic opportunities may emerge which will require research to tap them. This is not well appreciated, but countries that have a research culture and a sizeable pool of trained researchers are clearly going to be better prepared to reap the benefits from such new opportunities. Overall, one can say that while global knowledge is available for general use, development and innovation in a country will critically depend on its own research ecosystem which has the capacity to leverage global knowledge and global knowledge networks to their full potential in order to develop more relevant knowledge as well as to produce solutions for national as well as global challenges.

2.1.2.4 Signalling to the World and Soft Power

Global stature and voice at the international platform of deliberations and decision-making is the key marker for a progressing nation, which can be supported by a strong research potential. Research universities dominate the global R&D scene. Hence, it has a signalling value, which is sometimes also associated with national pride. Research universities can be the institutional umbrella that can support scientists who can achieve global fame, thereby providing icons for the country.

Nations are also respected in the world for their contributions to different aspects of life, as to the communality and health of our planet. As contribution to knowledge is one such aspect, nations that contribute adequately, through the scientific network, get recognized and respected in return.

2.1.2.5 Strategic Reasons and Self-Reliance

It is well established that research that is of strategic value to the nation may not be shared publicly. In other words, while the endeavour of science is to uncover the truth and disseminate it, nations routinely engage in proprietary research, results of which are not available in the public domain. Often this knowledge is in strategic areas of defence, national security, space, etc., and a country may share such knowledge (probably at a huge cost) only to partner or friendly countries. So it is not uncommon for countries to deny access to their knowledge and technology to others.

Clearly, a nation cannot rely only on public domain research for its strategic goals. It must therefore have sufficient R&D capability to address its strategic needs. There are also critical technologies for which a country may not want to depend on other countries. To be self-reliant in such areas also requires research. This need is vital for survival of nations and provides in itself a strong justification for having research capability within the country.

2.1.2.6 Addressing Local Problems

Engaging with particular topical issues is relevant and vital. Global research, done mostly in developed countries, focuses on their issues and problems. This is justified as those research studies are funded by their government and industry. Even academic researchers who have the freedom to engage in any research topic will normally choose to work on problems relating to their country or society as they are more familiar about those; their agendas are also often driven largely by the availability of research grants.

Hence, research problems that may be particular to a country, for example, the health problems of inhabitants of specific regions of the country and the challenges of developing low-cost products without advanced features for the poorer sections are not problems that are likely to interest global researchers. These problems can only be addressed by researchers from within the country. To address these research problems, it is imperative for a country to have research manpower which is well trained not only in research methodology but also in the current state of knowledge who can confidently take up unique research challenges from the society and country and even embark on collaborations with researchers in other countries if required.

2.1.3 Need for Research Universities

We have discussed the need for research even in lesser developed countries. Research can be carried out in focused research labs as well—an approach many countries, including India, have taken particularly for mission-oriented and focused research. In this section, we discuss why research universities are needed, particularly in poorer or developing countries. It is important to be clear on this fundamental question; otherwise, the 'relevance' issue keeps creeping up, either explicitly or implicitly, in discussions and conceptualizations about research universities and the need to allocate sufficient resources for them. The new NEP of the government of India has given due importance to research universities and considers them as a different type of universities which will lead the country in R&D and PhD production. It envisages about 100 strong research universities in the near future in the country and more than double this number in two decades (NEP 2019)

There are many reasons for having top class research universities—we discuss some of the key ones in this section. It should, however, be pointed out that only some of the universities in a country need to be research-intensive, commensurate with the needs of the research ecosystem of the country. In a large HE system, often less than 10 per cent of the universities may be research institutions.

2.1.3.1 The Core of the Research Ecosystem

As discussed above, even for developing countries, it is important to have research capability. Research in a country is largely conducted in universities, research labs and corporations. Research universities form the core of the research ecosystem in a country as they not only produce research but also researchers for other research organizations. Ongoing development of a new generation of researchers in itself makes research universities the core of the overall research ecosystem of a country. (Theoretically, the research manpower can be trained in universities overseas, but reliance only on that approach for developing the needed research manpower is clearly not desirable for a large country like India.)

In earlier centuries, much scientific research was conducted outside the universities. However, in the past decades, the centre of gravity for research has clearly shifted to universities. For example, a quick analysis of the Nobel laureates in the past 25 years show that the vast majority of the recipients are from universities—about 80 per cent for chemistry and physics, and about 70 per cent for medicine. Even in areas like computer science and electrical engineering, where industry R&D investments are huge, the recipients of the top awards are mostly from universities—in the last two decades, about two-thirds of Turing Award (top award in computer science) winners and about 60 per cent of IEEE Edison Medal (top award in electrical engineering) winners were from universities.

Universities provide a unique space which is highly conducive for research. There are many reasons for it. First, they bring together the wisdom and experience of the professors and the young, fresh ideas of PhD students. This mixture is extremely potent as young minds often have very new and innovative ideas which can be tempered with rigor under an experienced professor. Further, universities have engendered a hierarchy-less culture of open expression which encourages collaboration among people from different disciplines, making synergies feasible for new knowledge creation. As university researchers need not be tied to any goals or missions, the university provides intellectuals with the option of exploring uncharted avenues in order to investigate the not-so-well understood areas and develop something new. This unencumbered environment fosters creativity and true innovation.

New areas of importance emerge globally from time to time, which are important for economy and society (e.g., solar power, battery technology, artificial intelligence [AI], etc.). Often for new areas, researchers from existing related areas shift to address the problems in the emerging fields. For this, research capability in a wide range of disciplines is necessary, and that can only be done in the research universities in the country (as labs and companies will mostly focus on their mission needs). For example, AI has been identified as an important area of research for India, as its applications are immense. Most of the AI researchers today are ones who used to work on related problem areas such as image processing and analysis, algorithms and mathematics. Some of these areas were not considered very relevant in the country when these researchers were working in them. It is important that research capability in a wide range of areas be built to global levels, even if some of these areas are not too relevant in the current scheme of things. And this can be done only in research universities.

Research universities also are the most effective engines for research (Altbach 2009). Due to the education component of research universities, the investment in universities has a multiplier effect. It can be safely said that, except for strategic and mission-oriented research which are best carried out by focused research groups or labs, research universities are now accepted as the most efficient way to conduct research. Due to this, many countries are shifting from having separate research-only labs/institutes to embedding them within research universities (Altbach 2009). The NEP also observes the centrality of research and innovation in universities and that universities must support a culture of research and innovation while encouraging multidisciplinary research (NEP 2019).

2.1.3.2 Development of the Overall Education System

The HE system can be broadly divided as having institutions in three tiers:

- Colleges which provide education mostly at baccalaureate level (tier III);
- teaching-focused universities, which provide education at all levels, with emphasis primarily on bachelor's and master's programmes, but with decent PhD programmes (tier II);
- research universities, which have programmes at bachelor's and master's levels, but their main focus is on research and the doctoral programme (tier I).

It is a broad paradigm in teaching and learning that if one wants to teach at some level, he/she should have training up to higher levels. This is almost universally practised not only to ensure that the teacher knows more than the students but also because a deeper understanding of the subject is expected as one goes higher in expertise, which is often provided by higher degrees. To ensure that the faculty member has a higher level expertise in the subject, it is desirable if they are graduates from the higher layer. So teachers in colleges are expected to have postgraduate degrees from universities, and teaching-focused universities hope to have graduates from research universities as their faculty. The exception is, of course, the research university tier—faculty for this layer also come from the same level.

In other words, the overall education system can be seen as a pyramid with research universities at the top of the structure as shown in Figure 2.4. The research university layer fundamentally powers the HE system. It provides the faculty not only for the research universities themselves but also for the large number of other universities which then educate people and provide faculty for colleges. This type of tiering takes place in most developed HE systems—the universities get grouped into different layers naturally due to their mission, or due to their performance. The NEP also proposes a three-tier model like this.

Violation of the unstated principle in education—that a teacher is generally expected to possess a higher degree from a higher layer—has an impact on the quality of teaching at these levels. The lowering of education quality in colleges and

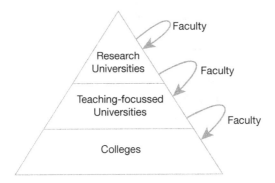

Figure 2.4 *Overall HE System and Role of Research Universities*
Source: Author.

universities then gets reflected in the lowering of teacher quality in schools. It should be evident that for the health of the overall education ecosystem and to ensure that good quality education is provided at all levels, it is essential to have a vibrant and high-quality research university layer, or else education at both the college and university levels, and at the school level, will suffer.

In India, effects of a relatively small research university layer are already visible. A vast majority of teachers in colleges do not possess a PhD and are the products of the layer in which they join as faculty. With a vibrant research university system which produces PhDs in requisite numbers to meet the demand, the availability of qualified candidates for faculty positions will help improve the quality of the overall education system. A research university also plays a key role in the overall quality of education in the HE system by designing new courses, improving course curriculums, providing teaching material and in many other ways. We will discuss this further in Chapter 3 on education. The NEP recognizes the importance of research universities in the overall education system, including the impact of university education on school education, and has made recommendations to enhance the PhD programme as well as teacher education for schoolteachers (NEP 2019).

2.1.3.3 Attracting and Retaining Talent

Often the best scientists are not only fine researchers but also creative innovators. Such talented people hugely value the freedom to explore (Arora et al. 2017) and are willing to work even at reduced compensation if such freedom is provided. So, gifted researchers are often attracted to organizations that provide such freedom as well as adequate support for research, along with an environment and culture for doing good work. World-class research universities inevitably provide an environment to attract and retain talent.

Talented researchers are global citizens who, regardless of their country of origin, have multiple opportunities across different countries. For a developing country like India, often the best and brightest scholars go to top universities across the world to pursue higher studies and PhDs, and after completion of their degrees, choose to stay in the same country. Such research talent can be attracted to work within their home country only if there are world-class research universities that can provide them the desired environment which is somewhat comparable to global standards. This can be seen empirically: top universities (e.g., IITs, IISc) that have a decent reputation and provide a decent research environment are far more successful in attracting as faculty those who have received PhDs from notable universities across the world. In other words, research universities are the organizations that can attract and retain the global talent for research, including the top indigenous minds which may otherwise migrate to foreign lands.

2.1.3.4 Global Cooperation in Science

Big problems are increasingly global in nature, where countries have to cooperate and work together. Examples are climate change, pollution, alternative energy, etc. It is important to have researchers in a country who can participate in these global collaborative efforts. Often research universities are at the forefront of knowledge in these areas. Researchers in universities have a long tradition of collaboration. Research universities also have mechanisms to support visiting faculty, invite scholars for short visits and seminars and organize student exchange programmes. As most research universities have somewhat similar systems for research, the global scholars find it easy and comfortable to visit a research university in another country and collaborate with students and faculty there. Many research papers come out of these visits, which also facilitate exchange of ideas on education and research. Overall, research universities provide a unique platform for global exchange of scientists and collaboration for science. No other type of organization can match what research universities from countries across the world have done for collaboration in science.

2.1.3.5 Having Neutral Experts

Policymaking is increasingly becoming more complex, particularly relating to use of new technology and services. Often corporations have their interests involved in this, and they have ways to influence decision making. It is therefore critical in these matters to get a non-biased view from experts, who are most commonly found in research universities.

Similarly, often for large works in specialized areas or technologies (e.g., selecting a new technology for the state or country), governments will receive proposals from vendors. These can be quite technical and evaluating them requires sound technical expertise besides commercial and other concerns. Often these experts are from research universities; not only are they well versed with developments in the field and technology, but they also provide a neutral view of advantages and pitfalls which can truly help in decision making.

2.1.3.6 World-Ranked Universities

Research universities are generating excitement across the world (Altbach 2007). So, even though research universities tend to be expensive—much more than teaching-focused universities—it is important for a country to have research universities, some of which should be operational at international levels.

World-class universities generally refer to those universities that are in the top 200 (or 500) as per the accepted global rankings of universities. Global rankings have become extremely visible in this century despite their limitations and certain criticisms levelled at them. Most global rankings depend on the research output and impact of the universities, though some weightage may be given to the teaching aspect as well. Consequently, all world-class universities are classified as research universities, though clearly not all research universities may be ranked highly.

A clear implication of this is, if a country aspires to have some universities ranked as world class, it must have good research universities. As only some of these research universities can make it to the world rankings, it will improve the chances if there are a reasonable number of research universities in the country which compete for research funding and talent with each other, while cooperating for research.

2.2 KEY CHARACTERISTICS OF A RESEARCH UNIVERSITY

As mentioned earlier, a research university is one whose mission and vision place a strong emphasis on research. While education remains a key objective of a university, a research university focuses sharply on research in its thinking, planning, culture, operations, policies, resource allocation, etc. What does this emphasis and focus on research actually mean? In this section, we discuss some of their key characteristics—many of these have also been discussed in Altbach (2007, 2009). These characteristics can also be guidelines for a university that aspires to be a research university.

2.2.1 Faculty Recruited and Promoted Primarily on Research

A research university must necessarily have faculty which is actively engaged in research, as faculty forms the core of the research capability of a university. This implies that only candidates with PhD in an appropriate discipline are considered for regular faculty positions. Focus on research potential during recruitment is a key characteristic of a research university. While a teaching-focused university will give importance to scholarship, ability to communicate and teach, and may look at research record only as an additional attribute, in research universities, it is the reverse. While communication and teaching are necessary in a candidate, the main assessment is on research record and potential. Due to this focus, the faculty recruitment process is rigorous with inputs from faculty of the relevant departments as well as from peers from across the world (in form of letters).

To keep the focus on research, it is not just important to recruit faculty with great research potential. To actually realize their potential, it is essential that promotion policies and practices be clearly tied to research output and impact. This means that faculty research performance is assessed on contributions such as research projects and funding, research publications, impact of research work (including reputation in peer community), PhD student supervision, etc.

Research universities must support meritocracy, where the research record and impact are the most important parameters for promotion as well as other rewards or benefits that may be given. The issue of faculty recruitment and promotion is discussed further in Chapter 7 in the book.

2.2.2 A Substantial and High-Quality PhD Programme

In many ways, the strength and quality of its PhD programme define a research university. Many other parameters can actually be subsumed in this. Having a large PhD programme is a significant investment. A PhD student is essentially an employee who is to be paid a fellowship or an assistantship, as well as provided support for their work in terms of facilities, travel, etc.

To ensure that the PhD programme aligns well with the overall objective of good quality research work, it is important

to have good systems and processes in place for doctoral programme. Universities that are not serious about research will
have lax systems, leading to average PhDs (and, of course, average research output). The PhD programme is discussed in detail
later in Chapter 6.

2.2.3 Active Research Programme

Most research universities motivate their faculty to get research
projects to support PhD students as well as other costs of research.
Most of the funding for research in research universities comes
through research grants. Besides bringing in funds for research,
success in getting these often indicates that the research in question is relevant and worthy of support while simultaneously
serving as a benchmark against others. So, even if other funds
are available, a research university should ensure that a thriving
sponsored research programme exists, and faculty vie for getting
these grants. For this reason, it is important that the faculty, as
well as universities, have strong incentives for seeking such funds.
These incentives can be in terms of overheads to the university,
travel and other support for faculty members, support for hiring
research staff or PhD students, summer salaries or some compensation for faculty, among others. The research funding that
a university gets indirectly defines the level of research activity.

To support research, a university needs to provide support
such as labs, library, R&D office, suitable IT infrastructure and
other necessary facilities. This is important and expensive. While
a library in a teaching-focused university needs mostly books, a
research university library needs other additional facilities like
subscriptions to journals and digital libraries, high-end IT infrastructure, etc. These are often very expensive. Similarly, labs for
research, as compared to labs for instructions, are often much
more expensive.

In modern times, it is believed that for good research output, it
is important to have research groups with multiple faculty (with
PhD and postdoctoral students) working long term on problems.

Such groups are able to make the most impact. Similarly, for interdisciplinary research, it is important to have structures that will encourage faculty from different disciplines and departments to work together for some common research theme. A research centre is a commonly used structure for this. Centres and research groups do not form on their own, they have to be actively supported and nurtured. A research university must have policies and funding to encourage formation of such research groups and centres.

A culture of curiosity and scientific exploration driven by self-motivation and peer recognition is an attribute difficult to define, but seminal for a vibrant research university. It is easy to publish research papers with insignificant contributions (sometimes even with incorrect results) in average conferences and journals, given the unholy proliferation of these forums. A strong culture of research will motivate faculty and students to aspire acceptance in venues that are known for quality work.

Such environments conducive to academic vitality also motivate faculty to stay active in research and continue contributing till late in their career. This is hard to achieve as often there is a propensity by faculty to give up or scale down research after becoming Full Professor, and perhaps seek administrative avenues. Since a majority of faculty members spend most of their time in the rank of a Full Professor (often a faculty member can become a Full Professor in about 10 years, while still having another 30 years till retirement), it is important that the motivation to remain active in research is sustained. This will depend to a large extent on the culture and systems of the university.

While a research culture generally develops organically, suitable policies for rewarding excellence in research in form of grants, awards, bursaries and such like, giving visibility and respect to research achievements of faculty and students, etc. can help the evolution of this culture. It can also be strengthened by having research seminars, conferences and workshops, supporting faculty to attend international conferences, and extending similar support to ensure participation in active research. Later

Chapter 4 will discuss various aspects of research management and promotion in a research university.

2.2.4 High-Quality Education

Almost all research universities have vibrant UG education programmes; often, two-thirds or more of the student population may be UGs. (UG tuition is a major source of revenue even for research universities). In the fast-changing technical fields, the best universities for UG education are often the best research universities, as there is a strong synergy between teaching and research for such fields. Due to the active research engagements of faculty, most research universities have some advanced courses whose syllabus is not only the established body of knowledge, but also the most recent developments in an area. Such courses may also lead to research projects and are available to both graduate and UG students. This unique aspect of education in a research university differentiates it from regular education and teaching.

It is often assumed that in research universities, only research matters and teaching are secondary. However, that is far from the reality—in most research universities, UG (and masters) education remains an important aspect. In fact, as we will discuss further in Chapter 3 on education, research universities are expected to take leadership in education, and they actually do so. Education is discussed further in Chapter 3.

2.2.5 Institutional Autonomy and Academic Freedom

Research is dynamic and complicated and requires academic freedom to operate. For these and other reasons, it is imperative that a research university has almost full autonomy of operation (with, of course, some expectations on its output and contributions). In many countries, this is a challenge as there is a strong political or bureaucratic control, and research universities are treated within the same framework as those which are more teaching-oriented. Autonomy is often difficult to obtain and sometimes universities have to struggle to obtain or maintain them, particularly when part of the financial support for these universities comes from public exchequer. Research universities need almost complete autonomy of operations and in selecting its governance team. In particular, they need the ability to select a suitable chief executive officer who remains accountable to the university.

Autonomy, however, comes with responsibility. Research universities need to be accountable to the society or the government, particularly if they take public funds. Safeguarding institutional autonomy while ensuring responsibility and accountability, particularly when the university may be funded in part by public funds, is a challenging issue, but one which has to be negotiated so that clear expectations are set from research universities, and in return, almost complete autonomy is supported.

A basic tenet of a research university is academic freedom, which ensures that a faculty member can pursue any line of research she wishes. Not only is it a key premise of a research university, compromising this opens risk of external intervention or stifling certain avenues of research. This is often not fully appreciated outside the academia—people and agencies fail to understand why a dean or a director cannot direct the faculty to take up some line of research, as, for example, the head of a research lab in a corporation can do. Academic freedom distinguishes a research university from a government or a corporate research lab, which may have some specific research mandate controlling the nature of research problems which can be worked on. We will discuss these issues further in Chapter 8 on governance of research universities.

2.2.6 Sufficient Financing

The high cost of research universities is very often underestimated. Frequently, plans are made for establishing a campus and for running expenses, but costs for research, which are often not clearly visible, are not incorporated. Sufficient finances are needed not only for the establishment of faculty and staff and running the campus but also for supporting research—labs, equipment, PhD students, travel support for conferences and meetings, digital library, etc. In a strong research university, the expenditure per faculty may be two times as much as in a teaching-focused university, and the number of faculty required for the quality of education that they provide may be twice as much as in teaching-focused places (as the teaching load has to be modest and the range of courses offered is large). It is safe to assume that the cost per faculty in a research university will be multiple times the cost in a teaching-focused institution. Clearly, without strong financial support, a research university cannot function effectively.

There is an increasing trend to charge the student closer to the actual cost of education, as subsidies seem to be declining world over. While separating education cost from research cost is complicated, it should be clear that the student tuition fee should go only towards covering education cost and supporting research through it is not fair. What this means is that even if the student is charged tuition fee to cover education cost, there needs to be financial support for research from the sponsor of the university. It should also be mentioned here that while research project funding can indeed provide some of the funds for research, the university still needs to invest considerably in PhD programme, labs, library and other infrastructure to maintain an active research programme. Financing of research universities is discussed later in Chapter 9.

2.3 CLASSIFYING RESEARCH UNIVERSITIES

A natural way to organize the HE system is to consider it as comprising of three tiers. In a three-tier system, at the top are the research universities—the main object of this book—which in addition to having education programmes at all levels, have a strong emphasis on research and perform research at an international level. They have strong PhD programmes and play a critical role in the research ecosystem of the country. At the next level are the master's universities (which we will refer to as universities), and they focus on providing high-quality UG education and master's programmes. To ensure that its education indeed is 'higher' and includes latest developments, they need to engage in research to some extent and so should have a small doctoral programme also. At the third level are baccalaureate institutions, whose focus is mostly on the UG programmes, though they may have some masters programmes also. Their programmes may also be based more on well-established body of knowledge. While a country needs and must have vibrant research universities, they cannot be institutions that satisfy the HE demand alone; otherwise, the cost to the students and society will simply be exorbitant.

The purpose of classifying universities is to group universities with similar objectives or mission (Carnegie 2000). A key goal of classification is to help understand complex systems with a heterogeneous population by grouping entities into subgroups such that entities in one subgroup share some common features, while differentiating them from entities in other subgroups (McCormick and Borden 2017). Classification can help separate the three tiers in a HE system. Here, we discuss some approaches for classifying universities with a focus on classifying research universities.

Classification is different from university rankings which, by definition, rank order the universities. Most rankings are based on multiple criteria, with different weightages assigned to each criterion for obtaining the final score for purpose of ranking. Ranking thus reflects a weighted sum of performance in teaching, research, service, perception, etc. This is different from classification, which is to categorize universities based on the characteristics they share. The class of research universities will get defined by characteristics relating primarily to research.

2.3.1 Research University Classification Frameworks

Carnegie classification is the oldest and most influential classification framework. Started in 1970, it classifies HEIs into a few broad categories: doctoral/research universities, master's colleges and universities, baccalaureate colleges, associate colleges, specialized institutions and tribal colleges and universities. Of a total of over 4,500 HEIs considered in the 2015 classification, the number of research universities is about 7 per cent of the total. (Carnegie 2016)

For classifying research universities, a two-stage process is used. A university is defined as a research university if it has graduated more than 20 PhDs per year in the recent past (in an earlier classification, this number was 50 PhDs per year). Based on this basic criterion, 335 universities are classified as research universities in the 2015 edition.

This basic classification separates research universities from the rest. However, this class itself contains a range of universities; for example, this set of research universities includes Massachusetts Institute of Technology, Caltech, UC Berkeley, University of Illinois, Georgia Institute of Technology, Carnegie Mellon University, etc. where the number of PhDs graduated per faculty per year is 0.5 or higher, and where sponsored research is in hundreds of millions of dollars, as well as many universities where the number of PhDs graduated per faculty per year is less than one-tenth of this. Hence, these are further sub-classified in the second stage of classification, in which the research universities are grouped into three subcategories: R1 (highest research activity), R2 (high) and R3 (moderate). The following features related to their research activity are considered while grouping the RUs into the three subcategories, namely R1, R2 and R3:

- Number of faculty members;
- research manpower;
- number of PhDs granted; and
- research funding.

These features are considered to be the most defining features of a research university and, therefore, used for the purpose of classification. In addition to research faculty, a research university also requires research manpower, so this factor is also included.

Globally, the main research manpower (besides faculty) is the PhD students. In advanced countries such as the USA, however, research universities also employ a considerable number of postdoctoral staff for research. (In Carnegie Classification post-doctoral fellows are counted as research manpower.) A large PhD programme is clearly needed for a research university. Finally, funding is needed to conduct research, including funds to support PhD students or employ research staff as also to develop and maintain lab equipment. Globally, while universities do provide limited support for research, much of the research funding comes in the form of externally sponsored research grants. The amount of research funding is a strong indicator of research activity.

For grouping into the subcategories, Carnegie does a cluster-ing analysis using these features to form three subcategories. The clustering approach first combines the features into two indices—aggregate (i.e., based on the values) and per capita (i.e., features normalized by faculty strength). The values of these two indices for each university are used for clustering the research universi-ties into the three subcategories termed R1, R2 and R3. Each subcategory has approximately one-third of the 335 research universities identified. More discussion about the methodology can be found in Kosar and Scott (2018); some ideas behind the Carnegie classification framework and challenges it faces are discussed in McCormick and Zhao (2005).

While Carnegie classification is the oldest and the most influ-ential, there have been classification efforts in other countries also. A two-step process for separating research universities was undertaken to classify Korean universities (Shin 2009). For basic classification, the criteria used was (a) the 'number of PhDs produced is more than 20 per year' and (b) the 'number of papers published each year in indexed journals is more than 100'. Using these basic criteria, 47 universities were identified. These were then grouped into different categories using a hierarchical clustering approach through key parameters such as faculty size, publications, research funding and PhD students graduated—the last three performance parameters being normalized with respect to faculty size. As a result, the universities were grouped into five clusters based on their research performance.

In the Chinese classification framework, four features were used (Liu 2007). These are: (a) total number of degrees awarded at different levels, (b) ratio between doctoral and baccalaureate students, (c) annual research income and (d) per capita of research articles in indexed journals. The universities are classified into a few different categories, with research universities being grouped into two subcategories: research universities I (7 universities) and research universities II (48 universities).

The EU classification framework aims to map the characteristics of universities to capture their diversity (Vught 2010). It does not group universities into a set of labelled categories. Instead, it categorizes them through a range of different characteristics. For mapping these, they have identified six dimensions: (a) teaching and learning profile, (b) student profile, (c) research involvement, (d) involvement in knowledge exchange, (e) international orientation and (f) regional engagement. For each of these dimensions, a few indicators are identified, with a total of 23 indicators. Based on the data for universities, they are grouped for each indicator into categories such as: major, substantial, some, none, small, medium, large, very large, etc. This type of classification across multiple dimensions allows universities to determine similarities and dissimilarities with each other along these dimensions.

2.3.2 Classifying Research Universities in India

For classifying research HEIs in India, a two-step approach, similar to the Carnegie framework, was proposed by Jalote et al. (2019). In the first step, a simple basic criterion is used to separate research HEIs from the rest. Then, in the second step, a more involved sub-classification is done using research activity measures and applying a clustering technique to separate research HEIs in two groups—ones with higher research activity and those with modest research activity.

Clearly, an HEI that is focused on research must have research faculty. The world over, research faculty predominantly hold doctorates. In fact, a hallmark of research universities is that they mostly employ as full-time faculty those that hold PhDs (Altbach 2007). Most classification approaches assume that all or most faculty in universities hold doctorates. In India, that is not the case; there are a large number of HEIs that have many faculty members who do not have doctorates. Consequently and necessarily, in order to identify research HEIs, the framework requires that at least 75 per cent of the faculty have doctorates before an HEI qualifies to be considered as a research HEI.

A fundamental difference between a research HEI and teaching-focused institution is the size and importance of its PhD programme. In fact, Carnegie considers this feature alone for classifying a HEI as a research HEI. In India, since focus on research in many universities is a recent phenomenon (as discussed in Chapter 1), and many of the HEIs that are focused on research have been created only in this century, for such a growing system, it is better to consider the strength of the PhD programme in terms of the total full-time PhD student population, rather than the number of PhDs graduated in a year. Since almost all full-time PhD students in India receive some form of scholarship, the number of full-time PhD students enrolled is a strong indicator of research activity as well as research investment. This criterion can be easily converted to number of PhDs graduated in a steady state.

A reasonable expectation for a research HEI is that each faculty member has on an average one full-time PhD student working with them. This should be the case for a research HEI regardless of whether it has a focus on social sciences, physical sciences, engineering or any other discipline. Hence this general criterion can be applied to both the categories of HEIs under consideration. This is used as part of the basic measure for defining a research HEI in India.

With this, the basic criteria for an HEI to qualify as a research HEI in India is:

- percentage of faculty with PhD >75 per cent of total faculty and
- ratio of number of full-time PhD students to number of faculty is >1.

This basic criteria is similar in spirit to the basic criteria used by Carnegie, in that it focuses on PhD students—except that an additional test on percentage of faculty with PhD has been added—an assessment necessary for HEIs in India.

This criteria was applied to the top 100 institutions in two categories of HEIs identified by the NIRF (NIRF 2015)—universities and engineering institutions. These two types of HEIs not only have the largest number of HEIs, but they are also the two main categories from governance perspective in India—universities generally have a Vice Chancellor as the Chief Executive while engineering institutions have a Director as the Chief Executive. The roles and powers of the two are somewhat different. The academic programmes also are often different—universities generally focus on offering 3-year bachelor programmes in natural Sciences, social Sciences, humanities, etc, while engineering HEIs predominantly offer 4-year BTech or BE degrees. They also have different regulating bodies: UGC for universities and AICTE (All India Council for Technical Education) for engineering institutions.

The NIRF site provides data of the 100 top HEIs in each of these two categories (for its 2018 exercise). As a result of applying the criteria, 40 universities and 32 engineering institutions were classified as research universities. The total number of HEIs that satisfy the basic criteria is 68—with 4 of these listed in both categories. This number of research universities seems reasonable—most academics in India will agree that the total number of HEIs that can be considered as research HEIs is definitely not very large. The number is also comparable to the number of research universities in China and Korea (as per their classification). The list of HEIs in the two types of institutions that satisfy the criteria, along with relevant data on total number of faculty, number of faculty with PhD and the number of full-time PhD students, is given in Jalote et al. (2019).

Of the HEIs that did not satisfy the criteria to be classified as a research HEI, the vast majority did not satisfy both the components of the criteria, though there were some which did not satisfy one or the other basic criteria. It is also worth noting that all the HEIs that satisfy the criteria for a research university are public institutions—23 universities and 28 engineering institutes are centrally funded, while the rest are funded by state governments (or a combination of state and centre). This is mostly due to the fact that private institutions are self-supporting and depend solely on revenue from tuition and other student fees. Consequently, they are not able to support research at any reasonable level, nor provide for at least one full-time PhD student per faculty. It is worth pointing out that private institutions are sometimes not eligible for research grants from some research funding agencies, making it harder for such institutions to support research.

For sub-classification of research HEIs using clustering, the main features considered are sponsored research grants, number of full-time PhD students, number of faculty and the number of publications in indexed journals. The features are combined into two indices—one for aggregate, and the other for normalized—based on the number of faculty. Given that the number of research universities is not too large, they are sub-classified in two clusters—R1 which represents the HEIs with higher research activity and R2 which represents those with modest research activity. The approach identified six universities and eight engineering institutions with the highest research activity. The list of research institutions that are in R1, along with the values of the features, are given in the paper of Jalote et al. (2019).

2.4 CREATING A RESEARCH UNIVERSITY

Let us briefly discuss how a research university may be established. For establishing a university, a common approach now being followed in many countries is through a legislative act—either of the central government or a state government. The legislative act establishing a university grants it powers for giving education, conferring degrees, conducting research, etc. In India, as explained earlier, besides being created through an act, an HEI may become a deemed university through a process which is executed by the UGC. However, in the recent past, the latter path had been taken less frequently, and most of the universities are now created through an Act. For the rest of our discussion, we will assume that a university is created through a legislative act. The NEP also recommends that universities be created through this route (NEP 2019). There are three main approaches for creating a research university.

2.4.1 New Greenfield Research Universities

Creating a research university from the ground up as a new university is something that is widely prevalent in India, which has a young and still rapidly growing HE system. IIIT-Delhi is an example of this—it was created by an Act of Delhi Government in 2008. India may have created one of the largest number of new universities in this century—more than half of its universities were established in this century.

A new university cannot be truly considered a research university for a decade or more, as only after a performance in research for a few years can a university be classified as a research university. However, a new university can be created with the 'intent' of being a research university, and then with the right policies and support and suitable execution, it can be considered a research university after a decade or so. While there are advantages in starting a new university in that new ideas may be easier to implement, starting such a university requires 'extraordinary leadership and abundant resources' (Salmi et al. 2018).

For a new university to eventually become a research university, the foundations have to be supportive—it is very easy otherwise to become a university with dominant focus on education. For a new university to become a research university, it should, right from the start, develop the key characteristics discussed above—recruit strong research faculty, build a high-quality and large PhD programme quickly, ensure, through policies and other mechanisms, that there is an active research programme, ensure to provide high-quality education and have a high degree of autonomy and academic freedom and sufficient financial resources. Some other factors for creating a world-class university, such as being a niche and interdisciplinary institution and favourable governance, are discussed in Salmi et al. (2018). In addition to these, there are a few essential aspects that a new university needs to focus on if it aims to become a research university.

- **Dynamic leader and a strong board.** There is no doubt that the initial leader of the university has a huge and lasting influence on its subsequent trajectory. The initial path taken and foundations laid have a long-lasting impact on a university and the direction it takes. Governance and leadership are discussed further in Chapter 8. The importance of a dynamic leader and strong board for a new university cannot be overstated—without a strong board and a visionary leader who is a respected researcher and has a good understanding of the research ecosystem, the chances are that the new university will become a teaching-focused university, as teaching can easily become the dominant goal, consuming much of the administrative cycles, particularly since there is the likelihood of many challenges in establishing the education programmes.

  Ideally, a few senior faculty from different disciplines should be taken on board soon after inception, who can then take leadership in planning and developing the discipline. However, it is important not to have senior people from other universities who cannot think beyond the existing systems and will only be able to develop the systems much in the same manner as in the institutions they are from. Due to this essential requirement, it may be a challenge to get the senior leaders, and the university may have to rely on external experts to develop its systems.

It is also desirable to take inputs from external experts from across the world, given that there are likely to be very few senior faculty. This is particularly important for designing the systems for the new university and its academic programmes. A new university must learn from the good practices, as well as from the bad or missing practices, of other institutions. It must learn to build upon what is good and in practice and avoid what may be in practice but is not desirable. To do this, consultations and help from experts are essential. It will be beneficial if committees with experts from the country as well as outside the country are formed for planning and designing systems and policies. This is facilitated if there is a strong vision for the university, along with a dynamic and open leadership and governance.

- **Faculty-led growth.** This is a critical planning factor which is often not given due attention. The plans for a new university are almost always student-led, that is, how the student population will grow. With the student numbers in mind, the faculty numbers are suitably computed. However, research faculty availability is very limited in India. As a result, if the student numbers continue to grow and faculty recruitment does not keep pace, then a strong pressure is created to recruit faculty, often leading to lowering of standards. There is another issue involved—for a new university, the plans typically focus on intake of students in various programmes. Taking a larger number of students initially has low impact, as in their first year, they need to be offered only a limited number of courses. However, when this same set of students reach later years of their programme, they require a range of specialized discipline courses to be taught by expert faculty. When the faculty recruitment does not happen in a satisfactory manner, the situation becomes challenging and then various approaches have to be employed to handle the situation. It is therefore better to start with a smaller intake and increase the student number slowly based on 'actual performance' of faculty recruitment, which may be different from the planned numbers.

It is essential not to relax faculty standards for recruitment, as the initially employed faculty can set the bar for future intake. If needed, it is perhaps better to start with visiting or contractual faculty (even if they have to be paid extra) while keeping the faculty recruitment bar for regular faculty at the desired level.

Even if these are in place, there are tremendous execution challenges like in a start-up. A new university has a huge advantage of having a clean slate without any historical baggage. This allows suitable policies and programmes to be conceived and implemented. However, newness also brings tremendous administrative challenges as almost all decisions are new with no past guidelines and with little policy and frameworks to help until they evolve over a few years.

2.4.2 Converting Existing Higher Education Institutions into Research Universities

It is possible for a teaching-focused university to convert itself to a research university with considerable effort and funding. Clearly, this transition will take time, perhaps decades, as it may require the current generation of faculty who are teaching-focused to be gradually replaced by research-focused faculty, and for some existing faculty to develop research capability. It should be clear that a college, which does not have the authority, and hence has not developed capabilities to design education programmes and courses, or do assessment for them, cannot directly move from being a college to a research university. Hence, for converting an existing institution to a research university, it will have to be an existing university, probably one which has some tradition of research.

From the set of universities, we need to group universities using some clear criterion for research activity (e.g., size of PhD faculty, PhD programme, research output), to identify research universities and other universities which are close to satisfying the criteria for research universities. The classification approach discussed earlier can be used for this purpose. From these universities, some universities which have a potential to ramp up their research can be supported for research strengthening. They should be provided multi-year block grants for research based on research performance and impact in previous years. PhD programmes should be supported heavily in these places.

It is neither desirable nor feasible to try to convert all universities into research universities. While over time some teaching-focused universities can move to being a research university by suitably enhancing their research activities and some universities can be supported every few years for this migration, most of them should remain education-focused and their mission should be to improve the quality of education at bachelor's and master's levels, keeping the educational programmes in line with new knowledge emerging in different subjects and disciplines.

Examples of converting teaching-focused institutions to research universities can be found across the world, as most universities created in the 19th century started with teaching as a focus. The USA has many examples of how teaching-focused institutions were converted to research universities once the movement for research universities was started. A more recent example is that of NTU. It started with a charter to train engineers and initially had programmes in three engineering disciplines—civil and structural, electrical and electronic and mechanical. It is now a broad-based research university with colleges in Engineering, business communication and information, education, biological sciences, humanities, social sciences, physical and mathematical sciences, and art, design and media. Recently, they established a new medical school. It has now a host of research centres and institutes, many in partnership with the industry.

The NEP recognizes that, in India, there are many very narrow-focused universities and that this is a hinderance to the evolution of high-quality research universities. It proposes to convert most of the central government universities and some state government universities into multidisciplinary research universities of decent size and envisages that in about two decades, there will be up to 300 such universities in the country (NEP 2019).

2.4.3 Mergers of Existing Higher Education Institutions and Organizations for Creating Research Universities

Merging of HEIs has been done in many countries such as Australia, South Africa, Europe, China, and USA. (Azziz et al. 2017). While reasons for mergers can be many, creating a large multidisciplinary research university is clearly one of the main drivers. China has perhaps had the largest number of mergers in recent times—in the last 25 years, it has had about 400 mergers involving about 1000 public HEIs in its attempt to move from specialized HEIs to having larger, globally competitive comprehensive universities (Azziz et al. 2017). We briefly discuss examples from Australia and France.

In 1987, Dawkins reforms took place in the Australian HE system. Under these reforms, amalgamation of colleges and institutes of education was done, some with the existing Australian universities, and some by creating new universities. One of the clear goals was to create larger, more comprehensive universities formed out of the amalgamation of various more narrowly focused HEIs with different goals.

Griffith University is an example where many HEIs were merged with Griffith over a few years to create a large research university. First, in 1990, Mount Gravatt Teacher's College and Gold Coast College of Advanced Education became official campuses of Griffith. Soon after, the Queensland Conservatorium of Music became a part of Griffith University. Finally, in 1992, the Queensland College of Art (QCA) became a part of the university. As a result of these amalgamations, Griffith, which was a small narrowly focused university of about 4000 students and a single campus, was transformed into a multi-campus university with more than three times the number of students and with a range of academic programmes within 4 years. Currently, Griffith has five campuses in three cities and over 50,000 students with UG, postgraduate and research degrees in almost all fields including engineering, science, business, law, education, environment, architecture, humanities, music and creative arts. It is also ranked in the top 300 universities in THE ranking. There were other such amalgamations, for example, with the University of Sydney and UNSW.

Queensland University of Technology (QUT) is an example of where mergers facilitated the creation of a new university. It was formally established as a university about three decades ago by merging two main educational institutions—Queensland Institute of Technology (QIT) and Brisbane College of Advanced Education. QIT itself had evolved over a century from various institutions—Brisbane School of Arts and Sciences, Brisbane Technical College and Central Technical College. Brisbane College of Advanced Education was a combination of multiple predecessor institutions such as Brisbane Teachers College, College of Advanced Education and a few other colleges focusing on teachers' training and advanced education. QUT is currently one of the top research universities in Australia with more than 40,000 students, two main campuses in Brisbane offering hundreds of degree programmes at all levels, and strong research in most fields. It is ranked in the top 200 universities in THE ranking. In the same manner as QUT, at least four other technical universities were created from amalgamations—Curtin, University of South Australia, University of Technology Sydney and RMIT University.

A recent example is that of the University of Paris-Saclay in 2014. It is an ambitious project to create a large university that will be among the top universities in the world. It brought together 2 universities, 10 Grandes Écoles (professional schools in engineering, agronomy, telecommunications, life sciences and management) and 7 national research institutions, fully or partially. All of them were previously autonomous and most of them are prestigious in their own right. They include the University of Paris-Orsay, the École Polytechnique, the École Normale

Supérieure de Cachan, the HEC business school, laboratories of the Centre National de la Recherche Scientifique (The French National Centre for Scientific Research). The university plans to focus on innovation and is linked to the technology cluster in Saclay. The campus is on the outskirts of the French capital and the government has allocated more than €6 billion for the project. The project has been in planning for many years and was also in response to relatively poorer performance of French HEIs in the global rankings. For planning, they had the ex-President of Caltech as the advisor for this project. The Université now has about 65,000 students from over a hundred countries, and has over 9,000 research professors.

2.5 SUMMARY

This chapter discusses research universities and their value to their countries and the world. The importance of research and the role of research universities in the research ecosystem of a country are explored. The key characteristics of a research university are enumerated, which not only help in the classification of an institution as such but can also be used to guide any university aspiring to be a research university. Classification frameworks for research universities are then discussed briefly, including the well-known Carnegie classification and its recent adaptation for India. The chapter concludes with a discussion on the multiple ways in which a research university can be created in India.

REFERENCES

Aggarwal, Varun. 2018. *Leading Science and Technology*. SAGE Publications. https://us.sagepub.com/en-us/nam/leading-science-and-technology-india-next/book261232

Altbach, Philip G. 2007. 'Empires of Knowledge and Development.' In *World Class Worldwide*, edited by Philip G. Altbach and Jorge Balan. Baltimore, MD: Johns Hopkins Press.

Altbach, Philip G. 2009. 'Peripheries and Centers: Research Universities in Developing Countries.' *Asia Pacific Education Review* 10 (1): 15–27.

Altbach, Philip G. 2011, April. 'The Past, Present, and Future of the Research University.' *Economic and Political Weekly* XLVI (16).

Altbach, Philip G., and Jamil Salmi. 2011. *The Road to Academic Excellence: The Making of World-Class Research Universities.* Washington, DC: The World Bank.

Arora, Ashish, Sharon Belenzon, and Lia Sheer. 2017. *Back to Basics: Why do Firms Invest in Research?* (NBER Working Paper No. 23187). https://www.nber.org/papers/w23187

Azziz, Ricardo, et al. 2017. *Mergers in Higher Education: A Proactive Strategy to a Better Future?* New York, NY: TIAA Institute.

Berman, Elizabeth P. 2012. *Creating the Market University.* Princeton, NJ: Princeton University Press.

Bush, Vannevar. 1945, July. *Science The Endless Frontier, A Report to the President by Vannevar Bush.* Director of the Office of Scientific Research and Development.

Carnegie. 2000. *The Carnegie Classification of Institutions of Higher Education.* http://carnegieclassifications.iu.edu/downloads/2000_edition_data_printable.pdf

Carnegie. 2016. *Carnegie Classification, 2015 Update—Facts and Figures.* http://carnegieclassifications.iu.edu/downloads/CCIHE2015-FactsFigures-01Feb16.pdf

Hawkins, Richard W., Cooper H. Langford, and Kiranpal S. Sidhu. 2006. 'University Research in an "Innovation Society".' In *Science, Technology and Innovation Indicators in a Changing World, Responding to Policy Needs.* OECD. http://www.oecd.org/science/inno/sciencetechnologyandinnovationindicatorsinachangingworldrespondingtopolicyneeds.html

Jalote, P., B. N. Jain, and S. Sopory, S. 2019. *Classification for Research Universities in India, Higher Education.* https://doi.org/10.1007/s10734-019-00406-3

Liu, Nian C. 2007. 'Research Universities in China.' in *World Class Worldwide*, edited by Philip G. Altbach and Jorge Balan. Baltimore, MD: Johns Hopkins Press.

Kosar, Robert, and David W. Scott. 2018. 'Examining the Carnegie Classification Methodology for Research Universities.' *Statistics and Public Policy* 5 (1): 1–12.

McCormick, A. C., and Chun-Mei Zhao. 2005, September/October. 'Rethinking and Reframing the Carnegie Classification.' *Change.*

McCormick, A. C., and V. M. H. Borden. 2017. 'Higher Education Institutions, Types and Classifications of.' In *Encyclopaedia of International Higher Education Systems and Institutions*, edited by J. C. Shin and P. Teixeira. https://doi.org/10.1007/978-94-017-9553-1_22-1

NEP. 2019. *Draft National Education Policy 2019.* Government of India.

NIRF. 2015. *A Methodology for Ranking of Universities and Colleges in India, 2015.* https://www.nirfindia

OECD. 2015. *Frascati Manual 2015, Guidelines for Collecting and Reporting Data on Research and Experimental Development.* OECD. https://www.oecd.org/sti/inno/Frascati-Manual-2015-Flyer-EN.pdf

Salmi, Jamil, Philip G. Altbach, Liz Reizberg, and Isak Froumin. 2018. 'The Art of Starting a New University: Lessons of Experience.' In *Accelerated Universities—Ideas and Money Combine to Build Academic Excellence,* edited by Philip G. Altbach et al. Brill Sense.

Shin, Jung C. 2009. 'Classifying Higher Education Institutions in Korea: A Performance-based Approach.' *Higher Education* 57: 247–66.

Stokes, Donald E. 1997. *Pasteur's Quadrant—Basic Science and Technological Innovation.* Brookings Institution Press.

Vught, van, et al. 2010. *U-Map: The European Classification of Higher Education Institutions.* http://www.u-map.eu/U-MAP_report.pdf

Chapter 3

Education
Delivering High-Quality Learning

Higher education was the original mission of universities, and remains the primary mission today, even for research universities. In fact, it is the presence of an education mission that distinguishes a research university from research labs. Manpower development through education is still the most significant and impactful contribution to society by universities, including research universities.

The importance of higher education is also increasing. As the world becomes more complex and more dynamic and is rapidly changing, businesses and societies are expecting universities to produce manpower that is adept at working with modern and fast-changing technologies in an increasingly complicated world.

Education is also the primary source of revenue for universities—even for many of the research universities. In UK, some of the universities support themselves largely through this per-student grant for education (Willetts 2017). The situation is similar in Australia, where the grant given to universities for education on a per-student basis accounts for the major portion of the revenue of a university, even for some of the top research universities. In India, most publicly funded universities get yearly grants from the government for their operation and expenses, and while grant for education is not earmarked separately, it is fair to say that most of the government grant is provided for the education in these universities.

While access to higher education has increased in India over the years, particularly with the large presence of private players running affiliated colleges, the quality of education has declined. There are various reports regarding the poor quality of education being imparted in most of the HEIs leading to only a fraction of the graduates being employable. There are many reasons for the decline in quality, including narrow focus, lack of culture of research, old and outdated curriculum and teaching methods, uninspiring teachers, lack of quality governance and leadership, poor quality of faculty, etc., as discussed in Chandra (2017).

Research universities tend to be among the best institutions for undergraduate education, particularly for professional programmes. Even a cursory look at the national or global rankings will show that the best research universities are also the most sought after for admission in their undergraduate programmes. This is broadly true in India as well—the most respected institutions for research (e.g., IITs, Delhi University, Jadavpur University, etc.) are also the most sought after for education. This trend is likely to remain so in future, as research skills become a necessary component of outcomes of even undergraduate programmes.

In this chapter we discuss some important aspects of providing high-quality education. The discussion in this chapter is largely for undergraduate programmes, though many of the ideas can be applied to master's programmes also. (We consider PhD as a research training programme and discuss it in a separate chapter.) In the chapter we discuss aspects of programme design, including programme outcomes, course design and learning outcomes, interdisciplinary programmes, etc., as well as feedback systems for ensuring high-quality education and learning. But before that, we discuss the special role of research universities in higher education.

3.1 EDUCATION IN A RESEARCH UNIVERSITY

What are the purposes of higher education? What is it supposed to do to the students undergoing it? These are a philosophical questions and answers can vary from developing responsible citizens and critical thinkers, to professional development for lifelong employment, to spiritual development. However, if we look at the impact higher education has on students, two key goals stand out—professional development and self-growth or self-development. This aligns with the framework of the European Union (EU), which states sustainable employment, personal development and active citizenship as three dimensions of relevant higher education (Vossensteyn et al. 2018), if we consider citizenship as part of self-growth. It is also similar to the framework discussed in Bridgstock (2009), which groups graduate attributes into two types—those pertaining to the capacity for citizenship and those pertaining to work productively.

Most students undertaking higher education, and often paying significant tuition fees, clearly expect higher education to provide them knowledge and skills which will help them in their professional career in life (which could be employment or self-employment). Hence, professional development is clearly the basic goal of higher education. The years a person spends in a university are perhaps the most defining ones in a person's life. For most students this period has a significant impact on their personality, interests, thinking, relationships, values, etc. All these we consider as part of self-development. For high-quality education, a university should provide development of the student in both these dimensions.

Most research universities take their education seriously and indeed are often the most sought-after for their education programmes also. While the education mission of a research university is similar to that of a teaching-focused university, the flavour and style of education in research universities is often quite different, and research universities often view education somewhat differently and as synergistic with research. Indeed, the objective of education in research universities can be argued to be somewhat different than that in teaching-focused institutions.

The number of students who will get their education in these research universities will be a small fraction of the total students. Given that these research universities, due to their high-quality faculty and prestige and other reasons, are also highly sought after, admission to these is highly competitive. In the Ivy League colleges in USA, it is often in single-digit percentages. In IITs in India, the acceptance is still just about 2 per cent of those seeking admission. Given that the intake in these universities is highly selective and the best minds join them, clearly, the goals of educating this cohort should be different than those of educating a general cohort. Let us start the discussion by looking at some special aspects of education in a research university.

3.1.1 Teaching–Research Nexus

Many have argued that there is a nexus between research and teaching, and that these two missions are not in conflict and can be synergistic. A considerable body of work exists on examining the teaching–research nexus. An example of how this nexus is supported in one university is discussed in Gibbons (1998), and a few types of connections between teaching and research are discussed in Neuman (1992). Though the debate about the nexus is not settled, it is possible to actively plan and support this nexus, and different approaches can be applied for this (Healey 2005)

Teaching benefits from research are generally quite evident. A teacher who is an active researcher will be well-versed with the latest developments in a subject, and hence while teaching that subject will be able to include the latest developments. There is also a qualitative difference in the teaching of a course when taught by a researcher in the field. With research faculty, advanced courses can be taught, which, besides covering the latest developments, may also provide students an opportunity to do some research. Moreover, such faculty will often offer projects, either as part of the courses or as capstone or final year projects, which are research-oriented—this can provide the students a deeper understanding of some areas and develop limited research capability. Overall, it is easy to see how teaching can benefit when the faculty are research-active.

However, it is not very evident how the research of a faculty or department can benefit from teaching. At the faculty level, conflicts can arise, since in pursuit of research faculty members may want to prioritize research over teaching for their time allocation and may view teaching as consuming valuable research time. Let us discuss some aspects of how teaching can support research.

At the most basic level, teaching helps solidify the depth of knowledge about a subject. As is acknowledged and experienced by many academicians, the process of explaining is one of the best ways to clarify things to yourself, and doing so to a class of bright students has the extra benefit of students potentially challenging the ideas or explanations or requiring further clarifications—which inevitably helps the faculty member in deepening his/her own understanding of the subject matter. As research universities tend to have top students and the ethos of such places encourages questioning and critical thinking, teaching in such universities undoubtedly helps the teacher also in further mastery of the subject.

Research universities are often at the forefront of introducing courses on emerging technologies and areas. Such courses are often intricately tied to current research and developments in the subject and may often start as 'special topics' or 'seminar' or 'advanced course'—with time, they may become standard courses. These courses are inevitably initiated by faculty working in the area and often start without a textbook in the area, with research papers as the primary source for the course. The format of the course is also often far more interactive, with students participating actively in researching on different topics in the subject, as well as often developing new ideas as part of their semester project or report. These types of courses further the research agenda of the faculty member in multiple ways.

First, it helps the faculty master the related work in different sub-areas of the subject and helps him/her conceptualize a suitable framework for structuring the knowledge—something that is often needed for a course. This directly furthers the research agenda of the faculty member. In academic circles, it is well-known that if a faculty member wants to get into a new area, he/she often prefers to teach a course on that area, with an important goal of developing mastery and depth in it.

Second, often offering such courses results in direct research outcomes. This can take the form of identifying important research problems to work on—something that a detailed survey and a deep understanding of the state of the field facilitate. These research projects can then be developed later. Sometimes, in these courses, students working on course projects or reports come up with interesting issues and solutions, which may then result in research publications and direct contribution to knowledge creation. Many faculty members have benefitted from this potential, and there are many research publications that have come out of such courses.

Third, such courses provide the students with an opportunity to go deeper into an area, and so if a student finds it interesting, he/she may choose to work in the area. The natural choice of selection of supervisor will then be the instructor of the course. In other words, such courses also provide a platform to attract good students to do their research work or thesis in the area and under the instructor, and their performance in the course also provides the faculty a better understanding of the students' capability and interest in the area. As faculty members in research universities are always keen to attract good students to do their research or thesis with them, such a course aligns almost directly with their research agenda.

In fact, such courses can be treated almost as a research activity. It is not surprising that there is generally a strong contention among faculty members to get an opportunity to teach such courses. Many departments have policies regarding how such courses are allocated. There are different ways in which the teaching–research nexus can be actively supported, and there are multiple ways in which such advanced courses which embed research can be organized (Healey 2005). A policy that directly recognizes the value of such courses and the teaching–research nexus, which is followed in IIIT-Delhi, is as follows. The standard teaching load of faculty is three courses in an academic year. Of these, while two courses are expected to be standard courses, the third course may be a special topic or advanced course directly aligned with the faculty members' research. This policy has helped institutionalize research as part of education—not only for students but also for faculty members—and explicitly recognizes the teaching-research nexus.

The benefits of research on teaching and those of teaching on research are widely acknowledged. The importance of faculty engaging in research to educate is widely acknowledged, and lack of research in many of the HEIs in India has been recognized as one of the causes of the poor quality of education (Chandra 2017). The NEP also recognizes and supports this connection and urges a strong research culture to be built in universities and a culture of research to be developed in all students.

3.1.2 Leadership in Programme, Curriculum and Course Design

All universities have a range of education programmes. For each programme, a curriculum in terms of courses a student may take in that programme is specified (along with other constraints and requirements). For each course, a syllabus is defined to ensure learning by the students in the subjects of the course. None of these three are static—new programmes and courses are often introduced, and syllabi for courses are often enhanced. Research universities are expected to take leadership in all these three.

New programmes are sometimes started by universities—while the starting of new programmes is not too frequent, it is a standard mechanism used by universities to respond to changing demands. New programmes are started generally in response to the changing needs of the society and industry and the consequent potential demand from students. The design of a programme is often a long process involving inputs from a range of sources, in particular from the industry or other potential employers. Often, data about the demand may not exist (as the programme does not exist). To create a programme that would produce manpower 4 years later which would be highly valued by society is an act of academic leadership, and the leading research universities are naturally expected to take this initiative. They are also well placed to undertake it as, besides having the leading subject matter experts in their faculty, they often also have strong linkages with the industry and other stakeholders to evolve a better understanding of the skills and capabilities that need to be developed by such a programme.

The curriculum for the programmes evolves over time, and all universities have mechanisms to review their curriculum and revise it as needed. As part of any revision exercise, it is common that universities will look at the curriculum of other leading universities. Generally, the curriculum of leading universities in the field inevitably influence the design. In other words, often, improvement in the larger education system may originate in what is being done in the leading universities. Given this, research universities play a leadership role in curriculum development— their curriculum can impact many other universities. These universities should be cognizant of this role which, even if they did not actively seek it, has been assigned to them.

Most universities will regularly add new courses on subjects of importance or include in the current education recent developments and advancements in knowledge. These leading-edge courses are often driven by the state of the knowledge. Since the research faculty in these research universities are often the leaders in their fields and are instrumental in the development of the fields and the furthering of knowledge, they are in the best position to design such courses and refine them based on their offering them to their own students. Such courses can then be taken up by other universities. Introduction of new courses, particularly in emerging areas, is a key role research universities have—not only for offering it to their students who have high expectations from their education, but also for helping introduce such courses in other institutions.

Another area in which research universities are expected to take leadership is research on education itself. Given the research capability and culture of research universities, and the fact that there always are open questions about education, it is natural for research universities to undertake research on higher education itself. Higher education has been a subject of research, and will continue to be so, as technological and societal changes require higher education to respond appropriately with changes in curriculum, support for learning, use of appropriate technology, etc. While all research universities are not expected to conduct research on education, some of them must do so. These universities are the most suitable hosts for doing this research. Not only do they have the research capability and culture and environment, but the university itself offers a platform to study higher education and conduct experiments where needed.

There are two key dimensions to research on higher education. One involves the higher education system itself and the related structures, frameworks, processes, etc. The other involves pedagogy-related issues in higher education (which are often different from the pedagogy issues of children or school students). There is a need to do research on both these aspects of higher education.

3.1.3 High-Quality Learning Experience

Given the highly selective intake, it is expected that research universities will provide a high-quality learning experience to their students through innovative and sound education practices. Indeed, given the selective intake, it is incumbent upon these universities that the learning environment and education practices are the best.

One of the aspects of education in these universities is that research is part of the education. While most undergraduate programmes generally focus on developing attributes that will develop the students for professional careers, one of the careers research universities must develop their students for is a career in research. Given their focus on research, and the research faculty that exists in these universities, this goal is natural. Some percentage of their graduates are expected to take up research careers.

Even otherwise, research capability is fast becoming a skill needed for most professional careers, given the pace of innovation and new-knowledge creation. Innovation rests often on the scholarship and research capability of the person—how well equipped the person is in reading and understanding research papers on the latest developments, in seeing the potential value of new developments for his/her work, to aid further development to make research results more suitable for the current job, etc. Research universities can develop these capabilities in their graduates by making research available even to undergraduate students.

Most research universities indeed have mechanisms for allowing undergraduate students to participate in research. These could be allowing some academic credits for undergraduate research, doing research for their UG project, research internships in labs and with faculty members, etc. This is often a unique offering of research universities—one that aligns well with its education goals as well as with the aspirations of its students.

High-quality learning experience, besides having the best curriculum, should also support learning opportunities outside the formal coursework and classroom. Experience indicates that while students learn in the courses which are taught by faculty, they also learn a lot outside the classroom and formal coursework. Many will argue that, in fact, it is the learning from peers that is the strongest in the best universities, as they have the highest quality peers. In other words, learning does not only take place in the formal coursework, but a lot of it also happens from the environment the university provides. Therefore, for high-quality learning experience, research universities need to provide such an environment.

The formal education programme, or the curricular aspects, usually focuses on professional development with some elements for self-growth. Much of the self-growth dimension is left to the informal processes that take place in corridors, hostels, student clubs and extracurricular activities, student–student interaction, student–faculty interaction, etc. These informal processes also support the professional development goals—for example, students learn a great deal from each other.

Generally, so much emphasis is placed on formal teaching that learning and growth that happen outside the formal curriculum have not been studied or understood well. The faculty and the universities like to believe the self-servicing view that what is taught in the programmes by the faculty is all that matters in education. Thankfully, universities have evolved as open and liberal communities which naturally provide a rich environment for significant informal learning and self-growth. A great university is one that provides a facilitating environment and strong support for development in both these key goals.

One way to encourage students to engage in such activities is to identify some activities and provide limited credits for these. Many universities follow this. For example, in IIIT-Delhi, students are required to earn two credits of 'self-growth' and two credits of 'community work' for graduation. These allow students to develop their interests outside the profession and learn to contribute to society. Both these have received tremendous feedback from the students on their learning and growth. (The community work credits were used effectively for conducting a summer camp for school children from poor neighbourhoods—discussed further in the chapter on the third mission [Chapter 5].)

3.2 CURRICULUM DESIGN

We now discuss the design of a curriculum for a degree programme. (Programmes are called courses in many contexts;

however, we use the term course to refer to units in a programme.) In this section our discussion will be around undergraduate programmes, though the same concepts apply for master's programmes also.

The design of a programme starts with what types of careers or roles it is trying to prepare its students for. We will refer to these as objectives of the programme. Often, these objectives may be common for a class of similar programmes—for example, BTech programmes may have similar objectives, while BA programmes (in social science and humanities) may have different objectives. These objectives may be stated in terms of what careers a graduate may be pursuing a few years after graduation, and are generally influenced by the mission and vision of the university.

As an example, let us consider the BTech programmes in IIIT-Delhi. The institute has stated that its programmes are preparing the students for careers in: Engineering, Research and Entrepreneurship. Stating the education objectives as specific careers has some clear implications on the programme design. A traditional programme is often designed for engineering careers and hence may focus mostly on developing engineering skills and foundations. With research and entrepreneurship careers also as the education objectives necessarily requires that all programmes should have opportunities for students to develop capabilities for these careers also in the programme. That is, there need to be courses, projects, industry interaction opportunities, etc. to support these. Also, stating these as education objectives does not mean that students cannot choose to later go into other careers like finance or management (e.g., by doing an MBA)—it only states that the education programmes will be designed to support these stated objectives.

With the overall objectives, specific outcomes for each programme are defined. These are the attributes of the graduates at the time of completion of the programme, or statements about the student's capabilities at the time of graduation, and are called programme outcomes or graduate attributes. Clearly, these should align with the objectives of the programme.

The programme outcomes are finally delivered though courses that are taught by faculty in semesters over the duration of the programme. Each course has to be designed to ensure some learning, such that together the courses can deliver the learning stated in the programme outcomes.

In the rest of this section, we discuss these aspects of the programme design. The designed programme translates to courses in the programme, which are the unit of teaching in a university. We will also discuss the effective design of courses. Following this discussion, we will discuss the design of interdisciplinary programmes and the use of open courseware. In the next section, we will discuss how the designed programme and courses can be delivered for effective learning.

3.2.1 Graduate Attributes (Programme Outcomes)

A degree programme can be specified in terms of what capabilities a student will have at the time of completing the programme, that is, the attributes graduates of the programme are expected to have. These are called programme outcomes or graduate attributes (sometimes, these terms are used with subtle differences; in our discussion here, we consider both of them as specifying the same thing). These outcomes should be aligned with the stated education objectives.

Clearly, programme outcomes will depend on the programme—so a BS in psychology will have different outcomes than a BTech in computer science. However, universities aim to develop some common attributes or capabilities in all their programmes, so graduates across different disciplines are expected to have some attributes that are common. These are sometimes called generic graduate attributes. These are skills and capabilities of graduates which are beyond disciplinary knowledge and often aim to develop the individual for being a responsible member of the society and develop skills that are transferable to different contexts (for a discussion on generic attributes, see Barrie [2006, 2007] and Bridgstock [2009]).

With general graduate attributes, programme outcomes can be divided into two groups: a general set of outcomes that apply to a family of programmes and a specific set of outcomes, one for each programme. For many professional fields, professional bodies also specify graduate attributes, which they expect the degree programmes to support. Often, having these attributes may be necessary for accreditation of the programmes. As can be expected, these graduates' attributes should be such that they will help in achieving the education objectives established by the university.

One common method of specifying the general attributes is to enumerate them as assertions about the graduates of the programmes. For example, in IIIT-Delhi, the general attributes for BTech programmes are:

- Ability to function effectively in teams to accomplish a common goal;
- An understanding of professional and ethical responsibility;
- Ability to communicate effectively with a wide range of audience;
- Ability to self-learn and engage in lifelong learning;
- Ability to undertake small research tasks and projects;
- Ability to take an idea and develop it into a business plan for an entrepreneurial venture; and
- Understanding of the impact of solutions in the economic, societal and environmental context;

The general outcomes play an important role in the holistic development of the student. Due to their wider and foundational importance, most good universities give careful attention to these outcomes. In India, often, the education is too narrow, with early specialization, thereby allowing students to graduate without the strong general attributes needed for a good citizen (Chandra 2017). The new National Education Policy (NEP) of the government of India has articulated the importance of education programmes moving from narrow, discipline-based education to one that is based on broader, more liberal education. The NEP envisages broad-based and multidisciplinary foundations to be provided beyond the disciplinary knowledge to develop well-rounded students who have good values and cultural literacy and general capabilities like critical thinking, problem solving, data analysis, communication, teamwork, social responsibility, etc. (NEP 2019).

While the general attributes are largely aligned with the broad goals of education, for a programme in a discipline, a fundamental goal is to develop competencies related to the discipline which can lead to gaining productive employment. Typically, these are evolved by experts in the discipline, with inputs from the end employers/users of the graduates. Most universities that explicitly state the programme outcomes will state these on their websites. For example, the goals of the Computer Science programme in IIIT-Delhi are to develop the following attributes in students (in addition to the general attributes mentioned earlier):

- Understanding of theoretical foundations and limits of computing;
- Understanding of computing at different levels of abstraction, including circuits and computer architecture, operating systems, algorithms and applications;
- Ability to adapt established models, techniques, algorithms, data structures, etc., for efficiently solving new problems;
- Ability to design, implement and evaluate computer-based systems or applications to meet the desired needs using modern tools and methodologies; and
- Understanding of and ability to use advanced techniques and tools in different areas of computing.

As can be seen, these outcomes are stated mostly in terms of the discipline, and so are different for different disciplines.

3.2.2 Programme Design

Once the programme outcomes are specified, the overall programme has to be designed for a degree programme. This is a challenging exercise, as for many practical and educational reasons, each programme is not designed in a stand-alone manner. Most programmes are designed within some overall constraints imposed by the university, which are influenced by the mission, vision and values of the university, as well as the constraints of the college or the school to which the programme belongs, which will generally require some common features in all the programmes. Within the constraints, programme design often comes down to decisions regarding:

- **General requirements.** These are courses that all students in all programmes need to take. These are largely driven by the general graduate attributes. They may be grouped into different subcategories and may even be divided among university-wide and school-wide general requirements. However, the essence of these requirements is that they provide a common foundation to all students, based on which students can essentially do any programme (and so programme switching is easier), and they also help develop some of the general attributes.
- **Programme-specific requirements.** These are what the specific programmes, which are mostly discipline-based, require. Some of the courses in these are mandatory for students enrolled in the programme, whose goal is to deliver the core or foundational knowledge about the discipline which forms the basis for advanced topics in the discipline. These are often called the programme's compulsory or core courses. Other courses are programme electives, that is, the student chooses courses on advanced topics in the discipline from the set of courses being offered (subject to the satisfaction of the prerequisites for the course). These courses may also be grouped into different buckets with some requirements that students must take some number of courses from some number of buckets. Collectively, the programme requirements of core course credits and elective credits aim to deliver the programme-specific learning outcomes.
- **Open credits.** These credits allow the student an opportunity to take any (with some restrictions sometimes on some of the

credits) of the courses in the university. This allows him/her to gain a deeper understanding of topics of interest which may not fall within the discipline of his/her programme. It also encourages a broader development of the student, providing him/her with a breadth that disciplines, by definition, do not provide. Moreover, in limited ways, it allows a student to customize parts of his/her programme as he/she wishes. These credits are often used for doing a minor in another discipline or doing another major. Due to these credits and discipline electives, most students will graduate with a transcript different from others, depending on the set of courses they have done.

There are generally some constraints on the programme design. First are the total credits for a programme and credits a student can enrol for in a semester. Let us take a typical undergraduate programme, which can be completed by a full-time student in 4 years or eight semesters. During a semester, a full-time student can be expected to spend a total of about 40 hours per week. This total effort puts a limit on the total number of credits a student can earn in a semester, which, in turn, puts a limit on the total number of credits in a programme.

While often no clear definition of credit is provided by universities, broadly, credits are understood to have a relationship with the total effort the student is expected to spend. In other words, one credit should translate to some overall effort, including the time spent in lectures, as well as tutorials and labs. This effort may be thought of as average in a week, or total in a semester, but should include all efforts a student is required to put, including efforts outside the class, which in many ways are more important for learning than the time spent on course lectures. Many universities have a standard credit for regular courses, with an understanding of the total hours and lectures per week that are expected in a course. For example, most regular semester courses in many US universities are of three credits (four credits in IIIT-Delhi). Such courses are expected to have 3 lecture hours every week and an average total workload of 8–10 hours per week. This means that a full-time student can effectively take four to six such courses.

The above discussion indicates the maximum credit or load that a student can take in a semester. Programmes often assume that most students, if they study full-time, have the learning capability to finish an undergraduate programme in eight semesters. However, it is well-known that the academic preparedness and learning abilities of students who enrol in a university in a programme may be quite different. While many students can handle this load, there are others who may find this level of full-time load hard to handle at the pace required for it. The approach in many countries, particularly in the West, for addressing this is to allow the student to take more than 4 years to graduate and take a load that he/she may be comfortable with.

This approach, however, is unacceptable in countries like India where there is a strong desire to finish the academic programme in the stipulated period. In such situations, having a fixed number of credits for graduation is tantamount to having a one-size-fits-all approach. Such a model can indirectly encourage the university to pitch its courses at a lower level so all students can complete, or have to face the problem of large number of backlogs, which pose another set of problems. Once a student is admitted to a university and a programme, it is somewhat the responsibility of the university to help the student graduate and achieve the learning outcomes. Hence, some flexibility in credits can be desirable, without violating the integrity or value of the degree.

One approach, which is used by IIIT-Delhi, is to pitch the main programme for the regular students admitted to the institute and provide a 'honours' option to those who are more motivated and can pursue higher levels of learning in their time in the programme. With this approach, the credit requirement is such that for a couple of semesters a student can work with a slightly reduced load, which also allows a student to make up for some courses he/she may not cleared earlier and still graduate in the desired 4 years. At the same time, the 'honours' student is required to do a few more courses and a thesis and must have a graduating cumulative grade point average (CGPA) above a respectable threshold. Given the CGPA requirement, the option is made available to only those who have shown through their performance in first few years that they can cope with the course load and are ready to take up more learning challenges.

Within these overall parameters, the programme for a degree in a university has to be designed. There are no rules for how many credits should be provided in each of the course categories or which courses should be included where. This is generally achieved through a process of discussion and iteration—often, programme design (or programme refinement) may take over a year, with different committees spending a considerable amount of time discussing and thinking and examining the programmes of other universities. Often, workshops may be held, in which external experts from other universities, as well as from the relevant industry, may also be invited to give inputs. Finally, the main academic body of the university discusses and approves the programme.

A broad principle that is being followed in many universities for their programmes now is to keep the compulsory portion of the programme as small as possible and allow a student more choices. This generally implies fewer credits for general requirements and fewer credits for the core courses of a discipline, with more credits left for discipline electives and open electives. It should also be pointed out that with more room for credits in the elective and open categories, the possibility of providing for minors and second majors increases, as often these credits are utilized to complete the requirements of a minor or a second major.

How do we know that the programme design is sound? The main test of the soundness of a programme design is that it should, at a minimum, achieve the programme outcomes and that the graduates should have the graduate attributes in them at the completion of the programme. As the programme outcomes are qualitative statements on what the student has learned in the programme and what capabilities he/she has developed, the assessment that the programme delivers to them also has to be done qualitatively. Generally, given the learning outcomes of each of the courses (discussed below) and the network of courses a student has to do in a programme, it can be demonstrated that achieving the learning outcomes of each course the student takes will lead to the student achieving the programme outcomes. Indeed, the course design is often influenced by the programme outcomes in that the learning outcomes of a course are decided upon so as to contribute towards the programme outcomes. How the network of courses satisfies the programme outcomes may be shown in terms of tables showing which course contributes to which of the learning outcomes, and how collectively the set of courses deliver a programme outcome.

3.2.3 Course Design and Learning Outcomes

Course design is a widely discussed topic in teaching and learning literature, as finally education for a programme boils down to teaching in courses, as a course is the basic unit for learning in an academic programme. Teaching of courses is also what teachers do—hence, for improving education, the focus is often on the teaching of courses. Due to the importance of courses in teaching, most books on effective teaching (e.g., Ambrose et al. 2010; Fink 2013) place strong emphasis on course design, as without a good course design high-quality teaching and learning are not likely to take place in the course. Often, a course is designed by enumerating a list of topics that should be covered in the course, generally called the course syllabus. This is a very teaching-focused approach, as the list of courses is often selected by the instructors based on their judgement regarding the importance of the topics. It is widely agreed that this approach, which is still quite prevalent, is not a sound approach for the design of courses. To help ensure good learning in a course, the course design should be learning-driven, first articulating the learning outcomes of the course and then designing the syllabus and its teaching. Besides the learning objectives and teaching plan to

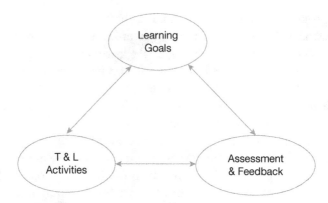

Figure 3.1 *The Three Elements of Course Design and Their Dependence on Each Other*

Source: Dee Fink (2013).

achieve them, another basic aspect of course design is assessment planning, without which the level of learning cannot be ascertained. An integrated course design then has three main elements, as shown in Figure 3.1.

These three elements are strongly dependent on each other and reinforce each other. Weakness in one will compromise the eventual goal of the course—to ensure that the learning outcomes are satisfied by most of the students. For example, if the course delivery plan is not aligned with the learning outcomes (for example, it does not cover all the necessary topics), then the student cannot achieve the stated learning outcomes. If the assessment plan is such that it focuses on assessing what can be assessed easily rather than on what are stated as the learning outcomes, then the students will align their learning towards the assessment rather than the learning outcomes, and the grades given to the student will not accurately represent the learning with respect to the learning outcomes. This again results in compromising the goal of teaching and learning in a course.

The design of a course, therefore, starts from stating its learning outcomes. Learning outcomes are statements about the knowledge and capabilities of a student who has successfully completed the course, that is, statements that assert what the student at the end of the course should know and what he/she will be able to do. The learning outcomes are critical in the design of courses, as from these it can be determined if the overall programme outcomes and graduate attributes are being delivered by the programme or not. As mentioned above, the programme is finally a network of courses that a student undertakes. The learning outcomes of the set of courses that a student undertakes in a programme should together ensure that the outcomes of the programme are satisfied. Hence, learning outcomes are not just what the instructor of a course decides for the course; they have to be aligned with the programme outcomes, particularly for the compulsory or core courses.

The type of knowledge acquired can be classified in many ways, and Bloom's taxonomy is the best-known technique for doing so (Krathwohl 2002). As per the revised Bloom's taxonomy, knowledge can be classified into six levels: remember, understand, apply, analyse, evaluate and create. Using the taxonomy, the statements about learning outcomes can be stated in terms of learning at different levels. However, for university courses, often the lowest level of knowledge are not the goals (unlikely to see learning outcomes for college courses state that a student shall 'remember x, y, z'). Generally, in courses in universities, especially in those in research universities, which are often pitched even higher, the learning outcomes are oriented more towards the higher levels of the taxonomy.

A simpler way to view the learning objectives is to focus on what the students will understand at the end of the course (conceptual knowledge) and what the students can do (skills). Using this simpler formulation, learning outcomes are statements of the type: At the end of the course, the student shall understand x, or be able to do y. It is desirable that most courses should have some learning outcomes of each of these—develop a better understanding of some systems, the world, people, how something works, phenomenon, etc. and develop some capabilities in the students to do something (e.g., critically analyse, write code, write a technical note or a critique, evaluate a system, create a design, integrate some technologies, etc.).

The second aspect of the course design is the planning of teaching and learning activities in the course. For this, a principle to be kept in mind is the quote by Herbert A. Simon: 'learning results from what the student does and thinks and only from what the student does and thinks. The teacher can advance learning only by influencing what the student does to learn'. In other words, the goal of any activity in the course, including lectures, should be to ensure that the student has something to think about or do—the only way a student can learn. Generally, the most visible aspect of this plan is the schedule of topics covered in lectures. While this schedule of topics is sufficient to ensure that appropriate topics are covered for the learning outcomes, it is an incomplete plan for ensuring the achievement of learning outcomes. For that, activities outside the lecture must also be included in the plan. As discussed above, typically, in a course, for each hour of lecture, the student is expected to put in a few hours of effort outside the lectures, in reading (lecture notes or text), doing assignments, doing lab activities, writing reports, etc. While lectures can form the nucleus of knowledge for learning in a course, most of the learning by students happens in the activities they have to perform outside the lecture. Hence, these must be included in the instruction plan for a course.

Finally, there must be a good assessment plan in a course. Assessment is an important and difficult aspect of teaching, and one that is often not enjoyed by teachers, as it is also generally cumbersome and time-consuming. However, it is an essential aspect of teaching and learning. Without a proper assessment plan, the effectiveness of teaching cannot really be judged, and learning levels achieved will depend only on the student's motivation and drive. Note that assessment does not mean only exams or tests—assignments, report writing, etc. can all be, and generally are, components of assessment. In fact, an assessment based only on formal tests/exams will be limiting in scope—it may not be able to test some of the learning objectives (e.g., the ability to set up an experiment), and it also encourages students to spend most of their effort on learning around the exams. Hence, assessment plans often use multiple instruments that are spread throughout the duration of the course. The final goal of assessment is to determine the level of learning achieved by the student, which is often captured in terms of the grade the student receives. In the current context, there is an increased interest in assessment and how automation and other approaches can be used. As delivery of lectures can now be done at a large scale through sophisticated tools on the Internet, assessments, which for many subjects have to rely on human effort for evaluating the students' learning, has become one of the key bottlenecks in scaling education through the Internet. Even otherwise, assessment is a challenging aspect, and books have been written on it (e.g., Angelo and Cross 1993).

3.2.4 Interdisciplinary Education and CS + X Programmes

Most degree programmes are aligned with disciplines—you get a bachelor's or a master's in some discipline like computer science, electrical engineering, economics, mathematics, etc. As discussed earlier, the overall curriculum of a UG programme generally ensures some amount of breadth and general foundations for the development of general attributes, while the bulk of the programme focuses on building competencies and knowledge in the discipline of study. Hence, a mathematics programme will have a lot of maths courses but also some general courses on communication, writing, sciences, etc., and an electrical engineering programme will have many courses in the various sub-areas of the discipline and also general courses in maths, computing, sciences, communication, etc.

This focus on discipline has emerged as a response to the increase in the breadth and complexity of knowledge. It simply is not possible for a student to acquire a decent understanding and knowledge of multiple disciplines. However, over the years, the expertise has tended to become too narrow, and the understanding and appreciation of related disciplines, which is needed for effectively working in multidisciplinary teams, has declined. While research and development problems in each discipline remain, the big problems that face societies, nations and the world clearly do not align with discipline boundaries, and their addressal needs expertise from multiple disciplines. To address these problems and, in general, work on innovations and complex problems that rarely fall within discipline boundaries, there is a need for developing manpower that has multidisciplinary capabilities. (Though the terms multidisciplinary and interdisciplinary have different technical meanings, we use these terms interchangeably, as they often are interchangeable.)

One standard approach to allowing students to develop multidisciplinary capabilities is to allow the students the option of doing a minor in another discipline. A minor requires the student to do a small number of courses in the minor discipline, which the students can often do using their open elective credits for them. A minor provides a decent understanding and capabilities in the minor discipline, as well as a basic vocabulary of the discipline. It is a common way to allow students to develop some capabilities in another discipline, without their having to spend extra time in the education programme. Most universities provide for minors.

Another standard approach is to allow students the option for a second major. Generally, requirements for both the majors will have to be satisfied. Usually, credits for a course can be counted towards the requirements for both majors, if the course is permitted in both the majors. As there may be many common requirements, or courses that can be included in both majors, the number of additional credits required to complete the second major might not be too high, particularly if the two majors have many courses in common. Hence, generally, second major will require the student to earn only some additional credits to complete the requirements for the second major.

These two are flexible approaches which leave it entirely to the student to decide what type of interdisciplinarity he/she wishes to pursue. Another way to approach interdisciplinary education can be to provide actual interdisciplinary programmes that are designed as such. In this approach, the programmes are designed and curated properly, and a student may choose to enrol in them; so, philosophically, this approach is quite different from the concept of a double major or a minor. Interdisciplinary programmes have been increasing in the recent past in universities (Knight et al. 2013).

The big challenge in having multidisciplinary programmes is, of course, that the size and duration of such a programme might become too large if a simplistic view that such a programme should be a combination of two majors is taken. If the design of this interdisciplinary programme has to fit in the overall credit requirements of programmes (as discussed above), then the key challenge is to balance the need to complete the programme in the defined time (or credits) and provide multidisciplinary capability, without diluting the capabilities of the disciplines. There are many different types of interdisciplinary programmes possible, depending on how the curriculum is structured and taught (Knight et al. 2013). Here, we discuss the approach taken at IIIT-Delhi.

Clearly, for such programmes, the disciplines being combined have to be chosen carefully. When considering which two disciplines to combine for such a programme (more than two is clearly not feasible), the disciplines should be chosen such that they develop complementary skill sets that collectively will be more valuable and sought after than only the skills of one discipline, for a range of jobs and careers. Further, the disciplines should also not be so 'vast' that combining them into one programme is simply not feasible. At least one discipline should be such that even with a small set of courses, reasonable skills and knowledge can be developed, which can help in improving the capabilities of other discipline also. Few disciplines will satisfy this—computing is one of them.

Computer science (CS) is a young discipline. However, with the easy and cheap availability of computing power, its use has become ubiquitous—there is hardly any discipline or any sphere of life which is not directly affected by information technology (IT). That is why computing is sometimes considered as the 'new physics'—it is useful in all disciplines, and its basic knowledge is essential. Today, in every discipline, knowledge of computing is an asset, and there is a demand for professionals in various disciplines who also have decent knowledge of computing.

CS is in some ways a simpler discipline. It is fundamentally about algorithms, software and systems. Hence, education programmes in CS focus on these: for software, there are courses like programming, data structures, software engineering, etc; for algorithms, there are courses on data structures, algorithm design, theory of these, etc; and for systems, there are courses like architecture, operating systems, networks, etc. Generally, a subset of these topics forms the core (or compulsory) part of an undergraduate programme, allowing for a relatively small CS core. These core courses, along with a few specialized courses, can provide strong knowledge and skills to students for them to apply computational techniques.

This ability to have a small core to develop useful skills and knowledge, renders CS for interdisciplinary programmes which combine CS basics with knowledge of other disciplines. Given the need for knowledge of computing in many disciplines, having an interdisciplinary programme with computing makes a lot of sense, particularly since further progress in many disciplines is highly dependent on the application of computing. A good example is biology; earlier, it was considered an experimental discipline, but now, without the use of computing, many aspects simply cannot be done (e.g., anything to do with genomics requires huge amounts of computing).

In fact, many senior computing academics have argued that while computing as a discipline must evolve, computing must be more tightly integrated with some disciplines for it to have more impact on society and on other sciences. This is another reason for having interdisciplinary programmes with CS. So, there are interdisciplinary programmes being launched with CS and other disciplines—these are sometimes called 'CS+X Programs'. IIIT-Delhi has launched a series of such programmes. UIUC and Stanford have their own such programmes. The discussion here is based on the thinking and experience of IIIT-Delhi.

One such programme is CS and Applied Maths. The basic motivation behind this programme is that for solving problems for complex systems as well as for big data, both mathematics and computing tools and techniques need to be applied. Hence, an engineer with training in both will be better prepared to handle such problems. Another programme is CS and Design, which aims to develop graduates who are not only well-versed with computing approaches, tools and technologies but are also experienced with design approaches and new media technologies and uses; it prepares students to work in the IT industry as well as in the digital media industry like gaming, animation, virtual/augmented reality, etc. CS and Social Sciences is another programme which aims to develop IT engineers with a strong understanding of relevant social science disciplines, as well as their methodologies. There is also the programme in CS and Biosciences—the need for this is easier to establish, as there are many master's and PhD programmes already in the field of computational biology and the need for combined knowledge of the two disciplines for solving problems in biosciences is well-established.

There are some guiding principles while designing such programmes. First, the set of core courses for the disciplines chosen for the interdisciplinary programme should be minimal, that is, the core should be as small as possible. Interestingly, it is possible to do so, since what constitutes a core is subjective, and when the programme is not for one discipline but tied to another, the core can be reduced considerably. Second, for electives for this programme, courses from both the disciplines should be permitted, and a balance should be achieved. Third, some of the courses taught in the programme should be interdisciplinary in nature.

Typically, in IIIT-Delhi, in any such interdisciplinary programme, a student will do the basic foundation courses in the first year, most of which are common for all programmes. These include courses on communication, critical thinking, programming, mathematics, systems, etc. Then, in the next few semesters, the student will do a small set of (about six) core or compulsory courses in each of the two disciplines, which will provide the grounding in the two disciplines. In the last few semesters, the student will choose a few electives (four to six) from either discipline. Broadly, such an interdisciplinary programme can satisfy the requirements of a BTech in CS, as well as the requirements of a 3-year BA/BSc programme in the second discipline.

Such programmes allow a student to pursue an exciting career at the intersection of the two disciplines and also prepare them to pursue higher studies and a career in one of the two disciplines, as decent knowledge of both disciplines is provided in these programmes. Many thinkers believe that interdisciplinary approaches for problem-solving is where the future lies, as siloed approaches of individual disciplines are limiting and often unable to take a broader view of a problem and its context. Such interdisciplinary programmes should help develop manpower that has the capabilities of at least two disciplines for problem-solving. The NEP also encourages interdisciplinary programmes and explicitly allows programmes to have a common core for general attributes and have one or two areas of specialization, thereby allowing disciplinary programmes as well as interdisciplinary programmes (NEP 2019).

3.2.5 Use of Online Courses

Over the last decade or so, there has been a lot of excitement on Internet-based delivery of courses, in particular, massive online open courses (MOOCs). The power of new technologies and the Internet has enabled the MOOC model. In its early years, there was an expectation that MOOCs may disrupt the established HE systems through the delivery anywhere-anytime courses by leading experts to masses of student at potentially a fraction of the cost of regular courses offered in physical universities.

The disruptive potential of MOOCs has so far not been realized, but the technology and methodology are now being widely used for teaching and learning, including delivering certificate or degree programmes. Many leading research universities have used the platform to offer their courses to students across the world. Many universities are involved in MOOC, and there are a host of reasons why universities are offering MOOC courses—main among them are to extend the reach of the institution, build the brand, improve the economics and improve education, innovation and research in teaching (Hollands and Tirthali, 2014). Experience indicates that most universities are producers or both producers and consumers, with a few being only consumers of MOOC. Platforms like Coursera and EdX offer a way to universities to host MOOC courses and for students to enrol in and take them.

We discuss here the use of MOOC and other such courses to enhance the education programmes, without being a producer of MOOC. In this form, the university is the consumer of the MOOC or open courseware. Surprisingly, using MOOC/open courseware within existing programmes in universities has turned out to be more challenging than expected. Most universities that use MOOC courses for credit employ some type of blended approach where a local instructor is present, and there may be some sort of assessment within the university (Sandeen, 2013). Here, we discuss an approach that was followed by IIIT-Delhi, as an example of how a research university may use these courses for its own education programmes.

First, let us clarify the objective of using MOOC courses. The institute took a view that it should leverage the top-class content being offered by globally renowned professors through online platforms like EdX and Coursera and Swayam (an Indian platform) for its education programmes. The goal was to augment the elective offerings of the institute, thereby making a wider variety of choices available to students for their elective courses. In other words, the courses the institute offered remained, and additional courses on newer topics were offered through this mode. This goal of augmenting the course offerings is somewhat different from what is commonly reported. There was a special keenness to make specialized courses available to students for which the institute did not have faculty to teach. To keep a control on this, the number of credits a student could earn thought this mode was limited.

For administering such courses, it was realized that it is easiest to 'offer' these courses as part of the course offerings in the institute. This not only simplifies their administration, registration, etc., but it is also easier for the students, as they are tuned to the semester rhythm. Consequently, only online courses that start and end within a semester are considered (though some relaxation is possible). To identify the courses, inputs from students are taken.

Once the courses are floated, an instructor is assigned for all the online courses being offered in the semester. For each online course, a teaching assistant (TA) is also assigned, who is required to enrol in the online course and take the course. The TA meets the students enrolled in the course once every 2–3 weeks to review the progress of students. Enrolled students may be required to submit suitable records to show that they are 'attending' lectures and doing the assignments. The TAs meet the instructor to brief about the progress of the courses.

As no formal assessment is done other than ensuring that the students are participating in all assessments of the online course, these courses are to be given only a pass/fail grade, so the problem is simplified somewhat. For giving the passing grade, the criteria are that the student has: listened to all the lectures, done all the assignments and taken all the exams and done well. When possible, the student should get a certificate of completion from the online course.

Generally, a few courses are offered each semester through this mode. The enrolment in these is not too heavy. However, the fraction of students who complete the course is almost 100 per cent, which is quite remarkable when compared to the completion rates generally published for such courses (less than 15%); even for paid courses/certificates, the completion rates are significantly lesser. The student feedback in these courses was positive; a vast majority felt that the course was 'very useful', and most felt that the course gave them an experience similar to or better than a regular course.

Use of courses available on various MOOC platforms is an excellent way to leverage their potential to expand offerings, particularly when there is a shortage of faculty. These are high-quality courses generally offered by the top experts in an area. The main challenge is to integrate these courses into a regular academic programme. The NEP also envisages leveraging the potential of open learning and MOOC for improving access to quality education and enhancing the offerings, and proposes a larger role of MOOC courses; it explicitly recommends the recognition and accumulation of credits earned through MOOC platforms (NEP 2019).

3.3 SUPPORTING EFFECTIVE TEACHING AND LEARNING

In the preceding section, we discussed how programmes and courses within programmes can be designed to provide high-quality learning for students, leading to graduates with well-developed graduate attributes. While the design of education programmes, and the courses within the programmes, indeed forms the foundation of good-quality education, for their expectations to be realized, they must be executed properly. In other words, courses must be taught effectively leading to good learning by the students in the courses. Effective teaching leading to good learning requires extra care to be taken by teachers, and there need to be systems in the university to support and encourage effective teaching. Over the previous decades, there has been a sharper focus on effectiveness in teaching which leads to the desired learning. The NEP also suggests universities to give attention to the teaching–learning processes to improve the learning outcomes of students (NEP 2019).

Any system to deliver high-quality output requires not only the people involved in the execution to perform their tasks as expected, but also needs feedback and quality systems to maintain and improve the quality—the law of entropy will ensure that if effort is not spent in properly administering the education delivery system, it is likely to decline in quality. There are a number of approaches universities can employ to improve the quality of teaching (Henard and Roseveare 2012). Focused efforts to orient teaching towards learning is known to improve the quality of teaching and student as well as faculty satisfaction (Kember 2009). Here, we discuss some approaches that universities can employ to help improve teaching, based on experience at IIIT-Delhi.

3.3.1 Training for Teaching

As stated in an earlier chapter, the faculty in a research university are recruited largely for their research potential. Such faculty are experts in their area, and their knowledge about their field is sound and deep. Earlier, the assumption was that if teachers had the required knowledge and understanding, they would be able to transmit their understanding to the students, resulting in good learning by the latter. This approach was adopted by almost all universities until a few decades ago—fresh faculty were assigned courses to teach with almost no training. This approach is no longer considered optimal. To ensure good learning in students, while subject matter expertise is necessary, it is recognized as not being sufficient. Teaching to ensure that students learn requires some effective teaching or pedagogical skills, besides knowledge about the subject matter.

Teaching and learning at the university level has been an active area of research for a few decades. Many traits and practices of excellent teachers (Sherman et al. 1987; Bain 2011) and of effective teaching (Devlin and Samarawickrema 2010) have been identified. While some people may naturally have the talent to be an effective teacher, it is now clear that there are some methodologies (e.g., active learning, project-based learning, etc.) that facilitate learning, which instructors can learn and apply. It is also now clear that for a teacher to be effective, he/she must have a decent understanding of students' learning processes and styles and student motivation, besides understanding the principles of course design and the basics of teaching.

As the PhD is largely the enabling degree for eligibility for a faculty position in a research university, and as the PhD is focused around developing research capability (see the chapter on the PhD programme), a newly recruited faculty member generally might not have even the basic knowledge about the pedagogical aspects of effective teaching. Hence, it is essential that the faculty, who are recruited largely for their research capability and potential, be trained in methods and technologies for effective teaching. While a few decades ago this was not appreciated, this is now widely accepted, and most large universities have established teaching-and-learning or teaching excellence centres. These centres, besides doing research on effective teaching and learning, offer training programmes for faculty to become more effective teachers.

While it is widely accepted by university administrators that such training programmes are important for faculty, particularly the new faculty, ensuring that the existing faculty also undergo some such programmes has been a challenge due to the culture and autonomy that exist in universities. Also, some of the senior faculty might have perhaps evolved through experience their own methods of effective instruction and may feel that they do not really need any further help. Universities have evolved various approaches to teach teachers about effective teaching methods. These involve requiring incoming faculty to necessarily take some such modules (since for new faculty this can be easily enforced), providing support to faculty for undertaking such programmes, looking at teaching qualifications also during faculty promotion and appraisal, etc.

As the importance of high-quality teaching also increases and many universities value teachers who are recognized as good, certificates programmes on teaching have also evolved. Having such certification from a globally recognized and reputed agency not only ensures that the teaching of the modules in a programme is effective, but it also helps motivate faculty to enrol in such programmes to obtain the additional qualifications that can make them more attractive for many universities. Faculty development programmes for improving teaching effectiveness have been generally found to be quite effective (Brawner et al. 2002; Hoyt and Howard 1978; Steinert et al. 2016).

3.3.2 Feedback Loops for Improving

Feedback loops are central to the improvement of any system—indeed, even maintaining the current level of quality requires feedback and continuous adjustment. For improving teaching, there need to be systematic feedback loops and actions taken based on the feedback for improving learning (Harvey 2003). There are multiple purposes for such feedbacks. For teachers teaching a course, feedback can help understand if they are proceeding as they had planned and if the teaching approach, speed, etc. are suitable for the current set of students. Feedback is also needed for the overall course, as course design cannot be static and its design cannot be assumed to be optimal—only with feedback can the design be improved—to either address deficiencies in design or accommodate newer developments. Even the design of a programme cannot be assumed to be optimal and should not be static; hence, feedback is needed on programmes. Finally, the teaching–learning methods being employed by faculty can always be improved, so feedback to understand the effectiveness of the approaches used by different teachers will help.

There are many feedback instruments that universities use; for example, end-of-the-course feedback from students is a standard in most universities. For different types of feedback, different approaches or questionnaires may be used (Harvey 2003; Richardson 2005). Here, we discuss the methods used in IIIT-Delhi for different purposes using structured questionnaires (with some open-ended questions)—they are likely to be similar in spirit and style to approaches used elsewhere.

- **Peer review of course design.** Most standard courses in a programme will have a design specifying the learning objectives, syllabus and assessment plan—the design would have been finalized through a process of discussion and review. However, it is desirable to provide some flexibility to instructors to adjust the topics covered, the assessment approach, etc., since even for a standard course some amount of evolution is desirable. If flexibility is provided to the instructor to modify the course design, it is desirable to ensure that the changes are appropriate and that the plan for course delivery by the instructor is sound in that it will deliver the learning outcomes and will assess them well. Given the autonomy and responsibility granted to the faculty for administering and running their courses—a freedom that is desirable and aligns with the faculty ethos—any approach for this has to be consistent with this ethos. Peer review of course plans is a feedback loop mechanism that attempts to achieve a balance. In peer review, the plan for a course by an instructor is reviewed by a peer (or a group of peers). The review comments are not meant to be on official record and are only given to the instructor. The institute only has to ensure that peer review has taken place, and so a record that it has been conducted is to be submitted. As it is a review by peers, it is a constructive exercise of improvement, with no threat of it becoming an assessment.
- **Mid-semester feedback.** The usual end-of-semester feedback on courses (discussed below), collected after the course has been finished, can only be used for improving the future offerings of the course and is of little value to the student enrolled in the course. To get feedback on the current course offering so any adjustments that might be needed can be made, an early mid-semester feedback instrument is employed—this is an online survey of students about a few key aspects of the course: the pace, the difficulty, their ability to understand and anything else the instructor may want to ask. The goal of this is to provide the instructor feedback on the current course teaching, so he/she can adjust it suitably, based on the inputs. This feedback is not an administrative instrument in

that the results are not recorded or used for assessment; it is meant exclusively for the instructor and to help him/her adjust the course. Hence, only the instructor receives the feedback, which he/she is expected to summarize to the class along with the actions he/she plans to take, if any.

- **End-of-semester feedback.** Most universities have end-of-semester feedback for courses. The main purpose of this feedback is to assess the quality of learning achieved by the student and the quality of teaching by the instructor (as perceived by the student), and obtain suggestions for improvement. Experience suggests that it is best to ask students precise questions that they can answer, rather than asking them summative questions (like: how good was the instructor, or how much learning did you acquire). Hence, it is desirable to have a set of questions regarding the teaching and a set of questions regarding the course and learning, and the student feedback on these can be combined into aggregate scores to assess the teaching and learning. Student evaluation of teaching has been found to be reliable and stable and useful for improving teaching effectiveness (Marsh and Roche 1997).

For assessing the students' view on learning, if the feedback form is an online instrument (as is generally the case now), there is a possibility to tailor the feedback form for each course, rather than have only general questions. In the online form used at IIIT-Delhi for a course, the learning outcomes for that course are stated, and the students are asked to share their views on how well they achieved the stated outcome. The average feedback on all the learning outcomes can be considered as the students' view on their learning. The direct method of assessing the learning outcomes has been promulgated by many scholars for assessment. This feedback approach takes this idea further and asks students to share their views on their learning with respect to the learning outcomes. A side benefit of this approach is that it reinforces the importance of learning outcomes in students, which often gets lost in the details and activities of the course.

- **Course summary.** Student feedback, it is known, is not an accurate reflection of the level of learning or the quality of teaching. Students are often biased and let other factors colour their replies. As is the general wisdom, while student feedback is an important input, it has inherent limitations. To address this and gain a holistic view of the course, for each course a course summary is prepared by the instructor and the teaching assistants. This summary also provides information about any special efforts and initiatives employed by the instructor to improve learning, any tools used, any other special practice, etc. This short summary provides the instructor's views on teaching. The information in this summary, when combined with the student feedback, can provide better insights on the practices that might be helping in students' learning. This can be used to determine the 'good practices' and 'teaching innovations' that faculty colleagues employ that seem to make their teaching more effective. These can then be shared with other faculty as 'lessons learned'—these can help transmit the effective practices more widely.

- **Feedback from graduating students, alumni, recruiters.** To get a broader student perspective, feedback can be taken from students at graduation time. These students have a full perspective of the education programme and also have a sense of what helped them during their job interviews or their graduate study applications. The focus of this feedback is more on the overall programme and learning experience (as well as other aspects of student life) and what can be done to improve it. Unlike other feedbacks which focus on a course, this is a more comprehensive feedback and is taken once a year—inputs from this can help in deciding on changes in the overall programme.

  Another useful feedback is feedback from alumni a few years after they have graduated. This is focused mostly on the overall programme and the learning environment—which courses they feel were useful, which courses they feel did not provide much value to them, which courses they feel they would have liked to take, etc. Again, for these inputs, the context of the alumni has to be kept in mind, as the views are inevitably determined by his/her experiences at his/her job—where he/she faced challenges and where his/her learning helped. While interpreting this, it has to be kept in mind that the education programme is designed for a range of job profiles and careers, and hence this feedback has to be interpreted suitably. Such feedback can also lead to a better empirical understanding of how the programme design supports the education objectives. However, getting such feedback is challenging—once students graduate, it is generally very hard to track them down and motivate them to participate in such studies.

In addition to these, feedback can be taken from recruiters on the strengths and weaknesses they observe in the students. These inputs provide valuable feedback from an employment perspective. However, it should be recognized that this perspective is often too narrow and focused on the objectives of the organization for which recruitment is being done, and that recruiters are unlikely to have a broad understanding of the education goals of the institute and the different career paths that the programmes prepare students for. Hence, such feedback cannot be taken literally, and any changes that may be suggested by this feedback must be supported by other needs and arguments.

3.3.3 Recognizing and Rewarding Teaching Excellence

Faculty members will often align their efforts towards what is perceived as valued by the institution and their profession. Though teaching and research are the two basic missions of a research university, in such universities, research performance is often what is most respected and what is most sought after by their faculty. In the quest for research excellence, the balance between teaching and research is sometimes lost in favour of research. There are some concerns that teaching has not been valued sufficiently by research universities, since in their own quest for prestige and rankings, they often send the message 'only research matters' to faculty. As mentioned earlier, teaching is the mission that society and governments value most and expect universities to excel in.

Therefore, there is a need to ensure that the message that teaching is important is communicated to the faculty (Efimenko et al. 2018). Along with it, a message needs to be sent to the students that teaching excellence is their right and not a favour by highly accomplished faculty.

There are methods established by professional bodies and societies to recognize and reward research excellence. There are prestigious awards, which often also have a financial incentive, to recognize great contributions in research. There are also prestigious fellowships established by professional bodies and societies which recognize research excellence. Additionally, of course, there are research funding schemes which provide grants for good research. Research contributions also get recognized through citations, invited seminars, keynotes, etc. Overall, there are many ways in which contribution to research is rewarded and recognized.

On the other hand, such channels are very few for teaching excellence. There is a fundamental challenge in this also—while research output is in public domain which the professional community of peers can assess and so can judge if the contributions over the years are worthy of recognition, such approaches are generally not possible for teaching excellence. Teaching is visible only within the university, and that too largely only to students (and indirectly, through their feedback and inputs, to others). Hence, it is hard for professional bodies to establish teaching excellence recognition and awards. Consequently, the university itself will have to identify and recognize teaching excellence— something it does not have to do for research excellence, for which it can rely on professional bodies. Recognizing teaching excellence through awards and prizes is now widely being practised in universities (Efimenko et al. 2018).

There will clearly be many ways to identify teaching excellence. Whatever method is employed, it must involve inputs from the students, as teaching is finally about the learning by students. Here, we briefly describe two schemes that are used in many universities, including IIIT-Delhi.

As hundreds of courses are taught each semester in a university and feedback is taken in each of these courses, one approach to recognizing good teaching is to recognize and reward instructors based exclusively on the student feedback on courses. Such recognition can be given to the 'top few' instructors in each discipline. For recognizing the top few, besides the feedback from students, other information can also be incorporated in the selection process—for example, size of the course, difficulty level of the course, innovations tried in the course (which are captured in course summaries), student comments, etc. This method has a drawback in that it relies too much on the student feedback, which is known to be not completely impartial.

A sounder approach can be to identify teaching excellence by taking inputs from graduating students and/or recent alumni. These groups of students have seen the entire programme and a range of teachers and hence are in a better position to identify those teachers whom they consider as having done the best job of helping them learn. These students would also not have any 'hidden agenda', as they would not be taking any more courses and would not be facing the faculty in the future. One approach for identifying recipients for teaching excellence awards as decided by the graduating batch (and/or alumni) is to have a process of nomination by the students, followed by subsequent voting. (This is the approach followed in IIIT-Delhi.) This method of recognizing teaching excellence has the drawback that as people tend to remember recent courses more, instructors of courses taught towards the end of the programme are likely to have an advantage. This can be alleviated by having separate categories for awards—some for the foundation courses, some for the core or compulsory courses, some for electives, etc.

Another way to respect and promote teaching excellence is to have workshops for sharing 'good practices' internally in the university. Recipients of teaching excellence awards, or those faculty who try some innovations in their teaching, can be invited to share their experiences and what they do with others. These workshops not only help in disseminate the good practices, they also help message that teaching excellence matters, and that excellent teachers are recognized and appreciated. They also support bottom-up innovation in teaching, which has been argued as an appropriate way to motivate and improve teaching and learning, with the workshops providing the platform to connect and share effective innovations and strategies across different disciplines. These can also provide inputs for top-down policymaking regarding teaching excellence, as well as for refining the modules that teaching excellence centres offer to faculty.

3.4. SUMMARY

Education is the first mission of universities, and remains perhaps the most important and relevant mission, even for most research universities. While all universities are expected to provide good-quality education, there are additional expectations from research universities as they are expected to take leadership in higher education and be the agents of change and upgradation. The chapter started with a discussion on this aspect of education in a research university.

The education function of universities has evolved over the centuries and decades. While in the olden days educating students on the classics, science, mathematics, critical thinking, etc. might have sufficed, it is now expected and desired that there should be clear objectives for education, that is, what types of careers is the programme preparing the students for. The education programme should be designed suitably, imparting the desired graduate attributes and learning outcomes that fulfil the objectives. The chapter provided a brief discussion on how a programme is designed—establishing the programme outcomes, designing the programme structure and designing individual courses.

It also discussed some special and contemporary topics like interdisciplinary programmes, in particular CS+X programmes. It also discussed the use of MOOCs and open courseware in university education programmes. Examples from IIIT-Delhi have been shared.

Finally, we discussed some approaches for ensuring effective teaching. These include providing training for teachers on effective teaching techniques, establishing feedback loops to ensure that the programme, course design and their delivery are achieving their objectives, and establishing awards and recognition for effective teaching.

We have not discussed admission into undergraduate programmes in this chapter. While admissions are not directly related to the processes of education, they have an impact on learning, as the peer group is known to influence the level of learning by students. Admission policies that help diversity can also help in improving education (as well as research), as they bring diversity of thought, different perspectives, cultural backgrounds, etc. which help in the development of students. Admissions in India have, over the years, become very rigid and largely based on exams, which does not encourage diversity. A discussion of admission approaches in India can be found in Chandra (2017).

Regarding admissions, IIIT-Delhi has championed an innovation that is quite unique in India. Instead of having admissions based only on the results of the common entrance exam, which is the prevailing method in almost all engineering institutions, IIIT-Delhi uses the score of the exam as the basis but gives bonus marks for achievements in various spheres, including sports, culture, chess, Olympiads, programming contests, class XII board exams, etc. In other words, admission is based on a score that is the sum of the score in the entrance exam and the bonus marks. This is a transparent and fair process that encourages diversity and recognizes the importance of multidimensional criteria for admitting students. This innovation of allowing a range of other aspects to be included in the decision on admission has paid off too—the students who come with bonus marks have, on average, a higher CGPA at the end of the first year (by almost 1 point). If such an approach is followed by some of the major institutions in the country, it can have a revitalizing impact on school education and the development of young minds, which currently is very focused on exams for admission.

REFERENCES

Ambrose, Susan A., Michael W. Bridges, Michele DiPietro, Marsha C. Lovett, and Marie K. Norman. 2010. *How Learning Works: Seven Research-based Principles for Smart Teaching*. San Francisco, CA: Jossey-Bass.

Angelo, Thomas A., and K. Patricia Cross. 1993. *Classroom Assessment Techniques: A Handbook for College Teachers*. San Francisco, CA: Jossey-Bass.

Bain, Ken. 2011. *What the Best College Teachers Do*. Cambridge, MA: Harvard University Press.

Barrie, Simon C. 2006. 'Understanding What We Mean by the Generic Attributes of Graduates.' *Higher Education* 51 (2): 215–41.

Barrie, Simon C. 2007, August. 'A Conceptual Framework for the Teaching and Learning of Generic Graduate Attributes.' *Studies in Higher Education* 32 (4): 439–58.

Brawner, C. E., R. M. Felder, R. Allen, and R. Brent. 2002. 'A Survey of Faculty Teaching Practices and Involvement in Faculty Development Activities.' *Journal of Engineering Education* 91 (4): 393–6.

Bridgstock, Rugh. 2009, March. 'The Graduate Attributes We've Overlooked: Enhancing Graduate Employability Through Career Management Skills.' *Higher Education Research and Development* 28 (1): 31–44.

Chandra, Pankaj. 2017. *Building Universities that Matter: Where are Indian Institutions Going Wrong?* New Delhi: Orient BlackSwan.

Dee Fink, L. 2013. *Creating Significant Learning Experiences: An Integrated Approach to Designing College Courses*. San Francisco, CA: Jossey-Bass.

Devlin, M., and G. Samarawickrema. 2010. 'The Criteria of Effective Teaching in a Changing Higher Education Context.' *Higher Education Research & Development* 29 (2): 111–24.

Efimenko, E., A. Roman, M. Pinto, F. Remião, P. Teizeira. 2018. 'Enhancement and Recognition of Teaching and Learning in Higher Education.' *Journal of European Higher Education Area* 2018 (2): 99–118.

Gibbons, Michael. 1998. *Higher Education Relevance in the 21st Century*. Washington, DC: World Bank.

Harvey, L. 2003. 'Student Feedback.' *Quality in Higher Education* 9 (1): 3–20.

Healey, Mick. 2005, July. 'Linking Research and Teaching to Benefit Student Learning.' *Journal of Geography in Higher Education* 29 (2): 183–201.

Henard, F., and D. Roseveare. 2012. *Fostering Quality Teaching in Higher Education: Policies and Practices*. An IMHE Guide for Higher Education Institutions. https://www.oecd.org/education/imhe/QT%20policies%20and%20practices.pdf

Hollands, Fiona M., and D. Tirthali. 2014. 'Why Do Institutions Offer MOOCs?' *Online Learning* 18 (3): 1–19.

Hoyt, D. P., and G. S. Howard. 1978. 'The Evaluation of Faculty Development Programs.' *Research in Higher Education* 8: 191–9.

Kember, D. 2009. 'Promoting Student-centred Forms of Learning Across an Entire University.' *Higher Education* 58: 1–13.

Knight, David B., Lisa R. Lattuca, Ezekiel W. Kimball, and Robert D. Reason, 2013. 'Understanding Interdisciplinarity: Curricular and Organizational Features of Undergraduate Interdisciplinary Programs.' *Innovative Higher Education* 38: 143–58.

Krathwohl, David R. 2002. 'A Revision of Bloom's Taxonomy: An Overview.' *Theory into Practice* 41 (4): 212–8.

Marsh, H. W., and L. A. Roche. 1997. 'Making Students' Evaluations of Teaching Effectiveness Effective: The Critical Issues of Validity, Bias, and Utility.' *American Psychologist* 52 (11): 1187–97.

NEP. 2019. *Draft National Education Policy*. New Delhi: Government of India.

Neumann, Ruth. 1992. 'Perceptions of the Teaching-Research Nexus: A Framework for Analysis', *Higher Education* 23: 159–171.

Richardson, John T. E. 2005, August. 'Instruments for Obtaining Student Feedback: A Review of the Literature.' *Assessment & Evaluation in Higher Education* 30 (4): 387–415.

Sandeen, Cathy. 2013. 'Integrating MOOCs into Traditional Higher Education: The Emerging "MOOC 3.0" Era.' *Change: The Magazine of Higher Learning* 45 (6): 34–9.

Sherman, T. M., L. P. Armistead, F. Fowler, and G. Reif. 1987. 'The Quest for Excellence in University Teaching.' *The Journal of Higher Education* 58 (1): 66–84.

Steinert, Y., K. Mann, B. Anderson, B. M. Barnett, et al. 2016. 'A Systematic Review of Faculty Development Initiatives Designed to Enhance Teaching Effectiveness: A 10-year Update: BEME Guide No. 40.' *Medical Teacher* 38 (8): 769–86.

Willetts, David. 2017. *A University Education*. Oxford University Press.

Vossensteyn, Hans, Renze Kolster, Frans Kaiser, Jon File, Jeroen Huisman, Marco Seeber, Martina Vukasovic, Kai Muehleck, Christoph Gwosc. 2018. *Promoting the Relevance of Higher Education*. European Commission, Directorate-General for Education, Youth, Sport and Culture. Available online at europa.eu.

Chapter 4

Research Management, Ethics and Culture

A research university focuses on research, and hence must promote and support research not only as part of its mission but also operationally. However, unlike education, which is a collective responsibility and effort of the university, research is largely done by small groups of faculty along with their students. Consequently, the role of the university is more about facilitating research. Towards this end, all research universities have management units for research—some large universities may have elaborate structures and multiple units looking after different aspects of research promotion and management. In this chapter, we will look at the key aspects of managing research in a research university. We will discuss research management at an institutional level, and not those elements of research management that are done by researchers themselves. (It should be appreciated that a considerable amount of research management is actually done by the faculty and staff executing research projects, usually within the frameworks defined by the institute-level research management (Kirkland 2008).)

The main goal of research administration in a university is to increase the volume and quality of research, especially sponsored research. For this, it has to perform key functions such as developing a strategic research plan, promoting sponsored research grant management and research advancement, providing research infrastructure, promoting the research done, etc. (Johnson 2013). We will discuss these in the next section. The research administration also needs to provide support for the commercialization and use of research in the society. We have discussed this aspect, which has become increasingly important, in more detail in the chapter on the third mission (Chapter 5).

Another function of the overall research management in a university is to provide support for research ethics and ensure that they are being followed. This is naturally a crucial aspect of conducting research involving live (human, animal and plant) subjects. Ethics has become increasingly important even in areas such as technology, as technology impacts all aspects of life and often has undesirable uses. Also, research sponsors often require that the ethical practices of research are strictly followed. We will discuss research ethics later in this chapter.

Finally, research thrives if a university can develop and support a culture of research. We will discuss this vital aspect also later in this chapter.

4.1 RESEARCH ADMINISTRATION

Research administration covers all aspects of managing and promoting research in a university. The funding in most research universities comes from sponsored research projects. Hence, providing support for managing such projects is a major goal of mainstream research management. Besides research projects, research universities often have research centres—these are entities that have focused research goals, which are sometimes interdisciplinary. Research centres may last for decades. They may have been created through some grants, but once created, they are the responsibility of the university and have to be supported till they are closed.

While providing support for projects and centres, the research administration should also proactively advance research. The goal is to promote high-quality research and research excellence and to help get more sponsored projects. This involves identifying emerging areas in which a research university should take a leadership role, obtaining funding for it and planning to develop it. Research administration should also promote the research done in the university among external and internal stakeholders, which indirectly helps the cause of research advancement.

Finally, the administration needs to provide a suitable infrastructure for research, which can be anything from space for labs, to high-performance machines, to digital libraries, and so forth. The administration can also support researchers in tasks necessary for the main research for which the faculty member may not have the expertise, for example, programs to be written to analyse data in a particular manner for some medicine-related research.

Universities also have to organize their research management structure suitably. We have not discussed this aspect here. The literature is available on this aspect. For example, how an organization managing university research might be organized and what might be suitable research management structures are discussed in Huong Nguyen and Meek (2015). Similarly, some issues related to managing research are discussed in Mintrom (2008). The OECD has also produced documents on this topic (Connell 2004; Hazelkorn 2005).

4.1.1 Strategic Planning

One of the responsibilities of the research administration is to develop a strategic plan for research (Bushaway 2003; Kirkland 2008). However, unlike a corporation, where research may be goal-driven and the research team can be asked to work on stated goals, in academia, the administration has no real authority to guide faculty members on the type of research they should pursue, and there are often no end goals for research other than generating new knowledge. Hence, all types of research have to be encouraged. In other words, there is an inherent tension between academic freedom and any centralized planning for research. Hence, the role of strategic planning is limited.

Although it is challenging to evolve a suitable and actionable strategic plan for research in an academic institution, not having a plan may lead to missing opportunities for getting research funding or becoming a leading player in some area.

At the institutional level, the main goal of strategic planning is to help an institution become a leading research centre in specific areas, which helps build its prestige, something that every university seeks. This goal often translates into plans for the establishment of research centres and groups in some areas where the university has some advantages and which are important areas.

In an established university, a new initiative for research is generally based on the availability of some talent in an emerging opportunity for research. For example, it may be that some existing faculty are working in an area that becomes more important, with more funding available. In such a situation, the university may wish to bring such faculty together to form a group and augment the faculty suitably. At other times, the university may plan to enter some new areas of research and then recruit some senior people to drive research in those areas—this may also require establishing new labs or centres or even departments in some emerging disciplines.

Strategic planning may also be opportunistic. For example, a university might be able to attract a senior faculty who has a well-established reputation in an area. In such a case, the university can develop the area around the senior faculty and include it in its strategic vision.

A basic strategic research plan is to identify a few emerging areas with some advantages for the university, for example, location, availability of talent, proximity to an industry, and so forth, and then plan to establish centres or groups in those areas. This plan has to align with the plans of the different departments involved. The plan may include providing and pursuing some seed funding for the group or centre from the government or from other funding agencies. The plan has to be reviewed periodically to ensure that it remains cognizant of the emerging opportunities.

Often, research groups for specific areas in a discipline are established within departments. However, at an institutional level, often, centres are set for significant research initiatives. These centres usually work on some problem areas which require multidisciplinary research. Thus, they become a unit that brings researchers from different departments together to work on the said problems. Often, incentives are provided to faculty with respect to PhD students, grants, support, and so forth, to contribute to the centre's research goals. Research centres are particularly useful for leveraging faculty strength from multiple departments to create an entity focused on some research areas.

A research university, therefore, needs special mechanisms to start research centres and operate them, as often, centres employ people who are neither university employees nor working on a project. A centre typically is provided some physical space and has a few administrative staff and a centre head, which makes its management quite different from the management of a typical project. This gives rise to a host of related issues—source of funding, motivation and incentives for the faculty to work in the centre, and so forth. If a certain source sponsors a centre, as is often the case for starting a centre, there must be plans to support the centre after the funding runs out, as such funding will typically support the centre for a few years. A research university must have specific guidelines for managing centres.

It is desirable to have the possibility of closing centres, perhaps when the research theme of the centre ceases to be an important research area. For this reason, most universities do not have regular faculty positions in the centre, but faculty are recruited from within the academic departments and participate in centres. Therefore, the space allocation for centres should normally be for some duration and should be reviewed after that. This can prevent situations wherein some old areas, though unimportant, with not much funding, still occupy space and the centre continues to exist.

4.1.2 Securing and Managing Research Projects

No research university can survive without successfully and aggressively competing for and getting research grants from various national and international agencies that provide funds for research. Most research-sponsoring agencies expect a central unit in a research university to serve as an interface through which they can monitor the appropriate use of funds. All research universities necessarily should have such a unit for managing research projects. In India, this unit is often the office of Dean of Research—also sometimes called Research and Development, or Innovation, Research and Development (IRD).

The IRD management needs to provide support for different phases in a project cycle (Kirkland 2008). The most fundamental support is to help prepare proposals with a suitable budget and submit them to a sponsoring agency. If a project is approved, the research management needs to provide necessary support for receiving funds and ensure their proper use, compliance with all regulations and submission of necessary reports, including the final project closure report, to the agency.

Sponsored projects are the main source of research funding, and in many universities, the overall sponsored project revenue may be as big as a quarter or more of their total yearly expenditure. The rules for the use of these funds are sometimes different from those of regular university funds. Also, the financial authority of approving the use generally rests with the principal investigator (PI) of the project. Therefore, the office of research usually has a separate accounting system and balance sheet, with dedicated staff for managing funds and accounts.

The support includes systems that can assist faculty in applying for projects and also facilitate the execution and closure of projects. Some of the requirements are:

- **Identifying project opportunities:** Often, calls for proposals are floated by agencies on their websites; faculty are not expected to monitor all such websites. The IRD unit should keep track of all such opportunities as they emerge and keep the faculty informed.

- **Facilitating proposal preparation and submission:** Although the PI is responsible for preparing the proposal, the IRD unit can help in various ways. For example, the IRD unit should save a copy of earlier proposals funded by different agencies and use them to prepare new proposals. Also, frequently, proposals may need some general information regarding available facilities, university support and administration. The IRD unit can also provide these standard details. Policies for many items are generally decided at the institutional level. The IRD unit can help in the budgeting and appropriate costing of these items.

- **Providing flexible support to execute projects:** Project execution, which is the responsibility of PIs, may require recruiting staff for the project, purchasing equipment, arranging meetings, scheduling visits, and so forth. All these activities require efforts. If the IRD unit supports the PIs in these activities, PIs can focus more on the actual research. The IRD unit can further support PIs in ensuring that the funding agency conditions are met, if there are any.

- **Helping in smooth project closure:** All projects close after their predefined duration (typically 1–3 years). Closure requires a host of activities, such as making the closure report, closing the account and balancing the funds, taking care of the equipment purchased during the project, and so forth.

All these are standard functions performed by different universities in their own way. We will not discuss them further.

4.1.3 Research Advancement and Promotion

The purpose of research advancement is to take initiatives to advance research in the university. One way is to seed research in some upcoming area, where either expertise in the university does not exist currently or research funding has not yet started in that area. Universities are keen to work on futuristic problems;

in fact, often, these problems are exciting and offer possibilities for new achievements. Often, funding for such emerging areas is lacking. Hence, a university may start some initiatives to get some faculty interested in these areas and develop research groups and leadership so as to tap research funds and projects when (and if) funding becomes available.

Research is no longer a solo effort, given the vast knowledge that already exists, the complexity of problems and the need for faster knowledge creation. Hence, a critical mass of research-ers must work on defined problem areas to make a mark in a shorter time. Forming research groups for problem areas is a proven method for making substantial contributions—multiple faculty working in similar areas along with their students form this group. A university can try to form research groups or labs in emerging areas by bringing related researchers together.

When taking this proactive approach towards research by identifying some research directions to pursue, often, such direc-tions may require interdisciplinary effort. In such cases, besides providing initial support, the university may also facilitate match-making across departments so that complementary strengths can be pooled for forming a strong interdisciplinary team suitable for the chosen area.

A university can follow a similar approach even if it does not currently have expertise in an area that it considers important. In such a case, the university may invest funds and recruit fac-ulty already working in that area. Further, the university can help some existing faculty members to migrate to or include this research area in their portfolio by providing them suitable support. With such initiatives, a new research group can emerge which can then bid for research funds.

These top-down approaches can be complemented with bottom-up approaches in which faculty can be asked to submit proposals for emerging areas or interdisciplinary work, particu-larly where some funding at an initial stage can help them reach a level where they can submit proposals to funding agencies.

Promising proposals can then be provided with some seed funding. Many universities have such funding programmes; the expectation is that some research proposals will be submitted to funding agencies as a result of the seed funding.

A research university needs to promote excellence. Though most research ends up making a modest contribution, if mostly mediocre-quality work is done, it is almost impossible to make a mark. Given the size of the research enterprise and the growing competition globally, as an increasing number of countries and universities are improving their research capacities, a university must have excellent research output to be noticed. Far too often, administration systems are geared towards the output, including papers published, and so forth. However, the goal of excellent research is actually to have an impact—impact on the body of knowledge or impact on the society, directly or indirectly, through the transfer of technology. Research advancement can support efforts for impactful research.

Another aspect of research promotion is to build industry partnerships leading to collaborative research on problems of interest to industries as well. This approach has been successfully employed by many universities in Australia, USA and elsewhere. However, these partnerships are not easy to build. Industries are preoccupied mainly with their business development. Their research needs are likely to be short-term in nature—opposite to academic research needs, which are long-term and more conceptual in nature.

For collaborating with industries, multiple approaches should be tried. Any progress in this direction can only be made if both sides acknowledge and accept each other's value systems and aspirations, identify common areas and problems that they can work on and develop mechanisms that facilitate the research, while working within the constraints of both sides. The most obvious approach is to have regular sponsored research projects from the industry. Another approach is to get into arrangements between a company and a university for funding research in certain areas, with some agreement about the intellectual property sharing. There are also models of industries supporting PhD and master's theses on specific topics, which can provide low-cost engagement to industries. Collaborative centres with industry, particularly if there is support in terms of matching grants available (as in the Industry-University Cooperative Research Centers (IUCRCs) in USA [Berman 2012]), is an excellent way to engage in long-term collaboration with industry.

The goals of research are helped if the research being done and its impact are visible to the society and various stakeholders. In other words, for advancing research in a university, the research done in the university has to be promoted. Promoting research is therefore another function in which the goal is to promote research done in the university externally among the public and other stakeholders, as well as internally among its faculty, staff and students. This can be in the form of newsletters, media posts, advertising, social media drives, and so forth. This function is sometimes handled separately.

4.1.4 Research Infrastructure

Clearly, research universities need to provide a strong research infrastructure. While funding and specialized equipment for research projects may come from research grants, researchers and funding agencies expect universities to have a strong and facilitating research infrastructure. The research infrastructure is essential to ensure that even areas that do not get sufficient funding from sponsors but are of interest to some faculty are supported. Most universities focus on broad-based general research infrastructure while relying on sponsored projects to get specialized facilities needed for specific projects. Some of the basic research infrastructures include the following:

- Computing and networking infrastructure, including high-performance computing;
- Library with journal subscriptions, books, etc.;
- Support for international connections and collaboration;

- Policies to support research; and
- Seed funding for research.

Another support that scientists often need is software support for their research project, which is different from IT support. All disciplines need various kinds of software support to do the work and answer their research questions—developing some software scripts for data processing or visualization, configuring some software systems, developing websites, and so forth. Researchers can focus on the main research questions if they are supported in all their software needs, as software development is often challenging for people from non-engineering fields. An example of this kind of support is the e-research unit of QUT in Australia.

Support for intellectual property (IP) management and commercialization is another area that has become increasingly important for universities. There is now an increased desire that while research generates new knowledge, where possible, the knowledge should be applied for the betterment of societies and peoples also. Commercialization of IP and its management needs support in terms of filing patents, protecting them, getting into IP-sharing arrangements with companies, and so forth. However, these are complex issues involving lawyers and dedicated IP management units. This aspect has been further discussed in the chapter on the third mission (Chapter 5).

Here it will be good to separate generating value, and benefitting from this value. Given the financial needs of a university, it may be important for a university to benefit from the value that may be generated from the research done at the university. At the same time, as a university is involved primarily in generating knowledge as a public good and is often supported through public funds, it can also be argued that the main goal of a university should be that the knowledge it creates must generate value for the society. This is different from the goal of new-knowledge creation by a company. A company is interested in generating value for itself, though it may also generate value for the society. For a university, it should be the reverse—the main goal is to generate value for society, and where possible, this value generation should also benefit the university financially. These two factors will have to be balanced by a university in its policies regarding the commercialization of the IP it creates.

4.2 RESEARCH ETHICS

Research is the pursuit of creating new knowledge through systematic inquiry. Ethics provides guidelines regarding what actions in the pursuit of knowledge are proper. Hence, ethics guides researchers and also provides the philosophical framework for universities to evolve their guidelines for their faculty, students and staff involved in research.

Ethics, in a very general sense of the term, refers to the study of what ought to or ought not to be done. It can consist of guidelines regarding right actions or decision-making. Research ethics is a form of applied ethics, that is, the study and formulation of guidelines for ethical behaviour in the context of research. Research ethics can define parameters and standards that will help researchers strive to maximize benefits and minimize harm in research activities (Anderson and Corneli 2018).

Ethical conduct of research is also commonly referred to as responsible conduct of research. Responsible conduct of research (RCR) is 'simply conducting research in ways that fulfill the professional responsibilities of researchers, as defined by their professional organizations, the institutions for which they work and, when relevant, the government and public' (Steneck 2006). For the responsible conduct of research, a way to view ethics is that it raises issues for the research project along three dimensions: (a) truth or scientific integrity; (b) fairness with respect to colleagues, subjects and the institution; and (c) wisdom or social responsibility for conducting the research (Pimple 2002). These three dimensions can be further divided into multiple domains.

A host of ethical issues come up when research uses human and other living subjects, and there is a risk of harm to the subject, for example, in medical research or some types of social science research. This is a big issue in itself—there are guidelines in countries on how human or animal subjects should be used for such studies, and there are books and articles which discuss them. Many of the dimensions relating to fairness fall in this category (Pimple 2002). We will not discuss this issue, other than saying that if living subjects are involved, a strong compliance with suitable frameworks should be the norm.

Research ethics can also be viewed as having two aspects— procedural aspects that deal with the processes to be followed for approvals, etc. and ethics in practice, which deals with issues that researchers face during their research (Guillemin and Gillam 2004). We focus on the practice aspects here and discuss some research ethics issues in the three main stages of research, namely, research problem formulation, execution of research and making claims and publishing research results. We then briefly discuss mechanisms a university should employ to support ethical research. For a deeper discussion on many of the issues, we refer the reader to Koepsell (2015).

4.2.1 Research Problem Formulation

This is the first stage of research—formulating a research question and planning the methodological stances that one would adopt to seek an answer to that question. In general, any question could be a research question if there is a good enough justification that it is 'research-able'. But there has to be an additional dimension to this stage of question formulation: Is the research in itself ethical? For example, it might sound interesting to a researcher to explore the hypothesis that states 'the number of girls in engineering colleges is less due to their poor math skills', but this research question formulation in itself is based on a gendered assumption of different intellectual abilities. Is that ethical? Does it carry the potential of misrepresenting a specific section of the society?

The main ethical issues that arise during this phase of research include:

- **Formulation of research questions or hypothesis that is fair and unbiased and is not intended to harm subjects.** This is the key issue while conducting research, and it relates to the social responsibility aspect of research. History has shown that, often, research questions are formulated in a manner that is not neutral and which leads to biases against groups (e.g., a question about whether people of some races have lower intelligence).
- **Methods or instruments used for answering the question.** It is the ethical responsibility of the researcher to ensure that the method used does not have inherent limitations or biases which can result in incorrect results. For example, the intelligence quotient (IQ) test used earlier to study the intelligence of people was itself shown to be biased against some groups of people. This issue is also related to scientific integrity.

While research in itself is a search for answers, it may or may not be beneficial for mankind to pursue some research questions. In such a case, while a scientist is clearly within his/her rights to pursue a question in the pursuit of science, he/she is faced with an ethical issue of whether it is worth pursuing (social responsibility dimension). There are many research questions that a scientist may have, but he/she pursues only those which according to his/her view and priorities are worth pursuing—this may be based on the possible impact, availability of funding, personal liking of the problem, etc. For research questions whose outcomes may harm mankind, the 'worth' question should also be asked from an ethical perspective.

4.2.2 Execution of Research

Once the research problem and questions are determined, the researcher may gather data pertaining to his/her research concerns. The data might be gathered through performing experiments involving subjects, compiling data from different sources, monitoring systems or people, etc. Then the data is to be analysed to obtain knowledge, which can be extracted. There are many ethical issues that come in during this phase of research. Some of the key ones are:

- **Use of human subjects.** Human subjects are also used in studies that have 'minimal risk of harm', for example, administering a questionnaire to study the habits or preferences of people. For such research also, research ethics dictates that some guidelines should be followed. This issue relates to the fairness dimension. We discuss some of these.

  Such research projects should follow a protocol which requires 'informed consent' by the human subject, that is, an acknowledgement that the human subject is fully aware about the research and the potential consequences of him/her participating in the research as a subject. Respondents should also be made aware of the rights they have as participants of the study. They should be informed about the possible steps of following up on how and where data/information extracted from them would be used.

  Another general guideline is that of privacy. The identity of the person should be kept hidden, and in no way should the privacy of the individuals be violated. Moreover, confidentiality of information/data gathered from the participants has to be ensured. Breach of confidentiality or sharing of information with third parties (not involved in the study) is a serious breach of research ethics.

  While the research may have minimal risk of direct harm, there may be other types of impact on the subject, for example, emotional, psychological, economic or interpersonal. Some psychological harms—sadness, embarrassment, anxiety—may be caused by the way data is collected. Other types of harms—breach of privacy, economic harm, harm to dignity—may occur if the researcher does not respect the will of the participants in terms of confidentiality of identity and data. It is important to identify the possible risks, consider the likelihood and magnitude of the risks and determine methods to minimize them. Further, the risk should be clearly explained to the subjects as part of informed consent.

- **Use of publicly available data.** There is currently a lot of data available on various platforms, which reveal much of it to the public. It is known that by combining data from various platforms, it is possible to find out more about a person— perhaps much more than what the person intended to make public. Should such data be inferred and made available? In such situations, an ethical response is that if the data reveals more than what the person had intended, then the consent of the person should be sought.
- **Fabrication or falsification of data.** A lot of studies start with some hypothesis that has to be established through data. Sometimes, some of the data that is collected (as a result of experiments or other data-gathering exercises) does not fully fit the hypothesis. If there are some data points that are 'the culprit', it is tempting for the researcher to ignore the data in order to prove the hypothesis, or worse, 'adjust' the data so it suits the hypothesis. The worst case of this is when data is not obtained but manufactured artificially to prove the hypothesis. All such falsifications or fabrications of data are clearly unethical. The ethical response should be to let the data speak for itself and not manipulate or manufacture it in any way, and if any data points are omitted (as outliers or special cases), this should be made clear when making research claims. In this discussion, data does not just refer to tables and numbers—an image is also data, and modifying images is also data manipulation.
- **Responsible management of the side effects of executing the research.** Research may result in waste. While not central to the research being pursued, it is the responsibility of scientists to ensure that waste and other side effects are managed properly.

4.2.3 Publishing Research Results and Claims

The final stage of research involves communicating one's findings with the larger academic community. Of course, there are possibilities that there might already exist research dealing with the same subject matter as one's own. There exists a proper procedure of acknowledging such prior works in one's own writing. Claiming someone else's finding as one's own is a serious ethical breach, and every researcher needs to be wary of it. Having said this, it is also a matter of concern that many a time, such incidents of plagiarism happen due to lack of awareness. Researchers require proper training on legitimate procedures of quoting and citing other research writings without coming under the risk of penalization for their own work being judged as plagiarized. There are many issues relating to communicating research results and making research claims. Some of these are:

- **Publication ethics.** There are some general rules which researchers are expected to follow when submitting their work for possible publication in a journal (of conference). The first is that the research paper should not be submitted to multiple journals at the same time—the ethical behaviour is to submit it to one place at a time. Second, the research paper should not be a 'rehash' of older works but should contain substantially new results. Third, the authorship for the paper being submitted should be claimed by those who have contributed significantly to the research results being reported and their writing. While the first two can possibly be checked by journals, the third issue can only be ensured by the researchers/ authors; this is also an area where, perhaps, violations are more common (it is known that some names are added in the author list—generally known as ghost authors—for extraneous reasons).
- **Plagiarism.** This is perhaps the most common violation of ethical standards. The plagiarism violation has a few different aspects. The first is what we will call as text plagiarism— picking up text (or a diagram, photo, etc.) verbatim from an earlier publication without permission and without attributing it to the source. This also often violates the legal copyright provisions. The second is what we will refer to as concept plagiarism—some earlier published ideas are used without giving credit to the original authors. The worst form of this

is when the main ideas or results in the paper are plagiarized but are claimed to be the author's own (e.g., an idea in a paper published in Russian/French is used by an author in a paper written in English, who claims it as his own). Finally, there is the concept of self-plagiarism—in this, text or ideas published earlier in works by the current authors are used without properly attributing them to the original publications. Most journals have clearly stated policies regarding plagiarism, including what actions it may take in case plagiarism is detected (e.g., guidelines by Nature).

- **Authorship and credits.** Researchers involved in a research need to ensure that in their paper, credits are given suitably. Any person who contributes significantly to a paper/research needs to be acknowledged as an author, while those providing minor support can be mentioned in the acknowledgements, and persons who have not contributed significantly to the research should not be listed as authors (this aspect is often violated, where a 'head' or a 'senior' person's name is added even if the person has not contributed to the research). The order of authorship—first, second, third or guest—has to be based on mutual consent among all the contributors involved. This holds true even if the contributor is a student.

- **Overclaiming and not clearly explaining the limitations.** Most often, research results are valid only in some circumstances. As an ideal for a researcher is to get general results that will hold true in a large range of circumstances, there is often a tendency to make larger claims than reasonable. It is the ethical responsibility of the scientist to not make an overgeneralized claim and clearly explain the limitations of the results and the assumptions made while conducting the research.

4.2.4 Institutional Mechanisms for Supporting Ethical Research

While it is the responsibility of the researchers/scientists to ensure that they follow the ethical guidelines of their profession and follow the standards/frameworks, it is the responsibility of the university (or the organization the scientist works for) to provide support for this. In addition, there are some issues that a scientist cannot himself/herself determine, as there might be a resultant conflict of interest—for example, if an experiment they want to conduct with human subjects is acceptable or not. In such cases, there is a need for an approving body, which can ensure that approval for a research is given only if it complies with their standards and there are no violations of the ethical guidelines. These committees are generally referred to as institutional review boards or IRBs. IRBs are present and functional in most research-based institutions to ensure that research is conducted safely and ethically.

The task of an IRB is to review, prior to its initiation, all research involving human participants. It has the authority to assess, approve, disapprove, monitor, make suggestions for or request changes in a research work per the ethical standards of the institute. The IRB usually has a few members from varying backgrounds to review a research's institutional, legal, social and scientific implications. For taking a holistic and unbiased view, the IRB should contain some scientists but also some non-scientists and someone with no affiliation to the institution. The requirements of a sound IRB composition are different in different countries.

Besides the IRB, an institution also needs mechanisms to investigate claims of unethical behaviour that might be brought to its notice and, based on the investigation, determine responsibility and recommend a course of action. Universities generally use committees for this purpose—often constituted based on the nature of the claim.

4.3 BUILDING A RESEARCH CULTURE

Universities have a culture that distinguishes them from other organizations, and the foundation of this unique culture rests on the unique missions of the universities—knowledge creation and dissemination. This culture is a shared set of values and beliefs that are taken for granted and which help the university faculty in defining who they are, what they are expected to do, the purpose of their work and how their community is different from others (Silver 2003). From this notion of culture, we can say that the research culture of a university refers to the set of shared beliefs, values, attitudes, practices, customs, etc. of the institution that support and promote research. The set of beliefs includes the views of faculty regarding levels of support for research, time for doing research (i.e., teaching load must be modest), importance of research in promotion, type of research expected, social norms in the university, etc. (Pratt et al. 1999). A supportive and thriving research culture is indispensable to achieve excellence and higher research productivity. All other things being equal, the universities having a strong culture of research will be more productive and conduct more impactful research than others.

The research productivity of researchers is influenced by their own capabilities and motivation and traits but is far more impacted by environmental factors (Bland and Ruffin 1972). Studies have shown that even very productive researchers become less productive if they move to environments that are not conducive to doing high-quality research. A study identified various environmental factors that affect research productivity. These include: clear goals and their communication, an emphasis on research, *culture*, group climate, participative and decentralized governance, leadership, etc. (Bland and Ruffin 1972). The NEP of the Government of India also recognizes that besides lack of sufficient funding for research, there is also a lack of research mindset and culture, which does not encourage the best minds to take up careers in research. It suggests that a basic goal of the national research foundation to be established should be to promote a culture of research in universities, besides providing funds for research in universities (NEP 2019).

Building a research culture is a concept involving social processes which are influenced by individuals and the past. Hence, it is hard and involves time and sustained efforts. Further, it requires commitment from all members of the university, particularly the faculty, PhD scholars and the leadership. Preserving and strengthening the research culture is even harder and also needs continuous effort and care. There are many examples in India and across the world where a flourishing research culture degenerates to one where mediocrity thrives. The various structures and stakeholders of the university have to be vigilant to preserve the culture and avoid the temptation of taking expedient steps and decisions that may avoid immediate unpleasantness but can damage the cultural fabric.

Higher education scholars have studied research culture over the years. The report of Hanover (2014) provides a background to the issue and some faculty and institutional characteristics. Some key characteristics of a research culture in a university are discussed here. These points are largely for the context of Indian universities, but most should be generally applicable.

- **Expectation of high-quality academics.** Any culture of an organization must start with what the organization expects from its employees. In a university, if the expectation is of high quality and excellence in academics, only then can it expect that people will try to achieve it. If modest expectations are set, then human nature will ensure that only small achievements are made. Therefore, to establish a thriving research culture, suitable expectations must be established. This means that internal policies for promotion and rewards are aligned with this expectation and that they are followed year after year. Just stating them and then not following them is of no value. Only when the expectations are consistently communicated and all internal systems and policies align with the expectations can excellence thrive. Most globally respected universities have achieved this. Often, the quality of venues of publication, impact of work, in terms of citations or other measures, and recognition of contributions by professional associations and peers are used to establish expectations.
  A key challenge in countries like India lies not only in articulating the expectations but also in aligning the policies and practices with these expectations. Sometimes, expedient

decisions are made, which can hurt the research culture. For example, if some faculty with mediocre records are promoted, it becomes a benchmark for future decisions and drives the expectations towards mediocrity. In such a situation, excellence survives only due to individual commitments and drive.

- **Strong motivations of faculty and research scholars for research.** There are umpteen examples of faculty and PhD students who have no strong reasons to be in the research profession—they may be there mainly due to the benefits they perceive. There are several examples of faculty in many universities across India and other countries who are in the profession mainly for teaching young minds and therefore engage minimally in research. Such faculty may be assets in teaching-focused universities, but they are not suitable for research universities. The faculty in a research university must be committed to conducting research and must have a strong personal motivation for the same, as only then can the drive be sustained over decades. The motivation can be enjoying research work and the respect that it accrues, collaborating with researchers across the world for exciting research, having a large research group and the name and fame associated with being a great researcher, having the fellowship of reputed associations, making an impact through research, participating in expert committees, and so forth. Ensuring suitable motivation requires care in faculty selection, so that only suitable candidates are appointed as faculty. Extra care should be taken during promotion and other evaluative processes to ensure that those who are excelling and improving their research performance are adequately rewarded.

Similarly, students having adequate motivation for conducting research should be enrolled in the PhD programme. Again, the motives can be varied, but students should have strong personal reasons that motivate them to conduct research and they should put in the necessary efforts to obtain a good PhD. Those who are pursuing PhD just to get a title, perhaps for their career progression, are likely to do the least required to obtain a PhD. While such candidates also need access to the

PhD programme, it is important to have a majority of PhD students with a strong motivation to do high-quality work and build and support the research culture.

- **Institutional respect for peer recognition.** Almost a defining characteristic of faculty from research universities is that they cherish and seek recognition from peers. This recognition comes in the form of fellowships from academies and professional societies, awards from these societies, awards for their papers given by conferences and journals that publish their work, prestigious responsibilities, such as being the editor of a journal or chairing an important conference, and so forth. These recognitions are often viewed as the pinnacle of a career by many. It is important for a research university to support and strengthen the peer recognition–based value system. In other words, the administration set-up should serve as a facilitator with necessary powers to facilitate and support the work of the faculty, hence leading to their greater peer recognition. Therefore, although peer recognition is outside the university's direct purview, the university and its administrative set-up can support this value system by internally recognizing and suitably rewarding achievers.

- **Opportunities for casual interaction between researchers and a hierarchy-less structure.** It is known that many of the great research ideas emerge at odd times, often during casual conversations among researchers. Most faculty members, being autonomous and independent agents, have private offices of their own. It is desirable for a research university to provide opportunities, spaces, events, platforms, and so forth to facilitate casual interactions and discussions among researchers—not social interaction but academics-related interaction. Many business organizations are supporting this by creating open spaces in which multiple people sit across each other at the same table. Since such mechanisms are not suitable for academics, regular interaction opportunities should be created through events and informal meetings.

    Such interactions are even more important for interdisciplinary research, which is needed to address some important problems in the world. For collaboration between the faculty of different disciplines, the faculty must meet each other and discuss their work informally, so that they understand each other's disciplines, vocabulary, motivations, and so forth. Ideas of projects that may involve the strengths of multiple disciplines can emerge when there is a decent understanding among faculty of each other and each other's disciplines. Hence, people with diverse ideas and from different disciplines should not only share their findings but also discuss conceivable new ideas and possibilities. While formal mechanisms can facilitate some aspects of this interaction, informal and casual interaction can supplement these.

Such interactions will thrive only if researchers form a flat, hierarchy-less group. Individuals should be allowed to express themselves freely, ask questions and raise doubts without feeling judged during these informal interactions.

- **Collaboration within and externally.** Many big challenges require multidisciplinary inputs for addressing them. Also, societal issues never align neatly along discipline boundaries. For many research challenges, researchers must work together to make a substantial impact. All these mean that collaboration between faculty within the department and across departments must be actively encouraged and promoted to have a vibrant research culture. While this is easy to state and understand, facilitating such collaborations needs suitable policies and encouragement. For example, a policy that attaches a substantial value to single-author publications (as was the case in a few disciplines earlier), or which insists that multi-author publications will be 'divided' among various authors for the evaluation of individuals, can go against the spirit of collaboration. Suitable policies and support/incentives for interdisciplinary projects or multi-researcher projects can help in promoting collaboration.

  Collaboration with colleagues at the global level is equally important. Research papers with authors from multiple countries are often cited more. Also, the pursuit of science and knowledge has been a global endeavour always. Hence, a university needs to have its faculty as part of the global community of scientists and collaborate with them. Collaboration can be particularly beneficial for junior faculty by enhancing their research capabilities and helping them imbibe the research culture (Tynan and Garbett 2007).

Ultimately, many research problems originate from the problems encountered by the society or by industries. Hence, a university should have good linkages with industries and the society, encourage discussions among their representatives and the faculty and facilitate a better understanding and resolution of the challenges. Such research challenges can then be worked upon by faculty and PhD students. Research work that addresses societal and industrial challenges is likely to have a direct impact on the society and economy. This is often a desired goal for researchers, and it helps the university be more directly relevant to the society at large. Hence, a thriving research culture should have platforms for collaboration with industries and the society on projects.

- **Active sponsored research programme.** Faculty must be motivated and incentivized to compete externally for getting research grants. Universities expect most of their research funding to come through grants; hence, applying for sponsored projects and trying to get grants must be an important part of the research culture and is a feature that is universal in all research universities. This should be ensured by providing good support for getting and executing projects and suitable policies also. For example, even if it is possible for a university to support more PhD students from its own funds, it should promote supporting most of the PhD students through project funds—this will motivate faculty to apply for research projects.

- **Rewards for good research.** It is sometimes thought, idealistically, that faculty are pursuing research only for the sake of research and that they are a different type of people for whom material rewards are of little consequence. This picture of a driven scientist is clearly an idealization. Barring some dedicated researchers, most are well-educated and deep-thinking professionals who want rewards and recognition for their contributions.

Hence, there must be rewards and recognition for good research in a broader sense—how research contributions are valued in terms of promotion, how excellent research is rewarded and how great researchers are recognized within the university. It should be noted that as only a few researchers achieve excellence while most can be considered as modest achievers, it is to be expected that this majority may want a more egalitarian system where all faculty are treated equally and excellence is not given any special treatment. However, without recognition, research excellence may not be sustained, and those who excel may move to other environments that recognize, respect and value excellence.

It should, however, be mentioned that faculty members as a community are indeed somewhat different from their professional counterparts in industries. Having chosen a profession with a flat structure and a tiny career ladder, they indeed highly value prestige from peers—from within the university and from the profession. Given the value system and the relatively flat structure, it is not desirable to consider financial incentives as the main form of rewarding, as is done in corporations. Such an approach may be counterproductive to the collegial and cooperative environment that a research university must have. Hence, the incentives for excellence should be a combination of prestige and recognition, extra support for the faculty member's research, compensation, and so forth.

- **Good work ethics.** It is almost impossible today to have significant research contributions with only a modest effort. A brilliant scientist, having reached a level, may be able to achieve a lot with a modest effort. However, for most, a modest effort can only lead to modest outcomes. While hard work and effort in themselves do not ensure success or more outcomes, a good work ethic is a necessary ingredient. As Hamming noted in his famous essay 'You and your Research' (Hamming 1986), effort goes a long way in the overall contributions a researcher makes in his/her career. Hence, a strong work ethic of putting in sufficient effort in the research (and teaching) endeavours is an essential component of a good research culture. This is extremely important in universities, because faculty are autonomous agents with a great deal of freedom and their efforts are never measured. In such a system, it is easy to slide into a minimal-effort zone—putting only as much effort as required to perform at an acceptable level in academics. Hence, the university and the faculty have to be vigilant to ensure that the work ethic is supportive and hard work is cherished and respected.

A thriving PhD programme is also essential to support and strengthen the research culture. Although there are many other ways to support the research culture and productivity (resources, suitable leadership, and so forth), having a strong PhD programme is indispensable. A large PhD programme with full-time PhD students, whose only goal is to pursue PhD and research, is essential to build a research culture. This also requires a good culture of interaction between PhD students and faculty and a culture of high aspirations among PhD students. The PhD programme has been discussed in more detail in a subsequent chapter.

Another aspect of a strong culture is having mentorship programmes and faculty development programmes for young faculty—these can really help the new faculty internalize the research culture and succeed in it (Tynan and Garbett 2007). These can be supported in universities if they have had a strong research culture for a long period of time and have senior faculty who live by that culture.

Many Indian universities have a weak research culture which supports and promotes mediocrity. A discussion of many aspects of the research culture in India is provided in Aggarwal (2018). It points out many aspects that come in the way of the strengthening of research in Indian universities, such as the research environment, incentive structure, PhD programme, relationship between faculty and PhD students, collaboration between researchers, international interactions and collaboration, lack of critical mass of researchers in any discipline, etc.

4.4 SUMMARY

Research is, of course, the main driving aim of a research university. However, unlike education, research is an endeavour of individual faculty or a small group. Hence, considerable thought and energy have to be put in not only facilitating research but also promoting research. This chapter discussed the various aspects of research administration, including strategic planning, managing research projects, advancing research, having a robust research infrastructure, and so forth.

Research ethics is an area that has become increasingly important with the increase in competitiveness, volume of research and number of researchers. The research management team has to ensure that research ethics are followed. This chapter discussed some key aspects of research ethics and how they can be supported in a university.

Finally, the chapter discussed the issue of research culture. Clearly, a vibrant research and innovation culture can enhance the quantity and quality of research. Hence, a strong culture of research is indispensable. Although the culture is built by the people involved in research (largely faculty and PhD students in a university), suitable policies and support can enhance it. The chapter discussed various aspects of a vibrant research culture and what a university can do to support them.

REFERENCES

Aggarwal, Varun. 2018. *Leading Science and Technology*. New Delhi: SAGE Publications.

Anderson, Emily E., and Amy Corneli. 2018. *100 Questions (and Answers) About Research Ethics*. Thousand Oaks, CA: SAGE Publications.

Berman, Elizabeth P. 2012. *Creating the Market University—How Academic Science Became an Economic Engine*. Princeton, NJ: Princeton University Press.

Bland, Carole J., and Mack T. Ruffin. 1992. 'Characteristics of a Productive Research Environment: Literature Review.' *Academic Medicine* 67 (6): 385–97.

Bushaway, Robert W. 2003. *Managing Research*. Managing Universities and Colleges: Guides to Good Practice. London: Open University Press. [Tata-McGraw Hill edition, 2011.]

Connell, Helen. ed. 2004. *University Research Management: Meeting the Institutional Challenge*. OECD. ISBN-92-64-01743-7.

Guillemin, Marilys and Lynn Gillam. 2004. 'Ethics, Reflexivity, and "Ethically Important Moments".' *Research Qualitative Inquiry* 10 (2): 261–80.

Hamming, Richard. 1986, March. *You and Your Research*. Bell Communications Research Colloquium Seminar.

Hanover. 2014, May. *Building a Culture of Research: Recommended Practices*. Hanover Research. https://www.hanoverresearch.com/media/Building-a-Culture-of-Research-Recommended-Practices.pdf

Hazelkorn, Ellen. 2005. *University Research Management—Developing Research in New Institutions*. OECD. https://www.oecd-ilibrary.org/education/university-research-management_9789264006966-en

Huong Nguyen, T. L., and Vincent Lynn Meek. 2015. 'Key Considerations in Organizing and Structuring University Research.' *Journal of Research Administration* 46 (1): 41–62.

Johnson, Alan M. 2013. *Improving Your Research Management: A Guide for Senior University Research Managers*. Elsevier.

Kirkland, John. 2008, November. 'University Research Management: An Emerging Profession in the Developing World.' *Technology Analysis and Strategic Management* 20 (6): 717–26.

Koepsell, David. 2015. *Scientific Integrity and Research Ethics—An Approach from the Ethos of Science*. Cham: Springer.

Mintrom, Michael. 2008, August. 'Managing the Research Function of the University: Pressures and Dilemmas.' *Journal of Higher Education Policy and Management* 30 (3): 231–44.

Nature. *Plagiarism and Duplicate Publication*. https://www.nature.com/nature-research/editorial-policies/plagiarism.

NEP. 2019. *Draft National Education Policy*. New Delhi: Government of India.

Pimple, K. D. 2002. 'Six Domains of Research Ethics—A Heuristic Framework for the Responsible Conduct of Science.' *Science and Engineering Ethics* 8 (2): 191–205.

Pratt, Michael, Dimitri Margaritis, and David Coy. 1999. 'Developing a Research Culture in a University Faculty.' *Journal of Higher Education Policy and Management* 21 (1): 43–55.

Silver, Harold. 2003. 'Does a University Have a Culture?' *Studies in Higher Education* 28 (2): 157–69.

Steneck, N. H. 2006. 'Fostering Integrity in Research: Definitions, Current Knowledge, and Future Directions.' *Science and Engineering Ethics* 12: 53–74.

Tynan, Belinda R., and Dawn L. Garbett. 2007. 'Negotiating the University Research Culture: Collaborative Voices of New Academics.' *Higher Education Research & Development* 26 (4): 411–24.

Chapter 5

Third Mission
Contribution to Economy and Society

The modern university initially evolved to provide higher education and certification of achievement to a select few. In the 19th century and early 20th century, research was added to universities as their second mission, in response to the need for new knowledge and technologies for society as well as the military, which is sometimes referred to as the first revolution in universities (Etzkowitz 2001). Over the years, the synergistic nature of education and research was recognized, and universities across the world included the second mission in their charter; those placing strong emphasis on research emerged as research universities. Through the research and education missions, universities helped national economies and societies by providing educated workforces and new knowledge which could be exploited commercially.

However, over the past few decades, universities are being asked to play a more direct role in society and economy, particularly by leveraging their core competencies in research and higher education. This is in response to the changing nature of the world where innovation-led industries are playing an increasingly important role in the economy of countries. As research is key to innovation, governments and society expect research universities to contribute more, and more directly to the innovation-based economy and entrepreneurship, giving rise to the third mission

(TM) of universities. Further, it is recognized that universities play an important role in their surrounding society and are expected to play a direct role in it as well. In this chapter, we discuss the TM, starting with a discussion on the nature of the TM itself.

5.1 THIRD MISSION, ITS RISE AND CHALLENGES

The TM of a university involves the broadening of its traditional missions to include activities to directly engage with various stakeholders and hence contribute to economic growth and social progress (Pinheiro et al. 2015). Another definition of the TM is that universities deliver benefits to host societies by engaging in social, enterprising and innovation activities (Zomer and Benneworth 2011). With the first two missions, universities engage with society by developing educated workforces, which then contribute to society through the roles they take up, and by generating knowledge, which is used by corporations to enhance economic activity. With the rise of the TM, universities are now expected to influence economy and society more directly. Despite the broad understanding that the TM implies directly engaging with and contributing to stakeholders outside universities and research communities, the scope of TM has not been clearly defined, and multiple perspectives have been presented in the literature (Pinheiro et al. 2015).

One perspective is to consider the TM contributing to eight different types of activities (Laredo 2007), which can be grouped into two basic dimensions: economic and social (Pinheiro et al. 2015). In the economic dimension, the TM activities are expected to contribute directly to the enhancement of economic activity in the region or the country. Four different aspects have been identified for this: human resources, intellectual property, spin-offs and industry contacts. In the social dimension, TM activities are expected to contribute to society at large. Four key activities identified for this are: public contracts, participation in policymaking, involvement in social and cultural life and public understanding of science. For our discussion in this chapter, we will use the economic and social aspects as the two broad dimensions of TM.

Another framework developed by a group of European scholars identified three core dimensions of the TM (as reported in Pinheiro et al. [2015]): technology transfer and innovation, continuing education (CE) programme and societal engagement. The first one is related to economic activity, while the second one helps in both economic activity and society. The framework in Roessler et al. (2015) identified four dimensions of the TM: university–economy interaction, social engagement, knowledge transfer in a broad sense and cultural and political engagement. Again, the last three can be considered as part of the broad social engagement dimension.

In this chapter, we briefly discuss the two basic dimensions of the TM: economic engagement and social engagement and outreach. As regards the economic dimension, we focus on innovation, entrepreneurship and technology transfer, and as regards social engagement and outreach, we discuss continuing education (which can also be considered as contributing to economic development) and social outreach programmes.

Although the TM may be an acceptable mission for a university, universities have to choose how much they want to engage with it, which depends on the overall mission and vision of the university. The situation is like the research mission; it is an accepted mission, but not all universities have to engage with it—different universities place different emphases on it. The same should be expected with the TM. As the research mission led to the emergence of strong research universities, a strong thrust towards the TM might lead to the emergence of entrepreneurial universities, which will have strong interfaces with the government and industry, an alignment of its other two missions with the TM, capabilities to assist in the creation of corporations, etc. (Clark 1998; Etzkowitz et al. 2000).

Many factors have given rise to the TM. We discuss some of the key ones here, some of them based on discussions in Zomer and Benneworth (2011). The new NEP of the Government of India also emphasizes the role of universities in innovation and entrepreneurship and also encourages universities to develop in their students a sense of community service (NEP 2019).

5.1.1 Changing Nature of Innovation

Universities have traditionally focused on creating knowledge and disseminating it through education. Knowledge was viewed as leading to the development of new products and services, and this conversion was expected to be done by the commercial world, facilitated by well-trained manpower, also developed by the university. In other words, the impact of research and education on economic activity was indirect and assumed a linear model of innovation wherein knowledge created by research was input for innovation.

The earlier linear model of innovation has given way to the networked model of innovation. It was observed that even when knowledge was published, there were some tacit knowledge components which made it hard for people not engaged in knowledge creation to fully appreciate and leverage the knowledge. It was also recognized that there were many sectors and corporations which did not have the capability to absorb knowledge or to change it suitably to facilitate innovation. It was also realized that innovation is an iterative process, frequently requiring research and development (R&D) in the loop. These types of observations led to the network model of innovation in which R&D is an important member (Laredo 2007). As universities are at the core of the R&D ecosystem, it is natural to expect that they become more integrated with the innovation ecosystem.

Consequently, towards the end of the previous century, the importance of knowledge creation as part of innovation was recognized, leading to the need to strengthen the linkage between knowledge generation and its commercial exploitation. In USA, this was given a boost by the passing of the Bayh–Dole Act, which gave universities rights to the intellectual property created through federal research grants. This led to the growth of patenting and collaboration with industry in US universities—a development which still implicitly saw knowledge production as helping firms in improving their products and services or in creating new ones. In other words, research was seen as an economic resource (Berman 2012). It was realized that while knowledge indeed has the potential to help existing firms, it also has the potential to drive economic growth through innovations leading to the formation of new companies. In other words, research started to be viewed also as an economic engine, and this view has been accepted and promoted by governments (Berman 2012).

Due to the importance of knowledge and innovation as economic engines that can drive growth, it is natural for universities with strong research capabilities and talented manpower to engage in the TM and directly contribute to the innovation-based economy. Moreover, it is natural for governments to expect, and promote, this engagement.

5.1.2 Resource Generation

We know that research universities are expensive. The education mission for most research universities is highly subsidized, with tuition fees covering only part of the costs. Moreover, research can always use more funding. Thus, a research university is perpetually in need of more funds. As government funding for universities is getting reduced in many countries, research universities need to diversify their sources of funding to ensure that their education and research missions are not compromised.

As innovation and knowledge have drawn great attention for their economic potential, universities see the possibility of generating funds by leveraging their research and educating capabilities, leading to initiatives to commercialize research and some educational activities (such as continuing education), with a key goal of generating more revenue for the university. As research and knowledge are critical components of the innovation process and ecosystem, and as utilization of the latest knowledge often requires tacit knowledge also, it is natural for universities who create knowledge and also have tacit knowledge to try to benefit financially from these. The hope is that it will generate additional resources for the university, thereby broadening its revenue base.

5.1.3 Changing Expectations and Universities' Desire to be Agents of Change

Universities have always viewed themselves as agents of change. Earlier, the focus was on changing thinking and mindsets through education and scientific knowledge. Although scientific knowledge has changed the world's thinking, it is the use of knowledge that has changed economies and societies. In today's world, much of the change is happening through innovative technologies and their creative applications. For universities to remain agents of change, it is imperative for them to directly engage in innovations and take them to society, in addition to creating knowledge and educating people. Expectations of society from universities is also changing.

Earlier, progress in science helped technology, which, in turn, helped in economic development. Now, societal challenges are more complex, requiring multidisciplinary approaches. The rapid pace of change in technology has led to undesirable side effects on society and people. Today, a more comprehensive view of technology has to be taken, one that has a better understanding of its impact on society and how society can benefit from it. The global challenges of today also require a multidisciplinary problem-solving approach. As universities have strong capabilities in many disciplines, societies are looking up to universities to address the challenges being faced.

The pace of change today is faster than ever before. Economies of countries are changing, and new companies are being formed and rising with amazing speed. The new economy is based largely on innovation to create new goods and services and to improve the existing ones. Therefore, governments want their countries to be innovative. Research is fundamental to innovation, and universities have research capability and comprise a combination of young students and experienced faculty. Hence, countries are looking up to universities to drive the innovation engines by directly participating in innovation, starting new companies, transferring their knowledge to existing companies, and so forth.

The world has changed. Now, entrepreneurs are icons and respected worldwide. Wealth creation and enrichment of individuals are lauded. Such a value system motivates academics also to become entrepreneurs, which changes expectations by faculty and students from research universities to accommodate and respect such aspirations and consider innovation and entrepreneurship as part of legitimate academic activity. At the same time, societies and governments are questioning the 'knowledge for its own sake' paradigm of research and expect knowledge to provide more direct and tangible benefits to society. These changed values and perceptions create pressure on universities to engage more in TM activities.

5.1.4 Challenges for the TM

The TM, which is a more recent addition for research universities, naturally faces challenges in acceptance and implementation. For research universities, engagement with the TM has some risks which must be mitigated. The main risk is that engagement with the TM may dilute its focus on its other two missions of teaching and research. This is likely to be the case if the TM is chosen as an additional mission that is separate from the other two missions. However, this risk can be mitigated if research and teaching support the TM and the TM is viewed as beneficial to them. Engagement with the TM cannot be a half-hearted effort by a few—all departments and faculty should imbibe the entrepreneurial culture, which should be supported suitably by the university through suitable outreach structures (Clark 1998).

Another risk is expectations from governments and society. As a university crosses the boundary from knowledge production to using knowledge for public good, expectations can rise.

Universities may be expected to start working on complex social problems, even though they may be squarely in the domain of political, social, administrative or business sectors. Earlier, universities posed research questions, and the answers provided were used by policymakers, government, corporations, etc. to take suitable action. Now, universities may themselves be expected to address the problem, and they are not organized or resourced for such direct action.

An important point to be noted is that not all universities need to emphasize the TM as a core mission, just like not all universities emphasize research as their core mission. How important the TM is to a university and the level to which a university should engage with it should be entirely the choice of the university. A university should ensure that engagement with the TM is not at the cost of its teaching and research missions, and should engage with it in a manner that supplements its other missions. This requires that a university should get into the TM in any significant manner only if it has complete autonomy over decision-making, so that it can control the level of its engagement with the TM. Otherwise, the university risks this engagement being forced upon it by external entities such as the government.

Significant challenges are faced for internally promoting the TM. Faculty are still generally aligned to disciplines, with journals and conferences, awards, peer recognition and review, and so forth all tied to the discipline. Also, disciplines are defined in a manner that they encourage in-depth exploration of the discipline rather than developing value or new methods by putting knowledge from diverse disciplines together. However, societal problems, particularly in a developing country, are never around disciplines. This poses a challenge of getting different disciplines together to work on some common problems, which is important for the TM.

5.2 INNOVATION, ENTREPRENEURSHIP AND TECHNOLOGY TRANSFER

Universities have been engaging with industry for a long time. However, earlier, it was a minor activity tolerated or even encouraged but not taken as an important dimension of a university, as the focus was on the two missions of education and research. However, with changes in time and the increased dependence of the economy on innovation, engagements of universities worldwide with the business and commercial world have increased, and universities are looking to find ways to commercialize their research findings. The framework of triple helix promotes a direct role in innovation and economic development by universities, in collaboration with industry and government (Etzkowitz and Leydesdorff 2000). The NEP also proposes to facilitate linkages of universities with government departments and universities, so research and innovation can help business as well as governance and create a synergy between the three important stakeholders for research and innovation: universities, government and industry (NEP 2019).

A study was conducted by the National Advisory Council on Innovation and Entrepreneurship (NACIE) in USA on what universities are doing to nurture innovation, entrepreneurship, commercialization of research, and so forth. The study found that while universities may pursue these activities for generating resources or making an impact, they have strong pedagogical value also (NACIE 2013). Of course, such activities have a direct impact on research being conducted in a university. In other words, activities related to the TM are not an add-on to the first two missions of a university but may be considered as a natural progression of the two missions and their alignment with the changing world and economic systems.

NACIE has identified a few different types of activities, including promoting student and faculty entrepreneurship, promoting technology transfer, facilitating university–industry collaboration and engaging with local economic development, which universities are engaging in for promoting innovation and participating in economic growth. We discuss these briefly in this section. Many of the concepts discussed are from NACIE (2013). Many of these are also encouraged in the NEP of the Government of India.

5.2.1 Innovation and Entrepreneurship among Students and Faculty

Many universities have shown considerable excitement in directly participating in the start-up ecosystem. While earlier this culture was present only in a few universities known for innovation and which were located in an entrepreneurial region (e.g., Stanford University and Silicon Valley, Massachusetts Institute of Technology and Boston area), it is spreading among many universities. If a university wants to be active in the start-up ecosystem, the university should promote innovation and entrepreneurship among faculty and students—who form the main intellectual manpower of the university. Many universities have developed policies and support to promote entrepreneurship among their faculty and students.

Three main components are required for a successful entrepreneurship ecosystem: a fertile innovation ecosystem, entrepreneurship culture and funding for new ventures (NACIE 2013). Universities naturally have a fertile innovation ecosystem, given the engagement of faculty and students in research and exploration, the academic culture of openness and new ideas and the questioning of old paradigms. Many universities have initiated programmes to address the other two factors.

Many universities have included entrepreneurship as part of their educational programmes to encourage the culture of entrepreneurship. These may take the form of a minor in entrepreneurship, or some courses on it, or some actual entrepreneurship projects involving direct experiential learning, etc. These provide good learning and experience of entrepreneurship to students and also engage the faculty who teach these more in entrepreneurship. As an example, in IIIT-Delhi, students are offered some courses on entrepreneurship; they can do an experiential summer course that engages them in the full process of entrepreneurship, ending with the creation of a company, and can do their final BTech/capstone project in entrepreneurship.

These for-credit initiatives are supported by activities like business plan and venture contests, talks by entrepreneurs, elevator pitch opportunities, internships in start-ups, mentorships by alumni who are entrepreneurs, entrepreneurship clubs, and so forth. Regional or national contests related to innovation also help. Universities are also providing innovation spaces to motivate students to collaborate for developing innovative ideas. Many times, the winning idea/project receives financial support, which can act as the initial capital for the start-up. To further provide student support, entrepreneurship fellowships are also being offered (e.g., in IIIT-Delhi, a graduating student can get a fellowship for entrepreneurship—they are effectively treated as PhD students for the duration of the fellowship and are provided a stipend, hostel accommodation, and so forth.)

For faculty, a different set of initiatives is needed. To promote entrepreneurship, a university needs to consider it as a legitimate part of faculty work and give weight to it in internal assessments and promotions, which is a fundamental change requiring a change in policies and mindset. This change is also reflected in how faculty members are assessed for recruitment; besides capabilities for research and teaching, capabilities for innovation and entrepreneurship are also assessed and given weight. Many universities are also providing leave for entrepreneurship to allow faculty to dedicate themselves fully for a few years to creating a venture. The faculty thus get an opportunity to engage with the world of business, which has a positive impact on their research and teaching and also encourages entrepreneurship.

Entrepreneurship is facilitated by networks and connections with corporations, venture capitalists (VCs) and angel funders, end-user groups in the community, and so forth. As universities often have good connections with all of these, they leverage them to support entrepreneurship. For example, universities may have programmes, such as entrepreneur in residence, in which some entrepreneurs spend a few days in a university and are available to faculty and students for discussions. Universities may provide a connection with the industry and VC networks, for example, by having an interaction day in which faculty can pitch ideas to some VCs and get their feedback, and possibly also financing.

Universities are also supporting these activities with awards such as 'innovation/entrepreneur of the year' for faculty, much like their counterpart 'researcher/teacher of the year' awards. With many such activities embedded in the academics of students and faculty, the culture of entrepreneurship gets strengthened.

Universities are also facilitating in the third component, namely, finance. Many universities have established incubation centres, which may provide space for the incubation of the companies of their faculty and students at a discount. The presence of an incubation centre in proximity also supports the transition from a university lab to a marketplace and continued engagement with professors and students. It also facilitates the hiring of manpower and interns from the university while getting ongoing consultancy from faculty. Universities are increasingly providing funds as well, from entrepreneurship fellowships for students to small seed capital from a fund created for this purpose, to venture capital through the network.

Incubation centres are quite common in India now, particularly in engineering institutions. These centres provide a seamless movement from academics/labs to the commercial world; the work/prototype/idea is moved from the lab where it was created to the incubation centre, to be incubated as a company. Incubation spaces may be provided to students, faculty and alumni at reduced rates, giving a further boost to their entrepreneurial dreams. The NEP also recommends that HEIs should establish such centres, and has proposed that, following the global best practice, the IP created from projects funded by the government agencies will rest with the university, which can commercialize them (NEP 2019).

5.2.2 Facilitating University–Industry Collaboration

Academia–industry collaboration has been a topic of interest for many decades. A key goal is to facilitate the use of knowledge created in the university by corporations for generating economic value. Another goal is to channelize research for directly address-ing challenges faced by industry. These collaborations are becom-ing even more important, as time for knowledge to be translated into innovations and generate value is shrinking. Earlier, this was done through the ecosystem of knowledge exchange, with some corporations and bodies facilitating technology transfer. Now, as the pace of knowledge generation and innovation is rapid, there is a need for both industry and universities to collaborate—productive collaborations can benefit both sides (Ankarah and Al-Tabbaa 2015).

One direct way of engaging industry, which has a long tradi-tion in academia, is to encourage faculty to provide consultancy. Most universities have policies to allow faculty to spend some time on consultancy activities, which helps in many ways. First, the knowledge available from the expert faculty is directly avail-able to the industry, which can leverage it to improve its own products and services. In return, the industry pays consultancy fees, which helps in improving the overall compensation of fac-ulty, which can help in retaining faculty and even attracting new faculty. If the consultancy fees are shared with the university, then some resource is generated for the university also. Such engage-ments may also lead to research problems, which the faculty, perhaps jointly with the industry partners, can work on. Regular interactions between the faculty and researchers in the industry can potentially lead to more extensive engagement in the future in the form of larger grants from the company or joint proposals. Given these and other benefits, most universities have provisions for faculty to engage in consultancy.

Another way to engage with industry, which is available in most universities, is through projects from industry. These can be like any other sponsored research project, although they may involve more deliverables and even some intellectual property protection. Some corporations have earmarked research funds for giving grants to universities.

Engagements such as consultancy and projects are on a need basis. It is also desirable to have a specific ongoing channel for collaboration. Often, efforts to establish ongoing collaboration did not succeed earlier, due to communication gap and misalignment of goals between the two sides. Lack of funding for these collaborations, which are risky for both sides, was also an issue. Realizing the benefits of strong collaboration between universities and industry, many governments started facilitating these through various means, including funding support.

For example, for the Industry–University Cooperative Research Centers (IUCRC) programme in USA, the National Science Foundation provided financial support for jointly created and operated centres, which resulted in many such centres across various universities in USA (Berman 2012). The basic objective of IUCRC was to encourage industrial innovation so as to support industrial growth. As universities have been at the core of knowledge creation and have the expertise, it was felt that academia–industry collaboration for innovation should be encouraged to promote industrial innovation. This collaboration facilitated some initial experiments in which centres were set up jointly by a university and a consortium of companies to work on problems of mutual interest. The government partially funded the centres for a few years, while the companies also contributed to funding. It was envisaged that, in due course, these centres would become self-sustaining, and many of them did. The model was then adopted by many states in and by 1990, hundreds of IUCRCs were operating in universities across USA (Berman 2012).

While a few types of collaboration have been mentioned above, there are many more possibilities, and such collaboration can take many different forms and for different reasons. A good survey of the types of collaboration is given in Ankarah and Al-Tabbaa (2015).

5.2.3 Technology Transfer and Patenting

It has become increasingly important that the new knowledge that research generates should be applied for creating value to society and firms. If the research has a potential commercial value, then the question is who benefits from this value, that is, who monetizes it? Earlier, universities were largely putting their research outputs in the public domain, leaving it to the larger society to leverage it for value. In other words, while a university created the knowledge, the value from the knowledge accrued to some other organizations; the university was satisfied with the fact that its research had helped the economic activity in society. As discussed earlier, given the need for resources and other reasons, universities are now increasingly looking to monetize the value of their research for themselves. To promote the commercialization of the research output, most universities have established a technology transfer office (TTO). This office helps in the commercialization process, which is often quite complex and tedious.

The main routes for commercialization of university research are to patent the invention or license the invention to some firm (including, perhaps, a start-up launched by the students or faculty involved) on some specified terms. Both of these are complex and time-consuming processes requiring careful negotiations and documentation, and most faculty members do not have the time or the inclination to engage in these. This has led to the need for an office such as a TTO, which is managed by experienced professionals who can drive these processes with some inputs from inventors (i.e., faculty and/or students). TTOs also often undertake workshops to sensitize faculty and other researchers about intellectual property laws and processes. Once inventions are patented, they need to be protected also, which often requires serious legal support. TTOs also help in this.

Although facilitation can reduce the tedium involved, in itself, it may not motivate faculty to license or patent their work, as most faculty are very focused on publishing their research so that their peers can appreciate their contributions. For this, universities have devised policies for revenue sharing from any royalties that may accrue from patents or any income that comes through other forms of commercialization. This incentive, along with the charm that the research may find its way into actual products and services, can go a long way in motivating faculty to commercialize their results.

In US universities, patenting is now quite common. Chapter 5 of Berman (2012) gives an account of how patenting has evolved in US universities. It should be noted that currently, though a few universities earn handsomely from patents and licences, most universities earn a very modest amount from these. However, most have mechanisms for patenting inventions by faculty and students, as universities do not want to miss any opportunity in the risky world of intellectual property.

Universities have followed a few different approaches for patenting (Berman 2012). One is to have a fully owned but separate entity that manages university patents and returns any income it generates to the university. Another is to have a third party take care of all the patenting, with some revenue sharing between the two. Several universities manage patents internally, through a unit specifically for that purpose, with certain committees helping in evaluation. For patents that may be used for creating new companies, a common method is for universities to take an equity in the start-up in lieu of royalties or the licensing fee, which helps the start-up to get going without requiring funds to pay for the intellectual property, and the university stands to gain if the innovation proves successful in the market.

5.2.4 Engaging with Regional Economic Development

The presence of a university itself helps in regional economic development, as a university is also a commercial entity, often with large budgets, which inevitably benefits the local economy by providing jobs, sale of goods, demand for local services, and so forth. It is of mutual benefit if a university can more actively engage and help in regional economic development. Universities have the ability of innovation, and their innovations can help in the development of industry locally. Moreover, as the regional economy grows, it provides a better surrounding climate that helps the university by making the region more attractive for faculty and students. This aspect of universities engaging in regional development is not actively pursued in India, and many universities actually try to isolate themselves from the surrounding society. However, now some efforts are being made to create R&D clusters in some cities with the intent of doing applied research, which can directly address challenges facing the city and boost the economic activity in the city through innovation, the starting of new companies, and so forth.

There are multiple ways in which a university supports regional economic development, and there have been studies to assess the impacts of different aspects, for example, Bramwell and Wolfe (2008), Drucker and Goldstein (2007), Murray (2004), etc. Encouraging entrepreneurship among faculty and students (discussed earlier) is one way which has direct benefits to the regional economy. The impact can be enhanced if the research and innovation parks and commercial spaces around are present to house the incubated firms as they grow. A university can also help in promoting entrepreneurship in the region by motivating and educating potential entrepreneurs, making university incubation facilities available to them, providing them technical help in their problems, providing student interns and part-time workers, and so forth. The university can also help in the growth of existing industries by helping them in technology and business improvement, making their labs and expensive resources available.

Overall, a university helps regional economic development in many ways, and many of the activities that universities engage in have direct advantages to the local economy. Of particular interest has been the issue of whether technology and science–led economic activity in a region can be boosted by research universities. It has been seen that it is indeed the case—technology and science–led firms are attracted to a region by the presence of strong research universities, and they engage with the universities in multiple ways to benefit; engagement methods involve leveraging the human capital of the universities, as well as the social capital that researchers and faculty earn by being part of the global network of scientists (Bramwell and Wolfe 2008; Drucker and Goldstein 2007; Murray 2004).

MIT has proposed a model to leverage a university for regional development, which is called the Regional Entrepreneurship Accelerator Program (MIT). This model envisages a partnership between the university, entrepreneurs (who may be from the university or outside), government, corporate and risk capital to help accelerate innovation-driven entrepreneurship. It tries to combine innovation from universities with entrepreneurial and venture capital agencies to create firms in areas of competitive advantage for the region. It is a 2-year structured programme whose design is tailored for the region, based on the specific strengths and weaknesses of the region, and which educates, trains and motivates stakeholders to collaborate for regional development.

It should, however, be understood that while research universities can act as a catalyst for developing the knowledge-based sector in the region, they by themselves are rarely sufficient to have such developments take place, even though many policies seem to wish that supporting various initiatives in universities can by itself spur regional economic development (Bramwell and Wolfe 2008; Brown 2016; Drucker and Goldstein 2007). Universities help regional economic development in many ways, but developing an innovation and knowledge-based economy requires many factors to align and other key stakeholders to also participate, as indicated by the Regional Entrepreneurship Accelerator Program (REAP) model.

5.3 SOCIETAL ENGAGEMENT

Universities have often distanced themselves from society to allow the mind to roam freely and explore the unexplored and not be constrained by the often harsh realities of the society around it. This situation is particularly true in developing countries such as India. The realities outside universities are often too harsh and complicated, and therefore universities try to create a full living community, sheltered from the realities of the 'real world'. Thus, often, universities not only build walls around their campus, but they also try to have all direct stakeholders to stay within the campus. With a fully residential campus, which many universities provide, even the connection with society through people staying there is minimized.

These walls are created to allow students and researchers to focus on academics and not worry about their daily struggles. However, this has also made universities in countries such as India more insular and disconnected from society, and a direct outreach is necessary for a university to engage with society and provide whatever benefits it can. Various attempts have been made to expose students to these realities so that they develop an understanding of issues.

The focus of the TM in most developed countries is to leverage research for economic benefits to society through innovation and incubation. A developing country such as India has many societal challenges. Hence, it may not be desirable for a university to limit its TM to innovation in the economic sphere only. A university can possibly contribute to some societal challenges in the region through social engagement. However, if this has to be done, it has to be ensured that the university does not compromise its first two missions of research and education, and indeed, TM activities should be synergistic and complementary. We later discuss an example of innovation from IIIT-Delhi which contributed directly to society in a very different way without diluting the research and teaching missions.

5.3.1 Continuing Education

A continuing education (CE) programme is an organized and structured education programme (which may involve lectures, labs, assignments, and so forth) for educating individuals who are not enrolled as students and providing them with knowledge and skills that can help them in their professional or personal life. By offering CE programmes, a university can extend the benefit of its teaching capabilities also to those who are not enrolled in degree programmes of the university. (In the context of CE, we will use the term programme generically to represent a course/module or a series of courses.)

CE plays a vital role in society. In the current age of rapid change, individuals need to update themselves with newer technologies and developments regularly. CE programmes facilitate this upgradation. Even without the changes taking place, given the breadth of knowledge in any field, no education programme can hope to provide all the necessary knowledge for a job. These knowledge gaps can be filled through CE programmes. In some professions, CE programmes may be required to be completed regularly to maintain a certain status (e.g., to continue holding the licence to practice). Indeed, CE programmes are a necessity in the modern world, serving multiple goals (Scanlan 1985; Cervero 2000).

In a broad sense, CE includes all types of education provided for different purposes such as preparation for a test, professional development, getting or renewal of a license, personal growth, credits for a degree, and so forth. Universities mostly engage in CE for professional development. Our discussion here is also limited to this aspect of CE.

For professional development, as a university has faculty members who are in touch with the latest developments (indeed, often, they may be driving them), they are in a good position to offer programmes for professional development. Moreover, as higher education is a basic mission of a university, CE becomes an extension of this mission, providing education to nonstudents.

CE for professional development has been around for a long time, which got a boost with the professionalization of various professions and jobs. It is also a big business; in some cases, a firm's expenditure in providing CE for its employees may be more than the budget of some universities (Cervero 2000). The focus of most professional development programmes is to update working professionals about the latest developments so that they can perform better in their profession.

In most universities, CE, while providing an important service, is also treated as a source of revenue generation for the university and the faculty engaged in it. CE programmes also provide a direct linkage with the professional world, which strengthens their connections with universities, and they can also offer useful interactions to faculty. Due to such benefits and others such as facilitating change and fostering growth (Scanlan 1985), most universities have CE programmes and some unit through which these programmes are offered. Universities and professional associations are most active in providing CE programmes, and they are collaborating to provide such programmes (Cervero 2000). Collaboration between universities and professionals is a natural way to combine academic rigour with practical insights to update professionals.

Of particular interest in India are CE programmes for faculty—particularly for colleges and universities. Most colleges and universities have faculty who are not very active in research and so are often not updated about the developments in the field, and who may often be teaching courses using a very old and outdated syllabus. As research universities generally lead the advancement of courses, as well as the development of new courses (as discussed in the chapter on education), their faculty are well placed to offer CE programmes on developments in the subject, how the courses on the subject should evolve and how they should be taught. CE programmes can be useful for school teachers also, though the purpose of such programmes will obviously be different. Such CE programmes of training the trainers have a clear multiplier effect on education. The NEP also suggests a strong teacher development programme by top research universities as part of revamping the education in the country (NEP 2019).

Traditionally, universities offered face-to-face CE programmes ranging from a few days to a few weeks. On successful completion of a programme, typically, a certificate of completion is issued. With the emergence of Internet-based education and the massive open online course, increasingly more CE programmes are being offered through the Internet. These allow a person to take courses from his/her home or office. Many universities, as well as businesses, are offering programmes through such platforms, and these are the major growth area for CE (Cervero 2000).

5.3.2 Community Outreach

Community outreach is a generic term to include all activities that a university may undertake to engage with the society and community around it to help them. Which type of outreach activities a research university engages in is contextual and depends on the needs of the surrounding community and society. Helping local business development has been discussed earlier; here, we discuss other types of activities.

As universities are in the business of education and admit students graduating from schools, one natural outreach programme that many have is engaging with local schools, which may be in the form of arranging visits to labs, showing demos, helping in organizing contests, and so forth. Another common activity is the promotion of science and scientific thought. Another engagement is organizing various cultural activities, sports and other programmes, such as lectures, workshops, and so forth, available to the local community. Some universities may also make some of their facilities available to the local community for events.

A different type of social outreach programme in which some universities engage is the short-term social immersion programmes. In these programmes, students of a university go and live in a community very different from their own and experience the cultural and social differences. In developed countries, such immersion programmes are often arranged in other countries. A key goal of these programmes is to provide students with a global and different experience (Gates 2014). While many view such programmes as improving their job prospects, for many others, it has a far deeper impact, even on the professions they pursue.

Immersion programmes can also help provide a better understanding of the challenges and problems being faced in the social context; students coming with no bias or preconceived notions for an immersion programme can see issues and problems differently, throwing new light on them. Some immersion programmes are designed specifically for this purpose. For example, in the rural immersion programme at the Indian Institute of Management, Udaipur, students spend a week in a village with the goal of studying a specific aspect deeply. They interact with local people through some local organization working in the village and survey them to understand better their context and the challenges they are facing. Their reports provide an understanding of and information about local challenges that can lead to interventions by local organizations or governments for resolving them.

Similarly, IIIT-Delhi conducts a programme in which students can spend their summer studying some social entity or community (referred to as domain) to develop a thorough knowledge of the functioning of that domain and to identify a few issues in which intervention through technology can help the domain. Examples of domains include a vegetable market, hawkers' occupation, milk distribution, garbage collection, a local government clinic or a primary health care facility, and so forth. Students work in groups in these domains during the summer term. They are expected to be highly interactive observers to understand the workings and identify problems within the domain. They are also encouraged to study the relevant literature on the domain. Once a set of problems has been identified, students are expected to take them up as projects in regular semesters.

5.3.3 An Example

As part of its undergraduate programme, IIIT-Delhi requires all its undergraduate students to pursue two credits for community work (CW). This aspect was included right from the inception to ensure that the education also supports the 'socially relevant' aspect of the mission of the institute. Most students usually choose to pursue their CW credits with some non-governmental organizations (NGOs). Reports from earlier students showed that most chose to work with NGOs working in the field of education for the young. (The NEP of the Government of India encourages universities to develop in their students a sense of community service for the benefit of society through active programmes organized by the universities [NEP 2019].)

The institute decided to contribute to the growth of government school children as part of its social outreach mission. The general situation in India is that children from poor families go to government schools, while those who can afford it send their children to private schools. Often, government school children do not get exposure to opportunities beyond schools and, due to their socio-economic condition and the peer group in the school, end up with low aspirations and confidence. The institute decided to hold a 1-month summer camp for children from these schools. The goal of the summer camp was to help build their confidence and aspirations and develop some life skills; providing remedial classes for subjects taught in the school was not a goal. The objective of the camp was to focus on developing:

- Communication skills and personality
- Self-confidence and aspirations
- Problem-solving skills
- Computer and Internet skills

Student volunteers run the camp, most of whom also use it to complete their CW credit requirements. A few coordinators are students with experience from previous summer camps. The camp objectives are achieved through a set of structured sessions, as well as through informal interactions between volunteers and children. Innovative approaches are employed to engage the school children so that they can learn better.

For the programme, the institute has partnered with a few government schools within a radius of a few kilometres of the institute. The partnerships were established through a few meetings with school principals and visits to the schools. The target group is students from sixth to eighth grades, as it was felt that exposure at this stage can have more impact (as from the ninth grade onwards, there is a pressure of board exams).

The delivery approach was also designed to suit the goals. A general tendency in academia is to convert any programme into a lecture-based format. It was clarified from the start that the goals of this programme are different and so this format is not to be used as the primary instrument. Some approaches used for the delivery are as follows:

- Interactive sessions with small groups are led by a few volunteers. (Groups of about 30 are formed, and six volunteers are assigned to a group.) Each volunteer covers a different activity.
- One topic is covered in a day, supplemented with some co-curricular activities. Each day, one particular goal is taken and all the sessions are geared towards that.
- No textbooks. The programme is completely based on experience and activity and motivates the children to think and reflect.

Coordinators, who have been volunteers in a previous summer camp, train the volunteers before the start of the programme. Modules are designed afresh every year by the volunteers after referring to the feedback received from the previous years and inculcating fresh ideas. At the end of the summer camp, some lessons learnt are captured, and materials for various sessions are archived for future years. As the coordinators of the next year are volunteers from this year (or the year before), there is some transmission of experience and knowledge through this method also.

Every year, about 150 children from about half-dozen schools attend the camp. The response and impact of this programme have been tremendous. School children love it, as the method of teaching is not classroom-based; their enthusiasm is reflected in the response they give to their mentors during the closing ceremony when volunteers are given their certificates. From the interactions, it is clear that they gain a lot from the camp; many of them may not have seen modern facilities, and interacting deeply over weeks with students of a premier institute also provides them with role models. It is not an exaggeration to say that this camp is possibly a life-changing event for many of them.

Although the camp is designed as a way to contribute back to society, it is clear that it also benefits the volunteers. For many of them, it is a once-in-a-lifetime opportunity. It opens their eyes to the fact that they are very fortunate to have what they have—a fact they probably did not appreciate before the camp. Most of them get a deep sense of satisfaction from their contributions towards helping underprivileged children. For some of them, participating in the camp is one of the high points of their stay in the institute.

It is worth noting that this direct action has no adverse impact on the regular academic activities of teaching and research, as it involves no faculty time. This approach of leveraging student talent for societal outreach is not common. Such societal outreach programmes, which can harness student power, have a huge potential for universities to contribute to society without adversely impacting their education and research missions.

5.4 SUMMARY

In this chapter, we have discussed the TM of universities. The TM is about making an impact on society through economic development and through direct societal engagements. Reasons for universities to engage with the TM include a need to generate new resources, the changing nature of academic research and innovation and expectations from society and governments of a more direct impact of university's research and academic activities. Universities have responded to this challenge, with many of them vigorously pursuing this mission. In this chapter, we briefly discussed two main aspects of the TM: contributing to economic growth through innovation, entrepreneurship and technology transfer and directly engaging with society for its welfare.

Regarding contributing to economic growth, we briefly discussed four key aspects: facilitating entrepreneurship among students and faculty, enhancing industry–academia collaboration, facilitating technology transfer and participating in regional economic development. For each of these, we briefly discussed what the objectives were and what approaches some universities were taking. In India, entrepreneurship among students and faculty is being promoted actively, with support from the government. Industry–academia collaboration is also something most universities pursue, though it has had a limited success in most universities for a host of reasons. Most research universities have evolved mechanisms for protecting intellectual property and for technology transfer. The regional economic development role of universities is a more recent thought—some attempt is being made to create clusters of research universities and other organizations to help development in the city.

For direct engagement with society, we briefly discussed two aspects: continuing education (CE) and community outreach. CE is in much demand due to the rapidly changing technology, which needs education of the current workforce in these changes. Universities are well positioned to help with this, given that they operate at the cutting edge of technology. They are partnering with professional bodies to deliver more relevant CE and, in the process, raising resources for themselves, as well as improving their engagement with professionals. As regards community outreach, we discussed a few different approaches being followed. We gave one example of how students in IIIT-Delhi are conducting a transformative summer camp for school children from economically weaker backgrounds.

REFERENCES

Ankarah, Samuel, and Omar Al-Tabbaa. 2005. 'University-industry Collaboration: A Systematic Review.' *Journal of Management* 31: 387–408.

Berman, Elizabeth P. 2012. *Creating the Market University—How Academic Science Became an Economic Engine*. Princeton, NJ: Princeton University Press.

Bramwell, A., and D. A. Wolfe. 2008. 'Universities and Regional Economic Development: The Entrepreneurial University of Waterloo.' *Research Policy* 37 (8): 1175–87.

Brown, R. 2016. 'Mission Impossible? Entrepreneurial Universities and Peripheral Regional Innovation Systems.' *Industry and Innovation* 23 (2): 1–17.

Cervero, Ronald M. 2000. 'Trends and Issues in Continuing Professional Education.' *New Directions for Adult and Continuing Education* 2000 (86): 3–12.

Clark, Burton R. 1998. *Creating Entrepreneurial Universities: Organizational Pathways of Transformation*. New York, NY: Emerald Group Publishing.

Drucker, J., and H. Goldstein. 2007. 'Assessing the Regional Economic Development Impacts of Universities: A Review of Current Approaches.' *International Regional Science Review* 30 (1): 20–46.

Etzkowitz, Henry. 2001. 'The Second Academic Revolution and the Rise of Entrepreneurial Science.' *IEEE Technology and Society Magazine* 20 (2): 18–29.

Etzkowitz, Henry, and Loet Leydesdorff. 2000. 'The Dynamics of Innovation: From National Systems and "Mode 2" to Triple Helix of University-industry-government Relations.' *Research Policy* 29 (2): 109–23.

Etzkowitz, Henry, Andrew Webster, Christiane Gebhardt, Branca Regina Cantisano Terra. 2000. 'The Future of the University and the University of the Future: Evolution of Ivory Tower to Entrepreneurial Paradigm.' *Research Policy* 29 (2): 313–30.

Gates, Lisa. 2014. 'The Impact of International Internships and Short-Term Immersion Programs.' *New Directions for Student Services* (146). DOI: 10.1002/ss.2008

Laredo, Philippe. 2007. 'Revisiting the Third Mission of Universities: Towards a Renewed Categorization of University Activities.' *Higher Education Policy* 20: 441–56.

MIT. *REAP (Regional Entrepreneurship Accelerator Program)*. http://reap.mit.edu.

Murray, Fiona. 2004. 'The Role of Academic Inventors in Entrepreneurial Firms: Sharing the Laboratory Life.' *Research Policy* 33 (4): 643–59.

NACIE. 2013. *The Innovative and Entrepreneurial University: Higher Education, Innovation and Entrepreneurship in Focus*. US Department of Commerce, National Advisory Council on Innovation and Entrepreneurship Report, NACIE, Washington, DC.

NEP. 2019. *Draft National Education Policy, 2019*. New Delhi: Government of India.

Pinheiro, Romulo, Paticio V. Langa, and Attila Pausits. 2015. 'One and Two Equals Three? The Third Mission of Higher Education Institutions.' *European Journal of Higher Education* 5 (3): 233–49.

Roessler, Isabel, Sindy Duong, and Cor-Denis Hachmeister. 2015. *Teaching, Research, and More?! Achievements of Universities of Applied Sciences with Regard to Society* (CHE Working Paper No 183). Gütersloh: CHE.

Scanlan, Craig L. 1985. 'Practicing with Purpose: Goals of Continuing Professional Education.' In *Problems and Prospects in Continuing Professional Education*, edited by R. M. Cervero, and C. L. Scanlan. San Francisco, CA: Jossey-Bass.

Zomer, Arend, and Paul Benneworth. 2011. 'The Rise of the University's Third Mission.' In *Reform of Higher Education in Europe*, edited by J. Enders et al. Rotterdam: Sense Publishers.

Chapter 6

Building a Strong PhD Programme

A PhD programme is the backbone of a research university, its most important facet, one which clearly separates it from institutions which focus on teaching. In fact, the basic definition of a research university in the Carnegie Classification framework for universities in USA is based on the size of the PhD programmes of these institutions (Carnegie 2000). In many countries, including India, PhD students are the main human resources, besides the faculty, for research in a university—while research is driven by the faculty, much of the work is actually carried out by its PhD students, who also provide a source of fresh ideas.

The PhD is a unique degree, quite unlike the bachelor's and master's degrees. While the goal of other education programmes is to build understanding and expertise in existing knowledge, the PhD programme's goal is to mould students into knowledge creators. Moreover, unlike the other education programmes where many students are taught together in a course, the PhD is fundamentally a programme wherein each student is 'taught' individually and progresses at an individual pace towards completion. It is more like an apprentice model for education, rather than the classroom-based model followed in other programmes. Due to its special nature, the programme often has a loosely defined structure. Further, while bachelor's and master's programmes are subjects of intensive discussions and debates in faculty bodies, boards and senates and attract central focus in university accreditations, PhD programmes often do not get such attention.

We briefly discussed the evolution of the PhD programme in India in Chapter 1; a detailed discussion on its evolution and challenges can be found in Jayaram (2008). In this chapter we discuss various issues related to the PhD programme, for example, the characteristics of a strong PhD programme, desired attributes of a PhD student, what is expected from a PhD programme, what research universities can do to strengthen it, an example of a PhD programme in India which has many of the desired traits, etc. We start this chapter by first discussing the objectives and learning outcomes of a PhD programme.

6.1 PROGRAMME OBJECTIVES AND GRADUATE ATTRIBUTES

Programme objectives and graduate attributes are standard formulations for undergraduate programmes but are not commonly articulated for PhD programmes. However, obviously, they are as important here as in any other educational course, and there are now active efforts to establish them (Denecke et al. 2017). We discuss these aspects in this section. We also discuss the desirable attributes of a PhD scholar, as for achieving the objectives it is essential that the students in the programme have the desired attributes to successfully complete a PhD.

6.1.1 Objectives

The main goal of the PhD programme is to develop researchers who are well equipped to undertake research challenges of the future for the benefit of the society. As it is almost impossible for someone to claim that he/she has become a researcher without a properly documented record of actual research, an important objective of the PhD programme is to extend knowledge about some topic—this knowledge is generated by the PhD scholar with the guidance of his/her supervisor and committees that may be part of the doctoral education of a university.

To be a sound researcher, it is imperative that the researcher not only has research skills but also has wide knowledge in the chosen area of research. Only with extensive awareness and a deep understanding of the work done so far can a researcher claim that the work he/she has done is 'new' (which is the basic premise for it to be considered research), 'worthy' and 'useful'. Hence, developing knowledge in the chosen area of research can be considered another objective of the PhD programme. This skill of building the knowledge base and identifying the gaps in it is a fundamental research capability and is essential for a long career in research, as a researcher will work in different areas during the course of his/her career.

These two objectives are sometimes stated as the two basic goals of a PhD programme (Sorensen 2016): to extend knowledge about an important topic through research and to provide training to the PhD student to develop competencies needed to be an effective researcher. These together can be considered as *research competencies*.

Traditionally, PhD programmes implicitly or explicitly tend to train the PhD scholars as if they are being prepared for an academic career. Perhaps, this bias is natural, given that the supervisor of the student considers an academic career as the highest calling for a researcher.

While earlier most PhDs may have joined academics, this has changed—for example, a large fraction of PhDs in USA want to work outside the academia and take up alternative employments (Nerad 2004, 2015a). In applied areas like computing and engineering, this is even more skewed—a study found, for example, that only 20 per cent of the PhDs in Electrical Engineering opt for academia. (In India, such data is not available; however, from IIIT-Delhi, of the graduates in computing and electrical engineering in recent times, about 10 per cent went for academic positions, more than 50 per cent went for industry jobs, and about 30 per cent went for postdoctoral research overseas.)

It is expected that this trend will continue and more and more PhDs will be employed in areas other than academia. As economies are becoming innovation-driven and new businesses emerge in newer areas that will be powered by R&D, they are likely to use more PhDs. Think tanks and policy bodies, which have traditionally employed research scholars for their work, will continue scouting for PhD graduates. PhDs are also expected to take up more leadership roles in corporations, research groups, policymaking bodies and other institutions.

Keeping these reasons in mind, besides cultivating their research capabilities, it is desirable that PhD graduates also possess transferrable and translational competencies, to enable them to have a successful career outside academia, which often require skills beyond creating new knowledge in a chosen field of study (Nerad 2012, 2015b). These are sometimes called professional competencies, and developing these can be considered as another basic objective of a contemporary PhD programme.

Researchers have always viewed themselves as a global fraternity, with the output of research treated as quintessentially public property, available to all, regardless of where the knowledge might have been produced. Research was globalized much before globalization became a buzzword—stories of researchers travelling and staying in different countries and collaborating with scholars of other nationalities are many. With the rise of globalization and global corporations, with the world shrinking through myriad forms of connectivity and the ease of travel, this trend will only accelerate. PhD graduates are expected to be global researchers who can work in multinational teams on global challenges, staying in different countries for periods of time. To facilitate this, it has been argued that a PhD programme should also develop suitable cultural competencies in its PhD graduates (Nerad 2012).

We can thus say that the basic objective of a PhD programme is to develop researchers who have wide knowledge about their area, have strong research skills that have been demonstrated by the generation of new knowledge, are well equipped with translational competencies to undertake a range of careers and have cultural competencies to work in different cultural contexts. In other words, a PhD programme should aim to develop research competencies, professional competencies and cultural competencies.

6.1.2 Graduate Attributes

The graduate attributes of a programme define the traits a graduate of the programme is likely to have. As discussed in the chapter on education, often, these outcomes are divided into general attributes, pertaining to the general capabilities and competencies of a graduate, and discipline-specific attributes, which specify competencies pertaining to a select field of knowledge. Unlike undergraduate programmes wherein discipline-specific attributes are key, for PhD, the general attributes are likely to be more important. This is because the main objectives of the programme, as discussed above, are independent of the discipline (in fact, in many universities, the PhD degree does not even specify the discipline). We discuss some of the desired general graduate attributes, many of them being based on the attributes for post-doctoral scholars given in Sorensen (2016).

1. **Independence**: A PhD graduate is expected to be an independent researcher in his/her own right, capable of forming his/her own teams and following his/her own research agenda. This, in some sense, is the most fundamental difference between a PhD scholar and a PhD graduate. As a scholar, one conducts research under the guidance of a supervisor, but after the PhD degree is awarded, the researcher is expected to work independently, and even guide some junior researchers (other PhD students, interns, master's dissertations, etc.).

2. **Innovation and creativity**: This might be understood as the ability to identify and formulate potential research problems,

as well as the approaches for addressing them. Identifying and formulating research problems are the core skills of a researcher—he/she has to be creative to identify research problems that are worthy of sustained effort and which may lead to good research outcomes and/or publication(s). Formulating research problems and pursuing them, particularly in the face of constraints and challenges, requires the ability to find innovative measures. Overall, having the creativity and imagination to spot a potential research problem, which is one of the most important challenges for researchers in many disciplines, is a key capability, along with the ability to evolve efficient and effective approaches for addressing the problem. A PhD graduate must have this competency.

3. **In-depth knowledge of the research area:** A researcher might have to work on different topics at different times. He/she must have the ability to quickly build the knowledge base and ensure that he/she has in-depth knowledge of related research and results. Without this, it is easy to spend time exploring problems whose results have already been published. This also requires developing a broader perspective and understanding of the different sub-areas of the research topic, including connections between the sub-areas.

4. **Ability to critically read research papers:** In-depth knowledge can be developed in a field by a researcher only if he/she has a strong ability to critically read research papers and understand the subtleties and nuances that might be involved in the work. For a researcher, the only way to be abreast of the latest developments in his/her area is to read research papers—textbooks are of no help here. Critical reading of papers also involves identifying the limitations of the work, how it can be applied or extended and what might be the related problems, among other critical concerns. It can be safely said that for many researchers, reading of research papers is also a source of getting ideas for their work, besides, of course, gaining knowledge about the latest developments.

5. **Ability to apply suitable research methods to rigorously explore a given problem:** Once a research problem is

identified, besides deciding on the approach for exploring it, a lot of effort has to be invested in applying recognized research techniques which can lead to robust scientific results eligible for publication in reputed platforms. Hence, a good understanding of research methods and the judicious discretion to apply them effectively is an essential capability of a researcher. This can also be considered as the ability to implement a high-level research goal—that is, to convert it into a sound research project and then see it through to completion.

6. **Aspiration to do high-quality work and publish in highly reputed venues:** Without the desire to do high-quality work and submit it for publication in critically acclaimed venues, average research is inevitable. All too often, PhD students are too focused on completing the thesis and acquiring the PhD degree, opting for an easy path of doing mediocre work of greater ease and lower risk, which is then published in low-impact forums. A PhD programme should try to develop high aspirations in the student.

7. **Ability to communicate effectively:** This is a critical capability of a researcher—to be able to communicate his/her work through writing (technical papers) as well as through oral presentation. Writing research papers is absolutely essential—without it, research cannot really be recognized. Often, researchers are requested to give seminars on their work in conferences, university departments and other intellectual gatherings. Hence, effective written and oral technical communication is an indispensable capability. Besides technical communication, it is also highly desirable that the researcher has the ability to communicate the problem and the results to a non-technical audience also—this is now needed not only to explain to a wider target group but also for collaborating across disciplines to address interdisciplinary challenges.

8. **Integration with the scientific community:** Research is essentially done by one global fraternity of researchers in an area. The union is preserved through its conferences, regular meetings, journals and digital interfaces. It is important for a researcher to be integrated into this fraternity—this not only

will help with staying updated regarding the latest developments, but engagement with the fraternity can also help in refining existing ideas or collecting new ones.

9. **Ability to collaborate with other researchers:** This is an essential cultural competency, as discussed earlier, as a researcher works in different contexts and with different collaborators who might often be of other nationalities and different cultural backgrounds.

These are general attributes, independent of the discipline, which a PhD graduate is expected to possess. It is expected that PhD graduates have some discipline-specific capabilities as well, which have to be developed by each discipline and will depend on the nature of the specific subject.

6.1.3 Being a Successful and Effective PhD Scholar

As the PhD is very different from other degrees, the traits that make an effective PhD scholar are likely to be different from those that make an effective student in, say, an undergraduate programme. An understanding of what attributes make an effective and successful PhD scholar can help a prospective candidate better assess whether PhD is the right option for him/her and if he/she has what it takes to successfully complete a PhD. It can also help PhD programmes in selecting the most suitable students in the programme.

First, let us clarify what we mean by an effective PhD scholar. We view a PhD scholar as effective if he/she can successfully complete the PhD with a good-quality thesis in a reasonable time (perhaps, the expected duration for the discipline) and who is able to secure a good position in the career of his/her choice after completing the course. In other words, an effective PhD student is one who (a) can complete the PhD in a reasonable time; (b) produces a good thesis demonstrating strong research skills; and (c) develops the professional competencies needed for the desired career. Such a PhD student is what PhD programmes also desire.

What are the key attributes of an effective PhD student? This is obviously a topic of great interest to prospective PhD students; consequently, there are many blogs, articles in the popular press and other forums which discuss this topic from different perspectives. If we look at the actual practices of selecting students for a PhD programme, perhaps, academic preparation is given the highest weightage by the committees who evaluate their applications. Although good academic preparation is necessary, it is also true that academic background as reflected in the CGPA, while a strong indicator of the readiness to do a PhD, is not the only factor that matters. Graduate admission committees routinely select students with a lower CGPA over ones with a higher CGPA based on a host of other factors like interest in the field of study, prior research experience, nature of academic preparation, etc.

Overall, what are the other attributes that make an effective PhD student? There are many perspectives on this question. Some of these attributes are discussed here (some are from Sorensen [2016]):

1. **Interest and motivation:** The student must have a keenness to undertake research towards a PhD, which might be demonstrated by their having attempted some research project in their education till this point. If a person has interest, he/she is more likely to be motivated and driven to work. It is also desirable that there is a clear and positive motivation to do a PhD, and PhD is not chosen simply because the student could not find a job or other opportunities.
2. **Initiative and independence:** This is a personal attribute or a work ethic as to whether the person takes initiatives on his/her own or is more dependent on the supervisor to give instructions. A person with initiative is also likely to be more motivated for doing the work. In general, people with initiative are more likely to achieve more than people who need direction.
3. **Creativity and ideation:** Research is about ideas—you cannot do research without having good ideas about what problems

to investigate, and ideas about how to overcome the challenges that might come in the way. One can say that great researchers are the ones who have novel ideas that others could not conceive of, and who have the ability and the traits to develop them and carry them forward.

4. **Integrity:** Research is in many ways a search for truth. While integrity is desired in all professions, this nature of research makes it even more important that researchers have the integrity to work ethically and report the results accurately.

5. **Ability to work hard and persevere:** For a researcher, these are perhaps the most important traits—it is well known that in research, while ideas are often what we talk about, to develop an idea to the level that it is accepted by peers and is recognized as a good contribution, a huge amount of work is often needed. Edison famously said, 'Genius is one per cent inspiration, ninety-nine per cent perspiration'. Besides hard work, learning to deal with failures and continuing to work after rejections is equally important. Whenever one is exploring the unexplored, failures are to be expected and will happen. A researcher will not always get the desired results, and an experiment might fail. Similarly, papers written on the research work done are, statistically speaking, generally more likely to be rejected than accepted (many journals have an acceptance rate of 25 per cent or less, implying that only one in four papers submitted are accepted). It should be clear that if one is mentally and physically not ready for this, a PhD, as well as a career in research, may not be suitable.

6. **Ability to work under uncertainty:** Research fundamentally is a risky venture—the outcome is not known. In fact, it is not even known whether there will be a successful outcome, and whether the research results will be accepted favourably is also uncertain. In the process of research, often, finding research problems to work on is also fraught with doubt. Overall, doing a PhD has many uncertainties. In undergraduate and master's degrees, the student can be certain that if he/she puts in the required effort he/she can complete the degree, but this

is not the case in a PhD; one might not even finish the PhD degree. Hence, having the ability to work under uncertainty is a key attribute of a good PhD student—having the confidence that finally, a positive outcome, though unknown at the start, is the most likely outcome if he/she perseveres.

7. **Interpersonal abilities:** Research is often done in teams, with multiple researchers working on a project and sharing results while still pursuing their own goals. Even during a PhD, often, the adviser will have a group of PhD (and master's) students and postdoctoral scholars working together on related problems. A good PhD student should have the interpersonal ability to work collaboratively with others in a team. Other things being equal, researchers who are good at collaboration are likely to do better in their research career than those who are weak at it.

6.2 CHARACTERISTICS OF A STRONG AND VIBRANT PHD PROGRAMME

Organizations routinely assess the quality of an individual PhD graduate—all universities and labs do this assessment during the recruitment process. In this assessment of graduates, the quality of the PhD programme of the university clearly plays a role—some universities are viewed to have strong and vibrant research programmes, and their graduates are often sought after. However, even the best of programmes produce mediocre PhD graduates, and there are graduates from average programmes who go on to excel. So how do we define the notion of quality for a PhD programme?

We will consider a PhD programme to be of a high quality if it consistently produces first-rate PhD graduates (as assessed by prospective employers). To ensure that more and more of its graduates are high-quality professionals, all the different aspects of a PhD programme—from admission of students to their thesis defence—play a role.

Traditionally, the quality of a PhD programme has been seen as largely dependent on the research reputation of the faculty.

While the quality of faculty undoubtedly plays a key role in the quality of a PhD programme, the quality also depends on a host of other factors: how well-designed the programme is, the level of mentorship and support provided to the PhD students, how well students are prepared for undertaking research, the guidance provided to the faculty for supervision, infrastructure, and so forth (Morrison et al. 2011). A study in USA considered a host of factors and their impact on the quality of doctoral education as perceived by the PhD graduates 10 years after their completion. The study found that graduates of the top-ranked programmes were only slightly more likely to assess the programme as excellent, as compared to graduates from other programmes. The study indicated that factors like academic rigour, clear programme requirements and support and guidance are viewed as being more conducive towards achieving excellence than the reputation of the faculty (Morrison et al. 2011).

In this section, we consider many different characteristics of a PhD programme, grouped around a few different themes or dimensions of the programme. However, before that, we discuss some of the expectations of prospective students in India regarding PhD programmes.

6.2.1 Expectations of Prospective Scholars from a PhD Programme

There are many studies about students enrolled in the PhD programmes—to better understand key aspects like time to completion, attrition, student experience and other related issues. While these studies help in understanding the PhD programme, they do not help in understanding what motivates people to join a PhD programme and what can be done to excite the brightest minds to take up a career in research by opting for a PhD. Developing countries like India have a special challenge in attracting students to PhD programmes in their institutions, as many of the graduates from their best institutions who want to pursue PhD opt to do it in overseas universities, most of which attract meritorious foreign students to their PhD programmes.

A few years ago, an informal survey of students who were about to graduate from BTech and MTech programmes of a few top engineering institutions was conducted (by the author) to get some data which could throw some light on the vexing problem of how to attract the best students to do a PhD in Indian institutions—a challenge that all top institutions in India have always struggled with.

The survey asked the students two questions. The first was why they may not want to do their PhD in India, and a set of reasons were presented to them from which they could choose as many as they wanted. The second was to understand what they would want in a PhD programme to seriously consider doing a PhD in India—for this also, a set of choices about what may be available from the PhD programme were given and they could select as many as they wanted. For these two questions, the choices given were decided based on discussions with faculty members and existing PhD students, as well as a general understanding of the prevailing situation. The students were also asked what they would prefer to do after graduation—a job, PhD, MBA, or master's. The survey was taken by about 275 students from three top engineering institutions, of which about 160 were BTech students and 115 were MTech students.

The first interesting observation was that while the vast majority wanted to do a job after graduation, over 15 per cent of them opted for a PhD. This number was higher than what many people expected. It revealed that there is a desire in a substantial number of graduates from the top institutions to do a PhD.

On the question of the main reasons why they would not want to join a PhD programme in India, the most common answers were:

- Have not thought about the PhD degree and career options after it;
- Job options after PhD are few;

- Do not want to be an academician; and
- PhD takes too much time.

The first three are career-related—these students do not understand what a PhD entails and the career possibilities after PhD, and might have been thinking that being an academician is the primary career (which many of them did not want to pursue). As discussed earlier, traditionally, PhD programmes have implicitly supported the view that after PhD, one should become an academic, and universities are often not aware of the range of possibilities that have been opening up for PhD graduates; hence, insufficient and incomplete information is given to the prospective PhD students which influences their perceptions about the programme.

It is also evident, as one may suspect, that prospective students are afraid that PhD takes a long time—implicit in this is also the fear of uncertainty about the completion time. In general, bachelor's and master's students perceive the PhD programme duration to be long and uncertain—perhaps strengthened by the anecdotes of students taking years to complete it and the jokes about the duration.

A considerable number of students also agreed with statements relating to the research scenario in India. Many students hold views like: the Indian PhD has a low market value, the faculty do not inspire them to take up higher studies, the range of research areas available in India is limited, as compared to foreign universities, etc. These are large research ecosystem challenges that a country like India faces.

Also, very few respondents chose the option that settling abroad was attractive. While experience—and some studies—shows that most students from India, when they do their PhD from universities in developed countries, choose to settle in those countries, this indicates that at least before they have actually moved abroad, the attraction of settling out of their country is not a strong motivator.

Students stated that they would consider doing a PhD in India if certain options are available, such as:

- If the PhD degree is jointly awarded by an Indian institution and a foreign university, with at least 1 year being spent in the foreign university; and
- If the PhD programme involves collaboration with R&D groups in companies, including an internship with these firms.

Two other career- and compensation-related options were found to be strongly favoured: if the job opportunities after PhD provide a good compensation, and if the stipend for PhD scholars is increased. Finally, one more option that was selected by many was that more information was needed about programmes and opportunities.

Results from a similar survey (also of engineering students) are given in Aggarwal (2018). This survey also identified many of the factors discussed above and discussed many challenges facing the PhD programme in India and some suggestions for addressing them. Though these studies are only of engineering students, some of the sentiments of these students will probably resonate with students in other disciplines as well, though there may well be other factors that influence their choices. Clearly, there is a need for similar studies for students in sciences, social sciences, humanities and other streams. However, an improved understanding of what prospective students are looking for can help in designing better PhD programmes in engineering. In fact, many of these studies directly impacted the design of the PhD programme at IIIT-Delhi, as will be explained later in the chapter in the case study section.

6.2.2 Admitting Scholars to the PhD Programme

While standard programmes are largely 'taught', the PhD programme builds upon what a student has already learned and aims to convert him/her into a researcher capable of creating new knowledge. Engaging in research requires different skill sets than learning. As discussed, while academic preparation (in terms of sound knowledge and understanding of the discipline and area) is necessary to undertake a PhD programme, there are other attributes relating to motivation, drive and creativity that may be more important for a PhD student. Students without proper skills and other attributes may not be able to complete the programme or may end up doing a mediocre thesis—both undesirable for a high-quality programme. Also, having unmotivated students in a programme can have a negative effect on the other PhD scholars, as the group size is generally rather small (particularly when compared to the size of bachelor's and master's programmes) and PhD scholars are often under pressure and self-doubt, which makes them more susceptible to negativity. Overall, selecting students from the applicant pool for the PhD programme needs careful consideration to ensure that the quality of the programme remains undiminished.

- **Holistic criteria for selection and proactive search:** A careful selection based on capabilities that are needed for PhD is extremely important. No PhD programme can thrive with mediocre PhD scholars. As discussed above, only academic achievements and preparation is not a strong predictor of success in PhD, and there are other attributes like motivation and drive that may have a larger influence on how well a student does. A good programme will take a rounded view of admission and will consider other important criteria besides academic achievement or scores in tests like Graduate Record Examination (GRE) (Kent and McCarthy 2016). What could be components of the criteria for admitting students to a PhD programme? This is something which each university, and departments within the university, have to specify, keeping in mind the expectations from the university and the discipline. Some of the attributes of an effective PhD student have been discussed earlier in the chapter—they can provide some guidance to evolving the necessary criteria.

In countries like India, there is a need to go beyond selecting from a pool using these determinants, as the graduates who are most suited for doing a PhD often choose to go overseas for pursuing their PhD. Hence, universities cannot expect to attract a large pool of applications of highly qualified candidates and selecting from this pool. When a good portion of the talent has gone to corporations (jobs) or for higher studies across the world, there is a need to find talent from the non-obvious sources. It is known that many universities and colleges that have average-quality education still often produce top-calibre graduates who go on to do exceedingly well in life. While the fraction of such students might be lower in such a university/college, such graduates do exist. In the light of the challenge that the best talent is not available, this 'hidden talent' has to be searched for and identified and 'recruited'. In other words, instead of selection, Indian research universities that aim to build a strong PhD programme have to adopt a 'recruitment' approach for PhD students and find the best and most appropriate talent, perhaps from somewhat unlikely sources.

- **Diversity**: Research can improve if there is diversity of thought. This can be provided in a PhD programme if there is diversity in scholars—diversity in terms of gender, background, nationality and culture. A high-quality PhD programme will actively build in diversity into itself.

- **Group size**: A reasonably sized PhD programme is needed to do the level of research that a research university desires. There is a need to have a reasonable cohort size for PhD for another reason. PhD scholars support each other, perhaps more than any other group in the university. Very commonly, in the acknowledgements of PhD theses, students are seen thanking their PhD colleagues. This is another important reason to ensure that there are sufficient numbers of PhD students in each department, so they can form their support groups.

6.2.3 Preparing for Research

Most PhD programmes have some coursework, though globally there are PhD programmes (e.g., in UK and Australia) which do not have any coursework. The main reason for having coursework in a PhD programme is to improve the preparation of the PhD student for undertaking research. In India, as discussed above, many PhD students may have graduated from universities and colleges with a mediocre-quality education that may not have adequately prepared them for undertaking a PhD programme. In fact, often, students may be weak even in the foundations of their discipline. Hence, in the context of a country like India, it is essential for a high-quality PhD programme to have a reasonable amount of coursework and to assess that the student is well prepared for undertaking research and completing the PhD programme.

- **Courses for preparing for research:** These are essential in India, as the students coming in are often not well-prepared. In fact, a strong coursework requirement can often be a good indicator of a sound PhD programme. In engineering education, for example, almost all of the main research institutes like the IITs and IISc, as well as IIIT-Delhi, have significant coursework. Some of this coursework is to strengthen the foundations and knowledge of students in their discipline so as to prepare them to undertake advanced courses and research. Some of these preparatory courses also train the students in research methods or pedagogy of research, including research ethics.
- **Advanced courses:** These are courses that are largely built around the current developments in an area rather than around the well-established body of knowledge. Often, these courses may not even have a textbook, and even if they use some books, these are commonly supplemented by recent papers and research results. These are also courses wherein the instructor's own research is often part of the syllabus of the course, integrating the research further with teaching. Some such courses help a PhD student in his/her research work.
- **Comprehensive exam:** There is a need to check, a few semesters after admission, if the PhD programme is suitable for the student, and if the student is suitable for the programme. PhD is not like a UG programme, where it is the responsibility of

204 | Building Research Universities in India

the university to ensure that the student learns and graduates. This is a special programme wherein only a few selected people are expected to enrol and succeed. Hence, it is important to check the suitability; if not found suitable, it is desirable that the student leaves the programme earlier, rather than later, so as to minimize the loss in terms of time and the resultant frustrations that can accrue. Comprehensive examination (which may be called qualifiers or with some such similar monikers) is a commonly used method to ensure that the student has the capability to withstand the rigours of the PhD programme. Sometimes, only after clearing this examination is a student considered as a candidate for PhD. There is no common view of this test (Walker et al. 2008), and its nature and scope varies from breadth in the discipline to grasp of the problem area of research to genuine creativity and other factors. However, a good PhD programme is expected to have such an examination.

6.2.4 Conducting Research and Monitoring Progress

A PhD programme is a long undertaking that can easily last 5 years or more. It is also a programme wherein there is minimal schedule or structure; hence, unlike a student in a bachelor's programme who has a weekly schedule of lectures, lab work, assignments, etc., a PhD student in many semesters might not be attending any course, and so might not have any of these structural forces to keep the momentum going. Often, the progress is left to the adviser. However, this is too personalized and not fully reliable; sometimes, a supervisor might not be able to take appropriate actions due to the strong one-to-one relationship that often develops. Often, a PhD student takes up many years, not due to the dearth of new ideas or hurdles in the process of research but due to a certain slackness which leads to the detriment of progress. For a good PhD programme, it is imperative to have rigorous progress assessment that is systemic and not exclusively dependent on the supervisor.

- **Rigorous and regular progress assessment:** The PhD is a programme in which losing a year or two is very easy. It is largely driven by self-motivation, and this is something most PhD scholars do not understand (as a large number of them still have a student mentality whereby the pace is effectively driven by instructors of courses). It is imperative that a regular review be done which is rigorous. At the start of the programme, the review should focus on how the scholar is honing his/her understanding and depth and building necessary skills, but after a year or so, its focus can be on progress made in identifying research problems, working on them, getting results and writing papers. One of these evaluations may involve the student presenting the thesis proposal and an assessment of the same. In the thesis proposal, the student explains what problem he/she wants to work on and the approach he/she wishes to take. Sometimes, the thesis proposal may be assessed by a separate review.

- **High expectations of research output:** PhD scholars, and their guides, will respond to the expectations that are set by the PhD programme of the university. These need not necessarily be hard-coded requirements stated as the nature and number of publications, but can be more about expectations, what the university expects from a PhD and what scholars should aspire for.

- **Research culture among PhD scholars:** It is not an exaggeration to say that the culture among the PhD scholars, which in turn evolves within the research culture of the faculty and the university, will have a strong influence on the work of PhD scholars. If the PhD students in the university support the aspiration to do good work and publish in reputed venues, encourage curiosity and knowledge seeking (for example by organizing and attending seminars and talks), motivate and support other scholars for doing good work (e.g., by giving presentations to each other, reviewing papers written by others, helping colleagues in problems when they may be stuck, providing ideas, etc.) and encourage initiative and exploration, it demonstrates a good and supportive research culture (Walker et al. 2008).

6.2.5 Preparing for a Career in Research

A graduate from a PhD programme is likely to pursue a career that will involve research. However, besides academics, research is important in a host of different environments and organizations, all of which can be potentially where a graduate may choose to build his/her career. For example, a PhD graduate may become a faculty member in a research university where teaching and research are both important, may become a faculty member in a teaching-focused university where teaching is the main job and research is given less weightage, may join a government research lab which may be working towards some national mission, may join an industry where research is done to help the business goals of the company, may join a think tank or an NGO which may be doing research to lobby or build public opinion around some important issues, may initiate or join a start-up to use research to create innovative products and services to generate value, may get inducted by government agencies where research-driven policies are being made—the possibilities are many. In future, it can be expected that opportunities are likely to expand. It is important for a PhD programme to prepare its PhD students for these diverse career opportunities.

- **Opportunities for research internships in the industry and other laboratory settings:** The close connection of research with industrial applications and, through it, with society is becoming increasingly important. Universities often are culturally inclined towards basic research, with less interest in exploring the potential applications for them or in deriving research problems from actual challenges in the field. To encourage the PhD scholar to take a wider view of research and also be cognizant of the possible impact of that research on innovation and business, a good way is to facilitate internships in the industry. Such internships will provide an exposure to the scholar about the nature of work in industry, as well as how research can be applied in that context. It can help in evolving research problems rooted in the industry practice or business.

- **International exposure:** Research is a global endeavour, and researchers can expect to work with multicultural and multi-national teams. Therefore, it is desirable that they have some international exposure during their PhD. This is particularly important for India, since its own ecosystem for research is still rather nascent. International exposure helps PhD scholars appreciate the research cultures of other countries, get different perspectives and also, perhaps, get the assurance that the work they are doing is at par with the type of work going on even in the well-respected universities. If a student can spend a semester or a year in some other research group in another country, the benefit of this would be tremendous.

- **Opportunities to present papers at international conferences:** During the course of the PhD, a PhD student should be able to present his/her work at international conferences. Such conferences provide a platform to present one's research to a global audience of scholars and experts in the field. They are also places where the latest results are shared, so they provide an excellent platform for students not only to hear great researchers present their work (and learn from this experience themselves) but also to find out both about the latest developments, as well as the open issues that the research community is excited about. This experience of presenting and listening to experts is immensely useful for improving the work the PhD student does, as well as his/her aspirations. As the top researchers in the field often come to these conferences, it is a great place to build connections with others and participate in the global network of researchers. Conferences often are the venues where job opportunities are shared and potential recruiters are present, which can help the PhD student in securing a good job after the completion of his/her PhD.

- **Developing teaching skills:** For a PhD graduate, academics provides an important career path, despite the other options discussed above. While the percentage of students joining academics has been declining, academics remains the career of choice for many PhD graduates. In some fields, particularly humanities and social sciences, academics is likely to be the preferred career for most of the graduates. In a university, teaching and research are the two main missions; faculty members are expected to teach a few courses each year, and teach them well. While researching skills are developed during PhD, the PhD programme must also prepare the PhD student for the other dimension of an academic career, namely, teaching. It is here that many PhD programmes fall short (Walker et al. 2008). While often PhD students have to do some TA duties, they are more often treated as ways to reduce the load of the faculty, rather than as training for teaching. For future faculty, it will clearly be desirable if they develop some effective teaching skills during their PhD. It can also help them better appreciate the academic career. A good PhD programme will provide active support and guidance to PhD students to develop their teaching capabilities. The NEP of the Government of India also recognizes the importance of developing teaching skills in future faculty and suggests that the PhD programme should actively develop these skills in PhD scholars by exposing them to good pedagogic practices and also provide them experience in teaching (NEP 2019).

- **Developing transferrable skills for non-academic careers and leadership:** It is desirable that the PhD programme also prepares students to undertake industry careers and develop leadership and entrepreneurship capabilities. While conventional academic skills are often developed through courses and mentoring, alternative approaches may be more suitable for developing such transferrable skills. For example, exposure to entrepreneurship can be provided through entrepreneurship clubs and their events (for example, hackathons and boot-strapping programmes), suitable lecture and discussion series, intensive workshops, etc. Similarly, for helping develop leadership skills, students may be given opportunities and responsibilities for managing some events (for example, organizing seminars), relevant workshops, aspects of PhD students' governance, and so forth. For developing their independence as researchers, they may be given opportunities to review papers, prepare research proposals, etc. If some patent is to be filed for a research project in which the student is involved, the student can be encouraged to take a leadership role in preparing the necessary documents, engaging with the lawyers and filing the patent. Much can be done to develop these attributes without diluting the academic rigour of the programme. Some more examples are given in Walker et al. (2008).

6.2.6 Supervision

A PhD programme is more like an apprentice-based individualized training. Therefore, its effectiveness depends considerably on the quality of advice or mentorship a PhD student gets. It should first be clarified that advising and mentoring are two distinct roles. An adviser helps the student progress towards completing the programme, ensuring that appropriate actions are taken at appropriate times and university requirements are fulfilled. A mentor, on the other hand, is a person who essentially guides a starting professional to develop skills and connections towards becoming a full-fledged professional.

- **Guidelines and/or training for supervision:** Generally, a PhD graduate who is recruited as faculty is free to take a PhD student and be a supervisor. As the PhD programmes themselves do not prepare the student for this role, it is expected that the experience of being supervised as a PhD student would have prepared a PhD student adequately for it. While this might often work, it is not sufficient and has no uniformity or consistency. It is therefore desirable that faculty members are provided with some training (through a workshop, for example) on different aspects of supervision. This is increasingly being taken more seriously in many universities. For example, in University of Melbourne, to be a supervisor, a faculty member has to undergo a training module every 5 years.

- **Multiple supervisors:** While the traditional apprenticeship model where the PhD student learns from one 'master' has worked quite successfully, it is broadly agreed upon that in the fast-changing and complex world, it is to the student's advantage if he/she has guidance and inputs from multiple supervisors. While it may not be desirable to legislate this as a rule, policies should support this so a good number of students are jointly supervised by a small group of supervisors.
- **Mentoring:** While the supervisor is often the primary mentor, having only one mentor has obvious limitations and risks, and a student is better served with multiple mentors (Walker et al. 2008). It is therefore important for the department or the university to provide mentoring to the PhD student, at least on how to successfully navigate the PhD programme and strategize career planning. It is sometimes done through a committee for the PhD student, which meets the student formally and regularly. Whatever be the mechanism for providing this, a good PhD programme is expected to provide good mentorship support to the PhD students, besides the support the supervisor provides.

6.2.7 Duration of the PhD programme and Attrition

Time to completion (along with attrition rates) is probably one of the most researched aspects of the PhD programme, particularly in USA, where the PhD programme is open-ended and, in many departments, time to completion tends to be rather long. Many studies regarding time to completion and attrition have been done (e.g., Bourke et al. 2004; Tuckman et al. 1989; Valero 2001).

While maintaining the open-ended nature of the PhD programme, it is possible to establish a reasonable completion time and then have support systems in place to achieve it, at least in most cases. A reasonable completion time, which is predictable for most candidates, is a desirable aspect of a PhD programme, which will also help attract more candidates.

It is important to have systems to achieve the desired completion times. It should be kept in mind that there is the possibility of a conflict between the interests of the student and those of the supervisor regarding this aspect. Towards the end of the PhD, the student is most productive, and if he/she stays longer, it can benefit the faculty in terms of more research output. It is therefore important that a reasonable duration for the completion of the PhD is established, perhaps suitably adjusted for different disciplines, and the PhD programme makes efforts to achieve it. The desired attribute for the PhD programme can be a clear articulation of the expected duration of the PhD programme. When a new cohort joins, counselling on this aspect—including what factors can delay graduation, what the student can do to keep the duration in control and what support the PhD programme provides for the same—can be provided. The time to completion should also be monitored and analysed from time to time to understand the effectiveness of the programme and to take any remedial steps needed.

Sometimes, for different programmes, tentative plans for finishing within a stipulated duration can be provided. Often, universities and departments will hesitate in officially providing such guidance, as clearly there are other variables that can affect the duration and, officially, a department or a university might not want additional challenges. However, informal guidance by senior faculty members, senior PhD students and other competent individuals can easily be provided based on experience. (An example of guidance for completing a PhD in Computer Science in 4 years can be found in the blog post by Jalote [2011].)

Closely related to completion time is attrition rate—the fraction of students who join the PhD programme but do not complete it. PhD programmes are likely to have the highest attrition rates; they are loosely structured and have inherent risks and uncertainties, often without clear actions that can be taken towards completion. Unlike bachelor's programmes, which are seen as basic and essential qualifications today, the PhD programme is clearly a choice, and that too a somewhat eccentric and difficult one. It is not uncommon for a student to join a PhD programme and then discover after a while that it is not what he/she wants to do, resulting in his/her opting out of the programme. There are clearly many other factors that affect the attrition rate, including the quality of support provided to students, level of guidance and culture of the department and the university, among others. Attrition is another factor that has been studied intensively, with many research papers having analysed the phenomenon (e.g., Bourke et al. 2004).

For a PhD programme, the goal is not to have zero attrition. Given the nature of the programme and uncertainties inherent in it, zero attrition is neither desirable nor achievable. It can also be argued that some amount of attrition is indeed desirable to allow the PhD scholar some room to revisit his/her earlier decision and plan for life—after all, doing a PhD is a long commitment which also alters the course of one's life and career. However, a large attrition rate is clearly indicative of issues in the PhD programme. What is desirable from a good PhD programme is that this parameter is monitored, the reasons for attrition are understood and necessary actions are taken to keep it in check.

6.2.8 Thesis Examination

Examining the thesis is the final check of quality. It is like the product acceptance test of a factory before the product is shipped out. In a production line, as is well established and known, the focus of quality assurance is to ensure that the production process is designed and geared towards producing a high-quality product. Still, at the end of production, before shipping the product out to consumers, most production systems will have a quality control check on the final item. The situation in a PhD programme is similar. Many of the attributes and dimensions discussed are to ensure that the process of the PhD programme has the desired features to produce a high-quality PhD. Still, before the student graduates, the thesis examination is the quality control check on the actual quality of the PhD work.

Actually, the methods followed for thesis examination are more than that and can impact the other attributes also. For example, if the thesis examination is lax, this message will be picked up by existing and future PhD students, as well as by their supervisors, and this may then affect what they aspire to achieve through the PhD. It is of utmost importance that the PhD thesis review process is rigorous, which ensures that if a thesis has been accepted, it is of good quality, but which also communicates to future PhD candidates and to advisors that this is a rigorous check and that a thesis whose quality is not up to the standards will not pass through.

Given the importance of this final check, often, a good PhD programme will have two steps in it: a detailed examination of the thesis by experts and an open thesis defence. Setting high standards for this is crucial, as PhD scholars and their supervisors respond to it through a self-check of quality. Thus, if the review is rigorous, the scholar and the guide will ensure that the thesis is of a high quality before it is submitted. If the review is easy and more of a formality, it is likely to lead to many average theses being submitted (and approved). The thesis review depends on the committee of experts that reviews it and, finally, on the guidelines for forming the committee. For example, some universities require a committee of at least three external experts, all of them having a certain reputation in the field, with some of them from other countries and none of the experts having any conflict of interest with the PhD student or the supervisor.

- **Thesis review:** A good-quality PhD programme should have a rigorous thesis examination by a panel of (at least three) independent experts who are not related to the student directly, with systems to ensure that the experts can give a frank assessment of the thesis work and have a clear idea of the standards the university expects from its PhD thesis. The review report should provide suitable flexibility and room to the examiner to not only give comments and critiques but also clearly express his/her view about the thesis quality. For example, if only a binary choice (accept or reject) is given, it might be hard for a reviewer to have the heart to reject a thesis. On the other hand, if options include something like, the thesis is not worthy of a PhD but is worthy of an MPhil/

214 | Building Research Universities in India

MS/..., it can provide the examiner another way of expressing negative views which may not be as hard to opt for. Similarly, the person(s) communicating with the examiners can impact the quality of the review; for example, if the supervisor is the negotiator, it might compromise the result.

- **Thesis defence:** If a thesis has been found acceptable during its review and changes have been made to address any short-comings identified, it is often a custom to have an open thesis defence. The idea of an open defence is that the candidate should stand in front of all interested parties and defend his/her work. Anybody in the room has an opportunity to raise objections to the work done in the thesis. It also provides the final check to ensure that all comments raised in the review have been addressed satisfactorily. It also becomes a communication forum to share within the university or a department and with the rest of the community the work being done in a PhD thesis, and provides the PhD student with an occasion to explain her work to a wider audience. It provides an excellent opportunity for other PhD students to see what type of work qualifies for a PhD and exposure to the last stages of the PhD programme. The tradition of a PhD defence is, however, not universal. However, given the benefits it can provide, and the fact that the time and effort required for it are not much, it is desirable that a good PhD programme should have an open thesis defence that is advertised widely (perhaps even outside the university) and which is attended by many. It is clearly desirable for all thesis reviewers to attend the defence in order to ask any other questions they may have and to confirm that all the concerns raised earlier in their evaluation have been addressed adequately.

6.2.9 PhD Programme Administration and Student Support

It is of utmost importance that the PhD programme is administered efficiently, keeping in mind the interests of the PhD student. As PhD students are partly like staff, there should be an administrative unit looking after their interests and grievances. In addition, there are many steps in a PhD programme (for example, comprehensive exam, thesis examination, thesis defence, etc.) which cannot be completed by the PhD student and the supervisor. They require inputs from the academic administration. It is not uncommon to find in some programmes delays in the graduation process of a PhD student by a few years, simply because of lack of reviews or delays in scheduling the defence. PhD students need a lot of support during the many years they work on their PhD. Some aspects of administering and assisting PhD scholars that are important for a high-quality PhD programme are discussed here.

- **An exclusive structure for administering the PhD programme:** It has been noted that PhD programme governance and administration cannot be left to just the non-academic staff. For a host of reasons, a senior academic should administer the PhD programme. The process should be bolstered by a range of policies and procedures; most of the aspects discussed earlier have to be documented and implemented in spirit and action.
- **Decent stipend/compensation:** PhD students, unlike the learners in bachelor's and master's programmes, contribute towards one of the main outputs of a university—research. They often help the regular faculty in education, which is the other important mission of the university. Therefore, they should be compensated suitably. In addition, there is an opportunity cost of doing a PhD—a graduate is not earning market wages while doing a PhD. If the opportunity cost is too high, it can strongly counter the incentives for joining a PhD programme. As it is, it is often hard for many people to choose to do a PhD. If the compensation is not suitable, it may dissuade them even further.
- **Career counselling and pathways:** This has been recognized as a common weakness in many programmes. Many universities just leave PhD students to their own devices or expect their supervisors to provide advice about career choices. Supervisors, having chosen academics as their profession,

may be out of touch with other professions for a long time and cannot always be expected to have the knowledge or skills to provide proper career counselling about all the new opportunities opening up. Hence, it is important for a PhD programme to provide suitable career guidance to its PhD students.

- **Infrastructure and other support:** PhD students need infrastructural support to do their work, including access to laboratories and libraries, hostel accommodation, computing resources, and others. They also need a variety of other assistance, for example, help in writing (thesis and scholarly papers), attending conferences, building a professional network and establishing their reputation. Many of these are often provided informally by the supervisor and mentors. It is also desirable to provide counselling support to these students. PhD is a very exacting degree, and students often go through very rough periods; having decent counselling support will help.

- **Setting the expectations:** What is expected from a PhD scholar for him/her to successfully complete his/her PhD? The answer to this question, unlike similar questions for a bachelor's or master's degree, is often not very clear. While the expectations cannot be articulated as precisely as can be done for an undergraduate programme, still, a department and a university should establish some expectations and articulate them clearly to the PhD scholars. Not being clear about the expectations is one of the most common complaints of PhD students. Similarly, there is often insufficient clarity about the rules regarding the different aspects of a PhD programme, in particular the rationale behind them (Walker et al. 2008). It is important that PhD students know the various stages involved during the PhD, the reason for the rules governing the different stages and the expectations of each of them.

- **Exit interviews and improvement:** It should be accepted that a PhD programme is not static and should continue to improve. As the goal of any programme is to deliver on its stated outcomes, feedback from graduating PhD students, as well as those who graduated a few years earlier, will provide excellent inputs for further improvement. Learning and improvement is facilitated if there are processes put in place for collecting data, analysing it, learning from it, using the insights gained for deciding upon the subsequent actions to take for improving the programme and, finally, implementing the actions. A good-quality PhD programme will have some formal process for this learning and improvement which it will execute regularly. As with other programmes, such analysis should be discussed and deliberated upon widely, including with the PhD students.

- **External review of the PhD programme:** A PhD programme is often not assessed carefully. Accreditation programmes generally focus on undergraduate programmes, and department reviews often look at general issues, particularly relating to faculty. It is implicitly assumed that a PhD programme will be reviewed and refined internally. One of the main challenges of an internal review is that faculty often have different views and may even have turf wars leading to positions that are hard to reconcile. In the absence of conflict resolution, the attempt should be to avoid such conflicts, which often leads to guidelines that are not necessarily in the best interest of the PhD programme but are added to maintain decorum (Walker et al. 2008). Given that internal mechanisms might not work, an unbiased external review by peers can be highly desirable. Such a review will inevitably meet with PhD scholars, as well as with faculty supervisors, and identify challenges faced by both groups—the first step towards refining the system.

6.3 CASE STUDY: PHD PROGRAMME AT IIIT-DELHI

The PhD programme at IIIT-Delhi was designed such that it could address some of the key issues uncovered in the survey of prospective PhD scholars, as discussed earlier. The entire cycle of the PhD programme—from admission to thesis defence—was carefully thought out so as to address the challenges PhD programmes in the country face. Partly as a result of this design, within a few years of starting the PhD programme in Computer Science, it became one of the largest programmes in the country. Data about placement of graduated students also indicates that the quality of PhD graduates is as good as the best in the country. We will discuss some key aspects of the programme.

6.3.1 Duration of the PhD Programme: Plan for 4 Years but Allow 5 Years

The duration of a PhD programme has always been a contested issue, and different models have been adopted. On one side is the model commonly followed in USA (and largely also in India), that the PhD is an open-ended degree, as creativity and new ideas and results are required, and whether sufficient work has been done cannot be predicted. Indeed, one cannot even predict if a scholar will complete a PhD. On the other side is the model often followed in UK and Australia, where a student starts the PhD with a good understanding of the problem he/she wants to work on and is given 3 years to complete it.

At IIIT-Delhi, a middle-of-the-road philosophy was adopted. The basic premise was that a PhD can generally be completed in 4 years, if progress is monitored carefully. However, there are situations wherein it may take longer, and while a longer duration should be discouraged, it has to be permitted.

This approach was implemented by an innovative approach. The fellowship of a PhD student starts from the first year and increases every year by a modest amount till the fourth year. In the fifth year, however, the fellowship reduces (to approximately the level of a first-year PhD scholar), and from the sixth year onwards, no PhD fellowship can be provided, even if the supervisor has projects from which he/she can provide support.

It should also be noted that, in the view of prospective PhD students, a duration of 4 years, which can mostly be achieved, is one of the most desirable attributes of a PhD programme—this was revealed in the survey discussed earlier and also comes up in discussions with prospective students. Overall, having strong policies in place to see that students complete their PhD in 4 years is hugely desirable, so both students and supervisors can align towards achieving this. It is also a goal that is clearly achievable, particularly with allowances for more time in special situations.

6.3.2 Admissions

As mentioned earlier, research universities in countries like India face a special challenge finding good students for their PhD programmes, and hence the open application-based approach, which is the most common approach used worldwide, will not suffice. Hence, it was felt that multiple channels must be created. The main channels that are used are:

- **Open application process.** This is the standard approach, in which students apply to the PhD programme in different disciplines, along with their resume, score in graduate admission tests (GATE in India), transcript, etc. After screening based on the available information, candidates are invited for a test and interview. As most entrance tests in India are subject-based and do not assess general aptitude (e.g., quantitative, reasoning, logical, etc.), the test focuses on this aspect. The interview is used to assess the level of interest and motivation and communication skills.
- **Rolling admissions.** In this channel, the candidates first engage with a faculty member for research. The faculty member may offer internship or training or use other means to assess the potential and suitability. If the faculty member is satisfied, then the candidate may apply, with the faculty member being the proposed supervisor. The candidate is assessed by a committee that may recommend admission. With this channel, effectively each faculty member is empowered to look for potential PhD students, which opens up new possibilities to identify PhD candidates.

- **Conversion of master's programme to PhD.** Most universities have procedures for permitting a master's candidate to migrate to PhD. In IIIT-Delhi, this was formalized and incentivized to motivate the best master's students to migrate to PhD. The idea is to identify those students who have already shown potential to do a good PhD in the two or more semesters that they have spent at the institute and invite them to join the PhD programme. If the student decides to migrate, then he/she is deemed to have joined the PhD programme from the time he/she joined the institute. This implies that the course requirement for PhD will be what it would have been at the time of joining the institute (this can save a semester or so of coursework). More importantly, as there is no tuition fee for PhD students, the tuition fee of the master's programme is refunded to the student. This is a significant incentive, as the tuition fee of a master's is substantial.

- **Campus recruitment.** As mentioned earlier, it is desirable to 'cast the net wide' to find the few candidates that might be there in places which are not generally considered as sources for PhD candidates. For this, a few colleges are visited where tests and interviews are conducted to identify deserving candidates, who are invited to the institute for the final interview. This is an effort-intensive exercise and so is done only occasionally. However, some research universities that want to consider this channel can easily expand and refine it by getting into partnerships with selected institutions, whose graduates have shown good performance in the past, for admissions, whereby the partner institution can do the initial screening.

6.3.3 Preparing Students for Research and a Research Career

Generally, after a bachelor's or a master's degree, students are not adequately prepared to undertake research. In fact, they often might not have even had exposure to research and current developments in different fields. To address this, there is a requirement in the PhD programme for a student to earn a certain number of course credits. The number of credits to be earned depends largely on the highest degree a student has. Such coursework requirement is common among the top research institutions in the country and helps not only in strengthening the background of PhD students, but also in developing an appreciation and understanding of research, before they undertake research themselves.

In India, it is widely recognized that even in the best research institutions, the PhD students often come from institutions which provide average quality education leading to students not even well prepared in foundations. To address this, some 'refresher modules' (which were introduced for master's students) are offered, some of which the students take during summer before starting their formal programme, and some like the module on 'Technical Communications & Research Methods' are taken during their first two semesters.

To develop teaching skills, all PhD students are required to be TAs for at least two semesters. To prepare them for their duties and help them leverage the experience to become better teachers, they are provided a short training. They are also given a handbook of best practices for TAs contains some strategies and best practices for conducting an interactive class, techniques for time-efficient grading and designing rubrics, some tips on the effective handling of score disputes, maintaining a professional conduct, handling academic dishonesty and student questions in office hours, etc. These are only initial steps towards using TA duties as training for a career in teaching—clearly, much more needs to be done so the TA experience can be leveraged suitably.

6.3.4 Progress Monitoring and Regular Reviews

The nature of a PhD programme is such it is easy for a PhD scholar to 'lose' a semester or two with minimal progress or contribution towards completion. To monitor progress and to send the message to students and supervisors that progress is expected so that PhD may be completed in the expected duration of 4 years, regular progress review monitoring is done.

To assess the progress of PhD students, some expectation of what progress means from year to year needs to be understood, as the expected progress in the first year of the programme will clearly be different from the expected progress in the third year. Also, a holistic programme of a PhD student should look at the knowledge acquisition as well as knowledge creation aspects. At IIIT-Delhi, a template is provided for reporting the yearly progress. It captures different aspects, including: courses taken, areas in which expertise has been gained, papers submitted, plan for the next year, performance with respect to last year's goals, etc.

The yearly review is done based on the report and a presentation by the PhD student to the committee. A feedback report is given to the student (and supervisor), which, besides capturing whether the progress is satisfactory or not, provides constructive inputs to the student for improving his/her work.

In addition to the yearly review, which is generally done at the start of the academic year, quick, stock-taking mid-year reviews are also done. This review is different from the yearly review, and the purpose is also different. In this review, each supervisor summarizes the progress in a couple of minutes to the entire department faculty. This review is also meant to inform all faculty members about the PhD work going on in the department, which has many indirect benefits. This might appear as be a tedious exercise, but if done well, it can be done in an afternoon for a small department.

6.3.5 International Exposure

As the aim of a good PhD programme is to produce high-quality global researchers who are comfortable working anywhere and with colleagues from different countries, it is important for a PhD student to get some international experience. This exposure is even more important for PhD programmes in a country like

India, where the research ecosystem tends to be smaller, with fewer opportunities for researchers to engage with international academics and researchers. International exposure, particularly exposure to institutions with a vibrant research culture and a large population of researchers, can have strong beneficial effects on PhD scholars' motivation, aspiration, etc. To facilitate this, a few different schemes are made available.

- **International conference travel support:** Each PhD student has a budget for this purpose. While the budget is limited, it can easily be leveraged to support more travels, for example, by utilizing the support to get grants from government/agencies, support from conference organizers, travel grants by research labs, etc. The support is for presenting papers, and only in reputed conferences.
- **External co-supervisor:** PhD students may have, besides supervisors from the institute faculty, external co-supervisors from reputed institutions and labs globally. These co-supervisors have almost the same role as supervisors and are recognized in the same manner as the supervisors from the institute. Having regulations to enable co-supervisors not only helps international collaborations but also facilitates joint PhD programmes. (Of the students who finished their PhD in the last 2 years, about one-fourth had external co-supervisors.)
- **Overseas research fellowship.** This is the most ambitious scheme, which is financially the most challenging. In this programme a student can spend up to 6 months in a research university or a lab. During the visit, the student must work with the collaborators in the host institution on research that will contribute to the PhD thesis. The duration can be extended, if the collaborator wishes and can sponsor the extension. It would be desirable if the host is also an external co-supervisor. (About half of the recently graduated students spent a semester or longer overseas.)
- **Joint PhD programmes.** Joint PhD programme between two universities are those in which the PhD student has supervisors from both universities and in which the PhD scholar spends

substantial time in both with the respective supervisors and a degree with both Institution's names is granted. Clearly, such a programme is highly valuable for a PhD student who can benefit from supervisors from two different universities and countries, as well as get substantial international experience. It is also valuable for universities to increase their international collaboration for research.

There are, of course, challenges in operationalizing this, as the regulations of two universities have to be satisfied. One approach (which IIT-Delhi has taken) is that the student has to satisfy the PhD requirements of both the universities. While this might look like it might overburden the student, in practice, it is not so, as, often, the requirements of collaborating universities are similar and are likely to have enough flexibility to be satisfied by another similar university regulation. Only minor adaptations are needed.

A key challenge for this programme is the funding—who funds the PhD student when he/she goes to work with the collaborator. This issue is particularly important for India, as the fellowship being provided here is clearly insufficient for staying in most developed countries. The current practice is that while the student is with the partner institution, that institution supports the student. The other main challenge in this is to form supervisor pairs who will guide the student. If some faculty members know colleagues in partner universities, this is not too hard. However, to increase the scope of the programme, it is desirable to facilitate the forming of supervisor pairs—this might require initial support for visits, workshops, etc.

6.3.6 Comprehensive Exam

The aim of the comprehensive examination is to check the understanding of the PhD student about his/her area of research (not just the problem on which the candidate is working). Though traditionally a comprehensive exam was meant to check whether the student has sufficient breadth, it was felt that this type of breadth should be fulfilled through courses and the comprehensive exam should be used to test the 'comprehensiveness' of the candidate's knowledge about his/her main area of research. Hence, the comprehensive exam at IIIT-Delhi is not for checking the comprehensiveness of a candidate's understanding of the discipline, but for checking the comprehensiveness of understanding of the area in which the student is working.

Effectively, the comprehensive exam becomes a checkpoint, which establishes that the candidate has comprehensively understood the problem area and has a solid understanding of the area around the problem, that is, the area to which the problem belongs. The report submitted for the comprehensive exam can also form parts of the 'related work' chapter of the final thesis, thereby making it contribute towards the thesis and PhD completion also, rather than just being an exam consuming extra time and effort (which helps in finishing the PhD in the expected duration). There are guidelines for by when the student is expected to complete the comprehensive exam and the committee constitution.

6.3.7 Thesis Examination and Defence

In many ways, processes set for the thesis examination, and how they are executed, have a significant impact on the quality of the PhD. Perhaps, the most important aspect of defence is the selection of the committee and the conduct of the defence itself. The thesis evaluation committee is formed from a panel of names submitted by the advisors of the student. There are clear guidelines for who can be included in the panel—in terms of seniority (Associate Professor or above), from within India and outside (at least one member of the committee must be from outside the country), conflict of interest (anyone with a conflict of interest with the student cannot be included), etc. For each name in the panel, a statement about the person's suitability and some publications in the area are also provided. From this panel, at least three persons are selected as external examiners, one of which must be from overseas. The names of the examiners are not revealed to the students or the supervisors (they are revealed only at the time of the defence).

The examiners are expected to send a detailed report on the thesis within a time limit. Based on the report, the student is required to provide a detailed response addressing each of the issues raised and what changes have been made in the thesis. Once the PhD administration is satisfied with the response, the thesis defence is scheduled. All examiners are invited to join—physically, if they can travel, or through electronic means. The supervisors also join the defence. The defence often lasts about 2 hours and is open to all—often, many PhD students attend it. After the defence, the committee submits its joint report using the template provided, which has multiple options like accept with minor changes, accept with major changes, reject, accept for an MTech, etc.

6.4 SUMMARY

A strong and vibrant PhD programme is the hallmark of a good research university. It is very different in its aim and methodology from the bachelor's and the master's degrees. Compared to these courses, however, it is also a programme that gets less attention from academic bodies as well as from accreditation frameworks.

The chapter begins by emphasizing the objectives and learning outcomes of the PhD programme and the desirable attributes of a PhD scholar. It then goes on to discuss the salient characteristics of a strong PhD programme. It first discusses, based on a study, what prospective students expect from a PhD programme. It then studies in close detail the PhD programme's many facets, starting from the admission process leading on to the preparation for research to the methods of monitoring progress effectively and mentoring scholars meaningfully. The proper procedures of examining the candidate and the final appraisal of the research done are foregrounded, with emphasis on the principles underlying each stage of assessment. The chapter also considers various aspects of administering the PhD programme.

The chapter ends with a case study, that of the PhD programme at IIIT-Delhi, in order to provide a specific real-life instance of a programme that embodies many of the principles examined earlier. Thus, from charting the broad ideals of the programme to highlighting a particular application of the same, the chapter provides both the educationist and the aspiring research scholar with a comprehensive overview, as well as an analysis, of the important aspects of the PhD programme.

REFERENCES

Aggarwal, Varun. 2018. *Leading Science and Technology*. New Delhi: SAGE Publications.

Bourke, Sid, Allyson Holbrook, Terence Lovat, and Peter Farley. 2004. *Attrition, Completion and Completion Times of PhD Candidates*. Presented at AARE Annual Conference, Melbourne, 2004.

Carnegie. 2000. *The Carnegie Classification of Institutions of Higher Education*. http://carnegieclassifications.iu.edu/downloads/2000_edition_data_printable.pdf

Denecke, D., J. Kent, and M. T. McCarthy. 2017. *Articulating Learning Outcomes in Doctoral Education: A Report from the Council of Graduate Schools*. Washington DC: Council of Graduate Schools.

Jalote, P. 2011. *Completing PhD in Four Years in CS After BTech/BE*. Blog Post on Jalote.wordpress.com

Jayaram, Narayana. 2008. 'Doctoral Education in India.' In *Towards a Global PHD?* edited by M. Nerad and M. Hegellund. Seattle, WA: University of Washington Press.

Kent, Julia D., and Maureen T. McCarthy. 2016. *Holistic Review in Graduate Admissions: A Report from the Council of Graduate Schools*. Washington, DC: Council of Graduate Schools.

Morrison, E., Elizabeth Rudd, William Zumeta, and Maresi Nerad. 2011, September/October. 'What Matters for Excellence in PhD Programs? Latent Constructs of Doctoral Program Quality Used by Early Career Social Scientists.' *The Journal of Higher Education* 82 (5): 535–63.

NEP. 2019. *Draft National Education Policy, 2019*. New Delhi: Government of India.

Nerad, M. 2004. 'The PhD in US: Criticisms, Facts, and Remedies.' *Higher Education Policy* 17: 183–99.

Nerad, M. 2012. 'Conceptual Approaches to Doctoral Education: A Community of Practice.' *Alternation* 19 (2): 57–72.

Nerad, M. 2015a. 'Confronting Common Assumptions, Designing Future-Oriented Doctoral Education.' In *Doctoral Education and the Faculty of the Future*, edited by Ronald G. Ehrenberg and Charlotte V. Kuh, 2009. Ithaca, NY: Cornell University Press.

Nerad, Maresi. 2015b. 'Professional Development for Doctoral Students: What is it? Why Now? Who does it?' *Nagoya Journal of Higher Education* 15: 285–318.

Sorensen, H. T. 2016. 'I-Determinants for a Successful PhD or Postdoctoral Outcome.' *Clinical Epidemiology* 8: 297–303.

Tuckman, Howard P., Susan Coyle, and Yupin Bae. 1989, October. 'The Lengthening of Time to Completion of the Doctorate Degree.' *Research in Higher Education* 30 (5): 503–16.

Valero, Yaritza F de. 2001, June. 'Departmental Factors Affecting Time-to-degree and Completion Rates of Doctoral Students at One Land-grant Research Institution.' *The Journal of Higher Education* 72 (3): 341–67.

Walker, C. M. Golde, L. Jones, A. C. Bueschel, P. Hutchings. 2008. *The Formation of Scholars—Rethinking Doctoral Education for the Twenty-First Century*. Stanford, CA: The Carnegie Foundation for the Advancement of Teaching.

Chapter 7

Faculty Recruitment and Management

Faculty and students are at the heart of any university. Students come and go after a few years, and even administrators often change once every few years. However, faculty remain—most of them for decades in the same university. Consequently, the character of a university is defined by the faculty it has and the culture that exists among its faculty. Faculty is even more critical in a research university, as the research is led almost entirely by faculty, who are also supervisors for PhD scholars.

It has been argued that research universities are organisms that work for prestige. The reputation and prestige of a university depend on the quality and success of its graduates and the quality and contributions of its faculty. As the former depends on the latter to some extent, the quality and contributions of faculty, in essence, become key factors affecting the reputation and quality of a university.

The situation in terms of faculty in universities is challenging in India, and perhaps in many other developing countries. The biggest challenge is the mismatch between the demand and the supply of faculty-calibre candidates. The lack of the supply of good-quality candidates not only affects recruitment but also restricts the nurturing of faculty to be high achievers.

Getting the best talent is necessary for a research university, but nurturing the faculty talent is even more important. Nurturing requires processes and systems to motivate faculty members to excel so that they can deliver to their potential. There are clear examples in India where faculty quality at the time of joining is as good as in some of the top global universities. However, if we look at the contributions of faculty after a decade or two, the achievement levels are often vastly different from those of their global peers.

Nurturing faculty so that they can achieve their potential and deliver to their level of capability is important not only for a research university but also from the perspective of faculty. Faculty in research universities are inevitably extremely talented, with the highest academic degrees, and often have a strong desire to make an impact. They are also among the smartest people, and their training provides them with strong analytical capabilities. Such people will frequently reflect upon their contributions and ask 'what they did in life'. A nurturing environment that motivates faculty to contribute more can also help the faculty feel more comfortable about their contributions through their academic careers. Unfortunately, in many universities in India, the culture and the environment are not conducive to high-quality teaching or research and are often demotivating for faculty. There are a host of factors that have led to this state of affairs, many of which are discussed by Chandra (2017), who also points out that faculty are one of the weakest links in Indian higher education today.

In this chapter, we discuss the recruitment of faculty, as well as various aspects of nurturing them. This discussion is mainly based on the policies and processes used in IIIT-Delhi, many of which are similar to those in other institutions. As the policies and frameworks regarding faculty management are strongly determined by the cultural and political context of a country, only a few references are provided in this chapter (there is very little literature about faculty management in India). We start the discussion with the nature of faculty work and the various types of faculty a research university often has.

7.1 FACULTY WORK

The work of a regular faculty in a research university is one of the most multidimensional and complex activities. A research university expects faculty to contribute to its core missions of research and teaching. However, faculty in a university often double up as administrators—faculty members handle many important administrative positions and most committees within a university. They are also members of the larger research community for their discipline. An important aspect of a faculty career is identification with the discipline and the professional community. This community functions largely based on the support from its members. Hence, a responsible faculty also provides service to the profession. In other words, faculty work has three dimensions: research, teaching and service.

With this, a key question is how a university expects its faculty to divide their effort between these three roles. Many research universities do not explicitly state what is 'normally expected' from a faculty in these three dimensions. The effort spent on different activities cannot be measured or accurately estimated. However, reasonable expectations can be established. For example, in some universities, the 'normal' expectation from faculty members is that they spend about 40 per cent of their time in research, 40 per cent in teaching and 20 per cent in service. Any such expectation is on an annual basis and not on a weekly or monthly basis. That is, some semesters, a faculty may end up spending much of his/her time in teaching-related activities, but in some other semesters with a lighter teaching load, or during breaks between semesters (often of about 4 months total), he/she may devote almost all their time to research. Many Australian universities use this 40-40-20 guideline. IIIT-Delhi has also articulated this as the guideline. The importance of this type of statement is not in the actual percentages but in the fact that teaching and research are both given equal importance and weight. This clearly has implications when assessing faculty contributions and performance.

7.1.1 Research

Faculty in a research university is expected to conduct research at an international level; this necessarily implies doing research, writing papers on results and communicating results through seminars, conferences, and so forth. However, for doing research, a faculty generally has to do much more, including applying for research grants, managing grants, guiding PhD students, managing research personnel, and so forth.

It is desirable to articulate the outcomes of research. Clearly, the main output of research is peer-reviewed publications. Sometimes, other forms of publications may also be considered, for example, patents.

While research publications are universally accepted as a recognized and primary output of research, other forms of outputs are also available. For example, getting and running grants is a significant activity for most faculty, which consumes a considerable amount of their effort. Universities also rely significantly on faculty getting these research grants. Thus, while one can view grants as inputs for research, they can also be viewed as outputs of the research activities of a faculty. A faculty may succeed in getting only some grants (just like research papers) after putting in considerable effort for developing research proposals.

Another reason for considering sponsored research projects as outputs is that these projects are generally granted by research-sponsoring agencies of the government. The types of projects they support often align with the current national agenda for research and development; only research efforts that are likely to advance the state of knowledge and technology in these areas are supported. These sponsored projects can therefore be considered as contributions to national research missions and as independent outputs of research.

Similar is the case for guiding PhD students. Guiding PhD students essentially helps faculty get fresh ideas and develop these into research results. Consequently, PhD students may be treated as inputs, with the final output being research publications. However, this is a narrow view; guiding PhD students is a significant work for faculty, which consumes a lot of their time. In fact, in the initial years of guiding, PhD students are mostly 'unproductive' in terms of output, and the effort is mainly in guiding and preparing students to undertake research. Besides the fact that guiding a PhD student is a significant effort, the graduation of a PhD student is an important output in its own right, one that is perhaps more significant from a broader research ecosystem perspective. Hence, it should be included as a research output.

Thus, the research activity of a faculty has many aspects. What may be considered as outputs of a research activity depends on the view taken by the university. One set of outputs of research by a faculty in a research university, which is employed in IIIT-Delhi, includes the following:

- Research publications;
- Sponsored projects;
- PhD students graduated; and
- Technologies and innovations developed and deployed/delivered.

We have discussed the first three and the rationale of including them as research outputs. The last one is perhaps more relevant in the current times and is closely related to the third mission of a university. Here, we use the word 'technologies' in a more general sense—virtually anything that can be used for the benefit of the society or a group in the society. It may be actual technology, or it may be a process, or it may be methodology—we refer to all of them as technology. The society and governments expect universities to provide new technologies and solutions for problems being faced by the society and to contribute directly to the economic development of the country, by leveraging their capabilities of generating new knowledge and converting them into innovations, products, processes and solutions. Universities can deliver innovations and technologies only if faculty aspire to do so. Hence, a university needs to articulate that these are valuable and expected outputs of faculty effort and will be recognized as such in evaluations, promotions, and so forth.

7.1.2 Teaching

All faculty are expected to contribute to education—the primary mission of a university. As the teaching of courses is the most visible activity in education, the contribution to education is often considered synonymous with teaching. We will use the term 'teaching' in a broader sense to mean not only the courses a faculty teaches but also other activities related to the teaching of students in which a faculty puts in effort to contribute towards the education mission.

The teaching of courses is perhaps the most important teaching function; it brings to mind the image of a professor delivering a lecture to a room full of students. In fact, it is much more than delivering lectures. It starts with the design of the course, which is an intellectually challenging exercise requiring establishing learning outcomes, designing lectures and other in-class teachings, planning out-of-lecture activities or assignments to ensure learning and planning for assessment. The lectures have to be delivered, and for each lecture, suitable preparation has to be made: assignments have to be given and graded in time, other assessment instruments have to be employed and checked, and feedback has to be given to students in time. Further, there are other course management tasks such as managing students, taking attendance, ensuring maintenance of academic honesty standards and code of conduct, holding sessions during office hours and, if needed, special sessions, to help clarify student doubts, managing the course-related website and discussion forums, and so forth. A large class (e.g., an introductory course with a few hundred students) requires additional tasks such as managing teaching assistants, coordinating different sections, holding tutorials, and so forth. All in all, teaching a course is a time-consuming activity, and for large classes, it can be exhausting.

Besides teaching courses, guiding students' work is another major teaching activity for faculty. Most universities have provisions for independent study or project work by students. All such work has to be guided by faculty. As this is one-on-one guidance given to students, it takes time, even with just a few students. Such guidance also involves reading reports that students may write, helping them with the reports and, perhaps, also reading the related literature.

Most research universities have programmes at the master's level which provide students the ability to do a master's thesis or a scholarly paper, or an equivalent. A master's thesis is substantial, often requiring some original work or analysis. It often spans a year, with perhaps one semester fully devoted to thesis work. Such a thesis requires a significant time commitment from the faculty who is guiding the student. Although a faculty might get some useful output from such a thesis, given the small duration, most of the time is spent in training the student. Thus, much of the effort is effectively a contribution towards education.

While teaching courses and guiding students are the main teaching activities, faculty also engage in other teaching activities, leading to desirable contributions to education. For example, a faculty may design a new course in an emerging area—something that is done not too frequently but regularly in most research universities. Any new course design and teaching involves a considerable amount of effort compared with teaching a course that has been in existence for a long time.

How to offer effective teaching that leads to learning by students is a question that has gained importance. No single answer to this has been accepted unanimously yet. Even accepted approaches to effective teaching might change with new technologies. Hence, teaching itself is a subject in need of constant innovation, and faculty who are involved in teaching are the ones who work on innovations by conducting research in teaching besides doing the teaching itself. Conducting research consumes extra effort but can generate valuable output for education. Hence, innovation and research in teaching is another teaching activity that faculty may engage in, which is often, and should be, encouraged by universities. This may lead to faculty publishing papers in the field of education.

Faculty members can contribute to education through other ways also, such as writing a textbook for a new course, developing courseware or lecture notes, projects, slides, online courses, and so forth. These contributions must be acknowledged and given due weight by the university.

7.1.3 Service

As research and teaching are the core missions of a research university, a faculty member is expected to contribute effectively to both. However, being an established researcher, he/she is also a member of a professional body of researchers. As these professional bodies function mostly based on volunteer effort in many of their tasks, faculty are expected to provide service to their profession—and most do.

At the simplest level, this may involve reviewing research papers submitted to journals or conferences; as a paper may be sent to two or three reviewers, voluntary reviewing itself involves a significant effort. The peer-review system, which has been honed over centuries by the scientific establishment, is widely regarded by all researchers as necessary and important. Researchers are morally obliged to do their share of work—if you expect your work to be rigorously and fairly reviewed, then you should be willing to do this yourself too.

However, the scientific establishment has many more roles undertaken on a voluntary basis by researchers and faculty. These include the editing of scientific journals, each of which has an editorial board that oversees the overall process of selecting papers for publication. Another example is organizing scientific conferences, which play an important role in the sharing of results and ideas and in networking and collaboration between researchers. Committees largely organize such events, and almost all members serve as volunteers.

There are academies with their own agenda and programmes (e.g., for recognizing research contributions), again mostly run by scientists volunteering their service. In addition, the government and society at large also often seek the services of faculty for various technical inputs, given their expertise and lack of alignment with any corporation or business interest.

Service to the profession is not only valuable to individual faculty members but also important for the prestige of the research university. Most research universities like to see their faculty work as editors of important journals or organize important conferences—these help in their reputation and prestige. While it is service to the profession and outside the university, it serves a purpose for the university also, and so universities encourage it.

Besides the service to the profession, faculty are also expected to do some administrative activities related to the university. Committees peopled by faculty take almost all academic decisions in a university. Any administrative role dealing with faculty normally rests with them. Faculty are also often involved in matters related to students. They provide much of the academic leadership in a university; we will discuss this aspect further in Chapter 8 on governance. Suffice it to say that a faculty member's role in service-related work in a university is significant.

Stating that a faculty may typically spend 20 per cent of their efforts on service has some implications on the university and the faculty. It implies that a faculty should not overcommit time and take too many professional responsibilities. It also means that a university distributes the service effort among faculty members and does not use too much time of any faculty member for its service work. It also has implications on the need for support staff. A university must provide sufficient support staff to handle much of the service activities, while needing only minimal inputs from the faculty.

7.2 TYPES OF FACULTY

It may sound surprising that while the faculty hierarchy is quite flat, with only three main levels (Assistant Professor, Associate Professor and Full Professor), a research university can have many different types of faculty. The general discussion on faculty revolves around the 'regular' faculty, who undoubtedly form the core of a university. However, universities have other types of faculty; in fact, in some cases, the other types of faculty have increased rapidly in recent times. Some of the types of faculty in a research university are as follows:

- Regular faculty;
- Research faculty;
- Teaching track faculty;
- Visiting faculty;
- Professor of Practice;
- Guest faculty; and
- Adjunct faculty.

These are 'position types' in that their roles and expectations are different and their employment contracts are also different. Various other titles also exist: Distinguished Faculty, Institute Faculty, Honorary Faculty, Emeritus Faculty, and so forth. These are more to show the respect for and stature of the person, although contractually, each of these may be one of the afore-mentioned types. Let us briefly discuss the role and responsibility of each of the faculty types.

Regular faculty are the ones who are on regular payroll and have a path to continue in the university until superannuation. Generally, such faculty are tenured, that is, their employment contract extends till superannuation, for most of the later part of their employment period. Before they become tenured, which generally entails an evaluation process, they are considered to be on the tenure track. This period typically lasts a few years. Regular faculty often spend their entire working life in the university.

Regular faculty effectively are the academic core of a university, providing continuity of thought and academic leadership, and strongly influence the culture of the university. They generally are the largest group among all types of faculty. Many academic leadership and management roles (e.g., Dean, Head of the Department, Chair of Committees, and so on) are handled by regular faculty.

Regular faculty are expected to engage actively in all three dimensions of faculty work: research, teaching and service. Although some dimensions may become more dominant from time to time (e.g., when one is assigned an important administrative task or some specific roles, e.g., Dean), the normal expectation is a contribution in all three dimensions.

The quality of regular faculty mainly determines the quality of a university, as they influence not only teaching but also research, as well as administration. The quality of this faculty group is also the magnet to attract new faculty and PhD students. They are the ones who bring research grants and industry projects to the university.

Regular faculty are expected to excel in both teaching and research. However, some may not be strong on both the dimensions, although they may be very good or even exceptional teachers. There are clear examples of excellent teachers whom students love and who can motivate students to achieve and learn but who are either not very interested in research or not very good at it. Such faculty may not 'fit the bill' for a regular faculty appointment, although they can contribute effectively to the university mission. Having teaching track faculty positions, in which the faculty is expected to engage much more in teaching and less in research, helps in leveraging the talent of such faculty effectively.

Teaching track positions in many research universities have been considered as different from that of regular faculty. Many universities, particularly in USA, often have different titles for such faculty rather than the regular titles of Assistant Professor, Associate Professor and Full Professor. This view, however, clearly gives more weight to research in its value system. For a research university that states equal importance to the teaching and research missions, the value of 'only or mostly research matters' is inherently contradictory to its mission.

An alternate way to view the situation is that strong contributions to research and teaching are expected from faculty, and some members can contribute more through teaching and less through research. In fact, the system should encourage this approach—to allow a faculty to contribute based on his/her strength and interests. In this approach, the expectation of contribution to teaching increases, and the expectation of contribution to research decreases correspondingly. For example, the number of courses a teaching track faculty teaches can be more than that taught by a regular faculty, while the expectations in terms of research can be correspondingly lesser. In other words, a teaching track faculty is a regular faculty with different expectations in the two dimensions.

It should be pointed out that this rebalance of expectations cannot become fully in favour of teaching. Not only would this be against the mission of a research university, but it can also compromise the level of teaching. Without research, it is hard to keep a course contemporary with the latest developments, which is a key aspect of teaching in a research university, setting it apart from teaching in other universities or colleges. Also, it can limit the teaching contributions a faculty member makes, as other dimensions of teaching (e.g., guiding master's or bachelor's student projects, starting new courses, and so on) will not get the adequate support they need from engagement in research. Hence, the total number of teaching track positions is best kept limited in a research university.

Let us consider the example of teaching track faculty positions in IIIT-Delhi. The objective of having these positions is to value education. Hence, a teaching track faculty should be just another regular faculty. For teaching track faculty, the number of courses to teach each year is one higher (from three to four), and the expectations on research are somewhat lower. The number of such faculty positions is limited. A faculty can move from teaching track to regular through the standard process. Therefore, for a faculty to opt for teaching track is conceptually not an irreversible decision.

Faculty can be recruited for teaching track positions. Some regular faculty may opt to shift to teaching track too. This is likely to be the case when an individual realizes with time that he/she enjoys teaching more and is not as excited about research and all that it entails. That is, with time, a faculty may find his/her strength in teaching and work according to his/her strength. With this, both regular track faculty and teaching track faculty form the regular, tenure track faculty of an institute.

Research track faculty are those who are typically recruited to work on research projects, and their salaries come from project grants, or 'soft money'. They may teach some course sometimes but are often not required to do so. This track is not widely used, and in India it is rarely used.

Visiting faculty, guest faculty and Professor of Practice are all positions to tap talent from different talent pools, mainly to contribute to the teaching function. A visiting faculty may be a full-time (or part-time) faculty, which means that the person is an employee of the university. A visiting faculty is expected to contribute not only in the teaching of courses but also in student

242 | Building Research Universities in India

guidance. As research expectations are minimal from such faculty, they are expected to teach more courses. They may be given some administrative responsibilities too.

A Professor of Practice is essentially a long-term visiting faculty, except that the source base for this is professionals with industry experience. Typically, these are people who have spent a considerable amount of time in the industry and, perhaps, got tired of the business and other related pressures, and who have the desire to teach young minds and share their experience with them. They might not have the necessary degree qualifications for a regular faculty position but might have a great deal of experience that can be leveraged for many technology- or application-based courses. Such faculty can bring in the real-world experience, which most regular faculty often lack, and are consequently very valuable for teaching such courses or introducing newer courses in cutting-edge technologies.

Guest faculty are people who are effectively given a contract to teach a course, that is, they are not appointed as employees. Their only commitment is to teach the assigned course and do all the work related to teaching the course. Given that guest faculty only need to spend a few hours every week, these people can be in regular employment elsewhere and may do this extra work. The motivations for taking up such a role are many: to contribute to education and be in touch with young minds, to stay connected with academia (perhaps to facilitate later transition to it), to earn some extra money, to add to their experience, and so forth.

In many countries, the number guest faculty (and perhaps visiting faculty) is growing rapidly—even faster than regular faculty. From a university's perspective, guest faculty are a lower-cost resource for teaching a course. Regular faculty are typically quite expensive and are expected to perform a variety of roles; hence, positions are created for them only with a long-term perspective in mind. Guest faculty, with the minimal role of teaching a course, only need to be paid modestly and can also be effectively used to take care of any short-term peak teaching demands. In India, many universities use 'ad hoc appointments' of faculty. These are temporary appointments, often for a year, with a lightweight process for selecting the faculty, who are like visiting faculty.

Adjunct faculty appointments are honorary; they are not given any salary. They are typically full-time employees of other organizations but want to engage with academia to give their advice and inputs and perhaps engage in research projects. A standard profile of adjunct faculty is that they may be working in a research lab for the government or in a corporation but want to engage with students and some research groups in a university. Being associated with a university might also provide added prestige to the person. To the university, they provide linkages to other organizations and their advice and inputs to various research projects. As they can co-guide a thesis, they also increase the capability of the university of guiding theses and projects. The main challenge in this appointment is that they have minimal expectations, and hence often do not result in much collaboration or activity.

Similar to adjuncts are honorary faculty positions. These are often given to distinguished faculty who may have retired after a long period of service to a university, or to famous scientists. Their role is largely whatever they wish to engage in. The benefit to the university is having the presence of these distinguished people, and the benefit to the faculty is that they have a home base in a university.

A university may have some other temporary or contractual positions for some supporting roles in teaching—teaching fellows, instructors, and so forth. These are not faculty positions in that, generally, these people cannot teach courses independently and guide theses, but they support faculty in various ways—conducting tutorials, taking a few lectures, helping in assessment, conducting lab sessions, and so forth.

7.3 FACULTY RECRUITMENT AND APPOINTMENT

Recruitment and appointment of faculty is one of the most important tasks of a research university. While large universities delegate this role, particularly at the entry level, to colleges or departments, it may be managed by the central leadership team in smaller universities.

An essential principle for an appointment is that the body that recommends appointment and the authority that accepts the recommendation should be distinct. Inputs from the unit where the faculty is to be placed must be widely taken and given due weight; although, sometimes, the views of a department that supports recruiting a person may not be accepted, it should not be the case that someone the department strongly recommends is not recruited.

7.3.1 Recruiting Regular Faculty at the Entry Level

Let us first discuss what a research university looks for when recruiting a new faculty at the entry level—typically an Assistant Professor or a lecturer. Then, we will discuss the process of selection and appointment. Research universities typically recruit PhD graduates from other research universities—this is to be expected, because the focus is on research, and so PhDs from research universities are likely to have a better alignment with the research goals.

7.3.1.1 Assessing a Candidate

It is evident that research universities are looking for faculty members who are excellent in research and teaching. A key point is that excellence is expected in the future, that is, recruiting faculty is about assessing their potential to excel in research and teaching. This is important to understand because, typically, the record of a recently graduated PhD, who is typically the candidate for consideration at the entry level, cannot really fully demonstrate excellence in either teaching or research; the record has to be supplemented with judgement.

For assessing the research potential of a candidate, the past research record, as demonstrated by the quality and quantity of publications, is looked at most carefully. In general, this is the primary contribution of the research work done during a PhD, as PhD students often do not get opportunities to explore other aspects of doing research, such as guiding other students, preparing research grant proposals, and so forth.

The quantity of research is generally measured in terms of the number of publications or the range of results achieved. However, assessing the quality of research work done is a challenge, as their work is recent and has not had sufficient time to show impact. Hence, the potential for impact and the significance of the research done have to be assessed. One proxy that is often used for this is the stature of the publication venue; a paper published in a highly reputed journal or conference (say with a high impact factor) is broadly assumed to be of a higher quality compared with ones published in less prestigious venues. Another indirect measure is comments by peers about the work—generally, recommendation letters for candidates comment on the quality of the research done.

Often, the assessment of research capability and past work is done by listening to a seminar given by the candidate to explain the work he/she has done. Through this seminar, administrators and faculty in the discipline gain a better understanding of the problems the candidate has worked on, their significance and importance and the quality of the results of the research. A seminar may be followed by interactions in which faculty may try to understand various other aspects of the work done. Often, some faculty members, particularly those working in the area in which the candidate has done a PhD, read key papers or reports of the candidate. Through these methods, the research potential of the candidate can be assessed reasonably well.

The teaching ability of the candidate has to be judged, because most PhD programmes do not offer opportunities to demonstrate or develop teaching capabilities. A PhD student might have been a teaching assistant in some courses. The exposure one gets in these roles, though valuable, is very limited. In other words, the résumé of the candidate itself can provide very little information for assessing his/her teaching ability.

There are two aspects generally assessed for evaluating the candidate's teaching capability. The first one is the communication capabilities, in a broad sense—good communication skills to communicate and explain difficult concepts. An important method for assessing this is the seminar the candidate gives, which gives some idea about his/her communication capabilities. In many universities, the candidate is often asked to give a lecture on a standard topic with which the candidate is familiar. This lecture is to assess the lecturing capability of the candidate directly. Besides these, communication skills are also assessed during meetings of the candidate with various administrators and faculty.

The second aspect is the subject matter expertise in courses the candidate expects to teach. A faculty has to often teach a few different courses on different topics, many of which may be outside the direct area of research. It is assumed that, for many courses, a faculty can gain the subject matter knowledge. However, a good foundation in the subject matter is often desirable. This is often assessed by looking at what courses the candidate has done during his/her master's and PhD programmes. The project and the research work the candidate has done, if closely related to the subject to be taught, provide other indicators that the candidate has a good understanding of the subject matter on which he/she can build upon to deliver a good course on the subject.

Besides the research and teaching capabilities, there are some other desirable personality traits which are hard to assess, such as taking initiative, getting along well with colleagues, having the ability to collaborate, and so forth. These are sometimes indicated by responsibilities the candidate might have been entrusted with, work he/she might have done that did not count towards the thesis, hands-on projects that might have been done by the candidate, and so forth.

7.3.1.2 Recruitment Process

Recruitment, of course, starts with candidates applying for faculty positions. Highly reputed universities may not need to be proactive in this step and can still expect the best candidates to apply. However, for most universities, a proactive approach can help. In today's world, where all talented people are essentially global citizens and good talent is being sought globally by universities, it is important to reach out to potential candidates and guide them to consider one's university. This proactive reaching out (for which various strategies can be evolved, such as engaging with PhD students in conferences) also communicates to the candidate that the university values talent and is excited about having him/her in the university. That he/she is wanted is often a factor in the decision-making by a young person who has recently completed a PhD, as many scholars want to work in an environment that values them and supports their efforts and aspirations.

Once candidates have applied, their applications have to be processed. Most established universities typically process these applications together; often, once a year, they look at applications and shortlist candidates to be invited. This might be suitable for an established university, which often has a few faculty positions and needs to look at all applications to decide. Large universities also, for logistical reasons, often want to process applications together. Again, a young university may respond quickly to applications as they are received. By processing each application on its own merit and soon after it is received allows the university to respond fast to the application, which is clearly an advantage in the struggle for talent. This approach is feasible for a young university, provided it has a good sense of the quality level of faculty it wants to recruit; each candidate can be assessed against this (unspecified but understood) quality benchmark, and decisions can be taken based on this.

A specific process should be followed while deciding on a candidate. The process should be thorough and rigorous; in the pursuit of talent, the evaluation process should not be compromised.

A candidate must prove his/her competence in all aspects. A shallow process that does not put the candidate through careful scrutiny and assessment might also communicate to the candidate that a university does not have the capability for rigorous evaluation. Also, it is psychologically well established that if a process of achieving something is hard, even painful, then the achievement is valued more, and conversely, if something is too easily achieved, it might not be valued highly. Hence, shortening the process to attract a candidate might actually backfire.

We have discussed how research and teaching are assessed. These imply that the candidate must give a research seminar, deliver a lecture and meet many faculty members, particularly those working in the candidate's area and in related areas. This necessarily should involve a visit to the university, with seminars and meetings scheduled. Also, letters of reference from people who can comment on the quality of the candidate's work must be sought.

Clearly, a department in a university should not invite all applicants to visit; only applicants who hold promise should be invited. Although this shortlisting can be done on the basis of the candidate's resume and teaching and research statements, it is better to interact with the candidate. Given the state of technology today, this interaction may be done on video, especially interaction related to the candidate's background, his/her teaching and research interests and plans. Such an interaction, perhaps with the head of the department and some senior faculty, is sufficient to assess whether the candidate has the potential to be invited for a formal meeting and full interaction. This interaction is also an important step to engage with the candidate and show to him/her how the university is suitable for his/her career aspirations.

The candidate's visit is another opportunity to strengthen or weaken the attraction of the candidate towards a university. A well-organized visit, which takes good care of the candidate and treats the candidate well and with respect, goes a long way in convincing the candidate that the university and the department value him/her and have effective systems to take care of their faculty.

In India, in most public universities, often, the final recommendation about a candidate is made by a 'selection committee', which generally has a few experts external to the university and one or two members from within the university. This selection committee meeting is often difficult to schedule. Therefore, universities often organize these once a year, during which all candidates are processed.

Organizing the interaction of the selection committee with the candidate and inviting the candidate for interaction with the faculty are often challenging. If these two are combined, it necessarily implies that one day all candidates will visit, give seminars and meet faculty, following which they will interact with the selection committee. This is a challenging process to manage and schedule and also leads to delays in processing applications. With technology, it is clearly possible to separate these two interactions, with one of them being scheduled during a visit and the other one organized through electronic means. Often, universities give more weight and importance to the selection committee interaction and have this scheduled in the face-to-face mode. However, for a decent research university with its own capability for assessment, it is actually better to use the physical visit for seminars and interactions with the faculty. This requires more time and is the more substantive part of the process. Given the statutory requirement that the final recommendation can be made only by a selection committee, the outcome of this visit is actually a recommendation to the selection committee itself, which uses its own assessment too. This makes the overall process more rigorous and preserves the ability to process each application as it comes while preventing the process from becoming cumbersome.

7.3.1.3 Focus Areas for Recruitment

A somewhat different aspect of faculty recruitment is deciding which areas faculty should be recruited in. This is clearly an important aspect, particularly when a department has many faculty in some areas and few or none in other areas. This is also important if the university or a department wants to launch a new educational programme or a research centre, which requires recruiting faculty with expertise in some specific areas.

Often, departments and universities have some focus areas for recruiting faculty. Having some such defined focus areas is desirable. A common and least conflicting approach to identify these areas is to see which areas are still not 'covered' by existing faculty and give preference to candidates in those areas. Although this might be a suitable approach for a teaching-focused university, this is not a smart approach for a research university. A research university should decide the focus areas based on the research areas it wants to strengthen—presumably, emerging areas where it may want to build strength or areas where it is already well placed and wants to strengthen further to take a leadership position. There must be faculty to teach the basic and important courses in different educational programmes, but a research university need not necessarily aim to provide courses on all topics; it is acceptable if some topics are left out, or if some faculty, though not working in the area, offer to teach it.

However, while strengthening an area, a teaching issue comes up. Faculty in an area want to teach similar types of courses, and if some faculty members are already active in that area, most of these courses might be already 'taken' or 'covered'. A faculty is required to teach a specific number of courses in a year. Hence, it should be ensured that he/she has courses to teach besides the possibility to teach some courses in his/her area. The incoming faculty member should clearly know at the time of recruitment what types of courses he/she might be able to teach and should plan for introducing some new desired courses. Due to this constraint on teaching, a group in an area cannot be too large in a university, unlike in a research lab. Therefore, even in a hot area (e.g., currently, artificial intelligence), where a research lab in a corporation can have many researchers working on various research projects, a department will probably have only a few faculty members in that area. This is also necessitated by the fact that there are limited faculty lines, whose numbers are decided by complex formulas or negotiations in the university. Further, a good department must have research groups in multiple areas and also provide sufficient breadth necessary for an academic department.

When recruiting faculty in an area that is already represented, a sound principle is to go for candidates who, while working in the area, bring strength and value in some aspects that are lacking. The case for candidates who bring nothing 'new' is weaker, because just replicating some capability adds little value. Hence, the view to keep in mind is that of overlapping circles—the candidate has knowledge and capabilities in existing areas but also has some additional capability and knowledge, so that the addition of such a candidate expands and strengthens the overall capability in the area.

There is one more aspect worthy of some thought. Although it is good to have focus areas, it should be kept in mind that these focus areas shift from time to time and that faculty themselves do not often remain in an area through their entire academic life—they may change their areas. In this context, it is important not to take focus areas too seriously; while looking for candidates in focus areas, a department and a university should always be looking for excellent candidates in any area within the discipline. Excellent faculty, regardless of the area, can strengthen the research culture and the academic and intellectual environment of the department. Moreover, if they later shift areas, such faculty are likely to be strong in their new area also. Thus, in the long run, often, such faculty can make significant contributions. Therefore, the opportunistic approach to faculty recruitment should also be taken—if an opportunity to recruit a top candidate comes, then it is tapped regardless of the area in which the person is working.

7.3.1.4 Recruiting Initial Faculty

For a young university, or one that is starting, how the university fares in the future depends on how it attracts and recruits junior faculty at the entry level while having some senior faculty to help provide the administrative depth and leadership. The first few recruits are critical, because a core of good faculty attracts other good faculty. Most candidates, when looking for a faculty position, inevitably see the profile of existing faculty and make judgements about the university based on that profile. Hence, it is critical to recruit high-quality faculty at the start.

As new institutions are often in a rush to start their educational programmes and expand, recruiting high-quality faculty is a big challenge. Once educational programmes are started and students are admitted, courses must be taught. Often, in an attempt to have faculty to teach these courses, the situation becomes desperate, and in desperation, average faculty is recruited. This can considerably damage faculty recruitment initiatives in the long run; the first few candidates often set the standard for faculty, and once the standard is lowered, its improvement becomes much harder and slower. Thus, the best approach is to give sufficient time to recruiting faculty before starting educational programmes. However, often, this does not happen in India—institutions are announced and then started in temporary premises within a short time (as was the case with IIIT-Delhi). In such a situation, an alternative is to have some arrangement with existing institutions to provide faculty for teaching initial courses and, through this, gain time for recruitment.

As the initial set of faculty members can be critical in future faculty recruitment, providing additional incentives to the initial faculty is a good practice. Besides, these faculty members are the ones who are taking a larger risk, which should be recognized and valued. Once some critical mass of faculty has joined a university, the risk for later joinees is less; not only has the university itself stabilized, the presence of a sizable faculty shows the stability of the university and ensures that the working environment is decent. In fact, the incoming faculty can check their interactions with the existing faculty about the working environment and support from the university. Another reason for not just having good initial faculty but also supporting them well is that they are the magnet and ambassadors for future faculty recruitment.

It is desirable to give as good a compensation and support as possible, and something extra for a limited duration to the initial faculty. While compensation helps, good junior people join a university only if they are attracted to the vision and mission of the university, its focus on and support for research and the leadership of the university. Most good-quality PhD graduates are excited about the possibility of making their mark in research and want to actively engage in it. Good PhD graduates are simply not available primarily for teaching positions, making it easier for research universities to attract such candidates. If a research university has an exciting vision backed by good leadership and suitable policies, it has a better chance of attracting good PhD graduates as junior faculty.

7.3.2 Recruiting Senior Faculty

The purpose of recruiting senior faculty is completely different than the purpose of recruiting junior faculty. Senior faculty are generally recruited to develop some research areas in the department and university. This works well for areas that are not well represented in the department and the university but where there is a desire to grow them. The traditional route is to make the area a thrust area and then recruit junior faculty in it. This route is slow and takes many years to build a credible group that is respected in the community of the area. An approach that speeds up this process is to recruit a senior faculty member, hopefully a well-established 'star' in the area, and then give him/her the responsibility to build the area. The presence of such people can then act as a magnet for getting high-quality junior faculty. The senior person can not only provide an anchor and visibility for the group but can also help mentor junior members of the group.

Although the technical process for recruiting senior faculty may be the same as that for junior faculty, the process of engagement is likely to be different. First, often, senior people do not apply; they have to be approached informally or through contacts to gauge their interest. The initial engagement and visits are often informal, during which the senior person assesses whether his/ her aspirations can be met in the potential host institution and the university assesses whether the prospective candidate will fit well in the culture and environment of the university and the department. Often, discussions are held regarding labs, support and other facilities that may be provided to the senior person. Following a broad agreement between the university and the senior person, the formal process may be kicked off to complete the recruitment.

In India, the culture of shifting at senior levels is virtually non-existent. A senior faculty is rarely seen to move from one institution to another. This is because the level of ease of mobility in the society, which is impacted by issues such as admission in schools for children, opportunities for the spouse, proximity of relatives and friends, and so forth makes it rather hard for people to shift after being in one place for an extended period. Also, some institutional rules and practices do not permit providing incentives for attracting a senior faculty, and without strong incentives, such a move is challenging anywhere.

7.3.3 Recruiting Other Types of Faculty

Recruitment of other types of faculty is relatively easier, as it does not involve long-term commitments. Internal processes for such recruitment may be less rigorous. Often, there may be a standing committee to consider applications for such types of faculty, particularly when offering contracts for a year or so, which is initially the case for most such appointments.

While the process may be shorter and quicker, such candidates do not naturally apply or approach a university for faculty positions. Since these positions are not very visible and are generally not advertised widely, people often do not know about these possibilities. Consequently, people who can be good guest or visiting faculty have to be sought out. This is even more so for Professors of Practice—practitioners are not really looking at universities for opportunities, even if they are inclined towards and interested in working with academia.

This means that such people have to be reached out to with proper messaging and through formal and informal networks. Then, there are retired professionals—they may sometimes contact a university but often have to be introduced. In other words, the methods used to attract these faculty are completely different from those employed for regular faculty. For regular faculty, the target is the research fraternity and PhD students—a community that is intricately tied to universities and which universities understand well. Here, the target is professionals and practitioners—a target group with which universities often have few connections and who also have a limited understanding of academia. Hence, different channels have to be explored and activated. These faculty clearly enrich the academic environment and course offerings.

Some of them have to be cultivated and developed so they can contribute effectively. As they do not know the needs of different programmes, they are often not able to even suggest what courses they may be able to teach. They often also have a different view of teaching, thinking that it is mostly about designing courses and giving lectures to students who are eager to learn. They may not be aware of many other aspects of teaching a course, in particular, assessment, which requires a lot of effort and which may not be as exciting as designing and lecturing. Therefore, expectations have to be set, and their course designs have to be carefully evaluated and guided well so that the course is pitched intellectually and content-wise at the right level. Without guidance, often, the course may either be too lightly loaded with some simple assignments or too heavily loaded with complex projects.

Leveraging this talent pool for education requires one to be flexible; often, such professionals may not be very interested in offering traditional academic courses. If one was to look for such professionals to teach from a set of defined courses, then the scope of engagement would be limited. On the contrary, if a university is flexible and willing to explore the possibility of designing courses that add value to academic programmes, and can leverage the strength of such resources effectively, then this engagement can be more fruitful. Programmes always have discipline electives and open electives, offering some special courses in the discipline and, in general, an interesting course that may provide a better understanding of a few aspects of the professional and real world.

7.4 FACULTY ADMINISTRATION

Managing faculty is not like managing human resources in the corporate sector—it is fundamentally different. First, faculty are essentially autonomous agents who largely decide their own work; they do not have a boss to whom they 'report' and who can assign them work. Although some work is assigned, for example, courses to teach and committees to serve on, these are often done in a collegial manner rather than being 'assigned by a boss'. The research work the faculty undertake is completely decided by themselves.

Faculty generally are adverse to authority; in fact, one of the reasons for joining an academic profession is 'not to have a boss who will tell what to do'. Faculty, like many other professionals, tend to be very competitive. Further, 'teamwork', which is practised in industry and in large projects, is not the norm in a university. Most research teams are headed by one or a few professors and consist of research staff on their projects and students working for them. All this makes people management a challenging exercise. Thankfully, the goals of a university are such that rather than delivering on a task, excellence is what is desired. Hence, light-touch management, expecting sound output and performance in research and teaching, works well.

The goal of this management is also somewhat different than what it might be for a corporate. Rather than having people contribute towards corporate goals, the objective of faculty management is to ensure that faculty achieve their expected goals of excellence in research and teaching. If most faculty can operate to their potential, the best possible outcome for a university is also achieved. Some of the tools that are often used for ensuring that faculty performance remains high are briefly discussed here—we use examples from IIIT-Delhi.

7.4.1 Yearly Review

Filing a yearly report of contributions by each faculty member in the previous year is a standard technique in many research universities across the world. As much of faculty work is not assigned and is self-determined, such a report is essential to clearly understand what a faculty has contributed. This differs from the processes in a company where the assigned job is well understood and the yearly appraisal depends more on how well a person has done. (In fact, even in a university, the non-faculty staff are not necessarily required to prepare a yearly report of their contributions.) Capturing the yearly contributions is required for faculty before an appraisal of their yearly performance can be done.

The accurate compilation of this report is in itself very useful. Faculty are smart and perceptive; an individual faculty looking at his/her own yearly report can make a fair assessment of how the year went. As faculty are frequently driven by intrinsic motivation, self-assessment, for which a detailed yearly report is useful, can itself often provide them the first level of feedback.

The criticality of an accurate system of yearly reports by faculty also needs to be understood. Almost all contributions to research, research grants, teaching, service, and so forth have faculty involvement. What a department or a university has contributed in a year is basically a sum total of what all has been captured in the yearly reports of the faculty. In this sense, yearly faculty reports provide the basic data for preparing any report about the department or the university's annual contributions. Without any comprehensive yearly report of faculty contributions, it is impossible to accurately assess the university's performance and how it has changed over the years. Most public universities have to submit their annual reports to government agencies. Moreover, such reports may also be needed for legal reasons. Analysis required for accreditation and other such agencies also often relies on the data from faculty yearly reports. Hence, a sound system of faculty yearly reports is essential.

In India, research institutions require data on publications, grants, and so forth for preparing the department report. However, requiring complete individual reports by faculty for yearly contributions are not a common practice.

For capturing the main contributions during a year, the template used for yearly reports should be such that it allows the capturing of various aspects of faculty contributions that align with the university's mission and vision. It must capture contributions made by faculty towards research, teaching and service. Some measures on impact can also be included in the template of yearly reports, although impact is better understood with longer time horizons than a year.

As an example, let us discuss the template used at IIIT-Delhi for reporting the yearly contributions. Besides different sections for research, teaching and service, IIIT-Delhi also has sections to report on impact, awards and recognitions received. Some important research aspects captured are:

Publications
Papers published in top-tier venues
Other papers published
Books and book chapters published

Sponsored projects
Sponsored projects sanctioned or submitted
Major consultancy projects

PhD students
Students who graduated in the year and where they are placed
Students currently working

Patents, technologies developed and deployed and spin-offs

List of patents filed

List of technologies that may be transferred to other companies

Any start-up that may have been started using the research work

Impact

Impact on research community—total citations and changes from the previous year

Impact on industry (number of users, licenses, installations, income, and so on)

Impact on the government or society

Awards and recognitions

Note that publications are listed in different categories. Assessing faculty research performance is challenging, with many issues (Braxton and Bayer 1986; Lim 2006). Assessing research publications has challenges, as there are many venues available, and there are many types of publications even in one journal. One approach is to group publications with respect to the quality of venues, for example, top-tier, second-tier, and others. Interestingly, although tiers are often broadly well understood by the research community, enumerating these for any formal purposes might be very challenging; sometimes, a favourite and an important venue for publication by a faculty might not be viewed favourably by the overall community. Separating venues into tiers, despite operational difficulties, helps in creating a culture and an environment of publishing in top-tier venues, which, in turn, necessarily increases aspirations of the quality of work. This message also gets passed on to PhD students, who then aspire to get their work in good venues. Using the quality of venues as a proxy for quality of research is not suitable for an in-depth assessment, though it can suffice for a quick yearly review. Counting book publication has its challenges, particularly on what is the weight of a book as compared to research publications (Braxton and Bayer 1986).

The portion of the report that captures services is straightforward—it requests the faculty to list all the services provided to the university and the profession the previous year, and any other service that might have been provided. Assessing service has its challenges and is influenced by how the department and the institute value service (Seldin 2006b).

Reporting on teaching-related activities is to capture contributions to teaching. As discussed earlier, teaching work involves not just teaching courses but also student guidance and other contributions. Student guidance is an important aspect of teaching, and the nature of it also depends on educational programmes. If programmes allow for an undergraduate thesis or independent study or project, then contributions to these should also be captured. As an example, some elements reported as teaching contributions in IIIT-Delhi are provided:

Course feedback
The number of students registered, number of responses, and average student feedback
Summaries of courses

Students guided
Undergraduate thesis, independent study/research/project completed
Master's thesis/scholarly papers, etc. completed

Other teaching contributions
New courses designed, special modules and lecture notes

As discussed in the chapter on education (Chapter 3), a course summary is also prepared for each course, which captures not only the student feedback but also innovations that might have been developed during the course, types of comments received, and so forth. This is a condensed form of teaching portfolios (Devanas 2006), and it provides more information about teaching, so the teaching assessment is not just dependent on student feedback, which has limitations (Pallett 2006).

The preparation of a yearly report serves an important goal of providing a structured input for self-assessment. However, the next question is what a university or a department should do with it. Any report on which nothing depends eventually becomes a chore, and submitters realize that it is merely a formality, inevitably leading to incomplete and shoddy reporting. This also compromises the accuracy of the annual reports of departments and universities.

One action that can be taken is to share yearly reports with colleagues in the department. This helps all faculty to have a view of what others are doing and encourages transparency about the functioning. This sharing permits an informal peer review of the yearly report by colleagues, motivating a faculty to ensure that the yearly report looks good.

Most research universities also have a specific type of yearly review based on the yearly report. The review, which has to be conducted by senior faculty from the discipline, can assess the contributions in the three dimensions, and feedback may be provided to the faculty on these. The contributions may also be assessed on a particular scale. Having a broad scale, rather than having a fine scale, is better to capture the level of contribution of a year qualitatively. However, whenever scales are used, guidelines for how performance is to be rated need to be evolved. Assessing the contributions of a faculty accurately is quite hard and challenging (Seldin 2006a). Also, the evaluation is always subjective and hence never uniformly agreed upon. However, the level of performance in the discipline is often not too hard to assess particularly by experienced faculty. Ensuring that the assessing committee is unbiased and is perceived to be so is important. Although disagreements may be there in the committee's assessment, its integrity and intent should not be in doubt in the minds of the faculty. (At IIIT-Delhi, the committee comprises some senior academics from other institutions also.)

What should be done with the review outcome? Of course, first, it is to be communicated to the faculty. This also provides a good opportunity for a university to have a formal one-on-one interaction with the faculty, understand their perspective or challenges and maybe even seek their views on some matters of importance to the university. These one-on-one meetings are best held at a department or centre level. Involving the Dean or the Director in such meetings is excellent and desirable, which provides the personal interaction and direct connection of faculty with senior administrators. In IIIT-Delhi, the Director meets each faculty member individually. This opportunity is also used by faculty members to provide inputs on some important issues. Overall, this yearly meeting of senior administrators with an individual faculty is an excellent practice with many potential benefits.

Given that there is subjectivity and that reviewers might err, allowing faculty to 'rebut' review comments is desirable, if they want to do so. This is much like how some journals and conferences allow for a rebuttal phase, whereby the author can explain or make arguments in favour of the submission. Such a process makes the exercise fairer and more transparent, although it makes the overall process longer and more complicated. Like in conferences, rebuttal comments can be reviewed and earlier comments and/or review ratings may be changed, or they may remain the same.

After communicating and discussing the review feedback in a one-on-one meeting, one possibility is to just leave it to the faculty to take suitable actions. In such a case, the yearly review really provides a moral force and does not have any 'teeth'. The risk of this approach is that it might become a mere formality that is not taken seriously, defeating the whole purpose. At the other extreme is to follow what companies generally do—yearly increments to the compensation depend on the performance. Some universities do this, but this approach is somewhat at odds with the academic culture and also tends to promote extrinsic motivation over intrinsic motivation. In a country like India, where the whole environment and the educational system are such that the yearly compensation is based on fixed formulas, implementing something like this is not only challenging but also undesirable, particularly since compensation information is not a secret.

An approach followed by IIIT-Delhi was not to let the compensation be affected by the review but make the yearly professional grant given to the faculty dependent on the outcome of the review. In other words, the professional grant was tied to the performance. As these yearly grants were not too large, the impact of the review outcome was not too much. However, this action based on review made the whole process of the yearly review formal—one that was taken seriously by the faculty—which was the main intent of the whole exercise.

7.4.2 Next-Year Plans and Mentoring

A sound performance management practice is to set reasonably ambitious plans for the future, translate them into plans for units or individuals and then try to achieve them. This is a standard approach used by corporations to achieve great results. In academia, such types of plans with targets are often not appropriate, particularly for research, as a university cannot assign research targets to individual departments or units and ask for specific outputs. Also, given the academic freedom, the research plan can only be made by an individual faculty. However, the process of planning and noting down the plan is in itself a beneficial exercise that can help faculty be productive.

Therefore, having some plans for the next year to help faculty achieve ambitious goals is desirable, which in turn can help them achieve their potential—the basic driving force behind faculty management practices. This can be considered more like a self-realization or self-improvement plan, rather than part of a 'corporate plan' to achieve organization-level goals. As most self-improvement pundits and consultants advise, having a plan of what one wants to achieve is almost an essential aspect of higher achievement.

Given that faculty have to make their own plans independently, the next question is what these plans should contain. Aligning with their main work, the faculty should try to specify what they want to achieve in the main dimensions of research, teaching and service. As faculty are often engaged in learning about new areas, which consumes time and may require active planning (e.g., attending a colleague's course or an online course), this can also be added as part of the plan. At IIIT-Delhi, the yearly plan template consists of four components:

- **Research.** Papers to be completed and their targets, projects to be completed, proposals to be written, books to be developed, and so forth
- **Teaching.** Any new initiatives/experiments planned to improve teaching and learning process, new courses planned, preparation of slides or notes for future use, and so forth
- **Service.** Goals in service for the institute and profession
- **Learning and self-growth.** New areas, concepts and technologies one wants to learn

Having a plan is a good idea, as with most such activities. However, if it is left entirely to individuals, such 'good-to-do' things do not get done. Hence, having the plan documented and submitted is desirable, which can enforce the discipline of thinking and documenting plans for the next academic year. If the plan is to be just documented and submitted, the exercise becomes meaningless and degenerates to just 'paperwork'. The whole idea of documenting a plan is to have not only faculty goals but also the possibility of providing advice and inputs on them. Mentors can play a useful role here.

Generally, it is senior faculty who mentor junior faculty. Discussing the yearly plan with the mentor is desirable, who can give inputs and provide guidance. The mentor can also review how the last year's plan panned out—how much of it was achieved, how much got missed, what changes were made due to new opportunities, and so forth. Mentorship can be very useful for the long-term growth of faculty. It needs to be done only in the initial years of a faculty's career; once a faculty has become a senior, this support is not needed. This type of mentorship can be provided only by senior and experienced faculty working in a related area. Often, this mentorship is established informally in a work setup where a junior faculty works closely with a senior faculty. In some places, this relationship may be facilitated. Rarely is it too structured or an administrative instrument.

7.4.3 Faculty Promotion

Promotions are standard in all organizations; generally, in corporations, promotions involve a larger role with more responsibilities. As discussed earlier, academia, having a flat faculty hierarchy, has one standard three-level system that comprises the Assistant Professor, Associate Professor and Full Professor. The normal job is the same at each of the three levels—teaching and research. The main thinking behind having a relatively flat hierarchy in academia is to reinforce the culture that essentially all faculty are colleagues, and a senior faculty is not the boss of any junior faculty. This is how academia has evolved; the hierarchy-less culture, where the importance of people is decided not by their title but by what they contribute and the quality of their work, is really deeply embedded in the academic mindset.

The selection for an entry-level faculty position is based mainly on potential, with the past record given some weight in the assessment of potential. However, for promotion, it is the record that matters the most. One can refine it even further. For promotion from Assistant Professor to Associate Professor, the past record is important, but future potential is also assessed, because the impact might still not be visible (particularly of more recent works). The weight of the record increases even more when a candidate is considered for promotion to Full Professor; the assessment is based almost fully on the record, with future potential given some consideration. (Going further, prestigious fellowships or awards are based exclusively on contributions and impact made.)

Policies for promotion and processes to implement them are needed, which should be such that they support the basic value of research universities, namely, excellence in research and teaching.

The processes for promotion differ from university to university. The discussion here is on the model employed in IIIT-Delhi, which is based on the system prevalent in US universities. (A discussion on promotion and yearly reviews in the US context can be found in [Diamond 2004].)

Technically, in India, most universities do not have a formal concept of promotion. The general approach is that at each level, there are appointments following the laid-out process for appointment. For example, for the 'promotion' of Assistant Professors to Associate Professors, advertisements for the post of Associate Professors are issued, in response to which anyone eligible can apply, including existing Assistant Professors. Then, the standard appointment process is followed, which involves a selection committee comprising mostly external experts who interact with applicants and give their recommendation.

Following this process means that promotions are based on the interview by the selection committee. As experience has shown, when senior people are entrusted with the task of making a recommendation about candidates, they rely mostly on the interaction they have with the candidates; the record of the candidate often becomes a secondary input. This process is suitable for the Assistant Professor position because the potential of the candidate is assessed, for which the opinion of senior experts is valuable. However, for senior levels, it is desirable that the record should speak for itself, and the 'interview' by the committee should not be necessary. Besides, some external inputs from peers can be obtained for more information on contributions to faculty. Then, a committee can assess the record. This type of assessment is consistent with the academic culture wherein assessment based on records is a standard practice—students are assessed and given grades based on their performance, papers are reviewed and their acceptance or rejection is recommended, proposals for possible funding are reviewed, and so forth. Generally, committee-based evaluation relying on suitable records and views from experts is well aligned with the academic system.

Some research universities have evolved methods to support 'promotion' within the framework of the selection committee (which is required). We briefly describe in the following text how this has been done in IIIT-Delhi—a few other institutes also follow a similar method.

Promotion should be based on the performance or past record of faculty. Clear criteria should be followed for promotion, so that faculty know what is expected of them. Quantitative criteria, though clear and unambiguous, are not feasible or desirable for faculty promotions. The combination of quality and quantity, which decides the overall contribution to research and its impact, cannot be captured through metrics. (The president of a US university very aptly captured this sentiment, saying, 'we can promote a person based on one research paper, and we may not promote a person with 20 research papers'.) Research contributions have to be assessed qualitatively, and the best way to assess them is to use the judgement of experts in the particular area about the nature and importance of the contributions, and also how the contributions compare with those of faculty at a similar stage of their careers globally (or any other such comparisons).

To ensure that key contributions are highlighted, a process followed in many universities is to get a focused summary of the contributions made by the faculty, in addition to the full resume. Asking the faculty to list their major contributions, particularly contributions to research, is desirable to focus on quality. Similarly, contributions to teaching and service can be summarized by highlighting the main contributions. For example, the summary to be provided by a faculty for promotion at IIIT-Delhi asks, among other things, for the following:

Key publications and impact
List five best papers (10 for Full Professor) and their impact
Give total citations and h-index

Technologies developed/deployed and patents received/filed
List up to two technologies/patents (five for Full Professor)
with impact

Sponsored projects summary
• Number of sponsored projects completed and their value
• Number of sponsored projects currently at hand and their value
• Total number of consultancy projects and their value

PhD students
• Number of PhD students graduated
• Number of PhD students currently supervised

Courses taught
A table containing key parameters about courses taught:
course name, year and semester; number of students enrolled;
student feedback scores

Students guided (non-PhD)
• Number of master's theses guided
• Number of undergraduate projects guided

Awards and recognitions
List of awards and recognitions such as best papers, journal
editorships, keynotes, well-known prizes/honours from professional societies, etc.

The summary focuses on research and teaching and the stature
of the faculty. To better understand the level and impact of
research contributions, letters from experts in that area to assess
research contributions of faculty, and how they compare with
academicians at a similar stage of their career across the world,
are sought. Different universities may require different numbers
of letters; about half a dozen is quite common. At IIIT-Delhi,
at least six letters are sought, at least half of which have to be
from those on a list of names provided by the faculty, while the
other half can be from those on the list or from other experts.
Also, a general guideline followed is that some experts should be

from within the country and some from outside, to gauge how the academic community within the country and how the global community perceive the contributions.

The summary, the full CV and other records and letters received are then discussed by a tenure and promotion committee of the department. These are senior faculty from within and outside the institute. They discuss contributions and letters and, based on that, prepare a short report for the candidate, which also contains the recommendation of the committee. The report gives their views about the research work (publications, impact, funding, PhD student guidance, etc.), sentiment expressed in the letters from experts, teaching contributions and service contributions. The report also makes an overall recommendation, based on the policy of the institute, whether tenure/promotion should be granted or denied or whether the person should be given more time.

The formality of the selection committee process includes the following: the candidate's record and the committee's recommendation are placed before a formal selection committee, which then may accept the committee's recommendations or modify them. In this process, only the candidate's record speaks; the candidate is not interviewed.

7.4.4 Preventing Faculty Complacency

Faculty complacency is perhaps one of the biggest challenges, particularly in India. There are many examples of faculty members who, at the time of joining as junior faculty after completing their PhD, had a record comparable to their peers in good universities of the world. However, a decade or two later, many of them find a comparison with the same peers much less flattering. The main reason for this is a complacency that often sets in. It is therefore important for the system to prevent complacency from setting in. In India, generally, salary scales and yearly increments are fixed, and therefore, compensation cannot be used as an instrument for motivation. As pointed out by Chandra (2017), there is no tenure system for faculty other than in a few places, and overall, evaluation systems for faculty work are weak. Such a system does not motivate faculty to perform; it rather encourages them to become complacent. Here, we discuss some measures that can be employed in the Indian context to prevent faculty complacency, based on experiences in IIIT-Delhi.

7.4.4.1 Yearly Review and Plans

Getting the best talent is necessary, but nurturing the talent a university gets is even more important. The basic goal of nurturing talent is to provide an environment and system that allows individuals and groups to reach their potential and, indeed, even exceed it. In other words, an academic system should be such that ordinary faculty do extraordinary work and extraordinary faculty do exceptional work. A mechanism of regular feedback on performance is indispensable for this. Without such a mechanism, it is very easy for an individual faculty to become complacent and be satisfied with ordinary achievements because he/she enjoys a very high degree of freedom and does not have pre-specified goals. For both the institute and the faculty, it is essential to have a proper review and feedback mechanism.

A yearly review of contributions made by a faculty is perhaps the single most important measure that can be employed to prevent complacency. As discussed earlier, for this, the faculty member prepares a yearly report of contributions. Feedback by senior people is then given about the contributions, based on this report. Just preparing the report itself helps, as the formal report provides the faculty member a method to self-assess the contributions. The value of the review is enhanced substantially with feedback from senior people. As discussed earlier, the yearly review should be not only of research contributions but also of teaching contributions and quality. It is important to recognize and communicate through these exercises that research and teaching are both important aspects of academics which support each other, and a compromise in teaching will in the long term hurt research.

The annual reporting of contributions and their review can be well supported with faculty yearly plans, which may be discussed with senior mentors for their inputs. Perhaps, the most important method to prevent faculty complacency involves reviewing, planning and mentoring. We have discussed yearly reviews and planning earlier in the chapter.

7.4.4.2 Tenure System

Faculty are often recruited after they complete a PhD, or after a few years of postdoc or other such experience. Just after PhD, neither the person nor the selection committee is fully sure whether the candidate is fit for an academic career with the twin objectives of research and teaching. There are PhD holders who are good at research but either do not like teaching or are not good at it. Also, there are those who can provide good teaching but are not excited about doing research. For the former, a career in a research lab is more suitable; for the latter, a career in a teaching-focused institution or a teaching track position is better. For those who can both do good research and provide good teaching, an academic career in a research-focused university is not only the most suitable but probably also the most rewarding and desirable option.

Whether a faculty can effectively manage a twin-objective academic career becomes clear only after a few years of experience in academia. Unfortunately, if the person is not suitable for such a career, the person does not leave to follow a more suitable and appropriate path but remains in the current job, often due to the 'permanent' nature of academic jobs in India. (As pointed out by Chandra [2017], very few universities in India have a tenure system.) Clearly, such a person is unlikely to succeed in this twin-goal academic career in a research university, and the institution is unlikely to derive the type of output it expects from such a faculty. Even the best academic institutions have faculty members who are not quite fit for the twin-objective career but stay on.

To ensure that only suitable candidates remain in the twin-objective career, it is important to systemically support some movement of faculty in early years. In other words, if a faculty or the institute finds that he/she is not suitable for the twin-objective career, the system should encourage him/her to leave the institution early to pursue careers more suitable for themselves. One of the best models for this is a tenure system in which a new faculty has some initial period to prove, both to himself/herself and to the institute, that he/she is suitable for this career before the job is made permanent. Championed by USA (a discussion of the approach in USA is provided by Diamond [2004]), it is now followed in some form in many countries.

In a tenure system, initially, a faculty is appointed for a specific duration, typically sufficient for promotion to the next level. After this period, an assessment of his/her contributions is done; if he/she meets the tenure criteria, he/she is 'tenured' in that the faculty has a permanent job until superannuation. If the criteria are not satisfied, he/she may have to leave the university.

The criteria for tenure is a major issue, and it must depend on the aspirations of the institution and the context in which the institute exists. In a country like India, where the research ecosystem is rather small and the concept of tenure is not common, it is not desirable to have a strict system of tenure often followed by some US universities, in which the duration given to become ready for tenure is fixed and that there are only two possible tenure outcomes: out or in. A fixed duration for being considered for tenure essentially implies that it is expected that all faculty ramp up their research and demonstrate their research capabilities during that period; it has no room for those who might want to build their research agenda somewhat slowly.

In India, the possibility of giving more time is desirable. Not all faculty ramp up their research swiftly. Also, given the overall higher education ecosystem wherein most faculty jobs are permanent, it is not desirable to have a harsh tenure system. Here, we briefly discuss a tenure system used in IIIT-Delhi.

An Assistant Professor is initially given a contract for 7 years. Normally, 6 years after PhD, an Assistant Professor may be considered for the tenure (and promotion too). A faculty may request, with reasonable reasons, up to a 2-year delay in his/her tenure evaluation. Some reasonable reasons for such a request are child-birth, serious illness in the immediate family, setbacks in work beyond one's control, challenges faced in initial years, and so forth. The tenure process is essentially the same as the process for promotion to Associate Professor, which was discussed earlier.

The outcome of the tenure is not binary; there are three possible outcomes. If a faculty satisfies the criteria, he/she is granted the tenure, and a new contract till superannuation is offered. If the evaluation suggests that the faculty is not fit for a career in a research university, the tenure may be denied (and no new contract is offered). The third option is that, if the faculty has shown potential and progress but has not yet satisfied the criteria, then he/she may be given another 3 years (this can be given maximum once). With this, essentially, only those who are not fit for a research-based academic career are screened out.

With a tenure system, it is necessary to have regular feedback on how a faculty is doing. Thus, a faculty can assess his/her performance on an ongoing basis and has a reasonable sense of what may happen during tenure assessment. Hence, a regular review and assessment of contributions made by a faculty is essential if a tenure system is in place. There are other reasons for having an annual review, as discussed earlier.

Interestingly, contrary to what might be expected, a tenure system does not result in many faculty being denied tenure. Often, if a faculty member is not suitable, he/she will choose to move on, as, with the yearly review, the person realizes his/her level of fitment. Hence, mostly suitable candidates come up for tenure, and so they are mostly successful. (This is the experience in most public universities in USA also.)

7.4.4.3 Large PhD Programme

The PhD programme is indeed a defining aspect of a research university. While not universally true, many successful academics have multiple PhD students working with them—how well PhD students perform gives also an indication of the quality of the research of a faculty. Hence, one of the best ways to keep a faculty active is to ensure that he/she is working with PhD students. For this, it is desirable to have a large PhD programme so that most faculty can attract some PhD students.

To ensure that almost all faculty can attract some PhD students, it is important to provide support or a fellowship for some PhD students. Thus, regardless of whether a faculty gets sponsored research projects, he/she can recruit PhD students. Some minimum level of support ensures that all faculty can have PhD students.

However, it is equally important for the university to not provide easy and unlimited support for PhD students; rather, faculty should be motivated to get sponsored projects to support more PhD students. This can help faculty remain active and avoid complacency.

7.4.4.4 Support for International Collaboration

It is known that international collaborations are a great facilitator of research. These collaborations can also help keep faculty members remain active researchers. If international collaborations are supported by a university, it helps improve the quality and quantity of research done by faculty and enhances the global reputation of the university. One way to encourage international collaboration is to provide support for faculty attending top international conferences—these are venues where often collaboration ideas are seeded.

Most disciplines have international conferences where the best researchers in the field meet; these are excellent forums to present one's work and gain global visibility, as well as establish connections and develop possible collaborations. In some disciplines, for example, computer science, the presentation of papers in conferences is now actually preferred over their publication in journals. Overall, support for presenting papers in international conferences is crucial for a faculty to build an international profile. Attending these conferences, listening to top researchers and finding out about the latest developments in the field also help faculty remain motivated and aspire. In countries like India, finding support for international conferences is quite hard; generally, even sponsored research projects having a budget for travel allow only domestic travel, not overseas travel, unless there is a separate budgetary provision for it. It helps if a university provides some support to young faculty for attending international conferences.

However, it is indeed true that such travels tend to be quite expensive. It is also true that finding a conference that accepts even a shoddy research paper is not very hard. Hence, ensuring that travel support is used mostly for presenting papers in high-quality conferences helps ensure quality, as well as good utilization of funds. Suitable policies have to be built to ensure this, such as separating conferences into different categories or tiers. Otherwise, there is a risk of funds being wasted in attending and presenting works in average conferences, which does not have the desired effect of meeting with top minds, getting inspired or motivated or developing collaborations.

7.4.4.5 Teaching-Research Balance

It is expected that faculty spend approximately half their academic effort on teaching and half on research to contribute towards the two basic missions of a university: teaching and research. Allowing a balance between the two is desirable so that those who are more productive and active in research can contribute more to the institute through research, while those who are less productive in research can contribute more through teaching. In other words, for allowing faculty members to contribute according to their capability/interest, those who are more productive in research should be given a slightly reduced teaching responsibility and those who are less active in research should be given somewhat more teaching responsibilities. This also motivates faculty to remain active in research.

The teaching–research balance—balancing teaching and research contributions so that faculty members can contribute according to their strengths—is one of the most important and controversial aspects in a research university. If the teaching and research responsibilities and expectations are not properly balanced, it might be hard to sustain the focus on research, because some faculty members might not contribute much to research and contribute only as much as others in teaching, leading to dissatisfaction or even demotivation among those who engage deeply in research.

One possible approach to address this is to adjust the teaching responsibility based on research contributions. Having too fine an adjustment is not possible or desirable, but adjusting based on multiple years' output can help strengthen both research and teaching—reducing teaching for those who have contributed excellently in research over time, and asking those who are not much engaged in research to take on more teaching responsibilities and expecting them to perform better at teaching. For example, in IIIT-Delhi, there is a policy that if the research output of the previous few years is excellent, the course-teaching responsibility may be reduced (from three courses per year to one course per semester); if the research output of the previous few years is average, the course-teaching responsibility may be increased (from three courses per year to two courses per semester).

7.5 SUMMARY

Faculty is the main pillar of a research university; everything else revolves around it. Faculty have twin academic goals: good research and good education. This makes them a very talented pool, which is generally in short supply. Hence, it is extremely important to carefully recruit faculty and nurture them. This chapter discussed various aspects of faculty management.

We first discussed the key aspects of faculty work—research, teaching and service. For each of these, we discussed various aspects. Research output can comprise research publications, sponsored research projects, PhD student guidance and technologies developed. Teaching includes classroom teaching, as well as guiding students, and activities that may promote education in the larger ecosystem. Service is the service to the profession as well as that to the university.

We also briefly discussed various types of faculty a university may have. Besides the regular faculty (Assistant Professors, Associate Professors and Full Professors), a university often also has visiting faculty, adjunct faculty, guest faculty, etc. While at the core are the regular faculty, other types of faculty are also valuable for achieving the university missions.

We then discussed faculty recruitment, with focus on recruitment at the Assistant Professor level, where most of the recruitment actually takes place. Recruiting someone at this level requires assessing the potential of the candidate, for which past record, letters from experts, interaction with faculty, interaction with selection committee experts, etc. are evaluated. We briefly discussed recruitment of senior faculty and other types of faculty.

Finally, we discussed the critical issue of managing the faculty. While appointing talented people as faculty is important, it is essential for the talent to be nurtured well. This requires suitable systems to motivate faculty to excel in research and teaching. We discussed a few approaches. Some of the most effective tools for helping faculty remain productive are holding a yearly review of faculty contributions in research, teaching and service, having a well-structured method of capturing their contributions and having a system of providing feedback. Faculty promotions must also be done suitably, with clearly articulated policies that support excellence in teaching and research. Finally, we discussed the critical issue of preventing complacency from setting in and discussed some approaches like the tenure system, yearly review, PhD programme, support for international collaboration, etc. which can help.

Interestingly, the national education policy of India (NEP 2019) also has suggestions regarding faculty, and many of the recommendations are along the lines of concepts discussed in this chapter. It recommends that rigorous and transparent criteria and process should be followed for faculty recruitment and that the criteria should include contributions to research, as well as understanding of the discipline, teaching capability, ability to work in teams, etc. It also recommends that career progression be also based on the evaluation of contributions, and for research, the quality of research should be given importance and only publications in credible and reputed journals be given weightage. It also recommends that the faculty body be a mix of academicians and field practitioners so that good connections with practice can be established, and encourages recruiting some faculty laterally from among practising professionals. There is also a suggestion of a form of tenure system having a probation period of 5 years, with employment becoming permanent based on a rigorous and comprehensive assessment of contributions in this period. The NEP also recommends mentorship of young faculty by senior academics, who can be from outside the university too.

REFERENCES

Braxton, John M., and Alan E. Bayer. 1986, June. 'Assessing Faculty Scholarly Performance.' In *Measuring Faculty Research Performance: New Directions for Institutional Research*, edited by J. W. Creswell. San Francisco, CA: Jossey-Bass.

Chandra, Pankaj. 2017. *Building Universities that Matter: Where are Indian Institutions Going Wrong?* New Delhi: Orient BlackSwan.

Devanas. 2006. 'Teaching Portfolios.' In *Evaluating Faculty Performance*, edited by Peter Seldin and Associates. Boston, MA: Anker Publishing Company.

Lim, Teck-Kah. 2006. 'Evaluating Faculty Research.' In *Evaluating Faculty Performance*, edited by Peter Seldin and Associates. Boston, MA: Anker Publishing Company.

NEP. 2019. *Draft National Education Policy, 2019*. New Delhi: Government of India.

Pallett, William. 2006. 'Uses and Abuses of Student Ratings.' In *Evaluating Faculty Performance*, edited by Peter Seldin and Associates. Boston, MA: Anker Publishing Company.

Seldin, Peter. 2006a. 'Building a Successful Evaluation Program.' In *Evaluating Faculty Performance*, edited by Peter Seldin and Associates. Boston, MA: Anker Publishing Company.

Seldin, Clement A. 2006b. 'Institutional Service.' In *Evaluating Faculty Performance*, edited by Peter Seldin and Associates. Boston, MA: Anker Publishing Company.

Chapter 8

Governance, Leadership and Administration

No organization can thrive without good management, and a research university is no exception. Universities are managed within the framework established by higher education policies of the state or the country. In this chapter, we focus on the internal management of the university and discuss key aspects of managing a research university.

The overall management of a university comprises governance, management or administration and leadership (Gayle et al. 2003). Governance means the structures and processes for decision-making at the institutional level (Middlehurst 2013) for establishing goals, values, policies and directions and overseeing that the decisions taken are implemented. Governance has two important dimensions: academic governance, which focuses on academics, and overall university governance, which looks at all other aspects, including finance and general administration. We discuss both in this chapter.

Governance structures establish policies and make decisions. However, these policies and decisions have to be implemented and followed in the day-to-day administrative functioning of a university, which is the backbone of running any organization.

Finally, leadership is about individuals who influence policies and decisions. Every university has a chief executive, who is expected to provide the main leadership to the university. Examples of how visionary leaders have transformed universities are found in the literature. Effective leaders for research universities now are highly sought after, as the world has realized that talented and visionary leaders can make a huge difference in how a university performs. Many universities often do a global search for the chief executive.

Governance and leadership are of particular importance for developing research universities in a country like India, where, often, universities do not get the benefit of good governance and strong and visionary leadership. The poor state of governance and leadership, and the related processes and structures that perpetuate it, are discussed at length by Chandra (2017). The new NEP of the Government of India clearly identifies this as an area for improvement. The NEP has observed that the governance and leadership of a majority of institutions of higher education in India have been plagued by external interference, which has compromised the autonomy of these institutions, and have not provided the leadership and governance that these institutions deserve. It notices that many decisions are imposed by the regulators or the government on universities, and appointments for leadership roles are made more to distribute favours rather than to find the most competent persons, which leads to a situation where people who do not have the vision or values for providing the inspired leadership and good governance that is needed are appointed as leaders. It also observes that public HEIs are often operated as extensions of government departments and that there is considerable interference in the selection and functioning of the leaders of these institutions (NEP 2019).

In this chapter, we discuss a few key issues related to governance, leadership and administration. Before that, we discuss some key guiding principles for the management of a research university.

8.1 SOME GUIDING PRINCIPLES FOR GOVERNING A RESEARCH UNIVERSITY

Research universities are now large and complex systems with, often, thousands of people in the system, and with a budget often exceeding that of many large corporations. At the same time, expectations from universities have increased—the society and governments expect universities to deliver more value and respond speedily to issues that might be raised or new situations and opportunities that may arise. Clearly, effective and efficient governance is required.

A few different approaches are followed in university governance (McNay 1995; Rowlands 2017; Trakman 2008). The most relevant approaches for contemporary universities in India are collegial, bureaucratic and corporation. Although sometimes these models are discussed as competing, all three operate in most universities today, perhaps in different spheres of university governance. The tension today is regarding the scope of each within the university, particularly the collegial and corporation models.

In the collegial model, also referred to as the university governance by the academic staff (Trakman, 2008), decisions are made by faculty bodies, such as the senate or committees of faculty. Freedom from external control, a democratic approach of decision-making based on views of the faculty, and academic freedom are the underlying concepts on which this model rests. This model of governance, while providing freedom and control to the faculty at large, has no clear responsibilities for individual leaders, making accountability harder. Also, as the primary goal of faculty is academics, governance becomes a part-time occupation for the faculty, which is not aligned with their professional goals. Such a model is also bound to be slow, because it requires extensive consultative processes for all decisions. This governance model has other perceived deficiencies.

In the corporate model, top managers are professional managers whose main responsibility is governance. In such a model, decisions are made by top management personnel and implemented in the organization. In such a model, the top management is responsible for all major decisions, and their own performance is assessed based on how well the organization performs. The corporate model is philosophically at odds with the collegial model.

The bureaucratic model is characterized by processes and procedures and is associated with suitable records and paperwork. This model, though often found cumbersome by users, is essential for the actual implementation of the managerial or collegial model. Hence, it can be seen as necessary for some aspects of university governance. This form of governance need not be in conflict with the other two—it actually supports them.

Although, earlier, some universities were run mostly with the collegial model, a clear trend towards strengthening the corporate-style governance in universities is observed over the last many decades. Many researchers have examined this shift from the collegial to the corporate style (e.g., Shattock 2013; Yielder and Codling 2004). This shift has been necessitated by the changing nature of universities, the context in which they operate and expectations from governments and the public at large of effective and efficient governance of universities.

Today, a combination of professional management and traditional academic approaches is needed in a university (Altbach 2011). This is often also called shared governance, in which both the executive and the faculty share responsibilities and the faculty is involved in most important decision-making (Birnbaum 2004; Stensaker and Vabo 2013; Taylor 2013). Often, the responsibilities overlap, and there is often some tension between the executive and the faculty. Therefore, some guiding principles need to be articulated for the governance and management of research universities. We discuss some of these key principles in this chapter, which have been organized around a few themes. The general principles of sound management of organizations, such as transparency, integrity, fairness, and so forth have not been discussed; the management literature will have much to say about them.

8.1.1 Autonomy and Accountability

Autonomy can be considered as a basic principle of operation for a university. As governments provide significant funds for research universities, there is always a tendency for increased government oversight and control. The governance structure of the university should preserve its autonomy so that all decisions regarding the university are taken within the university by its management structures.

The autonomy of public universities is often viewed as a struggle between the state and the university. Some degree of autonomy is granted to universities by their terms of operation and existing laws. However, the actual level of autonomy at which a university operates is also determined by the working equations between the government and the university that evolve over time. Universities play an important role in evolving these working equations. However, sometimes, autonomy is reduced by the university itself, for example, when difficult internal policy issues are not resolved internally and are referred to the government.

- **Autonomy.** The guiding principle for autonomy is that the research university must strive for greater autonomy.

Public universities are created by the state and supported through public funds. Consequently, it is expected that the state exercises a degree of control over these universities. Autonomy is the degree of control the university has over its matters *vis-à-vis* the degree of control exercised by public authorities. This balance between the degrees of control exercised by the university and public authorities regarding the affairs of a university is dynamic and evolving. In many developed countries, it is now broadly agreed upon that increasing the autonomy of universities is essential for a modern higher education system—the European Union has taken a formal view on this (Estermann 2015; Estermann and Nokkala 2009).

Experience and research indicate that autonomy helps a university in performing better and attracting more funds

(Aghion et al. 2010). The main reason why a state may hesitate in increasing autonomy is that it may lead to universities becoming less accountable to the public at large. However, in the modern context, research universities have become large and complex organizations, trying to respond to the forces of globalization, technology change, changing expectations from students and public, competition for global rankings and prestige, need for enhanced financial resources, and so forth. In such a scenario, providing a higher degree of autonomy to research universities is essential; the university is in the best position to govern itself to face the multifaceted challenges of the twenty-first century and provide desired academic outcomes to students and society.

What does autonomy mean for a public university? The European University Association has identified four key dimensions of autonomy: organizational, financial, staffing and academic (Estermann 2015; Estermann and Nokkala 2009).

Organizational autonomy means the degree of control a university has over its internal administrative structures. Some high-level governance structures are normally stated as part of the terms of establishing a university; these include bodies such as the governing board, senate, and so forth. We have considered these as part of the university's inherent organizational structure. Although these inherent structures must exist and a university might not be able to change them, autonomy with respect to these refers to the degree of control it has in selecting members of these bodies and their composition. Of course, autonomy over its internal administrative structures beyond these inherent structures refers to the degree of control the university has in defining and refining them.

A key aspect of organizational autonomy is with respect to the selection and appointment of the chief executive of a university. The main issue here is who decides who the next chief executive of the university should be. The chief executive may be elected in some manner or may be appointed (Estermann and Nokkala 2009). While election is used as a method in some older European universities, the common method today is that of an appointment. In this case, the question is who appoints the chief executive. If the appointing authority is a body of the university, for example, the governing board, then the university has autonomy in selecting its leader. If the decision rests with a body of the state, then the university does not have this critical autonomy. A person appointed to a post is answerable mainly to the appointing authority. Therefore, if the appointing authority is not the board of the university but some external authority, then, in many ways, the chief executive is answerable not to the university or the board but to the external appointing authority. To resolve this fundamental issue, the chief executive of a university, like the chief executive of business organizations, should be appointed by and answerable to the university.

In India, most research universities often might not have much authority in deciding the composition of bodies such as the governing board. In many cases, most members of the governing board may be some designated government officials or government-nominated members. In some cases, a university's governing board might have powers to nominate members to the board when the term of the existing members expires. Most research universities have no autonomy in the appointment of the chief executive; the state generally makes this decision. Only a few institutions now have this autonomy, and in these, the governing board is the selecting and appointing authority for the chief executive (e.g., IIIT-Delhi, some Indian Institutes of Management). Universities, however, have a fair degree of control over their internal administrative structures.

Financial autonomy is critical and challenging. It means that a university has full control of its finances, incomes and expenditure. Given that public universities take funds from the state, complete financial autonomy is not possible. However, even in this situation, financial autonomy can be enhanced to near-full autonomy if the funding provided to the university by the state is based on some transparent formula or method (e.g., based on the number of students). Such a mechanism effectively implies financial autonomy—while the funding comes from the state, it is predictable, and the university can rely on it and has full control over its financial planning and expenditure.

Staffing autonomy means a university has the control to decide the number of staff positions, recruit staff and decide the terms of employment. In many public universities, the number of staff positions is decided by the state, because it has direct implications on the budgetary support that may need to be provided. However, where formula-based funding is practised, exercising this control is not needed explicitly, and it may be left to the university to decide the staffing level. In India, most public universities get budgetary support from the government, and hence the number of staff positions often needs approval from the state. A few universities have this autonomy also (e.g., IIIT-Delhi).

Most universities across the world have a good degree of autonomy in selecting the staff, including junior faculty. In some European countries, however, appointments at senior levels might need to go through some government approvals. In India, most public research universities have autonomy in appointing staff, including faculty at all levels. Procedural stipulations need to be followed, but the university does the appointment.

The autonomy to decide the terms of employment refers to who decides the salary of faculty and other staff. In many countries, salary scales may be decided by the state. If formula-based funding is being practised, again, this autonomy can also be provided to the university. In India, almost all universities have to follow the government-specified pay scale for faculty and staff. Only a few institutions can decide their own scales (e.g., IIIT-Delhi), but even they are required to follow broad government norms.

Finally, academic autonomy is the ability of a university to make decisions regarding its academic programmes and decide on admission in these programmes. Decisions on academic programmes include introducing or terminating some degree programmes and deciding the structure and content of these programmes, way of delivering the programmes and quality assurance for the same. Most universities in India have autonomy over their academic programmes, although there are some broad national guidelines regarding degree names, their durations, etc.

Autonomy in admission is more complicated. On the one hand, in most US universities that have complete autonomy to decide their own criteria for admission and select students accordingly, often, the criteria are not fully transparent or made public. On the other hand, there are entrance exams in many countries, such as India, and the scores or ranks in these exams are used by universities for admission. In cases where the performance in entrance exams is the sole criterion for admission, universities really have little autonomy in establishing the criteria for admission; they have to admit students based on their performance in these exams. In India, most universities take admissions based on rank in an entrance exam or the school board exam. Some institutions, like IIIT-Delhi, have used their autonomy in admissions to define criteria that are based on the score in the entrance exam but which also give weight to student's achievements in various other dimensions. Performance of students has shown that students who have these other achievements to get benefit in admission, actually do better academically in the institute.

Autonomy does not exist without responsibility and accountability. Society ultimately funds public research universities and has expectations from them. While autonomy is desired, the autonomous governance should ensure that a research university is responsible and delivers value to society, which is necessary for the long-term survival of the university—the society that provides support must benefit from its support.

- **Responsibility**. The university should understand its role in society and its responsibility to stakeholders and should govern itself so that these are fulfilled.

If its societal responsibility is not fulfilled satisfactorily by a university, the state finds ways to enforce it, thus necessarily weakening the autonomy. Hence, it is in the interests of the university to use its autonomy to fulfil its responsibilities to the public and work relentlessly towards its mission.

One aspect of accountability is financial prudence and efficient use of funds. Universities use public funds. Such funds have to be used prudently and for designated purposes. This aspect of university governance has attracted much attention in the recent past, because costs of education have soared across the world. Going forward, universities might be expected to show stronger financial governance and cost reduction.

8.1.2 Shared Governance: Faculty Role in Governance

Given the complexity of managing a large university, and the need to be accountable and respond swiftly to the evolving environment, a research university clearly needs professional management. There are many other reasons for having a dedicated and responsible management team (the executive) working in a corporate-style management.

However, it is also true that academics have thrived in a self-governed environment, and universities are fundamentally different from corporations due to the nature of their goals. Therefore, although using modern governance practices is a need, ensuring that the academic ethos and values are preserved is also needed. Also, in a quest for efficient governance, the main goals of a research university—academic values and pursuit of excellent academics—should not be compromised.

Towards this, a trend that is almost universally followed to have corporate-style governance, while still ensuring that the faculty remain the main decision-makers, is to have an administrative route for the faculty. This has worked well across the world—some faculty members who have a flair and interest in governance can shift from being an academician, with research and teaching as the main pursuits, towards governance, where administration becomes their main task. While this ensures that most of the members of the executive team have a good understanding of academics and university governance, there is still a need for faculty at large to have a role in decision-making. This is achieved by shared governance.

Although the scope of faculty in governance has shrunk, they still play an important role in a university. The authority of the chief executive and senior administrators has increased; however, the collegial model involving faculty still operates in many subtle ways. For example, views of faculty and faculty committees often constrain the decisions the executive authority can take. Therefore, while theoretically the executive authority may take any decision it deems suitable, often, it is the collegial decision-making that influences the decisions. Similarly, while the executive structure can require faculty to teach in a certain manner, effectively, teaching remains mostly free from executive interference.

Shared governance is practiced in most research universities today, in which the power rests with both the executive and the faculty bodies, and none takes decisions unilaterally exercising the power vested in them, but work with a sense of common purpose (Taylor 2013). However, tension remains between the scope of executive and faculty. For a research university, it is important to have some aspects of governance that employ the collegial model with faculty controlling the governance. We point out two important aspects here.

- **Faculty administration by faculty.** Operationally, some roles in the governance structure are always needed to deal with matters related to faculty. Any administrative role that deals directly with faculty must rest with faculty members. Correspondingly, no administrative role having a professional staff leading it should have direct jurisdiction on any aspect of faculty affairs. According to this principle, a registrar who is typically a professional administrator should not have any direct jurisdiction on faculty matters. This principle also implies that a broader input of faculty must be taken on all policies and decisions relating to administration of the faculty.

- **Academic administration by faculty.** This principle is indeed foundational for university governance and is generally followed in all universities. Academics (related to education) is the basic purpose of a university, and faculty is its soul. Historically, faculty has debated long and hard over what should be taught to students and how it should be taught. This aspect is least likely to be understood by non-faculty. All aspects of academic administration must rest with the faculty, and policymaking for academics, including curricular issues, must involve a broad section of the faculty. It does not mean there is no need for professional staff to support or execute various functions of this administration; they are of course needed. As academics is the largest function of a university, the staff size may be substantial for helping in managing it. However, all policy matters related to academics must rest with faculty committees or members entrusted with specific roles.

These two are widely followed in research universities. As the scope of the executive and that of the faculty often overlap, there will still be many areas that will fall under the executive which should have inputs from the faculty. To enhance shared governance in such matters, an approach suggested is to have committees of members from both the executive and the faculty to provide an interface between the two bodies (Taylor 2013).

While there is a clear trend towards the corporate style of governance and increasing the power of the executive, there is a view that shared governance in which faculty have significant role in decision-making is critical for keeping the focus on the academic functions of a university, where academics is an end in itself and not a means to an end, as in businesses (Birnbaum 2004). As research universities pride themselves on their teaching and research, it is essential that shared governance be followed in spirit by the executive and top-level governance engaging with the faculty and taking their inputs for important decisions regarding the university.

8.1.3 Academic Freedom

Academic freedom is, of course, the basic foundation of all academics. This aspect makes universities different from other organizations such as corporations or government labs. Historically, academic freedom was a way to explore and teach as freely as possible and to avoid the restrictions that were often placed by the religious or civil authorities on what could be taught or what topics could be explored. In older times, academic freedom was limited, but it increased rapidly with the rise of research universities, though it has been, and remains, a contested area (Altbach 2001). Although the concept of academic freedom is applicable to both faculty and students, we discuss it here in the context of faculty.

Academic freedom does not seem to have a clear definition, and the degree of freedom enjoyed by universities varies across the world (Altbach 2001). We discuss here academic freedom in the two key missions of a university: how it applies to research and how it applies to teaching. For research, there is a general agreement on what academic freedom means; however, in teaching, the views are not uniform. Let us briefly discuss these two separately.

1. **Full freedom in research.** Faculty largely drive research in universities, and the pursuit of knowledge is the goal. Sometimes, the nature of research questions, or the answers, might be controversial, and sections of the society or governments may not like it. Complete academic freedom in all aspects of research should be maintained and supported in a university, implying that a researcher is free to pursue whatever questions he/she wants to pursue and disseminate the results as wished. It also implies that researchers can question or criticize other researchers' findings or established notions. However, it has another subtle implication, which is sometimes not

fully appreciated by governments or corporations. Given the academic freedom, a university administrator does not have any authority to demand that a faculty member do research on a certain topic. Hence, for any research that needs to be done, the concerned faculty cannot simply be assigned the work—they have to be motivated and suitably incentivized.

2. **Limited freedom in teaching.** Academic freedom can be interpreted as freedom to teach what faculty want in their courses and in the manner they want to. The main goal of education programmes is that students learn. Academic programmes are generally designed carefully, mainly by faculty themselves, to deliver the desired learning. Faculty members together largely control the design of the curriculum and courses in the curriculum, and once the courses are designed, the faculty member teaching a course has to deliver the learning outcomes of the course he/she teaches and does not have the freedom to modify it. The faculty member has the freedom to decide the approach he/she wants to take for teaching; however, it has to be consistent with the learning outcomes that have been established. Therefore, the faculty collectively have full academic freedom to decide the curriculum and the courses and their contents, but the freedom of individual faculty members in teaching a course is indeed limited.

These are the academic freedoms relating to the two key missions. However, academic freedom is a more general concept and applies to other aspects of life as well, particularly in expressing views. It is in this aspect of academic freedom where countries differ (Altbach 2001). This freedom, which is sometimes granted as a constitutional right, is of vital importance in a university, where the free exchange of ideas is a foundation. As universities are often supported by public funds and potentially subject to pressures from the government, it is important that this principle that faculty and students are free to express their views, even if the views are divergent from those of the university or the government in power, be enshrined in the rules and culture of the university. Universities generally support this with the caution that the person expressing the views should clarify that he/she is not speaking on behalf of the university and should show restraint when speaking in public. Related to this is that the beliefs of administrators, politicians and other powers cannot be imposed on students or faculty. It also means that faculty have a right to criticize the internal functioning or policies of a university, or a government, without any fear of reprisals. The concept of academic freedom adopted by the American Association of University Professors (AAUP) is given in AAUP (2001).

8.1.4 Light-Touch Management

Most modern universities have a corporate-style governance model in place. However, the functioning of these systems is hardly like that of a corporation. Indeed, although the structural aspects may have been borrowed, the actual operation of this set-up should be different from how it is practised in corporations. We mention some principles here.

- **Light-touch management.** Universities were, and remain, largely self-governed institutions, with faculty members being autonomous agents with a large degree of freedom in what they pursued and delivered. In corporations, the management approach is used to ensure that the work of individuals is aligned with the goals of the corporation, and for this, a tight management style is often exercised. In universities, given the autonomous nature of the faculty and the academic freedom they enjoy, such a style is inappropriate and likely to be counterproductive. Also, all faculty are expected to be leaders in their own right. Hence, the governance should ensure that faculty management is light-touch, where expectations are clearly articulated to faculty and micromanagement or detailed progress monitoring is avoided.
- **Limited professional management.** All universities need some professional management staff to manage their operations. The size of the management staff is often comparable to the

size of faculty. The role and responsibilities of the management staff have also increased. With the increase in the complexity and size of the management staff, their authority over and oversight of academic activities of research and teaching also increase, leading to bureaucracy, sometimes excessive. This bureaucracy is often disliked by the faculty who want to focus on academics, while the management often focuses on processes, compliances, paperwork, rules, and so forth. To avoid an overly governed system, which inevitably conflicts with the academic freedom ethos, it is important to ensure that the professional management staff size is limited. Also, it is important to ensure that all such management staff are clear about their supportive role in achieving the main goals of the university—research and education—and that their main role is to support faculty and students in achieving these goals.

- **Measure what is necessary.** All sorts of data about various functions and activities in a university are required to be collected. When data is available, different types of analysis can be done. Analyses can often shed light and provide useful insights and understanding. However, they often lead to significant overhead for data collection. This overhead largely falls on faculty already overloaded with their core responsibilities of teaching, research and service. Striking a balance between what data should be collected and how measurements are interpreted is important, keeping in mind that all aspects of academics cannot be effectively measured quantitatively.

8.1.5 Accepting Authority is Distinct from Recommending Body

In universities, committee functioning is the norm. For many policy matters, committees are formed to examine the issue and share their recommendations. Committees are also the norm for the selection or promotion of faculty. A committee examines the case and makes recommendations regarding selection, tenure, promotion, and so forth. Whenever committees are involved in making a recommendation, the recommendation goes to another body for possible acceptance and is then implemented. Often, a committee of experts, including the head of the department and some other functionaries, is formed to make a recommendation about faculty candidates. The experts on the committee may be from the university, perhaps with some members from outside the department. Alternatively, experts may be mostly from outside the university, as is the case in most universities in India. Typically, there is a chair of the committee. Recommendations of the committee are then sent to a higher authority, which may accept these.

Sometimes, this process might involve multiple layers. For example, in most universities in USA, decisions regarding promotion and tenure often go through many committees. A departmental committee may make a recommendation, which is then examined by another committee at the level of the dean, which makes its own recommendation, and this is further examined at the university level by the provost and/or the president for possible acceptance.

In most smoothly functioning systems, the trust relationship is built over years and the authority generally accepts recommendations. The recommender–acceptor framework then acts more as a method to maintain the integrity of the process, while still allowing for some room for correction in case the recommending committee has erred in its judgement.

For this model to be effective, the accepting authority must be fully distinct from the recommending committee. Ideally, there should be no overlap, so that the accepting authority takes a completely unbiased view. Therefore, in many universities in Australia, the recommendation for faculty appointment is made by a committee of faculty from the department and outside, which is then sent for acceptance to the dean (who is not a member of the recommending committee). Similarly, in USA, the recommendation for faculty selection is made by the department through a committee or a consultative process and sent to the dean for possible acceptance.

The same is expected for promotions. The committee recommending a promotion should not have any overlap with the committee empowered to accept recommendations. In many universities in USA that have multiple committee levels for promotion, if a faculty is a member of the dean-level committee for promotions, he/she is expected to excuse himself/herself from the department-level committee making the recommendation.

In many large university systems in Australia and USA, recommending committees are typically at the department or dean level, with no involvement of the chief executive. However, in India, where most universities tend to be small, often, the chief executive chairs the committee that recommends the selection or promotion of a faculty. In this case, the accepting authority must be above the chief executive, for example, the chairperson of the board of governors. This is followed in IIIT-Delhi and in all IITs.

If a committee recommending selection or promotion includes the chief executive, the chairperson of the board of governors should be different from the chief executive—an approach followed in most universities in Australia and many institutes in India. Clearly, if the chief executive also chairs the board, the situation violates the basic principle of separating the recommending and accepting bodies and is open to misuse. This happens to be the case in many universities in India that have not yet adopted this modern practice and rely on the old system of allowing much of the decision-making power to be concentrated in the chief executive.

8.2 UNIVERSITY GOVERNANCE

As discussed earlier, governance has two important dimensions: academic governance, which focuses on academics, and top-level, overall university governance, which looks at all other aspects, including finance and general administration.

The responsibility for the top-level, overall governance of a university rests typically with a governing board. This body may be called the board of governors, board of management, board of regents or board of trustees, or have some other name. Legally, this body is recognized as representing the university. We refer to this body as the board of governors or just the board. The board is the body responsible for formulating all the rules and regulations for university functioning.

While the board is the main body overseeing the university and has all the powers for acting on behalf of the university, in some universities, particularly those supported by public funds, there is often a body 'above' the board, which does not have executive powers but can be considered as a broader authority to which the university is answerable. This body may be called a 'court' or a council and is expected to represent the public to ensure that the university serves public interests. It often has political and government representatives in it. In UK, this body is generally called the court and may have hundreds of members (CUC 2009). In India, it is called the court in many universities and the council in many other institutions. The court or the council may be chaired by a 'chancellor', who is often the governor of the state for a state university and an appointee of the president of India for central universities. In IIIT-Delhi, this body is called the General Council and is chaired by the lieutenant governor of the state of Delhi, who is also the chancellor of the Institute. In most central government universities and institutions, there is also a 'visitor', who is usually the president of India, who has some authority for giving directions to the university. We consider a body like a court and a functionary like a chancellor, both of whom do not exercise executive powers, as representing the larger stakeholders of the university—the government and the public. We do not discuss these further.

The responsibility for academic and student governance generally rests with another body, sometimes called the academic senate (or board of studies or some other name). This body, which comprises of faculty from the university, as well as external experts, oversees the academic programmes of the university. The overall governance by both these bodies is governed by the act and statutes of the university. Hence, we start with a brief discussion on these.

8.2.1 Act, Statutes and Ordinances

All universities have some legal empowerment that allows them to engage in education and research and grant degrees. Although there are different ways in which this empowerment can happen, we have assumed that this is done through an act of some state government or the central government. In other words, some act of some government empowers a particular university to function as it does. Typically, this act lays out not only the scope of the university but also some aspects of the governance structure, responsibilities, and so forth.

The act typically is a high-level document specifying broadly what a university can do, its governance structure, its responsibilities, and so forth. Further policies regarding various aspects of governance and activities of the university are formulated separately while remaining in compliance with the act. We call these statutes, the term commonly used in India. Statutes are generally made by the university, except the first statutes, which are made along with the act. Often, new statutes, or revision of existing statutes, require the concurrence of the government that has enacted the act.

The governance of a university has to be compliant with the act and statutes. In other words, the act and statutes provide the framework within which the board of the university takes its decisions.

The detailed operational rules and guidelines for policies defined in the act and statutes, or decisions made by the board, may be specified in ordinances, which have to be formally notified. In other words, the governance of a university is driven by its act, statutes and ordinances, and the university is expected to comply with these.

Often, there is another layer below ordinances, called regulations. These are often codified details of the rules specified in ordinances. Often, details of academic programmes and their execution are also codified in regulations.

8.2.2 Overall Governance and Board of Governors

The main role of the board is to formulate policies for the university and ensure that they are executed. However, the scope of policies may have limitations, as defined in the act. For example, in many public universities, the number of faculty and staff positions that a university has may be outside the scope of the board and may be decided by the government.

Rather than discuss in generalities, let us illustrate the responsibilities of the board by taking the example of IIIT-Delhi. The act of IIIT-Delhi empowers the board with a wide range of responsibilities, providing it a large degree of autonomy. The board is responsible and empowered with the following responsibilities:

- Exercising general superintendence, direction and control in the affairs of the institute
- Laying down policies for the functioning of the institute and for the manner of implementation of these policies
- Making statutes and ordinances and approving any regulations that may be made by the senate or any other bodies of the institute
- Instituting academic programmes and reviewing the working of the senate (which is the main body overseeing the academics in the institute, as will be discussed later)
- Preparing the annual report, the annual accounts and the budget of the institute
- Creating positions, appointing persons to academic and other posts in the institute and determining the salary structure

and the terms and conditions of different cadres of employees; regulating and enforcing discipline among employees as the appointing authority; and appointing the director of the institute.

- Delegating any of its powers to the director or any other authority of the institute or to a committee appointed by it
- Exercising all the powers of the institute not otherwise provided for by the act, statutes and ordinances

As we can see, in this structure, the board is the main governing body responsible for all aspects of the functioning of the institute. It is the main decision-making body. It also has the responsibility of creating positions, appointing faculty and staff to these positions and deciding their compensation. Effectively, the board is fully empowered to make all decisions regarding the institute. Structurally, it has a great deal of autonomy in the operation of the institute and is perhaps one of the most empowered boards among public universities in India.

The autonomy of a university is strongly influenced by how empowered and autonomous its board is, which, in turn, depends on the composition of the board and who appoints the board members. If the government appoints most of the members or if there are many representatives from the government on the board, the board is likely to align with government policies and decisions. Therefore, the board should largely comprise members who are independent and committed to making decisions in the interests of the university.

A general structure of the board may include a chairperson and a secretary. The chief executive of a university is an important member of the board. Other members may be the following: officials from the government; some distinguished citizens and thought leaders nominated to the board by the government, the board or other stakeholders (e.g., alumni, faculty, and so on); some faculty from the university; and some alumni.

An important aspect is the size of the board. A large board makes decision-making hard, while too small a board is unable

302 | Building Research Universities in India

to provide diversity and multiplicity of views. Broadly, it can be said that a board comprising 12–24 members is appropriate.

Some key aspects of the structure and composition have a significant impact on the functioning of the board and autonomy of a university. Perhaps, the most critical issue is the presence of government officials on the board. Government officials have to take views aligned with the expectations and plans of the government and act in the interests of the government. Their presence impacts the autonomy of the university with respect to the state. Their presence is generally justified on the grounds that public funds are used and, therefore, some governmental oversight is needed. Ideally, there should be no government official on the board, so as to provide the university maximum independence from the state in its governance. If such presence is necessary, it should be minimal, and the expectation should be that these officials facilitate the interaction with the government that a public university might need.

The other important issue is who nominates distinguished citizens or thought leaders. Again, if the government makes the nominations, then the autonomy is likely to be compromised. (An interesting approach is taken by some universities in USA in which nominations are made by the government but for a very long period, so that they are effectively independent of the government for continuation.) It is best that these members are selected by the university itself, perhaps by the board through some consultative process.

As an example, let us look at the composition of the board of IIIT-Delhi. The board consists of the following members:

- The chairman, who is nominated by the chancellor
- The director
- Principal secretary, or secretary, Finance Department of the government
- Secretary, Technical Education Department of the government

- Four persons having special knowledge or practical experience with respect to education, information technology domain of the application of information technology to be nominated by the chairman from a panel of eight persons submitted by the director to the board
- Two professors of the institute to be nominated by the director
- The registrar, member secretary

As we can see, the board is quite compact. The term of the nominated board members is 3 years. Although the board has government representation, it is modest. The board itself selects the four experts on the board. These together make the board quite autonomous.

This structure of the board provides good autonomy to govern an institution, particularly in the earlier stages. However, it does not provide for including other stakeholders, which may be desirable at a later date. For example, it is desirable to have the option to include some alumni once its alumni base has expanded and matured. It is also desirable to have the possibility of having more independent experts as the institute expands. (This could have been addressed in the act, for example, by stipulating that, some years after its establishment, the board may be expanded to include some alumni and expand the number of experts.)

The NEP also recommends that all universities should have an empowered board of governors who feel ownership for the university and are empowered to take decisions in the best interests of the university. It suggests a compact board of less than 20 people, with one-third of the members being from the university (including the chief executive), more than half of the board members being experts who are independent of the government as well as of the university, and no more than three members from the government. It also recommends that the board should itself nominate these experts (NEP 2019). In other words, the recommendations of the NEP are along the lines of the structure at IIIT-Delhi, as discussed earlier.

Related to the structure of the board is the issue of who selects and appoints the chairperson of the board. Usually, the state or the board itself can appoint the chairperson. For the highest level of autonomy, the board should appoint its chairperson through a defined process, ensuring prompt execution of the process by a university when a new chairperson is to be selected, as it is in the university's interests to have a chairperson. However, for public universities, often, the government appoints the chairperson. In such cases, it is desirable if the appointment process is such that the views of the board and other university stakeholders are taken into consideration.

Continuing with the IIIT-Delhi example, its act stipulates that the chairman is to be appointed by the chancellor. The process specified later in the statutes for the selection of the chairman, however, provides means to take the views of the board and other stakeholders in the process. According to the statute for the selection of the chairperson, a search committee is to be constituted, with experts being nominated to the committee by the board and the chancellor in equal numbers. The search committee is expected to take suggestions from various stakeholders for its search. It finally suggests suitable names to the chancellor, from which the chancellor selects one to be appointed as the chairperson.

It is also important that the chairperson be different from the chief executive, as discussed earlier, and is not an employee of the university. Many institutions in India, including IITs and IIIT-Delhi, follow this. However, this important principle is sometimes not followed. The NEP explicitly suggests that the chairperson of the board should be independent and separate from the chief executive and recommends that the board should elect its own chairperson, either from within itself or from outside.

8.2.3 Academic Governance and the Senate

Academics are at the heart of a university. Governance of academics is in itself complex, particularly since it must necessarily deal with issues related to students. Inevitably, the responsibility for academic governance rests with a dedicated body separate from the board, which is concerned with the overall governance. This body is sometimes called an academic senate, or academic board, or may be known by different names. We refer to it as the senate.

The relationship between the senate and the board needs to be defined, as, for academic freedom, it is important that the senate be independent. Historically, in many universities, the senate, sometimes also called the faculty senate, controlled all aspects of academics, with essentially no role for the governing board. A current approach is that while the academic senate is entrusted with matters related to academics, it governs essentially on behalf of the board, and the board relies on the recommendations of the senate for academic and student matters. The nature of the relationship between the two bodies may be articulated in the rules of the university. However, in reality, the practice followed over the years defines the relationship between the two entities. In many institutions, the views of the academic senate in many matters related to the structure of programmes, courses, teaching, student matters, and so forth are taken as final. Such an arrangement is essential to ensure academic freedom.

For example, in IIIT-Delhi, as per its act, the senate is the principal academic body having the right to advise the board of governors on all academic matters. It is responsible for the maintenance of standards of instruction, education, examination, and so forth. It is also responsible for framing regulations for the academic functioning of the institute, student discipline, and so forth. In this model, while the board is the ultimate deciding body, it must seek inputs from the senate on all academic and student matters.

Although the term 'academics' in a broad sense includes research activities also, senates are mostly focused on educational aspects and academic programmes. The governance of the research mission is left to other governance structures. In the collegial model of governance followed earlier in many universities, faculty senates often also had research in their purview. The management of research was discussed in a previous chapter.

The design of academic programmes is a key task of the senate. Earlier, when higher education was limited to a small portion of the population, it was pursued for developing thinkers and generalists, with little concern about what skills might be needed by the industry or society. However, today, the scenario is different, and the society, including the industry and the students, expects higher education to provide students skills and knowledge to function effectively in the society and workplace. With this change, it is desirable to have external inputs in the process of designing academic programmes, particularly from the industry.

One way to ensure that there are good external inputs in academic programmes is to have representation from important stakeholder groups, in particular the industry, in the body making decisions regarding programmes (i.e., the senate itself). To have external representation in the senate, the constitution of the senate has to be such that it allows this. As an example, we can consider the structure of the senate of IIIT-Delhi. The statute for the senate states that the senate shall consist of no less than 20 and no more than 40 members, at least half of the members shall be full-time faculty members of the institute and at least one-fourth shall be members who are not faculty of the institute. It also specifies that external members may be academicians from other institutions, experts from industry or alumni of the institute. It specifies that there shall be at least two student representatives and provides the flexibility for co-opting others for a limited term or for discussing special issues. This structure clearly shows the intent—the senate shall have a majority from the faculty of the institute, and so the responsibility for all academics shall rest with the faculty. However, it also formally establishes ways to get external inputs. Academicians from other institutions help in bringing learnings and best practices from other institutions. Also, representatives from the industry and alumni help bring in the industry perspective in deliberations. The NEP also recommends that the main academic body should have members from the university as well as members from outside the university.

8.3 LEADERSHIP AND CHIEF EXECUTIVE

The main leadership of a university rests with the chief executive officer, often called the vice chancellor, director or president. As is often stated, leadership concerns itself with setting the direction and what needs to be done, while management is about efficiently doing what has been decided. The chief executive, however, is not only the main leader but also the chief operating officer responsible for implementing the decisions taken by the board and the senate.

Although a degree of leadership is expected from people appointed to a specific position of authority, people without authority can also often exercise leadership by championing a cause or a change. In a university, in some ways, all faculty are expected to provide a degree of leadership in their academics—in their research work and their teaching activities. Those who achieve a degree of respect and voice in the peer community due to their knowledge and contributions can be called academic leaders (Yielder and Codling 2004); they derive their 'power' not because of the position they hold but because of the respect they generate in their peers due to their knowledge and contributions. Individuals or groups of individuals can take up leadership to drive a change even in matters related to the university or a particular aspect of it. Keeping this in mind, the task of the appointed leader—the vice chancellor, president or director—is to not only provide the leadership at the top level for the university but also support and motivate others in the university to take up leadership for specific purposes or causes.

Due to the huge task of providing leadership and administration for various aspects of the university, the chief executive has a set of other leaders to assist him/her—these are typically deans, pro–vice chancellors, vice-presidents, etc. These titles and their roles differ from university to university and country to country. The team of senior leaders together is often referred to as the executive or senior management of the university. In this chapter, we only discuss the chief executive.

8.3.1 Main Responsibilities

The task of the main leader is complex and challenging—even daunting—in a research university, as the leader is supposed to ultimately provide the top-level leadership to all the missions of the university. The 21st-century universities have become complex organizations with multiple roles. Hence, an excellent and multifaceted leader is required to lead it, performing a range of functions (Altbach 2011). Let us look at some of the main responsibilities of the chief executive in the Indian context.

Chief academic officer. The main leader is essentially the chief academic officer of a university, in that he/she presides over academics. The chief executive is the chairman of the body that deals with academic issues—the senate.

Chief of finance. Finance officers may handle daily financial operations of a university. However, the chief executive is typically the ultimate authority for finance also—for example, approving the final budget and annual accounts of the university. The chief executive also may chair the finance committee of an institute, which advises the board on the financial matters of the university.

Chief human resources officer. In India, often, the selection and promotion of faculty and staff are done through committees often chaired by the chief executive. The delegation of these powers, for example to departments or deans, is not very common. Therefore, the chief executive is essentially the main person responsible for all faculty and staff appointments and their promotions. Departments are the main bodies that handle the details of processes related to appointment or promotion, but it is ultimately the responsibility of the chief executive to make an appropriate decision.

Chief leader. While the board sets policies, the chief executive is expected to provide the initiative and leadership for identifying what policies are needed and formulating them. Similarly, although the board may deliberate and discuss the direction the university is to take, it is the chief executive who is expected to conceptualize the trajectory of the university and seek support and inputs from the board. Essentially, the chief executive is the main person providing leadership to the university. What the university does is largely decided by the chief executive. That is why when histories of universities are written, chief executives who might have steered the university to greater heights are hailed as visionary leaders.

Chief facilitator for internationalization and collaboration. Universities are globalizing worldwide; in developed countries, they are already highly globalized. However, in India, globalization is at a nascent stage—the academic system is hard-pressed to satisfy the local demand itself. For a research university, internationalization is needed to excel in research and build a global reputation. Collaboration with other universities and institutions is not always easy and has to be driven by the top leadership.

Chief operating officer. Although there is always a team involved in the administration of a university, the chief executive, who is also the chief operating officer, is responsible for ensuring that the established policies and processes are being followed. Thus, monitoring the administration team, motivating the team, and so forth is finally the responsibility of the chief executive.

Chief estate officer. Universities have a large expanse of real estate. In India, a university may have accommodation for students, faculty and staff, besides academic facilities. Although there are always units to manage these, the final authority generally rests with the chief executive. In some universities, handling issues related to housing is a major time-consumer for the chief executive.

The chief executive has many other responsibilities. Effectively, all responsibilities for the effective functioning of the university finally fall on the chief executive. Given the range of responsibilities, clearly, the chief executive needs to have a team of senior executives (collectively often referred to as the executive) to share the responsibilities and duties. In the recent past, the powers and the role of the executive seem to be increasing, with even the top-level governance body (the board) often relying on the executive for many of their decisions (Shattock 2013).

8.3.2 Selection of the Chief Executive

Selecting the chief executive is clearly of great importance. Autonomy demands that the selection of the primary leader of the university, that is, the chief executive, should be left to the university itself. It is in the interests of the university that the chief executive is appointed by the university and so is answerable to the university. If an external body appoints the chief executive, the answerability also lies with that body, which is clearly not desirable.

Let us first discuss a few desirable traits for the chief executive of a research university, who is expected to provide the primary leadership to the university. The leadership of universities is a complex issue, particularly because there are talented, highly individualized and autonomous faculty who are top stars in their own right in their field and often have some contempt for authority. Given the complexities quite unique to the university system, it is now widely accepted that the chief executive for a research university should come from the university system. Some of the desirable attributes of a leader of a research university are as follows:

- **Good academician with a decent reputation.** The leader of a research university need not be a top researcher himself/

herself. The research output of a university depends on its hundreds of faculty and research staff. The goal of the chief executive is not to excel in research himself/herself but to support faculty and other researchers to excel. To be able to support the faculty in research, the chief executive must have been a decent researcher himself/herself so as to have had first-hand experience in key issues faced by faculty in teaching, guiding students and PhD scholars, writing research proposals, managing groups and projects, and so forth. Besides a better understanding of issues, a good academic and research background also provides the desired respect from faculty colleagues. Without a good academic reputation, it is hard to gain the respect of faculty or motivate them for excellence.

- **Vision.** Where a university goes, to a large extent, is driven by the chief executive. Further, where the chief executive wants to take a university is decided by the vision established and followed up by suitable policies and administrative support. In these times of rapid change and questioning about higher education and universities, the chief executive should necessarily be a visionary having the ability to evolve a clear direction of where to take the university to meet emerging and future challenges. Routine and efficient administration and management can keep the university running. However, without a clear vision of where to take the university in the coming years, the university is likely to remain in the current situation and might even lose energy and enthusiasm, as change is expected in today's environment from all stakeholders of the university.

- **Open and collegial, with the ability to build consensus.** This is extremely important, due to the nature of governance in a research university and the shared governance that is followed. If a leader wants to implement some changes, a top-down approach cannot work in a university as it might in a corporation. Although there is a chief executive, a university effectively has each faculty as an autonomous agent, with the chief executive having little control over them. Hence, though an idea may come from the leader, it must have support from key stakeholders to succeed. Due to this, the chief executive needs to have the ability build consensus for actions to be taken. Given the open nature of the university, it naturally follows that openness is cherished and desired in all aspects of university governance, and the chief executive must have the ability to convince colleagues about any initiatives and changes.

- **Ability to work with a variety of external stakeholders like the government, industry, funding agencies, other universities, etc.** Universities today work in an environment where many external bodies play an important role. For example, universities are expected to generate most of their research funding from sponsoring agencies and industry. They are also expected to play an important role in facilitating industry and local development and engage with the local community. Research universities also engage with other research universities across the world for research and academic collaboration. All these imply that a university cannot be an isolated ivory tower and must be far more externally focused than what may have been the case a century or so ago. Engagement with external agencies will often be led by the chief executive. Consequently, the chief executive should have a good ability to work with these agencies and build relationships globally.

- **Able administrator.** A research university has to be run efficiently and effectively, with all its complex operations running smoothly. This requires effective administration, which is led by the chief executive, as discussed earlier. Therefore, although the main goal of the university is to excel in academics, it rests on the effective administration of all support services and academics. There are, of course, administrative staff for running the organization, but leadership has a huge impact on how the administration functions, and for this, the chief executive must be an able administrator well versed with tools of administration.

These are some traits which need special attention in a research university. Some of these are also the desired characteristics of vice chancellors in UK, as reported by Middlehurst (2013), who also notes that the role of vice chancellors has been broadening over the years. There are, of course, regular traits of an effective leader that are desirable, for example, the ability to drive change or transformation, trustworthiness, transparency, fairness, the ability to take risks and experiment, encourage others' ideas and accept them when appropriate, behave as exhorting others to behave, and so forth. Many desired attributes of a leader for organizational effectiveness based on general leadership capabilities and special ones needed for universities are discussed by Pounder (2001). As a research university is expected to have many academic leaders in their domain, it is also the role of the chief executive to work with them and nurture and encourage such leadership (Yielder and Codling 2004).

Let us now return to the issue of the selection of a chief executive. Organizational autonomy starts with how autonomous universities are in appointing their chief executive, which is perhaps the most important aspect of organizational autonomy, because it impacts all other organizational issues. In many Western countries, this selection is done by different bodies of the university: the board, the senate, a search committee appointed by the board, and so forth (although the selection may sometimes be subject to approval, which is usually a formality).

In India, the chief executive is often selected by the government, though there is generally a selection committee to recommend a set of names from which the final choice is made. However, some public institutions have empowered boards that select the chief executive.

IIIT-Delhi is one such example. The act of IIIT-Delhi states that the 'Director shall be appointed by the Board of Governors in such a manner, on such terms and on such emoluments and other conditions of service as may be prescribed'. To specify how this appointment is to be made, a statute has been created, which specifies the process. The process is as follows:

1. Before the end of the tenure of the current director, the board discusses the issue of his/her continuation if he/she is eligible and has served only one term.
2. If the board decides that it is in the best interests of the institute that the existing director continue for another term, the board may appoint the existing director for another period of 5 years.
3. Otherwise, a search-cum-selection committee of at least four distinguished academicians/scientists/administrators may be constituted.
4. An advertisement may be placed, but nominations should also be solicited actively.
5. The search-cum-selection committee can follow a process to finally recommend names to the board, which deliberates upon the list and finalizes the order in which candidates are to be approached for the offer.
6. The chairman starts discussions with the recommended candidates about their availability and terms of appointment. After the interactions, the chairman informs the board about the candidate available and the terms agreed upon.
7. The chairman issues the letter of appointment to the selected director.
8. The registrar of the institute issues suitable notifications.

The process shows that the board is fully empowered to select the chief executive, with no role of the government. This process is somewhat unique in India, although such a process of open search by the board is regularly practiced by universities in many countries such as USA and Australia. It is worth pointing out that the NEP recognizes the importance of high-quality leadership and suggests that leaders for universities be chosen from faculty who have a good record in academics and service and possess leadership and management skills. It recommends that the board appoint the chief executive, that the selection be done using processes which will assess potential candidates for their promise of leadership, and that the chief executive report to the board. In other words, the NEP recommends an approach similar to the one followed at IIIT-Delhi.

While implementing this process, the search-cum-selection committee shortlists a few candidates from the list of nominations and applications it has received. These candidates are then invited to visit the institute, meet with various functionaries and faculty and make a presentation to the faculty. They are then invited to give a presentation on their vision and plans for the institute to the search-cum-selection committee. The committee takes inputs from the departments and faculty on various candidates. The committee then meets, deliberates and recommends three candidates to the board. The board then meets to discuss the recommendations and the candidates and takes a final view. The chairman then contacts the first-choice candidate regarding the terms of appointment. This is a simple and transparent process. Though not followed commonly in India, a process like this can be easily implemented; however, it requires suitable changes in the act and statutes to enable it. This single change can enhance the autonomy of universities tremendously, while making the chief executive fully answerable to the university through the board.

8.4 MANAGEMENT/ADMINISTRATION

The role of the management is to ensure that good support is provided to all those involved in delivering the main missions of an organization, which, for a research university, are education, research and the third mission. The management team also has to ensure that policies formulated by governance bodies of the university are implemented effectively and efficiently. For effective administration, often, universities have a large setup; the non-academic staff size is often as large as the size of the faculty. All well-functioning universities must have decent administration. Effective administration in a university is, in many ways, similar to effective management in any organization. Hence, we discuss it only briefly here.

316 | Building Research Universities in India

For administration, all complex systems are broken into units, with people given charge of running these units. Universities are no different. They have different units. Perhaps, the most important and visible units in a university are academic departments. These are the units, generally built around disciplines, which house faculty and run academic programmes. Departments are led by a head or a chair, who is typically one of the senior faculty members appointed for a period of 3–5 years. In a large university, departments may be grouped into schools, which are built around fields of study. A dean typically heads the school. In India, universities generally tend to be small and focused. Hence, the layer of schools is often missing, leading to a flatter academic structure comprising academic departments.

Departments are the bodies responsible for delivering education; they own education programmes. Also, they own courses and ensure that suitable instructors are assigned for teaching courses. Disciplinary research also takes place in departments. They may have research labs and research groups, typically led by one faculty and some other associated faculty members, and have multiple graduate students and other research staff.

Research universities often have centres. Centres are research units, which often may cut across disciplines. Centres are mostly run on research funds and may sometimes be sponsored for multiple years by some agencies or corporations. Typically, centres have faculty from various departments and do not have faculty lines of their own. Therefore, conceptually, centres can be started as needed and shut down when they outlive their purpose (or when the funding stops). Generally, centres do not own education programmes, although, in some places, they may run some postgraduate programmes, necessarily in partnership with some academic departments, because faculty for teaching come from these departments.

Departments take care of delivering education. However, a lot of administrative tasks need to be done for the education mission. These include guiding students, providing them grades and transcripts, registering students in courses, checking that students have completed the requirements for a degree, arranging for degrees to be distributed and the convocation in which degrees can be conferred, and so forth. For managing all these, there is typically an administrative unit, referred to as the academic section in a university. There is generally a university-level section that deals with all the administrative issues relating to the running of academic programmes. This section is often overseen by a dean. In addition to the university-wide structure, there may be a smaller unit in each department to help and guide students with education programmes run by the department.

Similarly, although research is done in departments and centres and these units may have some support for facilitating their administration, typically, there is a university-level unit to handle research, which is headed by a dean (or vice-president, or some other title) of research. We have discussed research and its management in Chapter 4. The unit to manage research must necessarily have a section to handle sponsored research projects, which generally provide the bulk of the yearly research funds. As they are from sponsoring agencies, they have some amount of compliance and reporting requirements. These are to be ensured by the unit managing projects. Typically, projects are submitted through these units; reporting back to the sponsor also happens through projects. Therefore, the unit becomes the interface between the sponsor and the university for administrative purposes, while faculty and other researchers are responsible for actually conducting the research.

For the third mission, the management structure is less standard. There may be some technology transfer cell, or industry collaboration cell, with a goal to provide support to departments and centres for putting their research to commercial use. The nature of the management structure to support the third mission depends on activities in this mission that are majorly focused on by the university.

Besides units supporting the main missions, there are other administrative units in a university which may not exist in other organizations or corporations. Examples of these include units for fundraising and alumni relations; these are functions specific to a university. These are not large units in public universities. However, in some of the most reputed private universities in USA, they can be large functions and may involve hundreds of people. In India, units for these two functions are generally quite small, because generally they are not given the level of importance they deserve in modern times.

A university has other administration units to support its activities and the running of the university. These can include units for finance and expenditure, security, facilities management, campus maintenance and development, student services, including sports and culture, health services, transport, travel, and so forth. These services are not much different from their counterparts in corporations and other organizations and can be managed in a similar manner using best practices for each.

The scope of this chapter does not permit a detailed discussion of the organizational structures for administration in universities. The administration is, in many ways, the same as in other complex organizations and corporations. However, universities are often focused on their key missions and hence may not sufficiently emphasize administration, sometimes leading to inefficient or ineffective administrative units. Although it is beyond the scope of this chapter to discuss how to manage universities effectively and efficiently (there is much literature on this), it is perhaps useful to discuss a few key principles for administration.

A key principle is that what you cannot measure, you cannot manage. There should be suitable measurements and reporting in place for each unit to ensure that it is working efficiently and is effective in achieving its goals—academic goals, service delivery goals or other goals. A useful concept here is to have reporting methods in place for units to regularly report on key performance indicators. As a general rule, it is always possible to have some measurement and reporting structures in place for almost any unit regardless of the nature of services provided by the unit.

Another principle is derived from the law of entropy. If a system is not actively managed by applying administrative oversight and energy, it degenerates to one providing a minimal level of service. Active management is required even to keep a system running at the existing levels of efficiency and effectiveness. In many systems, it can be seen how lax management of services leads to the degradation of service levels and satisfaction of those who seek the services.

A fundamental requirement to manage and improve the working of a system is that of having a feedback loop. Feedback is the only way of knowing whether the system is working well or not. Any system that has to be controlled must have feedback loops, according to the systems and control theory. One simple way to get feedback on services is to take feedback from customers (users of services) about the quality of services. This feedback can be obtained in various ways. In IIIT-Delhi, for example, yearly feedback is taken from users (students, faculty and staff) of various services. A simple online survey is conducted on the level of satisfaction of various services such as facility management, finance, R&D management, student support, support for academics, and so forth. Based on the survey results, the administration plans for improvements where needed. The results of the survey and the plans for improvement are discussed and presented to senior administrators or the governing board. The impact of these improvements is discussed after the next year's survey. This simple feedback tool can suffice for ensuring effective administration in a university.

One overall instrument for improving administration is university-level accreditation. Many countries now have accreditation frameworks for assessing the effectiveness of the internal functioning of an institution. Such accreditations are often perceived as unnecessary overheads by universities and academicians. However, they are an important tool for effective management. These are thorough and elaborate exercises carried out by a team of external experts using a fairly elaborate framework, which looks at all aspects of university management. Hence, they provide good feedback on systems in the university. Reports by these accreditation bodies also provide confidence to sponsors and external stakeholders about how well the university is being managed. Accreditation is also an excellent tool to bring about changes in a research university. Universities are notoriously conservative and resist change. Accreditation is often required, for example, by the government or by funding agencies. Universities can use the exercise to bring about desired changes and get the buy-in from internal stakeholders, particularly faculty.

The NEP also envisages that accreditation will become important and governments will rely more on accreditation to ensure that universities are well governed and fulfilling their mission. It also envisages that there will be separate bodies for regulating and financially supporting universities and that these bodies will rely on accreditation, which will be done by an autonomous authority, to provide information about the governance of universities for taking suitable actions. In other words, accreditation will become the basis of much of regulation and oversight by the government (NEP 2019).

8.5 SUMMARY

In this chapter, we discussed the main layers in the management of a research university: governance, leadership and administration. Before discussing these three dimensions, a set of principles for governing a research university were discussed. These included principles of autonomy and responsibility, shared governance, academic freedom, light-touch management and the presence of an accepting body distinct from a recommending body.

Governance includes a top-level, overall university governance, usually with a governing board, and academic governance, usually done by an academic senate. Governance is focused on making policies, taking high-level decisions and getting them implemented through leadership and management. We discussed the role of the board and its structure and what is desired to support autonomy. For academic governance, we discussed the main responsibilities of the senate and its possible structure.

Leadership in a university rests with many people; indeed, all faculty are expected to be leaders in their own right. However, the role of the chief executive, who may be called by titles such as vice chancellor, director, president, and so forth, is critical for the success of a research university. We discussed the various dimensions of the role of a chief executive in a research university and also some desirable characteristics the chief executive should possess. We then discussed the important issue of selection of the chief executive—who does the selection and appointment and how. It was pointed out that for maintaining autonomy and ensuring that the chief executive is answerable to the university, the appointment of the chief executive must be done by a university body such as the board. Policies and processes of IIIT-Delhi which support this were also discussed.

Finally, we briefly discussed management or administration in a university. It is often a large function in a university, and its main goal is to implement policies and decisions made by the governing bodies and leadership. A few guidelines on how services may be managed were also discussed. For various issues we also discussed the recommendations of the NEP.

REFERENCES

American Association of University Professors (AAUP). 1940. *Statement of Principles on Academic Freedom and Tenure*. Washington, DC: AAUP.

Aghion, Philippe, Mathias Dewatripont, Caroline Hoxby, Andreu Mas-Colell, André Sapir, and Bas Jacobs, 2010, January. 'The Governance and Performance of Universities: Evidence from Europe and the US.' *Economic Policy* 25 (61): 7–59.

Altbach, Philip G. 2001. 'Academic Freedom: International Realities and Challenges.' *Higher Education* 41: 205–19.

Altbach, Philip G., ed. 2011. *Leadership for World-Class Universities: Challenges for Developing Countries*. New York NY: Routledge.

Birnbaum, Robert. 2004. 'The End of Shared Governance: Looking Ahead or Looking Back.' *New Directions for Higher Education* 2004 (127): 5–22.

Chandra, Pankaj. 2017. *Building Universities that Matter: Where are Indian Institutions Going Wrong?* Orient BlackSwan.

CUC. 2009, March. *Guide for Members of Higher Education Governing Bodies in the UK*. Committee of University Chairs.

Estermann, Thomas. 2015. 'University Autonomy in Europe.' *Higher Education Trends*, University Education, No. 3.

Estermann, Thomas, and Terhi Nokkala. 2009. *University Autonomy in Europe—Exploratory Study*. Brussels: European University Association.

Gayle, Dennis J., Bhoendradatt Tewarie, and A. Qunton White. 2003. *Governance in the Twenty-First-Century University—Approaches to Effective Leadership and Strategic Management*. ASHE-ERIC Higher Education Report.

McNay, Ian. 1995. 'From the Collegial Academy to Corporate Enterprise: The Changing Cultures of Universities.' In *The Changing University*, edited by Tom Schuller. London: Society for Research into Higher Education.

Middlehurst, Robin. 2013, July. 'Changing Internal Governance: Are Leadership Roles and Management Structures in United Kingdom Universities Fit for the Future?' *Higher Education Quarterly* 67 (3): 275–94.

NEP. 2019. *Draft National Education Policy, 2019*. Government of India.

Pounder, James S. 2001. '"New leadership" and University Organizational Effectiveness: Exploring the Relationship.' *Leadership & Organizational Development Journal* 22 (6): 281–90.

Rowlands, Julie. 2017. *Academic Governance in the Contemporary University—Perspectives from Anglophone Nations*. Springer.

Shattock, Michael. 2013, July. 'University Governance, Leadership and Management in a Decade of Diversification and Uncertainty.' *Higher Education Quarterly* 67 (3): 217–33.

Stensaker, Bjorn, and Agnete Vabo. 2013, July. 'Re-inventing Shared Governance: Implications for Organizational Culture and Institutional Leadership.' *Higher Education Quarterly* 67 (3): 256–74.

Taylor, Mark. 2013, January. 'Shared Governance in the Modern University.' *Higher Education Quarterly* 67 (1): 80–94.

Trakman, L. 2008. 'Modelling University Governance.' *Higher Education Quarterly* 62 (1–2): 63–83.

Yielder, Jill, and Andrew Codling. 2004. 'Management and Leadership in the Contemporary University.' *Journal of Higher Education Policy and Management* 26 (3): 315–28.

Chapter 9

Financing the Research University

Research universities are expensive because large investments are needed to develop, support and nurture such universities. Many global research universities have an annual budget of more than US$1 billion and employ more than 10,000 people—they are larger than many large corporations. As we have focused on public research universities, a portion of the cost of running a university is expected to be borne through public funds (in private universities, the counterpart may be philanthropic funds). However, the allocation of public funds for universities has decreased worldwide. Consequently, even for a public research university, the financing has to be a combination of public funds and funds raised through fees and other sources.

Financing research universities is a complex topic; different countries have tried different approaches at the country level, while universities have pursued their own strategies for financial sustainability. In this chapter, we provide a brief, general discussion on the financing of research universities. A research university needs yearly support to finance its primary missions of education and research; activities for these two missions indeed consume most of the expenditure of a research university. Besides yearly financing for the education and research missions, the infrastructure of a research university also needs financing. We discuss the financing of these in different sections. We discuss the financing of the education and research missions separately, as they have different purposes and often are supported separately, even though it is often hard to fully separate the costs on these two missions. To begin with, we present a brief discussion on the source of money and the expenses in a research university in India so as to get a perspective of financial matters.

For the simplicity of discussion, we do not discuss the financing of other aspects of a research university: its third mission and outreach and other services it may provide. We assume that these activities are mainly self-supporting. We also do not discuss the raising of funds from alumni and philanthropists; it is a major activity in many universities, particularly in private universities in USA. In India, this aspect is still at a very nascent stage, though the new NEP envisages a greater role of private philanthropic funds for universities.

9.1 INCOME AND EXPENDITURE OF A RESEARCH UNIVERSITY

The main sources of annual income for a research university are grants from the government, tuition and other fees, sponsored research projects, income from endowment (which is typically small in the Indian context and for most public universities), income from other commercial activities, and so forth. To understand the sources of income in a research university, a rough income break-up of an older IIT (older IITs generally have about 500 faculty and about 8,000 students) for a recent year is shown in Table 9.1. We present the income for a year which is meant for regular, recurring or operating expenses; the funds for capital expenditure are separate and not included in the discussion here.

The main operating budget of the institution, which is based on funds from the government and internal sources such as tuition fees, is about ₹520 crores (approximately US$70 million). This covers the salaries of all staff and expenses on the regular running of the institute. As we can see, the government grant is more than 80 per cent of the income from internal sources and the government (which we call base funding). The income from

Table 9.1 *Sources of Income of a Premier Engineering Research Institution*

	₹ (crores)
Internal and government sources	
Tuition fee	45
Hostel and other fees (income from lands and buildings)	15
Interest (from corpus and investments)	15
Government grant	425
Miscellaneous (rent, guest house, fines, etc.)	20
Total income from internal sources/government	520
External sources	
Sponsored research projects, fellowships, etc.	300
Other external income	5
Total external income	305

Source: Author.

tuition and other fees is less than 10 per cent and that from the corpus is less than 3 per cent. In other words, the base funding for the institute predominantly comes from the government. In general, tuition fee still accounts for a small fraction of the total operating budget of public universities, though it varies from state to state (Agarwal 2009).

We can also see that, being a top research institution, it gets substantial income from research funding agencies, companies (consulting and other contract work) and other external sources. These funds are to be used for the purposes specified in the project proposals and can be considered as the research funding of the institute. In this particular year, the research funding is more than half of the base funding.

The base funding can be used to estimate the cost of education. A simple method is to take the total base funding and divide it by the number of students to get an estimate of the cost per student per year. This method provides only a very rough estimate, as parts of the main budget are also used for supporting research. However, separating teaching and research costs is extremely tricky, as faculty and resources, such as a library, that are supported by this budget are used for both teaching and research. However, for many public universities, it is assumed that the base funding is for education and general infrastructure and that much of the research is supported through external research grants. With this assumption, the rough cost of education can indeed be obtained from the base funding and total number of students. As is evident, education is highly subsidized in this institution.

Let us look at the rough expenditure of this institution. Expenditure from sponsored project funds is handled differently than that from the base funding, as these funds are not part of the operating budget and can be used only in the manner specified in the proposal for the project. Hence, expenditure from these two funds has a different pattern. Both are shown in Table 9.2.

Table 9.2 shows that almost 60 per cent of the funds from the government and internal sources (base funding) is used for salaries and pension, and more than a quarter of it is used for the maintenance and running of facilities (water, electricity, security, etc.).

Just about 6 per cent of the budget is used on PhD students—this can be considered as direct support towards the funding of research in the base funding. The rest of the expenditure on research is from the sponsorship of research projects.

More than half of the funds from research projects is used to procure equipment needed for research. Further, a good portion of these funds is used to pay staff hired specifically for the project. A substantial portion of these funds is used for supporting travel. Only a small amount is used to provide stipends to PhD students. (The expenditure from these funds is different from the external income, because the income for projects may be for more than a year and funds from a year are often carried over to the next years for expenditure.)

Table 9.2 *Expenditure Pattern in a Premier Engineering Institution*

	₹ (crores)
From internal and government funds	
Faculty/staff salaries, allowances and benefits, including travel	195
Pension and benefits	105
PhD student stipend and other allowances/expenses	35
Other academic expenses	20
Administration, including security, facilities, taxes, power, water, etc.	120
Repair and maintenance	30
Library	15
TOTAL: From institute funds	520
From external source funds	
Faculty salaries, allowances, and benefit	0
Other staff salaries, allowances, and benefits	35
PhD student + other student stipends and expenses	5
Equipment	125
Travel and related expenses	50
Other expenditures	15
TOTAL: From project funds	230

Source: Compiled by the author.

The aforementioned example from one major research university gives an idea about the income and expenditures in various research universities across India. A general pattern can be expected in many public universities: most of the income from government grants and fees are used for running the institution, including the salaries of the regular staff. In fact, the yearly budgetary support for a university is based on these committed expenses. Government funding is the dominant component in the base funding, though there are some state universities where this is not the case.

The research grant funds of this institution are quite high, as it is one of the top institutions in the country. The research grants vary drastically from university to university. As we have seen in Chapter 1, the average sponsored research funding is just about ₹20 crores per university for the top 100 universities and about twice this amount for the top 25.

The funding model of IIIT-Delhi is quite different from that of other public universities. In its model, education is expected to be made self-sustaining eventually. The government may provide some funds for research and for the infrastructure. Therefore, in the base funding, tuition fee accounts for about 60–80 per cent of the revenue, and direct annual support for education from the government is minimal. Some funding is provided by the government to support research—the model for providing support for research is that the government provides a grant equal to research funds raised by the institute, with some yearly limit.

9.2 FINANCING EDUCATION

Higher education is expensive, as it is still a people-based service. It is largely provided by highly educated and talented faculty, who are supported by teaching assistants, lab staff, instructors, etc., who are also skilled personnel. Further support is provided by administrators and other specialized staff involved in managing education, other functions and the infrastructure of the university. The costs of skilled human resources continue to increase faster than other costs, leading to an increase in the cost of university education globally, often at a pace faster than inflation.

This increase in cost is even more prominent in research universities, mainly because these universities require highly talented research faculty—who conduct high-quality research and provide high-quality teaching—to be recruited and compensated attractively for retention. Another reason is that the quality of education these universities aim to provide includes engaging with research and the latest technologies. Hence, the expenditure on labs and facilities is also significantly higher in such universities compared with other universities, as the latest technologies often require significantly more investments compared with established technologies, which often have become commodities.

How should the high cost of higher education be supported? In our discussion here, we primarily focus on the financing of undergraduate programmes. These are indeed the most sought-after programmes and degrees and are often perceived as necessary qualifications in today's world. The cost of education can be viewed as follows (Taylor and Morphew 2013; Winston 1999):

$$Cost = net\ tuition\ fee + general\ subsidy$$

In other words, the cost for higher education has two major components: the tuition fee paid by students and the general subsidy provided to all the students by the university through grants from the government, funds from donations and returns from endowment, income from other services, and so forth.

Traditionally, the net tuition fee (i.e., tuition fee charged minus scholarships and discounts given by the university) has been a small fraction of the cost; in many countries, education was either free or had a minimal tuition fee. However, the situation has changed a lot worldwide. The current situation is that a significant fraction of the cost is covered by tuition fee, and the general subsidy is reduced.

With the tuition covering an increasing portion of the cost and the cost of education continuing to increase, there is a need to ensure that access to higher education is not denied due to the lack of financial resources. This has necessitated the need for financial support to students, so that access to higher education is not limited to only those who can afford it and its benefits are not denied to students from financially weaker backgrounds. This support is therefore an integral part of the financing of higher education in a university. We discuss each of these aspects of financing education.

The level of subsidy and the costs students have to bear through tuition fee rest a lot on how higher education is viewed by society and governments. Hence, we start with a small discussion on the public-good nature of higher education and the phenomenon of cost increase in higher education.

9.2.1 Is Higher Education a Public Good

In economics, a public good is nonexcludable, that is, we cannot exclude some people from using it, and nonrivalrous, that is, consumption by one individual does not preclude consumption by another. On the other hand, a private good is one which provides positive benefits to only some people. The provider of private goods can exclude some people from it, and consumption by a person necessarily means that it cannot be consumed by another. The question we discuss here is whether higher education is a public good. Much has been written on this topic (e.g., Marginson 2011; Tilak 2009). We discuss it very briefly to reflect a widely prevailing view.

Education, in the sense of individuals gaining knowledge, is a public good, because anyone can get it and one person gaining knowledge in no way precludes others from acquiring it. However, education might not technically satisfy the economic definition of public good when delivered through institutions that limit the number of students admitted; students gaining admission exclude others from getting admitted, because seats are limited and other students cannot get them once they are filled.

However, in a broad and general sense, a public good is considered as one that is beneficial or useful to the society in general, or whose consumption by individuals leads to substantial benefits to the society, besides benefitting the individuals. On the contrary, the benefits of someone consuming a private good accrue largely, and possibly substantially, to the individual, even though the society may also benefit from the individual consuming it. When discussing higher education, the general notion of public and private goods is more suitable.

The reason for examining whether something is a public good or not is essentially to know who should pay for the good. A public good is expected to be paid through public funds, while individuals are expected to pay for private goods. Therefore, if education is a public good, then the government providing funds for it is clearly justified and expected. On the other hand, a government can be challenged for supporting a private good through public funds. Hence, from a public policy perspective, identifying whether something is a public good or not is important. Note that this is not a binary situation; in the complex world of today, some goods provide both public and private benefits. In such cases, discussion can help decide the level of support a government should provide, that is, the situation is not that either the government or the individual pays, but that it can be a combination of the two.

In modern times, basic education is a public good; it has huge benefits to society. A literate population leads to better citizens, a more efficient supply of services and communication, economic and overall development of society, and so forth. Basic education is widely accepted as a necessity for modern societies. In fact, in many countries, it has become a fundamental right, and children must necessarily be given basic school education.

The views regarding the nature of higher education, whether it should be treated as a public or a private good, are not as clear as those for basic education. For such a discussion, higher education and higher education institutions (HEIs) should be considered separately, as HEIs also engage in many other activities, including research and community outreach. Higher education essentially means the granting of degrees by HEIs to students who complete the requirements for the same and demonstrate that they have developed the required knowledge and skills for the degree. When discussing whether higher education is a public good or not, we discuss only about degrees that an individual gets and which are provided by an HEI, and the HEI incurs some cost for providing that higher education.

In earlier times, higher education was generally seen as a public good by most countries when fewer people opted for it. Having a more educated citizenry was considered good for the country, and the development of more skilled people was seen as beneficial to economic development. Higher education was also expected to provide leaders in various fields for tomorrow, besides many other benefits. The private benefit was often not substantial; indeed, employment needs often did not require higher education degrees. Hence, for a long time, higher education was considered a public good (Tilak 2008).

Two key factors have impacted the argument. First, public resources required for supporting higher education increased substantially with the massification of education. Second, many analyses have shown that higher education hugely benefits an individual, and those with degrees earn substantially more than those without and generally have a better quality of life. In other words, the private benefit of higher education is substantial—a view that is also reflected in the fact that students strive to get admission in the best universities because they know that education from these universities often leads to well-paying employment opportunities and provides long-term benefits in their careers. These two key factors have minimized the support for considering higher education as a public good: countries do not have the luxury of providing full budgetary support for larger numbers, and the fact that higher education provides private benefits is seen as a good justification to reduce the support.

However, higher education continues to provide large benefits to society, sometimes called externalities. These include producing a more informed citizenry, helping in the economic development, particularly for knowledge-based industries, developing leaders for tomorrow, improving cultural and political scenes, and so forth.

Given that higher education provides substantial private and public benefits, it is now treated in most countries as a mixed good or quasi-public good, and the broad trend is to have the beneficiary (i.e., the student) pay a good portion of the cost for the education. The same trend holds in India also: students are expected to pay a larger share of the cost for education, though earlier the tuition covered a smaller portion of the budget (Tilak 1993, 2008).

The new NEP of the Government of India recognizes that education has a high return on investment for individuals who gain from it in the form of increased earnings over their lifetime, as well as in the form of better health, better social and professional networks, increased life expectancy, etc. The NEP also points out that there are many societal benefits of education in the form of a more productive workforce, improved capacity of the society to innovate and participate in knowledge-based economy, lower crime rates, better public health and awareness, etc. (NEP 2019).

Clearly, if students are made to pay a larger portion of the cost of education, higher education will become less accessible, something that goes against the public-good nature of higher education and can lead to the denial of rightful opportunity for some. Consequently, the implementation of this view of tuition fees covering a substantial portion of higher education costs would necessitate some form of support to students from financially weaker backgrounds so that they have access to higher education.

9.2.2 Higher Education Cost Increase

Higher education costs have increased steadily and substantially over the years, often significantly faster than the increase in the inflation or income level. This increase has necessitated the increase in tuition fee for students, sometimes causing unrest.

An explanation for the increase in higher education costs rests on the basic economic constraint that, within the existing technology for delivery, a service/quality can only be improved by incurring extra costs (Archibald and Feldman 2008). In other words, depending on what it can afford to spend on education, which depends on the total revenue it generates, a university chooses a quality level that it can support with this level of funding.

334 1 Building Research Universities in India

If the university wants to improve the quality of education, then it must be ready to incur higher costs, that is, it must necessarily increase its revenue.

The traditional economic view is that cost reduction (for a quality level) takes place with changes in technology, which increases labour productivity. This increase in productivity also leads to higher wages for workers, though the productivity benefits are much more than the wage increase. Productivity gains are hard to achieve in services that do not render themselves easily to the use of technology for improving productivity, like producing a play or a concert. Hence, services such as higher education, where technology (including processes and methods) has remained unchanged for decades, cannot improve productivity; they can only do so by lowering the quality. However, they still have to compete within the larger economy for human resources and hence have to increase wages. Consequently, in higher education, the cost increases as the human resource cost increases, but without getting any productivity benefits, as technology is still the same. This is sometimes called the 'cost disease' of such services—incurring higher costs but without any productivity benefit (Archibald and Feldman 2008).

This explanation for the increase in costs is based on the assumption that technology cannot be used to improve productivity in the case of higher education. This has been the case in higher education for decades, or even centuries. However, with the development of alternative methods of education delivery, particularly Internet-based delivery, it is hoped that the decrease in costs can be managed. However, benefits of these new technologies are still to be realized, and costs of higher education still continue to increase.

Another reason for the increase in the costs of higher education in a research university can be attributed to the nature of such universities. Research universities desire global prestige, which often requires higher investments in more costly disciplines, the latest technology, the latest infrastructure, and so forth, which then increases the cost of education (Archibald and Feldman 2008).

Considering the nature of higher education, which suffers from the cost disease, the reduction in costs results in a corresponding reduction in quality. This can be in the form of an increase in the student–faculty ratio, thereby reducing the attention each student gets. Otherwise, it can be through reducing expenditure by increasing the hiring of part-time or guest faculty for teaching. The reduction in costs may also result in the reduction of non-teaching staff, thereby increasing the administrative load on the faculty and consequently reducing the time the faculty spend on academics. Consequently, forced approaches for cost reduction, for example, reducing subsidies without increasing tuition fees, may result in the lowering of education quality. Though low tuition fees are desirable and demanded by students, it should be understood that reductions in tuition fees should not result in cost reduction and are compensated by non-tuition revenues and grants; otherwise, quality will suffer.

9.2.3 Tuition Fee

In earlier days, higher education in many countries was supported mainly by the government through public funds. This situation has changed dramatically; higher education is now supported in part by a student (and the student's family) and in part by the government in most countries. This widespread shift has taken place in countries regardless of their political systems and ideologies. Some of the main reasons why most countries, even with different political and economic systems, have reduced their subsidy for higher education are as follows (Marcucci 2013):

- Enrolments in higher education have increased worldwide, and massification of higher education has happened, or is happening, in almost all countries. Massification of higher education is a well-documented phenomenon with many different reasons, including the demographic shift and increased complexity of the modern world requiring higher education for career advancement. With increased enrolment, the costs of subsidizing education have become much more significant.

- Budgetary pressures on governments have increased, with many competing demands on governmental funds for public services, including primary and secondary education, health, infrastructure, defence, and so forth. Consequently, providing allocations for higher education has become more challenging.
- The per-student cost of education has increased substantially over the years, as discussed earlier.

Perhaps, the main reason for governments reducing support for higher education is the change in the perceptions of governments and societies regarding higher education. As discussed earlier in the chapter, higher education is now treated more as a private good, with the recipient benefitting from it significantly more. Hence, it is expected that the beneficiary should pay more.

The student share of the cost of education is the tuition fee charged to students. The tuition fee means the fee for covering portions of the cost of education. For charging a tuition fee, two policies are commonly used: tuition fee for all and dual-track tuition fee (Marcucci 2013). In tuition fee for all, a common approach is to levy the fee upfront, at the beginning of the semester or academic year. This model is most commonly followed; it is easy to understand and simple to administer, and its accounting is also straightforward. The tuition fee level may change from university to university and even from programme to programme in a country such as USA, where there is no country-wide authority under which higher education comes. In countries where higher education is largely centrally funded and some central agencies are there for funding, fees may be uniform across universities, or adjusted for programmes (e.g., more fees for professional programmes) or for income.

The tuition fee payment may also be deferred, a model followed in Australia and UK. In this model, sometimes referred to as the Australian model, all students have to pay a fixed fee.

However, the upfront payment to the university is done by the government on behalf of the student, and the student is assumed to have taken a loan for the fee amount. The student has to repay this loan after getting employment, as a tax on the income if the income exceeds some threshold.

The dual-track tuition policy model is for charging different fees for different categories of students. One approach is to have some university seats on a reduced or zero tuition fee and charge full tuition fee to the rest. The subsidized tuition seats are often given based on merit, although they can be easily given on some economic criteria or merit-cum-means criteria. In this approach, the seats without any tuition reduction are sometimes called self-sponsored or self-financing seats, as they often charge the full cost of education.

Another approach for the dual-track tuition policy model is to have different fee levels for different students depending on their home state or country. For example, most state universities in USA have one fee structure for in-state students and another for out-of-state students. Similarly, many universities in the European Union (EU) and UK have some tuition fee for EU citizens and a much higher tuition fee for non-EU students. In Australian universities, the fee for international students can be many times the fee for Australian citizens. In some of these, one fee is regulated and often subsidized, as governments financing the university want a lower cost of education for their citizens. The second track fee may be deregulated and even be 'profit making' in that the fee charged may be higher than the cost of education; the surplus may be used to subsidize the education of citizens or the research function of the university. A good discussion of models existing in different countries is given by Johnstone and Marcucci (2010).

The dual-track approach is also indirectly employed by encouraging the growth of private universities and colleges, which are not under the control of the government and hence beyond any government policy for fee regulation. This approach leads to an elite public and mass private model of education (Marcucci

2013). In this model, the public universities financed by the government provide elite education to a relatively smaller section of students at a highly subsidized rate. Most of the students study in private institutions by paying the fees stipulated by the institutions, which often have minimal subsidy. This approach is followed in some Latin American countries such as Mexico and Brazil. In the last few decades, this model has spread widely in India, and currently, a majority of students get their undergraduate education from private colleges and universities, which charge fees to fully cover the cost of education.

In India, no uniform model for tuition exists. In private universities, effectively all seats are self-financing, although some scholarships may be provided for deserving or meritorious candidates. In affiliated colleges (which do not have degree-granting powers) the fee is generally regulated by the affiliating university; often, the fee is kept artificially low to keep education affordable, but as discussed earlier, forced lowering of costs results in the lowering of quality in higher education—something that is widely believed to be the prevailing situation in India. Public universities also have no uniformity, and the sponsoring government generally fixes fees, often on a university-by-university basis. Therefore, each state can fix the fee differently in each of its universities. In some central government–sponsored institutions having some overarching, common governing structure (e.g., the IITs with an IIT council, which has a say in common matters such as admission, fees, and so forth), there is a uniformity of fees. The dual-track fee system also exists, wherein some seats have tuition fees regulated by the government or the affiliating university, while others are self-financing seats. The deferred fee approach is not in use.

9.2.4 General Subsidy

Higher education is mostly a loss-making enterprise. A basic anomaly in the economics of higher education is that universities offer their primary service, namely education, at a price lesser than the average cost of production (Winston 1995, 1999).

There might be education providers for which this might not be true (e.g., for-profit colleges/universities), but this is almost universally true for research universities, including the well-known private not-for-profit research universities in USA. Most provide subsidies for education. (An analysis suggests that in USA, the average subsidy in public institutions is about US$7,000 and the average educational cost is almost US$10,000, while in private institutions these figures are US$5,000 and US$16,000, respectively [Winston 2004].)

The subsidy provided broadly has two components: a general subsidy given equally to each student in the university and a student aid awarded on a per-student basis depending on the student's merit, need or a combination of both. The student aid is generally quite visible, because these schemes are publicized, which individual students can avail. The general subsidy, on the contrary, is hidden and actually very hard to determine and quantify, and a student does not 'apply' for this subsidy—all students get it by virtue of studying in the university. Often, however, the general subsidy forms the dominant component, and for a research university, it is often ever higher than for other universities. Here, we discuss the general subsidy; student aid is discussed later.

The difference between the yearly expenditure on education and the total revenue from fees can be considered as the bulk of the general subsidy. There are, however, some other components in general subsidy, in particular the cost of the infrastructure. However, accounting for the cost of capital or infrastructure is quite challenging (Winston 1998). In most public universities in India, the cost of the infrastructure is accounted for separately and not included in the regular annual budget, and for most public universities this cost is absorbed entirely by the university and is not even reflected in the per-year expenditure or costs.

The key question regarding the general subsidy is what are the sources of funds to support this subsidy. For public universities, the subsidy is financed largely through government grants and other funds. It should be noted that as tuition plus subsidy must cover the cost of education, the fixing of these two cannot be done independently; if the support from the government is reduced, the tuition fee might need to be increased. In India, the general subsidy from government sources for public universities has been reducing, and a greater portion of the costs are borne by the student through the fees (Varghese and Panigrahi 2019).

Subsidies have an important role in education. First and foremost, the tuition fee for education gets reduced due to these subsidies—the higher the subsidy, the lower the tuition fee. Furthermore, as discussed earlier, generally, the higher the cost of education, the higher the quality. Therefore, higher subsidies often imply higher quality of education for the same level of tuition fee. With higher subsidy, the student demand is likely to increase, which allows universities to be more selective in admissions, which enhances the quality of input and thereby further improves the quality of output.

The general subsidy level also has an implication on the student decision-making process. Students are generally most influenced by tuition fees and the level of scholarship or fee reduction that is provided. However, rationally, they should pay close attention to the total cost of education relative to the tuition fee being charged, as the cost of education impacts the quality. Though general subsidy is often not visible, in various ways, the total cost of education and the general subsidy factor in student decisions; this is the reason why many major research universities, which often provide high levels of general subsidy, are sought after for undergraduate education.

The general subsidy is the cost of education per student minus the tuition fee. Unfortunately, determining the cost of education is not easy (Winston 1998). For a teaching-only university (i.e., where only one service is provided, namely, teaching), it is possible to get a good estimation of the cost of education by looking at the total expenses and the total number of students being taught. However, determining the cost is extremely challenging in a research university engaged in providing multiple services, including teaching and research. This is mainly because many of the resources or inputs used for these services are common, with faculty resource being the primary among them. Apportioning portions of these common resources to different services or activities to separate out the cost for the education service is extremely challenging.

Given the challenges in separating the costs of shared resources among teaching and research, often, governments supporting the university consider common resources, such as buildings, faculty and regular staff, and so forth, as primarily supporting education, and the annual expenditure of the university for faculty, staff, the running of the campus, and so forth (i.e., the base funding) as expenditure for education. If this approach is used, the cost of education can be determined using the total number of students enrolled in the university and the total expenditure, except for direct research expenditure incurred from research grants.

9.2.5 Student Financial Support

As discussed, the tuition fee for students has increased with cost sharing for education. A clear risk of this approach of having students pay a larger portion of the cost is that students from poor economic backgrounds can be denied access to the education because they are not able to afford it. Higher education is widely perceived to be the route to moving up in life, and therefore, closing that route for the people who have the maximum need to move up cannot be accepted. In other words, given the increase in the cost of education and that a larger fraction of this cost is covered through tuition fees, financial support systems for students are essential to ensure that higher education is accessible to all who want it. Hence, most countries provide financial support to students, largely with the broad goal that those seeking higher education are not denied due to the lack of funds.

The support generally has two forms: student loans and student grants. We discuss both of these briefly here. We discuss support to ensure access to education but not scholarships given based on merit, because the purpose of the latter is to attract meritorious students to join the university.

9.2.5.1 Student Grants

Financial constraints are known to be a significant hindrance in the pursuit of higher education for students from poor economic backgrounds, though other factors also might limit access to higher education by this section. There is a broad consensus regarding the need to provide grants to cover tuition and other costs, so as to increase access to higher education by students from poor economic backgrounds.

Student grants are conceptually simple. Students are given some financial aid based on some criteria regarding their socio-economic background; this aid can be used to cover parts of the tuition and living expenses. The aid received is a grant, which does not have to be returned. These grants may have different names (fellowships, tuition waiver programmes, etc.) and may be supported through different agencies such as the university itself or some other body outside the university (government schemes, philanthropic schemes, etc.).

One grant scheme often discussed, but not widely used, is the voucher scheme (Marcucci 2013). In this, the government gives out vouchers to a targeted group to increase access to higher education. The student can then use the voucher on any approved higher education provider. A key challenge with vouchers is that targeting seems difficult; often, other groups benefit, and hence these vouchers do not always increase access to higher education.

Although financial grants help in improving access, other factors also come in the way of access to higher education by students from poor economic backgrounds. One key factor is access to information about not only financial aid schemes but also benefits of higher education. Studies indicate that students often overestimate costs and understate benefits (Ziderman 2013), resulting in inappropriate decisions about higher education by students and their families.

India has many such programmes for student grants. In most public universities which have substantial fees (many public universities have minimal fees), many scholarship schemes are available for needy students. There are many scholarship schemes for students also by state and central governments—a summary of the schemes is given in Narayana (2019). Apart from government schemes, philanthropic organizations also give grants to students for higher education (e.g., the Vidyadhan scheme of the Sarojini Damodaran Foundation offers scholarships for higher education to thousands of students from poor economic backgrounds.)

Universities often have fee-waiver programmes generally tied to the income of families of students. An example of such a scheme is one used in IIIT-Delhi. The financial model of IIIT-Delhi is that the recurring cost of education is borne mostly by a student. In this model, the tuition fee has to be higher than that in other public universities where the government might provide higher subsidies. Three levels of fee waiver are provided to ensure that access is not denied to any eligible student: full fee waiver, half fee waiver and quarter fee waiver. The criteria for each of these levels are tied to two factors: the income level of the family and the fee paid by the student in high school. Therefore, students whose family income is high, or those who paid a high fee during their schooling, are deemed to have the capability to pay the full tuition fee. Other students whose family income is less than some threshold and the school fee was less than a certain level can apply for fee waiver. (A challenge in India is checking for income levels, because, traditionally, income reporting is not considered good. By putting the second check, the scheme reduces the scope for misuse.) This scheme has been very successful and has been converted into a state government programme, wherein students studying in any higher educational institution are now eligible for the fee-waiver scheme.

9.2.5.2 Student Loans

Unlike targeted student grants, student loans are mostly general schemes available to all students. Consequently, they are generally government-sponsored. Education loans to students are different from the commercial loans given by banks for all sorts of purposes. Students might not have collateral to offer, and the asset being created by the loans is human capital, returns on which are unpredictable. Hence, they need government sponsorship.

One of the most effective loan schemes is the one used in Australia and also in UK and some other countries, which is sometimes called the Australian model. In this approach, the government pays the university directly the subsidy for education, which is considered as a loan to a student. The student is required to start repaying it a few years after graduation. This recovery is through an additional tax, and it is levied only when (and if) the income is above a certain level. In other words, until the graduated student earns 'enough', the loan does not have to be repaid. Effectively then, the unpaid portion of the loan becomes a grant to the student. The government has to suitably plan for this and recognize that some of the loans will have to be written off.

This model is widely appreciated because it not only provides support for students but also addresses the issue of government support to universities for education. Loans given to students actually become a grant supporting the education mission of a university. Moreover, the university is completely shielded from formalisms of loans and its recoveries. The implementation and accountancy of this scheme requires suitable structures. In England, this has been done by creating a separate student loan body, initial capital for which has been provided by the government (Bolton 2019). In Australia, the grant is currently directly administered by the government.

Another model for providing student loans is the one followed in USA. The loan is given to a student by a commercial bank and subsidized by the federal government to the extent that the government pays interest on the loan while the student is in college and for a short grace period after that. No support is provided for the principal amount. As the loan is guaranteed, the government provides a safety net for lenders, though not for students, who are expected to pay back the loan and are not absolved of it even in bankruptcy (Williams 2013). This model, where the lender's risks are mitigated while the student remains indebted, has many economic and social consequences and has already led to the student loan crisis in USA: the average debt at graduation time has gone up many times to more than US$30,000, the total education debt is set to cross US$2 trillion, and an estimated 40 per cent of students may default in the coming years. A lot has been written about this in the US context, in both the popular press and research journals. Suffice it to say that this model has some inherent difficulties.

In India, there is a government scheme for providing higher education loans. In this scheme, commercial banks give out higher education loans to students at their standard commercial rates. Loans up to some amount are to be given without any collateral, generally on the personal guarantee from parents. For loans to students from financially weaker backgrounds, the government provides subsidy for the interest for the period of study plus 1 year. Similar schemes are employed in countries like China, Korea, and Canada (Ziderman 2013). In India, while the total value of education loans disbursed continues to increase, the number of students taking loans has been declining, per reports in the press. The default rate of education loans is also high among the different retail loan categories (around 11%). (Interestingly, in the 1960s, when there were government loan schemes, recovery rate was very low—estimated to be less than 15% [Tilak 1993].) An analysis of the student loan scheme in India is provided by Krishnan (2017).

9.3 FINANCING RESEARCH

Research is expensive. The costs can be daunting even without counting the cost of the regular faculty who lead much of the research but whose salary may be covered as part of the education cost. The research cost includes the cost of PhD students, staff hired specifically for the research project, labs and equipment, library facilities, travel support, fieldwork costs, administrative support needed for managing research projects, and so forth.

How is the research of a university to be funded? Using tuition fees to cover parts of research costs further increases the cost of education, and it also does not seem fair to charge for education and use portions of that to support research. Hence, research should be supported by other funding sources. Indeed, that is the case in public universities: research is largely supported through funds from research-granting agencies funded by the government and the industry. (In some countries, while tuition fee for citizens is subsidized, the fee for foreign students is high, and parts of it are used to cover some proportion of research costs.)

In this section, we briefly discuss some funding methods for research. However, before that, we discuss whether research is a public good or not. If it is a public good, the claim for public funds is justified.

9.3.1 Is Research a Public Good

As discussed earlier, higher education was previously considered as a public good, but it is now increasingly considered as a mixed good with substantial private benefits. Hence, students are asked to pay a larger portion of education costs. Universities also engage in research and have to spend resources to support the research. A natural question then arises: is research a public good?

Research, fundamentally, is about creating new knowledge for a better understanding of the world or for economic exploitation. The output of research endeavours is generally scientific publications, which may include data, development of prototypes, and so forth. If the research is published, which is still the predominant, preferred and most respected channel for academicians, the new knowledge contained in the research paper is available to the entire world, with no restriction on its access or use. Further, use by one does not exclude anyone else from using it. Therefore, this research is not executable and is nonrivalrous and is truly a public good. In fact, knowledge can be considered as a global public good (Stiglitz 1999).

Research by a private company might not be fully a public good, because the company is not obliged to publicly share the knowledge its researchers create. Often, however, even when researchers share their research results as patents, which provides an exclusive right to the inventor of its use for some time, such research still has many public benefits and can be considered as an impure public good (Stiglitz 1999). (That is why while corporate research is generally not supported by public funds, often, governments provide some tax and other incentives to corporations for research.)

We can consider research being conducted in research universities as a public good, and therefore, support for it should be provided through public funds. Furthermore, basic research, which historically has had a huge impact on the world and continues to have large social benefits, due to its nature, is not an activity in which private companies can invest much, as it is hard to keep its benefits private, and hence the government must invest in it to obtain the social benefits that such research provides (Nelson 1959).

However, with any claim on public funds, the next question pertains to the value of research and the benefit it brings to the society or public—this type of analysis finally decides how much of public funds should be allocated for research. There is no clear-cut answer to this dilemma; it depends on the country's context. For developed countries, research is critical for their economies, because their developed and technologically advanced corporations depend on innovations and new knowledge. In countries such as India, there is a need for research, but the amount of research that needs to be done is debatable. The amount of research that should be done in universities, which are generally not mission-oriented, is sometimes even more questioned. However, given that the modern world is complex and rapidly changing, it is clear that countries such as India need to do more research. There are many reasons to have strong research support for universities, as discussed earlier in Chapter 2.

The new NEP of the Government of India recognizes that in the modern world, heavy investments in research are essential to tap the economic opportunities of the knowledge-driven era. It notices that levels of research investment in India have dropped and are well below those of other countries and makes a case for increased investment in research and innovation. It recognizes that in universities, there is a lack of funding for research, as well as a lack of a research mindset, leading to young minds not opting for careers in research or going overseas for such careers. It proposes establishing a national research foundation whose goal would be to strengthen a culture of research in the country, and which would fund research in universities using peer-review-based best practices for competitively supporting good research proposals (NEP 2019).

To support research through public funds in research universities, an approach used by some countries, including India, is as follows. A basic budgetary support is provided to public universities for education, which (along with tuition fees and other incomes) covers the operating costs of the university, including the salaries of faculty and staff, much of the costs of maintaining and running the infrastructure and the university, as well as the costs of resources that also help the research endeavours, for example, the library, some labs, etc. In other words, some amount of research costs, particularly those of shared resources like the library, faculty, etc., are also covered in the budgetary support for education. Direct support for research projects is provided through research-sponsoring agencies, which are funded through public funds. This competitive and open approach for research funding ensures that public funds are being used for research that is considered of high quality and high value. By having targeted research programmes for funding, this mechanism also allows the government to direct public funds towards areas that it deems more important.

9.3.2 Funding Research

As discussed earlier, as research is considered a public good, most countries provide support for research in universities through funding agencies that support research projects. Some industries might also support focused research projects, although the bulk of the research in universities is funded through research-funding agencies supported by the governments.

However, research takes place outside of sponsored projects as well: not all research in a university is sponsored through research grants. There needs to be support for this type of research also. Even when research is supported by a research grant, the grant generally only covers direct costs involved in conducting the research project, such as equipment for the project, human resources employed on the project, and so forth. However, executing a project also incurs some indirect costs or overheads. These are expenses not directly attributable to specific projects but are needed nonetheless to support research—such as administrative costs for research, space, utilities, security, maintenance, and so forth. These indirect costs of conducting research are referred to as 'overheads'. Research overheads have increased over the years due to the increased cost of various support activities, the need for more oversight, and so forth. (Brown [1981] and Ledford [2014] discuss these issues in the context of USA.)

However, research overheads provided for by sponsoring agencies often do not adequately cover the actual overhead costs of executing a research project. As computing overheads is complex, most countries fix some percentage to be awarded as overheads. Japan has 30 per cent, while the EU has 25 per cent (Ledford 2014). In USA, the rate is negotiated by each university separately to reflect the different circumstances of different universities. In India, it is generally 20 per cent or less, with a modest overall cap.

Hence, the full research overheads of sponsored projects often do not get covered. Further, as discussed, some research is not funded through research projects, but which a university must encourage and support. The question then is how the balance cost of research should be supported in public universities. One method is that some of the balance cost is absorbed by the education support provided—common facilities and resources, support for some PhD students, etc.

An alternate approach taken by UK and Australia is to directly finance these other research costs through a government grant for research, which is not an award for a specific research project. A university gets a block grant for research, which is separate from grants for education and sponsored project grants. The quantum of this grant depends on the level of research activity in the university, as well as on the quality and impact of the research. This method for supporting research also lends itself to promoting excellence, because it rewards universities conducting high-quality and impactful research. In both these countries, an elaborate exercise is done every few years to assess the research quality and impact of universities, based on which the annual block grant is given. This is called the 'Research Excellence Framework' in UK and 'Excellence in Research Australia' in Australia.

In India, the first approach is followed for most public universities—budgetary support provided by the government also covers some research costs, particularly manpower and basic infrastructure. For direct funding of research, some funding agencies provide project-based research funds. However, research funds provided through research agencies are modest, as discussed in Chapter 1. The NEP of the Government of India suggests a significant increase in research funding. It envisages establishing a national research foundation which will provide project-based research funds to universities and will also provide funds for centres of excellence and for supporting research excellence (NEP 2019).

9.4 FINANCING THE INFRASTRUCTURE

Much of the discussion and writing on the financing of universities focus on the recurring expenses for education and research.

The costs of infrastructure (e.g., costs of constructing a building, a facility and a lab) are one-time costs incurred in building the infrastructure. The infrastructure costs can be accounted for in the recurring expenditure using the norms of depreciation (in accounting, depreciation of capital assets essentially provides a way to convert capital expenditure into a yearly recurring expenditure). However, many universities in India do not include depreciation of capital as a recurring expenditure and work largely with recurring or yearly income and expenditure. Often, universities separately account for capital expenditure and also have separate fundraising for capital expenditure for infrastructure. Generally, in public universities, capital and recurring expenditures have to be handled differently; capital expenditure is provided separately by the government. We have discussed earlier the recurring costs of education and research and how they are financed. We briefly discuss the approaches universities follow for financing the infrastructure.

For established universities, much of the infrastructure is already built, and hence the costs are mainly for the incremental addition of infrastructure: a new building for a centre or a department, a new facility, and so forth. For a new university being established, of course, the infrastructure costs are substantially higher, because even the basic infrastructure has to be constructed, land has to be acquired, and so forth. If a new public university is being created, the initial capital expenditure for infrastructure is normally borne by the government creating it.

Financing infrastructure augmentation in existing universities is different from financing the infrastructure for a new university, because already-existing universities have revenue streams and are perceived to have the potential to raise capital. In such cases, different approaches are employed for financing the infrastructure.

The most common approach taken by a public research university for financing any new or additional infrastructure is to request special grants for the same from the government. This is the approach followed in India. The government may require a detailed project proposal and consider financing it using public funds. As for any public expenditure, funds may be granted if the perceived value being provided to the public is worth the expenditure. Hence, universities often need to explain not only the need for the capital but also benefits accrued from this investment.

The second approach is for a university to use its own accumulated funds for financing the infrastructure. This possibility depends on whether a public university is permitted to accumulate its savings from its income; a major portion of it might be from the grants it receives from the government. This approach is not feasible if there are limits on accumulating funds and the surpluses are adjusted against future grants from the government. However, it is feasible if the university receives grants based on some formula and is allowed to keep any surplus as a saving due to its efficient functioning. Indeed, this approach can encourage public universities to become operationally more efficient.

Another approach for funding infrastructure is to take loans from banks or other agencies for the infrastructure. As universities have strong and predictable revenue streams, securing bank loans is not much of an issue. However, loans from banks need to be repaid with interest, in the form of regular loan repayments to the bank. In other words, the capital is financed through the recurring budget of the university, implying that the tuition fee, which is an important source of revenue, now covers a part of capital costs. However, this approach is challenging, because it might require further increasing the tuition fee, which might not be acceptable.

A part of the special infrastructure that might be for some special R&D initiative can be funded from the research grant obtained for the initiative depending on the granting agency and on whether such infrastructure is permitted. Providing for infrastructure other than the equipment needed for research is generally not encouraged in regular research grants. However, special initiatives or proposals (e.g., for specific centres) may allow for covering a part of the infrastructure cost, with the remaining being covered by the university through its own internal accruals and other sources.

Another approach is to seek donations from philanthropists, corporations, alumni, and so forth for the infrastructure. Generally, these generous donations are sought for specific infrastructure projects: a new building for a department, a new centre in emerging technology, and so forth. Often, the support provided by a donor is acknowledged by the university naming the building or the asset created in the name of the donor. This public and visible acknowledgment of the support provided by the donor is sometimes a motivating factor for donors. This approach has been championed by old private universities in USA but is now being used in public universities as well.

The capital expenditure on the infrastructure should normally be used to compute the full and actual cost of services the university provides, that is, education, research, and so forth. However, accounting for this has many challenges (Winston 1998), and often, universities do not account for it while determining the cost of education.

9.5 FINANCING A PUBLIC RESEARCH UNIVERSITY

Public research universities need financial support for their two core missions: higher education and research. We have earlier discussed approaches for financing education and for financing research. Here, we combine these concepts for the financing of the research university as a whole.

The most common method of supporting public universities in India is through yearly budgetary support in the form of block grants to universities to cover much of their basic costs. While block grants are easier to operate, it is generally believed that formula-based funding models are more suitable. Such approaches are more transparent and provide a direct mechanism to align universities with government goals of increasing education opportunities and conducting research that benefits society.

For such an approach, it is desirable to separate the funding for the education function from the funding for the research function of a research university, as both serve different public purposes and separating them provides better control over the financing of the two functions.

The NEP also envisages funding for education and research being provided separately by different agencies. It envisages a higher education grants council which would provide the base funding to the universities. Its role would be to provide financial support for education and the running of the university but not for research. This funding is to be predictable and fair, with the university having the freedom to decide the optimal use of these funds. The NEP envisages much of the research funding coming from the national research foundation, which would grant funds for research projects based on peer review, as well as funds for establishing centres and for excellence (NEP 2019).

We propose a simple conceptual approach for the yearly financing of public universities in a country such as India, based on the approaches that exists in various countries and have been discussed above. We assume that the financing of capital expenses would be handled separately, as is often the case.

Moving to formula-based funding from the block grant approach can be challenging and might require a specific method for transitioning. This can be done by having a small block grant component in the yearly support provided to the university, which can also cover any special needs a university might have. With this, the public support for a university is expressed as:

Public funding = block grant + formula-based yearly support for education + formula-based yearly support for research

The block grant can be based on some proposal for special needs and historical data or can even be discretionary. We discuss the two formula-based components further.

9.5.1 Funding for Higher Education

As discussed earlier, higher education, particularly in professional disciplines, is now viewed as providing benefits to students and, hence, should be partly supported through the tuition fee. However, higher education serves a public function also; therefore, some subsidy should be provided through public funds. This subsidy is best viewed in terms of per-student subsidy; basing the total funding for education on the number of students directly encourages universities to increase the number of students. With this, the yearly funding for education for a university is expressed as:

Yearly support for education = number of students × yearly subsidy per student

A more detailed model is to have separate subsidy amounts for different programmes. This approach is easier to articulate and implement and also encourages universities to expand education (which governments want) and to improve quality (which also governments want) in order to attract the best students.

With this subsidy, the education is effectively covered through the tuition fee paid by students and the yearly grant provided by the government for education. The tuition fee has to increase with the decrease in this subsidy. In fact, even if the subsidy amount remains the same, the tuition fee has to increase to cover the increase in the cost due to inflation and other forces. If the subsidy amount remains unchanged, then the tuition fee increase has to cover the full cost increase (including the portion covered by the subsidy), and hence the rate of increase in the tuition fee might be faster than the rate of increase in the cost of education itself.

This subsidy amount for students can be viewed in two ways: it can be treated as a subsidy or as a loan to a student which the student has to pay later. If it is treated as a loan, then mechanisms to recover it have to be devised by the government, as done in UK and Australia.

Even with the subsidy, the tuition fee might be high enough to be a barrier for many to enrol in education, which must be handled to ensure that access to higher education is not denied to deserving candidates. For this, two types of support must be provided: income-linked fee waivers or scholarships and education loans. The scholarships should take care of students whose families cannot afford to pay tuition fees, and hence they should be income-linked. Education loans are for the rest of the students. Such schemes exist in most countries, including India.

Although the yearly subsidy by the government is a very direct and visible form of subsidizing education, it should be noted that there is another significant subsidy being provided by the government, namely the cost of capital. In countries such as India, where the capital is expensive, this capital subsidy can be substantial. Hence, even if the government does not provide yearly subsidy for education but bears the capital cost, a student still gets a substantial subsidy for education.

9.5.2 Funding for Research

As discussed earlier, much of the research support for universities is assumed to come through research projects, which are funded by various agencies. As discussed earlier in Chapter 1, the research funding available for universities through sponsored research projects is currently modest in India.

However, as mentioned, a university cannot be engaged only in sponsored research, as funding is not always available for all types of research. The academic freedom and ethos of a university should allow researchers to explore even esoteric areas. This needs non-project-based funding for research. Also, as discussed earlier, the funding provided for overheads in sponsored projects often do not cover the actual overhead costs—support for the balance is also needed.

Therefore, there is clearly a need for yearly support for research to a research university beyond the availability of sponsored research grants. Again, formula-based funding can be most transparent. For education, the formula is quite straightforward, because it is based on the number of students, which is the key indicator for the education function of a university. The formula for research funding will be more complicated, because determining the level of research is not easy. Broadly, the formula can be based on key indicators of the level of research being done in a university. Some of the key indicators are: (a) size of the PhD programme and the number of PhD students graduated; (b) research output, such as publications and patents, and their research impact in terms of citations; (c) impact on industry, innovation ecosystem, economy, and so forth; and (d) research funding received through funding agencies and industry. There can be other indicators, and the weight for different indicators can change with time, reflecting the value associated with research by society.

Applying the aforementioned approach for determining the level of research funding is an arduous task. Also, assessing the level of research for a university can only be done by considering the output and impact over a substantial period. Hence, this formula should not be applied on an annual basis. This exercise should be done every 5 years or so, based on the performance of the university in the previous 5 years. The grant is given yearly; however, the level of grant is decided based on the application of the formula until the next exercise. Hence, universities can predict the research funding for a few years, which is hugely desirable, because many research bets can take many years of investment before the results show and the investment pays off. (It might never pay off, because research is fundamentally a high-risk activity with the chance of impact being very low.)

As this funding is based on research performance, it provides incentives to universities to improve their research. This is desirable, particularly in the current environment of accountability. The funding also rewards the better-performing universities, which can further help them improve their research and become world-class universities.

As an example of this type of funding, let us consider the approach followed in IIIT-Delhi. The state of Delhi decided to have a very simple formula for this funding. It chose only the key parameter of research funds raised by the institute from funding agencies and industry and agreed to match the funds raised. This simple model can be applied yearly and does not require an elaborate exercise for assessing research. It is suitable for a state that might have only a few research universities but might not have the necessary infrastructure needed for conducting an elaborate performance evaluation exercise. For a larger system or one at the federal government level, it is better to look at all the key indicators of research activity, as is done in UK and Australia.

9.6 SUMMARY

Research universities are expensive in both of their main functions: education and research. Higher education is now widely considered a mixed good with private and public benefits, while research is largely considered a public good. Hence, research universities get considerable support from public funds globally. In this chapter, we have briefly discussed how the education and research functions of a university can be supported.

Globally, the costs of higher education have increased, partly because it suffers from a 'cost disease'. Governments have reduced support for education due to the high costs and massification of higher education. This reduction is further supported by the fact that higher education should be viewed more as a private good, because it provides substantial private benefits. Consequently, the share of the cost of education paid by the student through the tuition fee has increased. However, despite the higher tuition cost, a substantial subsidy is provided to students for education in all public institutions and even in many private institutions.

The increased cost-sharing by students has led to a need to provide financial support for students so that access to higher education is not denied. Financial support is provided mostly through two approaches: grants and loans. Grants are generally for targeted groups and are given to students to defray education costs. Grants are not to be recovered. Student loans are usually available to all students and are often supported in some manner by governments. The Australia model of providing support is to pay universities education subsidy for each student and treat it as a loan for the student, which is later recovered by the government through an additional tax on the student. In India, loans are provided by commercial banks but with some subsidy and guarantees by the government. There are many schemes to provide grants to students from financially weaker backgrounds.

The research function of a university generates public good, because research results in an increase in public knowledge. Hence, research is largely supported by government funds. The most common method of funding research in universities is to provide project-based funding through research-sponsoring agencies, which get budgets from public funds. Sponsored projects form a major portion of the research revenue for most research universities. However, they do not cover all the research expenses in a university. One approach to support these other research costs is to provide a yearly grant to the university for research, based on the research performance of the university. This approach is followed in UK and Australia.

In conclusion, we briefly discussed a conceptual model for providing support through public funds to a public research university, in which education is supported through a per-student subsidy; it implicitly encourages the university to admit more students, thereby increasing the availability of education. Research is supported largely through research grants, which can help in directing research towards areas deemed as more important. Extra support for research is provided to a university based on its performance in previous years, thus helping it achieve excellence and obtain more funds for research.

REFERENCES

Agarwal, Pawan. 2009. *Indian Higher Education: Envisioning the Future.* New Delhi: SAGE Publications.

Archibald, Robert B., and David H. Feldman. 2008. 'Explaining Increases in Higher Education Costs.' *The Journal of Higher Education* 79 (3): 268–95.

Bolton, Paul. 2019, January. *Higher Education Funding in England* (Briefing Paper). London: House of Commons Library.

Brown, Kenneth T. 1981. 'Indirect Costs of Federally Supported Research.' *Science* 212 (4493): 411–8.

Bruce Johnstone, D., and Pamela N. Marcucci. 2010. *Financing Higher Education Worldwide—Who Pays? Who Should Pay?* Baltimore, MD: The Johns Hopkins University Press.

Krishnan, K. P. 2017. 'Financing of Higher Education in India.' In *Navigating the Labyrinth—Perspectives on India's Higher Education*, edited by Devesh Kapur and Pratap Bhanu Mehta. New Delhi: Orient BlackSwan.

Ledford, Heidi. 2014, November. 'Keeping the Lights On.' *Nature* 515 (7527): 326–9.

Marcucci, Pamela. 2013. 'The Politics of Student Funding Policies from a Comparative Perspective.' In *Student Financing of Higher Education*, edited by Donald E. Heller and Claire Callender. New York, NY: Routledge.

Marginson, S. 2011. *Higher Education and Public Good.* Wiley Online Library.

Narayana, M. R. 2019. 'Scholarship Schemes for Student Financing.' In *India Higher Education Report 2018: Financing of Higher Education*, edited by N. V. Varghese and J. Panigrahi. New Delhi: SAGE Publications.

Nelson, Richard R. 1959. 'The Simple Economics of Basic Scientific Research.' *Journal of Political Economy* 67 (3): 297–306.

NEP. 2019. *Draft National Education Policy.* New Delhi: Government of India.

Stiglitz, Joseph E. 1999. 'Knowledge as a Global Public Good.' In *Global Public Goods—International Cooperation in the 21st Century*, edited by Inge Kaul, Isabelle Grunberg, and Marc Stern. New York, Ny: UNDP.

Taylor, Barrett J., and Christopher C. Morphew. 2013. 'Institutional Contributions to Financing Students—Trends in General Subsidies, 1987–2007.' In *Student Financing of Higher Education*, edited by Donald E. Heller and Claire Callender. New York, NY: Routledge.

Tilak, J. B. G. 1993. 'Financing Higher Education in India: Principles, Practice, and Policy Issues.' *Higher Education* 26: 43–67.

Tilak, Jandhyala B. G. 2008. 'Transition from Higher Education as a Public Good to Higher Education as a Private Good: The Saga of Indian Experience.' *Journal of Asian Public Policy* 1 (2): 220–34.

Tilak, Jandhyala B. G. 2009. 'Higher Education: A Public Good or a Commodity for Trade?' *Prospects* 38: 449–466.

Varghese, N. V., and J. Panigrahi. 2019. 'Financing of Higher Education, An Introduction.' In *India Higher Education Report 2018: Financing of Higher Education*, edited by N. V. Varghese and J. Panigrahi. New Delhi: SAGE Publications.

Winston, Gordon C. 1995. *Costs, Prices, Subsidies, and Aid in US Higher Education* (Discussion Paper 32). Williams Project on the Economics of Higher Education. Williamstown, MA: Williams College.

Winston, Gordon C. 1998. *A Guide to Measuring College Costs* (Discussion Paper no 46). Williams Project on the Economics of Higher Education. Williamstown, MA: Williams College.

Winston, Gordon C. 1999. 'Subsidies, Hierarchy and Peers: The Awkward Economics of Higher Education.' *Journal of Economic Perspectives* 13 (1): 13–36.

Winston, Gordon C. 2004. 'Differentiation among US Colleges and Universities.' *Review of Industrial Organization* 24: 331–354.

Williams, Jeffrey J. 2013. 'The Teachings of Student Debt.' In *Student Financing of Higher Education*, edited by Donald E. Heller and Claire Callender. New York, NY: Routledge.

Ziderman, Adrian. 2013. 'Student Loan Schemes in Practice—A Global Perspective.' In *Student Financing of Higher Education*, edited by Donald E. Heller and Claire Callender. New York, NY: Routledge.

Chapter 10

The Road Ahead for the Higher Education System and Research Universities

The success of research universities in a country depends critically on the overall higher education (HE) system in the country. However, their success also depends on the larger ecosystem comprising stakeholders such as industries and professional bodies. For example, the presence of research- and innovation-driven industry gives a boost to research universities, as much of the applied research finally benefits through products and services delivered by businesses. Similarly, respectable professional bodies help research tremendously. These bodies often give awards, prestigious fellowships, and so on to recognize achievements in research, which go a long way to support research excellence, as the respect of peers often drives researchers. Society has an important role to play as well: if researchers are highly respected and a career in research is valued, it will help the development of research universities. While many factors play an important role, the most critical support needed by research universities is from the overall HE system.

Previous chapters have discussed various aspects of research universities. In this chapter, we discuss some desirable changes that can help research universities thrive in India. As research universities cannot thrive unless the overall HE system in the country supports research universities, this chapter has two sections. The first section discusses the desired changes in the HE system to support research universities, and the second one discusses some desired changes within research universities. However, only a few key desired changes have been discussed; no comprehensive discussion has been conducted on the set of desired changes. As the new draft NEP of the Government of India (NEP 2019) also has proposals and recommendations on various aspects of research universities and the overall higher education system, where suitable, suggestions of the NEP are also mentioned.

10.1 FOR THE HIGHER EDUCATION SYSTEM

All universities exist within a society and derive support from society, both financially and motivationally. For example, if most universities are supported by the state and the focus of the state is only on education, then research universities will find it hard to justify the investments needed for research. Therefore, the larger HE ecosystem, with its policy frameworks, should support research universities and not focus only on education. As discussed in Chapter 2, some strong research universities are needed, even in poorer countries such as India. In this section, we discuss some key support needed from the HE ecosystem for research universities to thrive.

10.1.1 A Differentiated System for Higher Education

The overall HE sector in a country is typically much larger than the set of research universities. With the massification of higher education, the HE system has expanded rapidly in the last few decades in India and is one of the largest in the world. Any extensive HE system will have to be a differentiated system; there is simply no way all universities in an extensive HE system like that of India can be research universities. Not having strong research universities is also not an option, as discussed in Chapter 2. While education and research are the two main objectives of a university, all universities need not be, indeed, cannot be, research universities. To satisfy the educational needs, while still supporting a smaller number of research universities, a differentiated HE system is required. Without a differentiated system, all universities would be treated uniformly, which is counterproductive, as research universities have a different ethos and purpose and have to be supported and treated differently from universities that may focus more on education (Altbach 2007).

As discussed earlier in Chapter 2, a natural way to organize the HE system is to consider the system as comprising three tiers, with one tier focusing on research and doctorate, another tier focusing on postgraduate and undergraduate education and the third tier focusing on undergraduate education. This is how the famous California Master Plan for Higher Education was organized. This is also how the Carnegie Classification for Higher Education Institutions categorized the institutions in USA: research universities, masters colleges and universities and baccalaureate colleges. (There are a few other categories as well, such as associate, tribal and specialized colleges.) This is also how the NEP suggests that the Indian HE system should be organized.

In such a three-tier system, the research universities are at the top (tier I), which, while having education programmes at all levels, have a strong emphasis on research and perform research at an international level. They have strong PhD programmes and play a critical role in the research ecosystem of the country. At the next level (tier II) are universities that focus on masters and undergraduate education and may have a small PhD programme. The main mission of these universities is higher education. High-quality education requires that the latest developments are included, for which these universities will need a modest research and doctoral programme. At the third level (tier III) are colleges; their focus is mostly on the undergraduate programmes, though they may have some master's-level programmes also. Their programmes may also be based more on a well-established body of knowledge.

A differentiated system of higher education, such as the three-tier system, is necessary to keep education accessible while still having research universities. As the cost of education is necessarily much higher in research universities than in teaching-focused universities, and is higher in teaching-focused universities than in colleges, the role of tier II and tier III is critical in keeping higher education accessible. Research universities cannot be the institutions to satisfy the full HE demand, as the cost to the students and society will simply be exorbitant. Only a small percentage of students get their education in these research universities. Moreover, getting the faculty talent for such a large number of research universities is simply not possible.

In India, the current HE system is effectively a two-tier system, with universities and colleges. This stratification is not based on education goals but on the ability to design education programmes and grant degrees; universities are given this authority, while colleges are not. Clearly, out of about 900 universities in India, only some conduct good-quality research and publish in reputable international venues and thus may be considered research universities. The rest mostly focus on education. For having top-quality research universities that are at par with global research universities, research universities need to be identified and then supported so that they can achieve global standards.

Research universities can be separated from the rest through a classification system. The Carnegie Classification of USA is the best-known method. It was created in 1973, and the classification is done by a foundation instead of a government body and is widely accepted by both the government and the HE community (Carnegie 2000). The Carnegie Classification is not a ranking system. Rather, it is constructed to place all HE institutions in USA in appropriate categories. This classification system for separating research universities from the rest was adapted for India in a recent paper entitled 'Classification for Research Universities in India', written by three former vice chancellors/

directors (Jalote et al. 2019). This framework has been discussed in Chapter 2. To recap, the basic criteria for a university to qualify as a research university in India is:

Percentage of faculty with PhD >75 per cent of the total faculty and

The ratio of the number of full-time PhD students to the number of faculty >1.

These are reasonable criteria, and this is a suitable adaptation of the Carnegie Classification framework. A university that is focused on research must have research faculty. All over the world, research faculty predominantly hold doctorates. A hallmark of research universities is that they mostly employ as full-time faculty people who hold PhDs (Altbach 2007). Given that a significant fraction of the faculty in many universities in India do not possess a PhD, the criteria require that at least 75 per cent of the faculty have doctorates before the university qualifies to be considered as a research university. A reasonable expectation for a research university is that each faculty member has on average one full-time PhD student working with him/her—hence the second condition. As India's HE system is rapidly expanding, with so many new universities created within the last two decades, instead of PhDs graduated, it is better to include full-time PhD students, which also represents an investment in research, as full-time PhD students are paid stipends.

With such criteria in place, research universities can be separated out from the set of universities and institutions. This classification helped identify about 70 universities as research universities from the set of top 100 universities and top 100 engineering institutions per the Indian ranking agency, National Institute Ranking Framework (NIRF) (2018). This number is quite reasonable and comparable with the percentage in USA, and comparable in numbers with China and Korea. This number will increase with time, as it should, in an expanding system like that in India.

With research universities identified, they should then be assessed for their research contributions and capability and then be provided strong research support so as to help them reach global rankings. Funding for research universities is modest, as shown in Chapter 1, and needs to be enhanced; we discuss it further later in this section.

Research universities should be expected (and supported) to produce the majority of the PhDs in the country. In USA, just the top 50 universities produce about 50 per cent of the PhDs. The ratio produced by its research universities (which are less than 10% of the total) is probably over 90 per cent. In India, a large number of PhDs are produced outside research universities (as shown in Chapter 1). As research universities have the best capability for research, they are the ones that can produce the best-quality PhDs in the country. Hence, the effort should be to ensure that the bulk of PhDs are produced in these universities, with a modest number being produced in other universities (which can also allow some of them to become research universities in due course).

Trying to convert all universities into research universities is neither desirable nor feasible. While over time some universities in tier II can move to become research universities by suitably improving their research, the rest should continue focusing on education, and their mission should be to improve the quality of education at the bachelor's and master's levels and keep their educational programmes in line with new knowledge emerging in different subjects and disciplines. By expecting tier II universities to also do good research, their focus is unnecessarily divided, often leading to mediocre research and mediocre education.

The NEP also envisages such a three-tier system for higher education in India. It suggests that about 100 universities can be identified soon to form the initial set of research universities and these can be expanded to become large multidisciplinary research universities, having between 5,000 and 25,000 students each and producing a large number of PhDs. Over time, it feels, some from tier II can move to tier I and the number of research universities may expand from 150 to 300. It recommends abolishing the affiliating college model and suggests that all colleges become autonomous, with full academic powers, particularly for the designing and teaching of courses and for assessment (NEP 2019).

10.1.2 Autonomy of Research Universities

Research universities are complex entities engaged in teaching, research and the third mission, as well as many other activities. They have a unique environment not found in other organizations. Moreover, they compete and collaborate at the global level with research universities across the world. These universities can only be run effectively if they have complete autonomy of operations (within the overall HE policies). If a country wants its research universities to compete at the global level, these universities should be provided as much autonomy as possible.

Autonomy implies that the university takes all decisions related to all aspects of its operations and its management. As discussed in the chapter on governance (Chapter 8), the university management can be viewed at three levels: top-level governance body, which makes policies and oversees their implementation; leadership, including the chief executive; and management and administration. Autonomy in research universities in India needs to be strengthened at the first two levels, as, generally, a fair amount of autonomy is already present at the management level. Research has shown that universities with a greater degree of autonomy and accountability and with competition perform better (Aghion 2010). The EU has taken up the cause of autonomy for universities and has developed a scorecard for autonomy to help (Eastermann 2015; Estermann and Nokkala 2009).

At top-level governance, the main body for overall governance is the board of governors (or equivalent), which we refer to as the board. The board forms all policies related to the university and is responsible for its effective functioning. Typically, the size and constitution of this board are specified in the act and statutes for a university. Autonomy at this level means that the board should have all the powers to take decisions for the university, including the power to appoint its members (on expiry of the term of some of its members), and there should be minimal representation in the board from the government or government appointees.

A related issue is the selection of the chairperson of the board. The chairperson holds a crucial position, as he/she often represents the board, is empowered to take decisions on its behalf and is often the accepting authority for recommendations of the chief executive. With full autonomy, the board should elect its chairperson. Where some external body (e.g., the government) has to appoint the chairperson, the selection should be from a set of names suggested by the board (which can seek inputs from the faculty and other internal stakeholders) or a committee with strong board representation. It is essential that the chairperson is not an employee of the university and is independent from the chief executive.

Autonomy regarding the selection of the chief executive means that the chief executive is selected and appointed by the university itself. This will normally mean that the board of the university appoints the chief executive. Only if the board appoints the chief executive will he/she be accountable to the board. If the government makes the appointment, then necessarily, the chief executive is answerable to the government and not to the university. This aspect has many subtle ramifications. In the chapter on governance (Chapter 8), we discussed an existing model in a state university in India regarding how this autonomy can be provided to public universities. It is perhaps the foundation of autonomy that the leader of an organization is selected by the organization itself.

Public research universities must have financial autonomy despite getting financial support from the government. This is essential, as otherwise, financial support can become an instrument of impinging on the autonomy. Financial autonomy, with good accountability, is facilitated if formula-based funding is provided yearly for education. The formula to decide the level of funding could be based on the number of students in different fields, or can include some other parameters also. Australia and UK follow this model for supporting education while providing full autonomy to their universities on the use of the funds. This approach of having funding based on the number of students also ensures an incentive for the university to expand its education and thereby be more responsive towards the needs of students. Importantly, a university gets committed funds for its educational function, so it can adequately run its education programmes from the funds it gets from the government for education, the tuition fee it collects and the other revenue it generates.

The NEP also recommends full autonomy of governance for universities. It recommends an autonomous board of a modest size with limited government representation and which has the power to appoint the chief executive, as well as to identify the chairperson. It also recommends that there be a transparent and fair method of funding HEIs so that they have predictability of finances and suggests that as the capability of these institutions develops, more and more financial autonomy be granted to them in terms of how they spend the funds.

In addition to funding for education, research universities need robust research funding. Research is expensive and has to be supported at global levels to reach international standards. Research funding has to come primarily from governmental sources, with some support from corporations. Funding for research is discussed further in the following section.

10.1.3 Research Funding for Research Universities

Research universities employ the best and most talented faculty who need to be compensated well. Moreover, to support research work, expensive research labs, high-quality computing infrastructure, a library, PhD students, travel support for conferences, and so forth have to be provided. While the government support for education can be reduced by increasing tuition fees, no such handle for research exists. Research must be supported in the universities by the government; private sector contributions even in developed countries are very small and can at best be viewed as supplementing research income and making research more applied. In most countries, universities rely primarily on funding from government sources for research.

The level of research funding available to Indian universities is modest. An analysis of data of the top universities and engineering institutions (using the 2018 NIRF data) shows that the research grant per faculty in the top universities is about US$7,000 per year. In USA, the Carnegie Classification for 2015 (Carnegie 2016) identified approximately 330 research universities and grouped them into three categories: R1 (highest research activity), R2 (high research activity) and R3 (modest research activity), each having about one-third of the research universities. The R&D expenditure per faculty per year is more than US$300,000 for the R1 universities, about US$150,000 for the R2 universities and US$30,000 for the R3 universities. In the top 100 institutions in India, the R&D support per faculty is one-sixth of the R&D support per faculty in the R3 institutions, and less than 2 per cent of the support in top global universities. Even after considering the fact that manpower and some other costs are lower in India (though research equipment, international travel, digital library subscriptions, etc. all cost the same as in other countries), the level of expenditure and R&D investment is significantly lower than even the R3 category research universities in USA.

For India's top universities to be included among the top global universities, the investments in their research will have to increase substantially. For research universities to thrive, two types of research funding are needed:

- Long-term block research funding, based on the research performance of the university and
- Sponsored research project funding, granted based on proposals for research.

Long-term block funding is followed in UK and Australia with a great degree of success. This funding is given for 5–7 years based on the evaluation of research contributions and impact. The universities have to improve their quality and quantity of research to get a more significant portion of this funding pie. Moreover, they get an opportunity to prove themselves and get rewarded suitably every 5 years or so. This is an excellent model, as it supports performance; better-performing universities get higher funding. This block grant also covers the overheads of the universities for executing research projects, which are not fully covered by the typically small overheads provided for in research grants, and provides support for research in areas for which grant funding may not be available.

The best practice for supporting sponsored research in universities is to have a system of giving competitive research grants to the faculty based on research proposals. This is a standard method being followed in almost all countries, including India. The challenge in India is that the overall funding for sponsored research is rather small. As shown in Chapter 1, on average, a university in the top 100 (per NIRF rankings) only gets sponsored research grants of about ₹2,000 lakhs in a year (approximately US$3 million). The total research funding available and the size of each project need to be substantially increased. It should be simultaneously ensured that for most PhD students, support comes from such grants; this will motivate the faculty to compete for such grants vigorously.

A vast system of competitive grant funding is essential for research universities to thrive. In India, the funding to universities comes as extramural funding from about 20 or so research agencies. As shown in Chapter 1, of the total research funding to these agencies, less than 10 per cent is extramural funding, of which universities get a significant share. In other words, more than 90 per cent of the government spending on R&D is spent by various research agencies, and less than 10 per cent goes to universities as research grants. This situation is vastly different from that in many developed countries (as discussed in Chapter 1), where research funding to universities from government sources is often more than that to other agencies. The extramural funding of each agency in India needs to be increased substantially to increase the research funding available to universities. An increase in extramural funding can also facilitate more collaboration between the labs of these agencies and university researchers. Other ways to enhance R&D funding to universities can also be explored, for example, requiring government departments that can benefit from R&D to have an explicit research budget for sponsored research.

The NEP has clearly identified lack of research funding as a major area for improvement for the higher education system in India. It has recommended the formation of a National Research Foundation (NRF) which will have a substantial budget for supporting research in universities. It will set up divisions in four areas: technology, science, social science and arts and humanities. Research grants will be given based on peer review of proposals to support high-quality research based on merit. Besides supporting projects, NRF will also provide support for setting up centres of excellence in different universities, as well as provide support to those whose performance has been excellent. This aspect of supporting centres and excellent performance can easily be operationalized into performance-based funding for research for universities, as discussed earlier.

10.1.4 An Association of Research Universities

Out of about 900 universities across India, only some conduct good-quality research and publish in reputable international venues and thus may be considered research-intensive or research universities. The rest are largely teaching-focused universities doing little and potentially mediocre research. This situation is similar to many other countries in which only a fraction of the total universities are research-intensive. Earlier in this chapter, we discussed how research universities need to be separated and how they can be identified from the set of universities through some classification criteria.

Another challenge in the development and support of strong research universities is that no voice exists to represent the interests of research universities. Research universities exist within the society and derive support from the society at large and give back to the society in a variety of ways while pursuing their academic missions. The health of public research universities is hugely influenced by the support from the government and the public at large. Due to this, they need a voice to communicate with the government and society about their role and contributions to the society and government and what is needed for them to thrive.

While each research university maintains an interface with the government and the public, an association of research universities is essential to ensure that there is a collective voice that represents the views of the research universities as a system.

Most advanced countries have such associations; in fact, many countries have many associations of universities. In USA, the Association of American Universities (AAU) is the most prominent association for research universities. Its members are 62 top research universities in North America (60 from USA and 2 from Canada). The mission of AAU, as given on its website, is that its member universities 'transform lives through education, research, and innovation.... seek to address national challenges and contribute to economic strength, ... educate tomorrow's leaders ... help shape policy .... promote best practices in education.... contribute to American society' (AAU). The Association of Public and Land-Grant Universities (APLU), which has over 200 members, states on its site that it is a policy and advocacy organization for public universities in USA, with the mission 'to expand access .... deliver workforce of tomorrow.... advance and promote research to improve society, foster economic growth, and address global challenges...build vibrant communities ...' (APLU).

There are other university associations in USA. For example: the American Association of State Colleges and Universities is an association of nearly 400 public colleges and universities; the Association of Jesuit Colleges and Universities has 27 Jesuit colleges and universities in USA; and the Association of Catholic Colleges and Universities represents the collective voice of Catholic HE systems in USA.

In UK, the top research universities form the Russell Group, which represents 24 leading UK universities. It aims to 'help ensure that our universities have the optimum conditions in which to flourish and continue to make social, economic and cultural impacts through their world-leading research and teaching. We provide strategy, policy development, intelligence, communications and advocacy for our member institutions' (RussellGp).

University Alliance is a network of British universities offering technical education, professional training, R&D, enterprise and innovation. It covers about 20 per cent of all UK students and accounts for over a quarter of UK's research in engineering (UniAlliance). The N8 Research Partnership comprises eight research-intensive universities in Northern England (N8). Universities UK's members are chief executives (vice chancellors or principals of universities in UK), and as stated on its site, it 'is the voice of universities, helping to maintain the world-leading strength of the UK university sector and supporting our members to achieve their aims and objectives' (Universities UK). Moreover, its work includes advocacy, analysis, advice, and so forth. UK has other associations as well.

In Australia, which has only about 40 universities, the Group of Eight (Go8) comprises leading research-intensive universities in Australia. According to its site, Go8 'is focused on, and is a leader in, influencing the development and delivery of long-term sustainable national HE and research policy, and in developing elite international alliances and research partnerships' (Go8). The Australian Technology Network (ATN) is made up of four of the country's most innovative and enterprising technical universities, with a focus on industry, practical impact of research, industry-oriented education, and so forth (ATN). Innovative Research Universities (IRU) is a coalition of seven comprehensive universities in Australia. Its members' 'research focus is on the translation and commercialization of research on issues of critical importance to the communities in which they are based and addressing problems of national and global scale' (IRU). Other associations also exist, including Universities Australia, which is the voice of universities of Australia, with most public universities being its member.

These countries have multiple university associations, each having members with some common views and each representing the collective views of its members. At least one of the associations is of the top research universities of the country, which represents the collective views of these top research universities to the public and to the government so that their collective inputs provide weight to the government policymakers. These associations have representations only from their members and not from the government, so they take views in the interest of their members. Also, they are largely financed by the membership subscription of their members.

Currently, India does not have any such organization of research universities. These universities have different challenges, and a general association of Indian universities, which is open to all universities, cannot represent these universities' views and can lead to pertinent issues of research universities not getting due attention from the government and policymakers. For such an association to be effective, this body should be kept modest in size so that it can work coherently. It should be self-selective, using clear metrics for inviting new members to join the association and for terminating the membership of existing members. Of course, it should only have membership and representation from chosen universities and should be completely independent of the government, as is the case with associations in other countries (e.g., AAU, Go8 and Russel Group) discussed earlier. Typically, for funding, these associations are run on membership subscription from its members and may also raise funds from other agencies. They should not get any regular government grant. How such an association can be started is discussed in Altbach and Jalote (2019).

Research universities have the highest-quality PhD programmes in a country. It is also expected that they produce the largest number of PhDs in the country. Like other education programmes, PhD programmes also need to evolve and improve with time, as discussed in the chapter on PhD programmes. While institute and programme accreditation are instruments that can be used to assess and improve institute governance and undergraduate programmes, they typically do not look at PhD programmes carefully, as they are quite distinctive and different from other education programmes. USA and Australia have an association of graduate deans, which discusses issues related to PhD programmes. The association of research universities in India can form this type of a committee of its deans to spearhead changes needed in the PhD programme in the country. It can look at various good practices in research universities to evolve useful frameworks for managing and organizing PhD programmes so that the quality of PhD graduates improves with time. Frameworks created by an association of research universities are likely to have strong credibility and can help other universities also in improving their research and PhD programmes.

10.1.5 Professionalize the Administrative Functions of Universities

A university typically employs a large number of non-academic staff for managing different aspects of its operations. Often, the staff size is as large or larger than the size of the faculty. The staff provide critical support for key functions of the university. Academics management itself is typically quite large, with staff needed to manage records, provide guidance to students, issue transcripts and other records, address student concerns, help in organizing thesis evaluations, address faculty concerns regarding classes and tutorials, provide support to faculty for exams, and a host of other activities. Student-life management is another important and often a large function dealing with student hostels, facilities for student clubs and other activities, dining facilities and other support to student life. Human resource management in universities is also very different from that in corporations and is rather specialized. Also, some other functions such as fundraising and alumni relations, which are very specific to universities, are quite specialized and require a considerable amount of domain knowledge about HE and its operations and management.

To develop properly trained people for managing university operations, the higher education departments in many universities in USA offer master's and PhD programmes in HE administration. The goal of the master's programmes is to shape professional staff for different functions in universities. A typical master's in higher education administration has courses on academic advising, alumni relations, sports administration, enrolment management, financial aid, government and community relations, student support services, study abroad, policy research and analysis, and so forth. In addition to the courses, it provides experiential and hands-on training through internships and assistantships, during which students work in the university itself and get to practise what they have learned and experience the concepts in practice. Several universities offer such master's, including many of the top universities.

A good fraction of a university's staff in USA, particularly in specialized university functions, have a master's in HE administration. Many of them may start a job in a university and then do the master's part-time, building the competencies and knowledge that help them in their career advancement. Also, professional bodies of HE administration professionals exist that organize conferences and meetings, further promoting and developing the profession of university administration. Many university staff positions, in their advertisements, clearly state that preference is given to candidates with master's in HE administration.

Similarly, many postgraduate courses on educational leadership and administration (names vary) are offered in UK. The goal of these programmes is to prepare future leaders and administrators, and past graduates have gone on to make careers at universities in UK and across the world, as well as in many other sectors. Australia also has many master's in education leadership programmes.

Currently, in India, such programmes are missing, and most of the staff in universities have general degrees in a variety of disciplines. They learn about the profession of university administration on the job, as they have little prior knowledge about the profession or competencies required for the profession. Lack of professional associations for the administrative staff leads to the staff not being able to share good practices and discuss challenges and issues facing the profession. Moreover, lack of professionalization has also led to most of the management functions, often even routine ones, being handled by faculty, thereby effectively wasting the talented faculty's time over such tasks when their focus should be on academics.

For a large education system like that of India, it is desirable to treat university and college administration as a profession and have educational programmes that can build suitable competencies, so that HEI administration can be considered as a career option after graduation. Also, professional bodies should evolve, which can strengthen the profession. Having education programmes and professional bodies for university administrators can go a long way in improving the management of universities. It can also help reduce the administrative load on faculty, which will be an added advantage.

Such programmes must be offered in reputed universities so that the students can also do internships in the university and experience the profession in practice. Such degree programmes can be suitably recognized and given weight in appointing staff in universities and colleges. Part-time options should be provided for the currently working professionals so that they can upgrade themselves for more leadership roles and improve their effectiveness. PhD programmes should also be started, so that people seeking to become administrative leaders, such as registrars or even principals of colleges, can have their highest degree in HE, rather than in some non-related discipline, as is currently the case.

10.1.6 Create Some Large, Multidisciplinary Research Universities

As discussed in Chapter 1, a comparison of the top 200 universities and engineering institutions in India with the top 200 institutions globally revealed that the top Indian universities are much smaller in size. The analysis showed that 90 per cent of the top 200 universities globally have more than 10,000 students and 1,000 faculty, and only 2 per cent have a faculty size of less than 500. In India, it is very different; more than half of all institutions have a faculty size of less than 500, and only a few have a faculty size of more than 1,000 (Jalote 2019).

Broad-basing universities to become comprehensive universities has now become a trend worldwide. This trend is visible in many countries, and institutions that started with a narrower focus (e.g., on technology) have over the past couple of decades expanded their scope and become multidisciplinary universities. One can view a comprehensive university as one with departments in various disciplines of natural sciences and mathematics, social sciences and humanities, and also in various applied fields, such as engineering, business, law, pharma and medicine. The prevailing wisdom is that for conducting impactful research, a university needs to have expertise in many fields and disciplines, as the important research problems in the current times and in the future will require expertise from various disciplines to be satisfactorily addressed. Although different universities can theoretically achieve interdisciplinarity with narrower but complementary fields of strength, it is far more challenging and often impractical for different universities to collaborate effectively. Collaboration between faculty of different disciplines is facilitated if they are in the same university and share the same governance systems, space and other systems.

In India, the HE system has grown in terms of creating a large number of smaller and more focused institutions. Smaller institutions are easier to manage and easier to create and support. Although having smaller and focused educational entities can have advantages and not all institutions need to become large, there is a need for some of the top institutions to become multidisciplinary and global in size. This can be achieved through creating such universities; however, it is a much slower process, and such large multidisciplinary research universities might come up only after a decade or two.

A more pragmatic approach is to motivate some of the top universities and institutions to become large and broaden their scope. Many of the top universities/institutions have a faculty strength close to about 500, and some of these can be challenged to expand their faculty strength to more than 1,000 within the next decade. Many of the top universities/institutions have vast land area, though it will have to be redeveloped heavily for such growth. Such an expansion of research universities will require tremendous resources, not only to build the infrastructure for handling the large size but also to redevelop the existing infrastructure. It should also be understood that the existing models of governance and organization within the university might need to change to support the size.

Examples of converting focused institutions into broad-based research universities can be found across the world. For example, Georgia Institute of Technology started with a single degree in mechanical engineering and then expanded to start degree programmes in a few other engineering disciplines such as electrical, civil, textile and chemical. As late as till 1988, it had only three colleges: the College of Engineering, the College of Management and the College of Sciences and Liberal Arts. Today, it has six colleges, with 28 schools (departments), most offering undergraduate programmes in their discipline. It has over 25,000 students and is considered one of the top universities in USA and is highly ranked globally. A more recent example is that of Nanyang Technological University (NTU) in Singapore. It started as a teaching university in 1981, with programmes in three engineering disciplines: civil and structural, electrical and electronic, and mechanical. It is now a broad-based university with colleges in engineering, business communication and information, education, biological sciences, humanities, social sciences, physical and mathematical sciences, art, design and media, and so forth. It now has a host of research centres and institutes, many in partnership with industry.

The NEP has also noted that India has too many small and narrowly focused universities and has suggested this approach for broadening and expanding some of them. It envisages, in the short term, about 100 universities being identified, which can then be supported to become multidisciplinary and large research universities with 5,000–25,000 students. Later, more universities can be identified and gradually moved to this group of research universities.

A more difficult, but possible, approach is to try merging some colleges and research labs in an existing university. Though this has all the challenges mergers bring, this can immediately expand the size and scope of the university. As discussed in Chapter 1, the merging of educational institutions has been done in many countries, and one main reason for merging is creating large, multidisciplinary research universities. China has perhaps had the largest number of mergers in recent times; in the last 25 years, it has had about 400 mergers, involving about 1,000 public HEIs in its attempt to move from specialized HEIs to having larger, globally competitive comprehensive universities (Aziz et al. 2017).

Australia followed this approach in its Dawkins reforms, which were started in 1987. Under these reforms, an amalgamation of colleges and institutes of education was done, some with the existing Australian universities and some through creating new universities. One of the explicit goals was to create a larger, more comprehensive university formed out of an amalgamation of various more narrowly focused HEIs with different goals.

Griffith University is an example where many HEIs were merged with Griffith over a few years to create a large research university. As a result, within a few years, Griffith transformed from a university of about 4,000 students and a single campus into a multi-campus university with more than three times the number of students and with a range of academic programmes. Currently, Griffith has five campuses in three cities and over 50,000 students, and is one of the topmost research universities in Australia.

QUT (Queensland University of Technology) is an example where mergers facilitated the creation of a new university. It was established as a university by merging two main educational institutions, the Queensland Institute of Technology (which itself had evolved from various institutions earlier) and the Brisbane College of Advanced Education (which itself was a combination of multiple institutions focusing on teachers' training and advanced education). QUT currently is one of the top research universities in Australia, with more than 40,000 students, two main campuses in Brisbane, offering hundreds of degree programmes at all levels, and strong research in many fields. It is ranked among the top global universities.

A recent example is that of the University of Paris-Saclay. It was the result of an ambitious project to create a large university that would be among the top universities in the world. It was in response to the relatively weaker performance of French HEIs in the global rankings. It brought together many autonomous and prestigious institutions, including two universities, 10 *grandes écoles* (professional educational institutions in engineering, life sciences management, and so forth) and seven national research institutions. The government has allocated more than ₹6 billion for the project. For planning, they had the ex-president of Caltech as the advisor for this project. The university now has about 65,000 students from over a hundred countries and over 9,000 research professors. It is already ranked well globally. France has other such projects, mostly in large cities with multiple institutions engaged in research and HE.

In India, we have experimented with breaking up large institutions into smaller institutions, perhaps to make them more manageable. It is worth experimenting with the merging of some professional educational institutions (in engineering, management, pharma, law, and so forth) with some research labs, and maybe some colleges. Of course, suitable planning and care have to be taken to only merge institutions that have a research focus and culture, and detailed planning must be done on a case-by-case basis. There cannot be any general template for merging. Institutions in major cities can be examined to evolve suitable plans of amalgamating some. This type of merger can also unlock the potential of the land they currently occupy. Such an alliance can create large universities that can make it to global levels within a decade.

10.1.7 Develop Some Higher Education Research Centres

HE itself is a subject for research. Many top-quality international journals on HE are present, and many universities have research centres on HE. Also, a large number of books on various aspects of HE are available. The breadth of the research is quite extensive; research areas include doctoral training, financing of HE, education and learning, role of HE in innovation and economic development, research and its impact, changing nature of academia, sociology of academia, and so forth.

As HE is an object of research, countries such as UK, USA and Australia, which have highly reputed and large HE systems, have research centres working on HE. A couple of examples of HE research centres in a few countries are as follows:

- **Australia:** Centre for the Study of Higher Education, Melbourne
- **UK:** Centre for Higher Education Studies, University College London; Centre for Comparative and International Education, Oxford; Centre for Higher Education and Equity Research, University of Sussex

- **USA:** Center for 21st Century Universities, George Tech; Center for Studies in Higher Education, University of California, Berkeley; Stanford Institute for Higher Education Research, Stanford; Center for International Higher Education, Boston College

Most of these research centres are present inside a university. Research centres on HE should be housed in universities whose primary mission is education and research, so that the university itself can provide the data and information and platform for analysis and research in HE. Research universities also support a culture of research. (Stand-alone and separate institutions for HE research are also useful; some of these are also present in these countries.)

In India, no major university/institution has a research centre on HE. (The National Institute of Education Planning and Administration is a stand-alone institution for providing analysis and data for policymaking to the government.) Hence, while India has one of the largest HE systems in the world, HE remains a highly under-researched field. Although the governments (central and state) invest so much on education, hardly any investment has been made for HE research. It should be noted that, unlike science and engineering where knowledge is global and applies universally, research in HE is, by its very nature, contextual. The HE system of India is like no other country's system, and the needs and evolution are very India-specific and do not follow the trajectory of those of any other country. Therefore, if we are to better understand our past in HE so that we are better prepared with research and analysis for improving the efficiency, effectiveness and reach of our HE system, we need to conduct serious research on it and cannot rely only on global research in HE.

For this, we must establish a few HE research centres in different parts of the country in reputed research-focused universities/institutes and charge these centres to build research competency and suitable research manpower and conduct research on HE in the country, as well as on the global HE context and trends. We invest so much in HE; we must invest a small percentage of that on HE research to get better returns on our HE investment and to protect our future. These centres can then also help in running professional educational programmes for developing administrative human resources, as discussed earlier.

10.2 FOR RESEARCH UNIVERSITIES

We now discuss some of the initiatives that existing research universities can take to become stronger and improve their standing in the global association of research universities. Although the ecosystem and the policy framework support research universities, they cannot take a university to greater heights. The university has to leverage the available support from the government and ecosystem to strive for excellence in research and education, for which it will need suitable practices in place. In this section, we discuss a few initiatives that an individual research university can take by itself.

10.2.1 Strengthen Research Culture and Ethics in the University

Although sufficient resources are essential for research, a supportive and thriving research culture is indispensable to achieve excellence and higher research productivity. Universities having a strong culture of research will be more productive and conduct more impactful research than others, even with the same level of resources.

The research culture of a university refers to the set of beliefs, values, attitudes, practices, customs, and so forth of the institution that support and promote research. Strengthening the research culture will require a strong commitment to excellence from the administration, faculty and research scholars, and it will take sustained efforts. Many examples in India and across the world can be cited where a flourishing research culture degenerated to one where mediocrity thrived. The various structures and stakeholders of the university have to be vigilant to preserve the culture and avoid the temptation of taking expedient steps and decisions that might avoid immediate unpleasantness but can damage the research culture.

The issue of building a research culture was discussed in the chapter on research management. Some of the key characteristics of a strong research culture include the following:

- **Expectation of high-quality research.** Only if the expectation is high quality and excellence in research can a university expect that its researchers will try to achieve it. A key challenge in countries such as India lies not only in articulating the expectations but also in aligning the policies and practices with these expectations. Sometimes, expedient decisions are made that can hurt the research culture. For example, if some faculty members with mediocre records are promoted, it becomes a benchmark for future decisions and drives the expectations towards mediocrity. In such a situation, excellence survives only due to individual commitments and drive.

- **Encourage collaboration.** Many big challenges require multi-disciplinary inputs for addressing them. Also, societal issues never align neatly along discipline boundaries. For many research challenges, researchers must work together to make a substantial impact. All these mean that collaboration between faculty within the department and across departments must be actively encouraged and promoted to have a vibrant research culture. While this is easy to state and understand, facilitating such collaborations needs suitable policies and encouragement. Appropriate policies and support/incentives for interdisciplinary projects or multi-researcher projects can help in promoting collaboration.
  Collaboration can also be facilitated if there are spaces and opportunities for formal and informal interaction on academics between faculty from different disciplines. Such interactions are even more important for interdisciplinary research. Informal and relaxed academic discussions are known to

lead to research ideas. Such interactions will thrive only if researchers are free to express themselves and raise doubts and questions without feeling judged. A key difference between an active collaborative research culture versus one with a low level of collaboration is in what faculty discuss during these opportunities to meet and discuss. In the latter, mostly, other topics are discussed (e.g., politics of the country, world, university, etc.), while in the former, often, discussions will be about research-related issues, which may start over a cup of coffee or lunch and then carry on.

Collaboration with global colleagues is equally important. Research articles with authors from multiple countries are often cited more. Also, the pursuit of science and knowledge has been a global endeavour always. Hence, a university needs to have its faculty as part of the global community of scientists and collaborate with them.

- **Active sponsored project programmes.** Faculty must be motivated and incentivized to compete externally for getting research grants. Applying for sponsored projects and trying to get grants must be an important part of the research culture and is a feature that is common to all research universities. This should be ensured by providing good support for getting and executing projects and suitable policies also. For example, even if it is possible for a university to support more PhD students from its own funds, it should promote supporting most of the PhD students through project funds. This will motivate the faculty to apply for research projects.

- **Rewards for good research.** Good research in a research university should be rewarded and recognized. Recognition and celebration of research can strengthen the culture and importance of research. Without recognition, research excellence might not be sustained, and those who are excelling may move to other environments that recognize, respect and value excellence. The incentives for research excellence should be a combination of prestige and recognition, extra support for the faculty member's research, compensation, and so forth.

- **Good work ethics.** It is almost impossible today to have significant research contributions with only a modest effort. Hence, a strong work ethic of putting in sufficient effort in research endeavours is an essential component of a good research culture. This is extremely important in universities, because faculty members are autonomous agents with a great deal of freedom, and their efforts are never measured. In such a system, it is easy to slide into a minimal-effort zone, making only as much effort as required to perform at an acceptable level of academics. Hence, the university and the faculty have to be vigilant to ensure that the work ethic is supportive and hard work is cherished and respected.
- **High-quality and large PhD programmes.** A thriving PhD programme is indispensable for having a healthy and vibrant research culture. An extensive PhD programme with full-time PhD students, whose only goal is to do PhD and research, will ensure that faculty are also actively engaged in research. However, it is also essential that the rigour and quality of the PhD programme are maintained and high expectations from PhD scholars are established. This was discussed in more detail in the chapter on PhD programmes (Chapter 6).

Although a high level of research activity is needed, it is also essential that ethics for research be followed scrupulously by all researchers in a university. As research is the pursuit of truth, it is even more important that high ethical standards be maintained. The research community and the government have evolved various frameworks and codes for ethical research. These codes cover the full life cycle of research, from the selection of problems to conducting research and publishing research results. We have discussed research ethics in the chapter on research management (Chapter 4). The entire research community in the university should be sensitized about ethical conduct, and ethical practices should be followed as part of the research culture.

A university should provide support for ethical research in the form of workshops, training, lectures, and so forth. Besides, a scientist might face issues that he/she cannot solve because of a resultant conflict of interest, for example, whether an experiment they want to conduct with human subjects is acceptable or not. In such cases, an approving body is needed which can determine rules to ensure that approval for a research work is given only if it complies with their standards without any violation of the ethical guidelines. These committees are generally referred to as institutional review boards (IRBs). IRBs are present and functional in most research-based institutions to ensure that research is conducted safely and ethically. Besides the IRB, an institution also needs mechanisms to investigate claims of unethical behaviour that may be brought to notice and, based on the investigation, determine responsibility and recommend a course of action. Universities generally use committees for this purpose, which are often constituted based on the nature of the claim.

10.2.2 Establish a Teaching and Learning Centre and Focus on High-Quality Education

In the pursuit of research, there is a risk that education might get ignored. As research universities are prestigious and well-ranked, top students will always vie to get into them. These students need to be prepared well in their education programmes to take on leadership roles in the future. Given the highly selective intake of these universities, it is essential to have dynamic and contemporary programmes that are sufficiently challenging and which develop the capabilities of the young students who enrol.

Education is what the society and government expect from universities, including research universities. In fact, the expectation on education from research universities is even higher, given that significantly more public funds are spent on these universities. As discussed in the chapter on education, research universities are expected to provide leadership in education to the whole country. This can only be done by providing the best education possible to the students in the university.

Higher education has been shifting its focus from teaching to learning over the last few decades. Earlier, with smaller classes and a much smaller HE system, a teaching-led education sufficed. Universities decided what should be taught overall, and teachers often decided what was to be taught in a course and generally did a sincere job of teaching. Smaller classes allowed attention to individual students and the ability to help if a student faced difficulties. Also, the expectations on what was learned by a student were modest, as the world which employed them was simpler. In fact, often, the graduates were 'over-educated' for the jobs they took up after their education.

The situation is very different now. Due to the massification of HE, class sizes are much larger now, not permitting individual attention. The world has become much more complex, and the skills required to be effective in the workplace are more sophisticated and multidimensional. This situation often leads to the situation where what is learned in HE by students is not sufficient for working in the real world. Consequently, demands regarding what students learn in educational institutes have soared, and the focus of education has shifted from teaching to learning by students, with the learning outcomes and graduate attributes being driven mainly by the workplace of the future. In this changed scheme of things, it is indeed essential to understand that learning is the goal of education, and effective teaching has to ensure that students learn what they are expected to in a course.

A teacher teaching a course on a subject needs two basic competencies for effective teaching: subject matter expertise (SME) and an understanding of effective teaching techniques. SME is necessary (though not sufficient) to teach a subject in a manner that students can learn that subject. A teacher who himself/herself has a limited understanding of the subject cannot be expected to teach the subject well. Till recently, and even now, in many universities, SME was considered sufficient. Consequently, faculty members with the most advanced degree, that is, a PhD, were recruited even in universities that did not have a strong research agenda. It was believed that a teacher with SME, which he/she must have obtained by doing a PhD, would naturally do what was needed in a class to ensure learning by the students.

While this approach sufficed when learning expectations were modest, and indeed has served well for many decades, it is not sufficient now. For advanced learning by students, teaching has to be much more than 'brilliant lectures by experts'. This is what effective teaching techniques focus on—what a teacher can do to ensure deep learning by the students.

Though the set of techniques that can lead to effective teaching is evolving, and it remains an area of research, some of the methods (e.g., active learning) are now well established. The knowledge of and use of effective teaching techniques by a teacher can lead to good learning outcomes in students. In fact, one can say that even with good SME, without employing effective teaching techniques, the learning outcomes achieved will be modest. Universities are filled with examples of such professors who have SME and conduct good research but are not good teachers. In research universities, the faculty members have good SME, as they generally have a PhD from a good university and a good background. These institutions, if they want to improve the quality of their education, can focus on improving the capability of its faculty in effective teaching.

Many global universities have established a teaching and learning centre (TLC, which might be called teaching excellence centre, or centre for innovation in teaching, or some other name) to improve the knowledge and capability of faculty in effective teaching techniques. The key goals of these centres are to help faculty members in making their teaching more effective and to conduct research in HE effectiveness. Even universities with the most talented faculty, for example, all the members of the AAU (which are the top research universities in North America), have such centres, which clearly shows that expertise in a subject matter is not sufficient for effective teaching. In UK, some time back, considerable investments were made to develop over 70 Centres for Excellence in Teaching and Learning.

Most such centres have short training programmes for the faculty, perhaps a few modules focusing on topics such as learning theories, student motivation, learning outcomes for courses, designing courses and experiences, effective lecturing and active learning. Most of these modules have a few sessions that might be conducted over a few weeks, that is, the time involved in the learning of these topics by faculty is quite small. Often, a certificate is provided on the completion of a module. These centres often have staff who have degrees and experience in teaching and learning, though faculty from other disciplines might also join as an adjunct of part-time members of the centre. Besides offering these training modules, such centres might also provide one-on-one help and guidance to faculty, arrange for the videotaping of lectures and/or teaching observations in class by experts, arrange workshops and seminars for sharing good practices and forming a community of faculty wanting to improve teaching, and so forth. They also study the effectiveness of these programmes, for example, by checking if the teaching feedback for faculty improves after these modules. Evidence indicates that, indeed, such modules help the faculty be more satisfied with their teaching efforts and help their student evaluations improve.

One of the key challenges in training faculty in effective teaching techniques is to make them realize that their teaching can improve with the application of some techniques and with a better understanding of the teaching and learning process, and to make them attend these programmes to learn these concepts and methods and apply them in their teaching. A couple of approaches are employed to overcome this. One method is to make it mandatory, but this can be done only for the incoming faculty. Another approach is to favourably consider the achievement of these certificates for teaching modules in the promotion process. Of course, the most effective method to motivate the faculty to take these programmes is to demonstrate the effectiveness of these programmes, so that the faculty members want to attend them, as all teachers fundamentally must want to be more effective in their teaching.

The role of these centres is increasing rapidly, with online learning deployed by many universities. The centres have, in many places, expanded their scope to include new technologies and innovations as part of their agenda. Most are also conducting research in effective learning and teaching. Some of them also have graduate-level programmes. Overall, it can be asserted that a research university, which is expected to take leadership in education, should have such a centre.

This area is, unfortunately, virtually ignored in India, and well-respected research universities need to take leadership in this area by establishing such centres. It should be clear that such a TLC must be set up within a university, as it requires access to students, faculty and the actual teaching and learning process. Research universities are eminently suitable for having these, not only to improve their education but also to conduct research on effective teaching, particularly incorporating the local context and attributes of the local learners. A TLC can also provide suitable training to PhD students for preparing them for taking up the role of next-generation faculty. Research universities have large PhD programmes, and also the most prominent source for next-generation faculty, and can leverage a TLC for suitably enhancing their PhD programmes. A TLC in a region in a respected research university can also become a resource centre for that region, helping other colleges and other universities, which might not be able to set up such centres, in improving their teaching and learning practices by transferring the knowledge and best practices. The NEP has also recommended a strong focus on quality education and the establishment of centres in universities to help in the continuous professional development of faculty, particularly for teaching.

Some of these centres may have a broader scope of being research centres for higher education. As discussed earlier, HE itself is a subject of research, and developed countries have a few centres in universities that conduct research on HE, in addition to performing the functions related to effective teaching techniques. Some of the major universities can seek support to establish such centres.

10.2.3 Strengthen Internationalization

HE and research were globalized centuries before globalization became a buzzword. Scientists and scholars travelled to knowledge centres across the world to study and share knowledge. For example, ancient universities in India hosted scholars from around the globe much before modern universities started emerging. The movement of scholars and sharing of knowledge across countries have been an important part of the development of civilizations.

However, the global movement of students in larger numbers became regular and systemic mostly in the previous century. This exchange has only accelerated in this century. This movement has mostly been students from lesser-developed countries going to developed countries with a high-quality HE system. While earlier the movement of some of these students was facilitated by richer countries through scholarships to help development in lesser-developed countries, currently, much of the global movement of students is viewed by universities and governments as an issue of trade and economic development (Rizvi 2011). In fact, in Australia, HE is the third largest export industry.

While often the discourse on internationalization revolves around the movement of students across countries for HE, internationalization for universities takes place at multiple levels. The main ones are international collaboration for research, exchange and visits of faculty, admission of students from other countries in education programmes and student exchange. For a university, reasons for engaging in these can vary, and the reasons of Indian universities might be different from those of universities in developed countries. Currently, in India, internationalization is playing out mostly in the form of Indian students going abroad for higher studies—referred to as Mode 2 of internationalization in Kapur and Mehta (2017). However, research universities in India are in a good position to enhance their engagement in many or all of these.

Regarding research, there is a broad agreement that trans-national research collaborations are advantageous and much needed. A key argument for this is that many problems facing the world now are global in nature, and hence collaborative research efforts across countries, involving scientists from diverse cultures with a better understanding of impact in their countries, are more likely to evolve suitable approaches and solutions. Such collaborations also help deepen understanding across countries and are broadly in alignment with the paradigm of a globalized world. Consequently, many countries promote collaborative research, and many universities in these countries are vigorously pursuing international collaborations for research. Growing evidence suggests that the volume of transnational collaboration in research is increasing; in all the top research-producing countries, the fraction of papers published with at least one author from a different country has been increasing.

Besides benefits at the national and global levels, international collaboration has many advantages at both the individual researcher level and the university level. At an individual faculty level, international collaborations can help increase access to expertise, specialized equipment, data sets and cultural and social environments; participate in global scientific networks and stay on top of the latest developments; tap the bilateral or multilateral funding opportunities; raise international visibility, which is sought by all researchers; increase research productivity and quality; and so forth. Internationalization of research can also help a research university in multiple ways. It can provide a method of augmenting the research capabilities and facilities through partnerships and collaborations and enhance the global visibility of the institution. It can also help in improving a university's global ranking, as such rankings consider internationalization as a factor. Overall, for research universities, it is valuable to engage in international collaborations for research and evolve mechanisms to facilitate their faculty.

Reasons for the exchange and visits of faculty include all reasons discussed earlier, as these visits are likely to lead to research collaborations among researchers. In addition, such visits facilitate the exchange of ideas about education, as visitors often actively participate in teaching and can help the research culture of the university by learning about the good practices in the visitor's country. Through formal and informal discourses on education, good practices from a visitor's countries get shared, and the visitors may take back practices from the host to their home country. These discourses also help in developing a better understanding and appreciation of other countries and their systems. However, supporting visits for international collaboration, both for faculty visiting outside and external faculty visiting the university, is challenging and requires resources, proper facilities, support for visa, and so forth.

One possibility for international research collaboration is to have joint PhD programmes with universities in other countries. Many of the top universities in the world are now open to such programmes, and many already have partnerships with some Indian universities. Typically, in such a programme, a student has a supervisor from both institutions, and the student is required to spend 1–2 years in the partner university also. Such a programme, while enriching the PhD programme of the university, also helps in reducing the migration of students to other countries for PhD by providing them an exciting collaborative PhD. It also helps expand the PhD guidance capability of a university. A key challenge in such programmes is to find financial support to encourage the visits of faculty, so that they can identify problems to work on jointly, based on which the PhD students can later work, and to financially support the student to spend time in the partner university.

Movement of students to another country for HE has, for India, generally been a one-way movement—students from India go to a host of developed countries for HE. It is the movement in the other direction that research universities in India need to apply themselves to. This movement is currently minimal. Carefully designed programmes need to be in place to initially encourage students from other countries to come and do their postgraduate degrees in India. It is unlikely that these students will come from countries having highly evolved HE systems, but it is quite feasible to evolve programmes to attract students from some other developing countries (e.g., those in Asia and Africa). However, these programmes have their own challenges. The university has to learn to host these students and take care of their well-being (besides education). This might require not only suitable infrastructure but also the sensitization of domestic students and healthy interaction among the foreign and domestic students. Many subtle cultural and diversity issues come up when foreign students are present on campus. These issues should be resolved, and in the process, should enrich the university and make it more global.

Finally, student exchange between universities is an approach where students from one university visit another university, typically for a semester or a year. It is expected that, broadly, the number of students in both directions should balance out. Globally, student exchange has been an accepted approach for students from one country to spend significant time in another country. Student exchange programmes have not picked up to any significant level in India. Students face challenges in both directions: students going from India might find the cost of living too high, and students from overseas might find the overall infrastructure inadequate for them.

Support from the government will be needed for facilitating internationalization by universities, particularly for visas and for financial support for some of the schemes. The NEP has also recommended the internationalization of universities and encourages collaboration between institutions across countries for joint programmes, student and faculty exchange, etc., as well as attracting students from other countries to India for higher education.

10.2 4 Strengthen Autonomy

We have discussed the autonomy of research universities earlier in the chapter as a desired change from the overall HE policies and ecosystem. We have discussed the key aspects of autonomy—what authorities a university should have to be more autonomous. While the degree of autonomy a university enjoys is constrained by the HE system (and the act and statutes of the university), the university also plays a role in it. As mentioned in the chapter on governance (Chapter 8), the autonomy of a public university is a source of tension between the state and the university. The university should ensure that the full degree of autonomy provided is exercised. Often, autonomy is eroded by universities themselves, for example, by their not fully exercising the authorities provided (e.g., to be 'safe') or by heeding to directives in matters that fall within the purview of the internal governance of the university. Research universities should attempt to exercise as much autonomy as possible and keep pushing the boundary to get more autonomy. It may be desirable for research universities to also lobby the government and HE regulators for enhancing the level of autonomy. An association of research universities (discussed earlier in the chapter) can do this more effectively than individual universities.

10.2.5 Increase the Size and Scope and Encourage Interdisciplinarity

As discussed in Chapter 1, globally respected research universities are mostly large. A large university, along with a broader scope, supports research, particularly interdisciplinary research. In India, most universities tend to be small, as discussed in Chapter 1. For many research universities, it is important to be larger and have research activity in multiple disciplines. This helps the research activity in multiple ways. We have discussed this issue of size earlier in this chapter as an initiative of the HE system to develop large research universities. While a push from policymakers can help, a push is also desirable from some research universities themselves for expanding their size.

For research universities, growing in size will require a significant amount of funding. For public universities, this funding mostly comes from the government. While the government's policies have traditionally been towards creating small universities that are perhaps easier to manage, growing in size is also dependent on the university. Research universities have generally shied away from growing in size. While growing to an internationally competitive size will require substantial changes and may require newer internal governance structures (e.g., instead of the flat hierarchy that currently exists, another layer of governance might need to be added, as is the case in most research universities in the world), the top universities and institutions in India are capable of doing the needful for this, with experiences from across the world on how to manage large research universities helping them in this endeavour.

The importance of multidisciplinary universities and research in the Indian HE system has been emphasized in the National Education Policy (NEP 2019), as well as in other writings (e.g., Chandra 2017; Hatakenaka 2017).

10.2.6 Prevent Faculty Complacency

The complacency of faculty is perhaps the most critical impediment in achieving greater success in research in Indian research universities. Faculty are at the core of research activities, and all research is effectively driven by faculty. Therefore, if faculty are complacent and satisfied with their modest achievements and do not have the drive to pursue bigger research challenges, there is no hope for the university to excel. Complacency often starts with senior faculty, who might slow down or stop pursuing research. As in a mature university a vast majority of the faculty might be at the professor level, where they spent almost two-thirds of their tenure as faculty, complacency at the senior faculty level is hugely detrimental. It also establishes undesirable messaging to the junior faculty about the possible trajectories of their academic career.

Faculty complacency is the main source of underachievement in many top universities. In many top universities in the country, faculty at the entry level are often at par with their peers in globally respected universities. Yet, a decade or two later, the trajectories of the faculty in globally ranked universities and those in Indian universities often diverge substantially, and achievements and research contributions vastly differ.

If there is one drive that a research university needs to embark upon, it is to do whatever is needed to ensure that complacency among its faculty is prevented. This issue can be addressed in multiple ways; some of these have been discussed in the chapter on faculty management (Chapter 7). However, in an existing university, implementing any of these will require a change in the culture and the existing scheme of things, which is always a big challenge. The challenge is heightened by the fact that the appointment of the chief executive is often made by the government and is typically for a term of 5 years, perhaps too short to bring about the substantive changes that will be needed to address faculty complacency, and certainly too small a period to see the effects of the changes proposed.

One clear approach to help in preventing complacency is to ensure that all faculty members submit a report on their annual contributions and that feedback on the contributions is given to the faculty through a due process. As discussed in the chapter on faculty management (Chapter 7), just having individual faculty members prepare a good annual report has advantages. If a review of the contributions is done, it can really go a long way in helping prevent complacency. While review and feedback themselves might suffice, their impact can be further strengthened if some, even small, incentives are granted when a faculty has had a highly productive and successful year; the positive reinforcement can motivate the faculty to remain vigilant and continue to aspire for good academics. Some other approaches for preventing complacency are discussed in the chapter on faculty management (Chapter 7). These include having a tenure system, having a large PhD programme, supporting international collaboration and ensuring teaching–research balance.

10.2.7 Enlarge the Third Mission

With the first two missions of education and research, universities engage with society by developing educated human resources, who then contribute to the society through the roles they take up and by generating knowledge that is used by corporations to enhance economic activity. The third mission of a university is broadening its traditional missions to also include activities to directly engage with various stakeholders to contribute to economic growth and social progress, in other words, deliver economic benefits to host societies, through engaging in innovation, entrepreneurship and technology transfer activities, and social benefits, through more outreach programmes. The third mission of research universities was discussed earlier in Chapter 5.

Universities across the world are embracing the third mission in a big way. They hope to not only make a direct impact on society and economy and continue to be agents of change but also generate revenues. It is appreciated that innovation and knowledge is no longer just a resource for economic growth but also an engine of growth. Universities with their strength in knowledge creation and innovation are well positioned to participate.

The pace of change today is faster than ever before. The economies of countries are changing, and new companies are being formed and rising with amazing speed. The new economy is based largely on innovation to create new goods and services and to improve the existing ones. Hence, governments want their countries to be innovative. As research is fundamental to innovation and as research universities have research capabilities and a combination of young students and mature faculty, countries are looking to universities to drive the innovation engines by directly participating in innovation, starting new companies, transferring their knowledge to existing companies, and so forth.

Universities can take a few initiatives to help economic development, as discussed in the chapter on the third mission (Chapter 5). These including promoting student and faculty entrepreneurship, promoting technology transfer, facilitating university–industry collaboration and engaging with local economic development. To support the entrepreneurship ecosystem, universities naturally have a fertile innovation ecosystem and an academic culture of openness, new ideas and the questioning of old paradigms. They need to enhance support for the funding of new ventures and enhance the entrepreneurial culture.

Contribution to economic activity is also facilitated by improved academia–industry collaboration. A key goal is to facilitate the process of knowledge being used by industry for creating economic value. Another goal is to channelize research for directly addressing challenges faced by industries. It is desirable to have some ongoing channel for collaboration, which can help overcome the challenges of communication gap and misalignment of goals between the two sides. One successful approach is to establish cooperative research centres. Such centres will need some initial support from the government. The success of such a programme in USA—the IUCRC—in which the National Science Foundation (NSF) provides support, can be used as a starting point to guide the establishment of such centres.

A university can more actively engage and help in regional economic development also. This is a much bigger challenge and can only happen through concerted efforts by many universities and other stakeholders. Massachusetts Institute of Technology's (MIT) regional entrepreneurship accelerator programme provides a way forward for this. This model envisages a partnership between the university, entrepreneurs, government, corporate and risk capital to help accelerate innovation-driven entrepreneurship. It tries to combine innovation by universities with entrepreneurial and venture capital agencies to create firms in areas of competitive advantage for the region.

Universities often distance themselves socially from the surrounding communities to allow for the mind to roam freely and explore the unexplored and not be constrained by the often-harsh realities of the society around them. However, this has also made universities in countries such as India more insular and disconnected from society. Just as walls are necessary for a host of practical reasons in the current world we live in, there is also a need for a research university to have direct outreach to society, so that it can engage with the latter and provide whatever benefits it can.

In a developing country such as India, there are many societal challenges; hence, it may not be desirable for a university to limit its third mission to innovation in the economic sphere alone. Many other societal challenges might be present in the region, to which a university can contribute through social engagement and outreach. However, if this has to be done, it has to be ensured that the university does not compromise its first two missions of research and education; indeed, third-mission activities should be synergistic and complementary. An approach can be to harness the power of the large and talented student body for social outreach programmes. Such programmes can deliver good benefits to the society and also benefit the students in their own growth. An example of how students volunteer in a summer camp for children from disadvantaged backgrounds was discussed in the chapter on the third mission (Chapter 5).

10.3 SUMMARY

In this chapter, we discussed a few key initiatives that can be taken to have thriving research universities in India. We have divided them into two groups—one for the overall HE system and one for the universities themselves.

We discussed a few initiatives in the overall HE ecosystem that can help research universities thrive. These include having a differentiated HE system which can clearly separate out research universities from the rest, providing a greater degree of autonomy to research universities so they can compete more effectively with their global counterparts who already enjoy much more autonomy, having special funding for research in research universities based on research performance, having an association for research universities that can voice a collective opinion of these universities, starting education programmes to professionalize university administrative functions, creating a few large multidisciplinary universities by expanding some existing ones and by merging some institutions together, and developing a few centres for higher education research that can critically examine issues relating to Indian HE and provide information for policymaking.

We also discussed some initiatives that research universities can take. These include strengthening the research culture of the university, improving the quality of education and establishing a teaching and learning centre, strengthening the internationalization of the university, strengthening the autonomy of the university, increasing the size and scope, preventing faculty complacency and enlarging the third mission activities of the university.

REFERENCES

Aghion, Philippe, Mathias Dewatripont, Caroline Hoxby, Andreu Mas-Colell, André Sapir and Bas Jacobs. 2010. 'The Governance and Performance of Universities: Evidence from Europe and the US.' *Economic Policy* 25 (61): 7–59.

Altbach, Philip G. 2007. 'Empires of Knowledge and Development'. In *World Class Worldwide*, edited by Philip G. Altbach and Jorge Balan. Johns Hopkins Press.

Altbatch, Philip G. and Pankaj Jalote. 2019. 'Forget Top 100 list, India doesn't even have a Mechanism to Identify Research Universities, *The Print*.

Azziz, Ricardo, Guilbert C. Hentschke, Bonita C. Jacobs, Lloyd A. Jacobs, Haven Ladd. 2017. 'Mergers in Higher Education: A Proactive Strategy to a Better Future?', TIAA Institute, 2017. https://www.tiaainstitute.org/sites/default/files/presentations/2017-09/TIAA%20Institute_Higher%20Ed%20Mergers%20Report_Azziz_September%202017.pdf

Carnegie. 2000. 'The Carnegie Classification of Institutions of Higher Education'. http://carnegieclassifications.iu.edu/downloads/2000_edition_data_printable.pdf

Carnegie. 2016. 'Carnegie Classification, 2015 Update—Facts and Figures'. http://carnegieclassifications.iu.edu/downloads/CCIHE2015-FactsFigures-01Feb16.pdf

Chandra, Pankaj. 2017. *Building Universities that Matter: Where are Indian Institutions Going Wrong?* Orient BlackSwan.

Estermann and Nokkala. 2009. University Autonomy in Europe: Exploratory Study, European University Association, 2009. https://eua.eu/component/publications/publications/79-report/408-university-autonomy-in-europe-i-exploratory-study%20.html

Eastermann, Thomas. 2015. 'University Autonomy in Europe', *Higher Education Trends, University Education*, No 3. https://core.ac.uk/download/pdf/197252400.pdf

Hatakenaka, Sachi. 2017. 'What is the Point of Multidisciplinary Research Universities in India'. In *Navigating the Labyrinth: Perspectives on India's Higher Education*. Orient BlackSwan.

Jalote, Pankaj. 2019. 'India's Quest for World-Ranked Universities'. *Current Science* 116 (9). https://www.currentscience.ac.in/Volumes/116/09/1479.pdf. A shorter version appeared in International Higher Education as 'India's Research Universities and Global Rankings.' (99; Fall 2019) https://ejournals.bc.edu/index.php/ihe/article/view/11659/9723

Jalote, P., B. N. Jain and S. Sopory. 2019. 'Classification for Research Universities in India', *Higher Education*. https://doi.org/10.1007/s10734-019-00406-3

Kapur, Devesh and Pratap Bhanu Mehta. 2017. 'Introduction'. In *Navigating the Labyrinth: Perspectives on India's Higher Education*. Orient BlackSwan.

NEP. 2019. *Draft National Education Policy*. Government of India. https://www.mhrd.gov.in/sites/upload_files/mhrd/files/Draft_NEP_2019_EN_Revised.pdf

NIRF. 2018. India Rankings 2018. https://www.nirfindia.org/2018/Ranking2018.html

Rizvi, Fazal. 2011. 'Theorizing Student Mobility in an Era of Globalization.' *Teachers and Teaching* 17 (6): 693–701.

Index

About the Author

Pankaj Jalote is the Founding Director of Indraprastha Institute of Information Technology Delhi (IIIT-Delhi). He worked as the Director of IIIT-Delhi from 2008 to 2018, during which it reached the list of BRICS top 200 universities. Prior to this, he has been a Chair Professor at IIT Delhi, Professor in the Department of Computer Science and Engineering at IIT Kanpur, where he was also a Head of the Department, and an Assistant Professor at University of Maryland at College Park. From 1996 to 1998, he was Vice President at Infosys Technologies Ltd., and from 2003 to 2004, he was a Visiting Researcher at Microsoft Corporation, Redmond. He has a BTech from IIT Kanpur (1980), MS from Pennsylvania State University and a PhD from University of Illinois at Urbana-Champaign (1985). He has served on the editorial boards of *IEEE Transactions on Software Engineering*, *Empirical Software Engineering* and *IEEE Transactions on Services Computing*, and was the General Chair for the International Conference on Software Engineering (2014).

He is the author of five books. His books *CMM in Practice* (Addison Wesley) and *Software Project Management in Practice* (Addison Wesley) were highly acclaimed and were translated in many languages, including Chinese, Japanese, Korean and French. His textbook *An Integrated Approach to Software Engineering* (Springer, three editions) was very popular, and its Indian edition was declared as the bestselling computer science book by its local publisher (Narosa). The book *A Concise Introduction to Software Engineering* was published by Springer, and its Indian edition by Wiley India. The book *Fault Tolerance in Distributed Systems* (Prentice Hall) was the first graduate-level book in the area. Currently, he is a Distinguished Professor at IIIT-Delhi. He is a Fellow of the Institute of Electrical and Electronics Engineers (IEEE) and Indian National Academy of Engineering (INAE).

CPSIA information can be obtained
at www.ICGtesting.com
Printed in the USA
LVHW090931241220
674513LV00012B/2